ELEMENTARY STATISTICS

IN CRIMINAL JUSTICE RESEARCH

ELEMENTARY STATISTICS
IN CRIMINAL JUSTICE RESEARCH

JAMES ALAN FOX
Northeastern University

JACK LEVIN
Northeastern University

MICHAEL SHIVELY
Northeastern University

LONGMAN

An imprint of Addison Wesley Longman, Inc.

New York • Reading, Massachusetts • Menlo Park, California • Harlow, England
Don Mills, Ontario • Sydney • Mexico City • Madrid • Amsterdam

Acquisitions Editor: Janice Wiggins Clarke
Marketing Manager: Wendy Albert
Electronic Page Makeup/Project Coordination/Text Design: WestWords, Inc.
Cover Design Manager: Nancy Danahy
Cover Design: Keithley and Associates
Full Service Production Manager: Eric Jorgensen
Print Buyer: Denise Sandler
Printer and Binder: The Maple-Vail Book Manufacturing Group
Cover Printer: Phoenix Color Corp.

Library of Congress Cataloging-in-Publication-Data

Fox, James Alan, 1951–
    Elementary statistics in criminal justice research / James Alan Fox,
  Jack Levin, Michael Shively
      p. cm.
    Includes bibliographical references and index.
    ISBN 0-321-02463-X
    1. Social sciences—Statistical methods.   2. Criminal justice,
  Administration of.   3. Criminal statistics.   I. Levin, Jack.
  II. Shively, Michael.   III. Title.
  HA35.L456   1999
  519.5'024'364—dc21   98-8602
                                        CIP

ISBN 0-321-02463-X

12345678910–MA–01009998

We dedicate this book to our loving families.

CONTENTS

PREFACE   XII

CHAPTER 1

WHY THE CRIMINAL JUSTICE RESEARCHER USES STATISTICS   1

The Nature of Criminal Justice Research   1
Major Data Sources in Criminology and Criminal Justice   5
Why Test Hypotheses?   7
The Stages of Criminal Justice Research   8
Using Series of Numbers to Do Criminal Justice Research   8
Functions of Statistics   12
Summary   17
Terms to Remember   17
Problems   18

PART ONE

DESCRIPTION   21

CHAPTER 2

ORGANIZING THE DATA   23

Frequency Distributions of Nominal Data   23
Comparing Distributions   24
Proportions and Percentages   25
Ratios and Rates   26
Simple Frequency Distributions of Ordinal and Interval Data   28
Grouped Frequency Distributions of Interval Data   29
Cumulative Distributions   33
Percentile Ranks   35
Dealing with Decimal Data   41
Flexible Class Intervals   42
Cross-Tabulations   44
Graphic Presentations   50
Summary   64
Terms to Remember   64
Problems   65

CHAPTER 3

MEASURES OF CENTRAL TENDENCY   69

The Mode   69
The Median   70
The Mean   71
Taking One Step at a Time   73
Comparing the Mode, Median, and Mean   74
Obtaining the Mode, Median, and Mean from a Simple Frequency Distribution   78
Obtaining the Mode, Median, and Mean from a Grouped Frequency Distribution   80
Summary   83
Terms to Remember   84
Step-By-Step Study Guide: Mode, Median, and Mean for Raw Scores   84
Problems   85

CHAPTER 4

MEASURES OF VARIABILITY   88

The Range   89
The Mean Deviation   90
The Variance and Standard Deviation   92
The Raw-Score Formula for Variance and Standard Deviation   96
The Meaning of the Standard Deviation   97
Comparing Measures of Variability   100
Obtaining the Variance and Standard Deviation from a Simple Frequency
   Distribution   101
Obtaining the Variance and Standard Deviation from a Grouped Frequency
   Distribution   104
Summary   106
Terms to Remember   107
Step-By-Step Study Guide: Variance and Standard Deviation for Raw Scores   107
Problems   107

PART TWO

FROM DESCRIPTION TO DECISION MAKING   111

CHAPTER 5

PROBABILITY AND THE NORMAL CURVE   113

Rules of Probability   114
Probability Distributions   117
The Normal Curve as a Probability Distribution   121
Characteristics of the Normal Curve   121
The Model and the Reality of the Normal Curve   122

The Area Under the Normal Curve   124
Standard Scores and the Normal Curve   129
Finding Probability Under the Normal Curve   133
Obtaining Percentile Ranks from the Normal Curve   137
Summary   140
Terms to Remember   140
Step-By-Step Study Guide: Probability Under the Normal Curve   141
Step-By-Step Study Guide: Percentile Ranks from the Normal Curve   141
Problems   141

CHAPTER 6

SAMPLES AND POPULATIONS   145

Sampling Methods   146
Sampling Error   150
Sampling Distribution of Means   151
Standard Error of the Mean   158
Confidence Intervals   159
The *t* Distribution   165
Estimating Proportions   171
Summary   174
Terms to Remember   174
Step-By-Step Study Guide: Confidence Interval for the Mean Using *z*   174
Step-By-Step Study Guide: Confidence Interval for the Mean Using *t*   175
Step-By-Step Study Guide: Confidence Interval for the Proportion   176
Problems   176

PART THREE
DECISION MAKING   179

CHAPTER 7

TESTING DIFFERENCES BETWEEN MEANS   181

The Null Hypothesis: No Difference between Means   183
The Research Hypothesis: A Difference between Means   183
Sampling Distribution of Differences between Means   184
Testing Hypotheses with the Distribution of Differences between Means   188
Levels of Significance   191
Standard Error of the Difference between Means   196
Testing the Difference between Means   197
Comparing the Same Sample Measured Twice   201
Two Sample Tests of Proportions   204
One-Tailed Tests   207
Requirements for Testing the Difference between Means   213
Summary   214
Terms to Remember   215

Step-By-Step Study Guide: Test of Differences between Means for
    Independent Groups   215
Step-By-Step Study Guide: Test of Differences between Means for the Same
    Sample Measured Twice   216
Step-By-Step Study Guide: Test of Differences between Proportions   216
Problems   217

CHAPTER 8

ANALYSIS OF VARIANCE   222

The Logic of Analysis of Variance   223
The Sum of Squares   225
Mean Square   231
The F Ratio   233
A Multiple Comparison of Means   238
Requirements for Using the F Ratio   240
Summary   241
Terms to Remember   241
Step-By-Step Study Guide: Test of Differences between Means for Several
    Independent Groups Using Analysis of Variance   242
Problems   243

CHAPTER 9

NONPARAMETRIC TESTS OF SIGNIFICANCE   245

One-Way Chi-Square Test   246
Two-Way Chi-Square Test   250
The Median Test   269
The Mann-Whitney U Test   272
Kruskal-Wallis One-Way Analysis of Variance by Ranks   275
Summary   278
Terms to Remember   278
Step-By-Step Study Guide: Test of Differences between Groups for Nominal-Level
    Data Using Chi-Square   278
Step-By-Step Study Guide: Test of Differences between Groups for Ordinal-Level
    Data Using the Mann-Whitney U Test   279
Step-By-Step Study Guide: Test of Differences between Several Groups for
    Ordinal-Level Data Using the Kruskal-Wallis Test   280
Problems   280

CHAPTER 10

CORRELATION   284

Strength of Correlation   284
Direction of Correlation   285
Curvilinear Correlation   286
The Correlation Coefficient   286

Pearson's Correlation Coefficient   288
The Importance of Scatter Plots   296
Partial Correlation   298
Summary   304
Terms to Remember   304
Step-By-Step Study Guide: Testing the Strength of Association between Interval-
        Level Variables Using Pearson's Correlation   304
Problems   305

CHAPTER 11

REGRESSION ANALYSIS   308

The Regression Model   309
Interpreting the Regression Line   314
Prediction Errors   316
Regression and Pearson's Correlation   319
Regression and Analysis of Variance   320
Multiple Regression   325
Summary   328
Terms to Remember   328
Step-By-Step Study Guide: Testing the Effect of an Independent Variable on a Dependent
        Variable Using Regression Analysis   328
Problems   330

CHAPTER 12

NONPARAMETRIC MEASURES OF CORRELATION   332

Spearman's Rank-Order Correlation Coefficient   332
Goodman's and Kruskal's Gamma   339
Correlation Coefficient for Nominal Data Arranged in a 2×2 Table   344
Correlation Coefficients for Nominal Data in Larger than 2×2 Tables   346
Lambda   349
Elaboration   352
Summary   356
Terms to Remember   357
Step-By-Step Study Guide: Testing the Strength of Association between Ordinal-Level
        Variables Using Spearman's Rank-Order Correlation   357
Step-By-Step Study Guide: Testing the Strength of Association between Cross-Tabulated,
        Ordinal-Level Variables Using Goodman's and Kruskal's Gamma   357
Problems   358

CHAPTER 13

APPLYING STATISTICAL PROCEDURES TO RESEARCH PROBLEMS   361

Research Situations   363
Research Solutions   376

Appendixes 385

Appendix A: Crime and Criminal Justice Internet Sites   387

Appendix B: A Review of Some Fundamentals of Mathematics   391

Appendix C: Tables   396

Appendix D: List of Formulas   412

Glossary   418

Answers to Problems   425

Index   431

PREFACE

Elementary Statistics in Criminal Justice Research provides an introduction to statistics for students in criminal justice and criminology. This book is not a comprehensive reference work on statistical methods. On the contrary, our first and foremost objective is to be understandable to a broad range of students, particularly to those who may not have a strong background in mathematics. Although this is technically a first edition, this text has in an important sense been tested and retested on virtually tens of thousands of students spanning a broad range of colleges and universities. That is, this volume is a thorough adaptation of *Elementary Statistics in Social Research,* which over the past 25 years has undergone refinements and improvements in responding to instructor and student feedback through seven editions. While the statistical procedures and conceptual explanations remain essentially unchanged for the criminal justice edition, practically all of the illustrations and examples pertain to crime and justice concerns.

Like its predecessors, this textbook contains a number of pedagogical features. Most notably, detailed step-by-step study illustrations of statistical procedures are located at important points throughout. We have also attempted to provide clear and logical explanations for the rationale and use of statistical methods in criminal justice research. In this edition, we have included a large number of end-of-the-chapter problems, almost all of which are answered at the end of the book. Finally, for all major statistical procedures we have included step-by-step study guides at the end of chapters.

Following a detailed overview in Chapter 1, the text is divided into three parts. Part One (Chapters 2 to 4) introduces the student to the most common methods for describing and comparing data. Part Two (Chapters 5 and 6) serves a transitional purpose. Beginning with a discussion of the basic concepts of probability, it leads the student from the topic of the normal curve as an important descriptive device to the use of the normal curve as a basis for generalizing from samples to populations. Continuing with this decision-making focus, Part Three (Chapters 7 to 13) contains several well-known tests of significance, procedures for obtaining correlation coefficients, and an introduction to regression analysis. Part Three concludes with an important chapter in which students learn, through example, the conditions for applying statistical procedures to criminal justice research problems.

The text provides students with background material for the study of statistics. A survey of key Internet sites which provide criminal justice data and related documents appears in an appendix. A review of basic mathematics, statistical tables, a list of formulas, and a glossary of terms are also located in the appendixes at the end of the book.

Additional supplements are available separately with this text. There is a student workbook written by Jeb Booth and Michael Shively, which contains a number of criminal justice data sets for use by students. A computer disk containing three criminal justice data sets and documentation for each has been prepared by Michael Shively. An instructor's manual and test bank written by the authors and Jeb Booth provides a test bank and handouts for classroom use. The testbank is available in printed and computerized versions.

We are grateful to the following reviewers for their insightful and helpful suggestions:

Dr. Richard Anson, Albany State University, Dr. Roger Barnes, University of the Incarnate Word, Dr. Paige Gordier, Lake Superior State University, Professor Michael Turner, University of Cincinnati, Dr. Kimberly McCabe, University of South Carolina, Dr. Libby Deschenes, California State University, Long Beach.

We are also indebted to the Literary Executive of the late Sir Ron A. Fisher, F.R.S.; to Dr. Rank Yates, F.R.S.; and to Longman Group, Ltd., London, for permission to reprint Tables III, IV, V, and VI from their book *Statistical Tables for Biological, Agricultural and Medical Research,* 6th ed., 1974. Finally, we acknowledge the important role of our personal computers, without "whose" assistance this book would not have been possible.

James Alan Fox
Jack Levin
Michael Shively

1

WHY THE CRIMINAL JUSTICE RESEARCHER USES STATISTICS

- **THE NATURE OF CRIMINAL JUSTICE RESEARCH**

- **WHY TEST HYPOTHESES?**

- **THE STAGES OF CRIMINAL JUSTICE RESEARCH**

- **USING SERIES OF NUMBERS TO DO CRIMINAL JUSTICE RESEARCH**

- **FUNCTIONS OF STATISTICS**

- **SUMMARY**

- **TERMS TO REMEMBER**

- **PROBLEMS**

A little of the social scientist can be found in all of us. Almost daily, we take educated guesses concerning the future events in our lives in order to plan for new situations or experiences. As these situations occur, we are sometimes able to confirm or support our ideas; other times, however, we are not so lucky and must face the sometimes unpleasant consequences.

To take some familiar examples: We might invest in the stock market, vote for a political candidate who promises to solve domestic problems, play the horses, take medicine to reduce the discomfort of a cold, throw dice in a gambling casino, try to psych out our instructors regarding a midterm, or accept a blind date on the word of a friend.

Sometimes we win; sometimes we lose. Thus, we might make a sound investment in the stock market, but be sorry about our voting decision; win money at the craps table, but discover we have taken the wrong medicine for our illness; do well on a midterm, but have a miserable blind date; and so on. It is unfortunately true that not all of our everyday predictions will be supported by experience.

THE NATURE OF CRIMINAL JUSTICE RESEARCH

Similar to our everyday approach to the world, social scientists attempt to explain and predict human behavior. They also take "educated guesses" about the nature of social reality, although in a far more precise and structured manner. In the process, social scientists examine characteristics of human behavior called *variables*—characteristics that differ or vary from one individual to another (for example, age, social class, and attitude) or from one point in time to another (for example, unemployment, crime rate, and population).

Not all human characteristics vary. It is a fact of life, for example, that the gender of the person who gave birth to you is female. Therefore, in any group of individuals, gender of mother is the *constant* "female." A biology text would spend considerable time discussing why only females give birth and the conditions under which birth is possible, but a social scientist would consider the mother's gender a given, one that is not worthy of study because it never varies. It could not be used to explain differences in the mental health of children because all of their mothers are females. In contrast, mother's age, race, and mental health are variables: In any group of individuals, they will differ from person to person and can be the key to a greater understanding of the development of the child. A researcher therefore might study differences in the mental health of children depending on the age, race, and mental health of their mothers.

In addition to specifying variables, the researcher must also determine the *unit of observation* for the research. Usually, social scientists collect data on individual persons. For example, a researcher might conduct interviews to determine if the elderly are victimized by crime more often than younger respondents. In this case, an individual respondent is the unit to be observed by the social scientist.

However, researchers sometimes focus their research on *aggregates*—that is, on the way in which measures vary across entire collections of people. For example, a criminologist might study the relationship between the average age of the population and the crime rate in various metropolitan areas. In this study, the units of observation are metropolitan areas rather than individuals.

Whether focusing on individuals or aggregates, the ideas that social scientists have concerning the nature of social reality are called *hypotheses.* These hypotheses are frequently expressed in a statement of the relationship between two or more variables: at minimum, an *independent variable* (or presumed cause) and a *dependent variable* (or presumed effect). For example, a researcher might hypothesize that socially isolated children watch more television than children who are well-integrated into their peer groups, and he or she might conduct a survey in which both socially isolated and well-integrated children are asked questions regarding the time they spend watching television (social isolation would be the independent variable; TV-viewing behavior would be the dependent variable). Or a researcher might hypothesize that the one-parent family structure generates greater delinquency than the two-parent family structure and might proceed to interview samples of delinquents and nondelinquents to determine whether one or both parents were present in their family backgrounds (family structure would be the independent variable; delinquency would be the dependent variable).

Thus, not unlike their counterparts in the physical sciences, researchers in criminal justice and criminology often conduct research to increase their understanding of the problems and issues in their field. Research takes many forms and can be used to investigate a wide range of problems. Among the most useful research methods employed by researchers for testing their hypotheses are the experiment, the survey, content analysis, and participant observation. For example, a researcher may conduct an experiment to determine if arresting a wife batterer will deter this behavior in the future, a sample survey to investigate political opinions, a content analysis of values in youth magazines, or a participant observation of an extremist political group. Each of these research strategies is described and illustrated in this chapter.

THE EXPERIMENT

Unlike everyday observation (or, for that matter, any other research approach), the *experiment* is distinguished by the degree of *control* a researcher is able to apply to the research situation. In an experiment, researchers actually manipulate one or more of the independent variables to which their subjects are exposed. The manipulation occurs when an experimenter assigns the independent variable to one group of people (called an *experimental group*) but withholds it from another group of people (called a *control group*). Ideally, all other initial differences between the experimental and control groups are eliminated by assigning subjects on a random basis to the experimental and control conditions.

For example, a researcher who hypothesizes that drug abuse treatment prior to release from prison reduces subsequent criminal behavior might randomly assign a number of subjects to the experimental and control groups by flipping a coin (heads they're in the experimental group and receive drug treatment; tails they're in the control group and receive no drug treatment). This random assignment ensures that the groups do not differ initially in any significant way. The experimental group might receive six months of intensive treatment to address their substance abuse issues, while the control group resides in the same prison and is handled no differently *except* that they do not receive the drug treatment. The researchers would then follow the progress of both groups for two years after their release, examining state and federal records for indications that the released inmates were convicted for crimes committed during this period. If the conviction rate of the experimental group was lower than the control group, the difference would be attributable to the drug treatment program since the only known difference between the two groups was the program. The conclusion would be that drug abuse treatment prior to release from prison reduces subsequent criminal involvement.

THE SURVEY

As we have seen, experimenters actually have a direct hand in creating the effect that they seek to achieve. By contrast, *survey* research is *retrospective*—the effects of independent variables on dependent variables are *recorded* after—and sometimes long after—they have occurred. Survey researchers typically seek to reconstruct these influences and consequences by means of verbal reports from their respondents in self-administered questionnaires, face-to-face interviews, or telephone interviews.

Surveys lack the tight controls of experiments: Variables are not manipulated and subjects are not assigned to groups at random. As a consequence, it is much more difficult to establish cause and effect. Suppose, for instance, in a survey measuring fear of crime, that a researcher finds that respondents who had been victims of crime tend to be more fearful of walking alone in their neighborhoods than those who had not been victimized. Because the variable *victimization* was not manipulated, we cannot make the logical conclusion that victimization *causes* increased fear. An alternative explanation that the condition of their neighborhoods (poverty, for example) produces both fear among residents and crime in the streets is just as plausible.

Surveys also have advantages precisely because they do not involve an experimental manipulation. As compared with experiments, survey research can investigate a much larger number of important independent variables in relation to any dependent variable. Because they are not confined to a laboratory setting in which an independent variable can be manipulated, surveys can also be more *representative*—their results can be generalized to a broader range of people.

For example, a survey researcher who hypothesizes that frustration increases aggression might locate a number of severely aggressive individuals and interview them to identify the frustrating events in their lives, such as isolation, physical disabilities, poor grades in school, and poverty. Obviously, survey researchers cannot manipulate the variables by introducing these frustrating life events themselves; but they can attempt to discover and record them after they have occurred. To study the relationship between frustration and aggression, Stuart Palmer interviewed the mothers of 51 convicted murderers. He found many more frustrating circumstances in the early lives of these killers than in the lives of their brothers who had not committed murder. Specifically, the research showed that the murderers as children had been subjected to more serious illnesses, operations, accidents, beatings, physical defects, frightening experiences, and disapproval from their peers than had the comparison group.

CONTENT ANALYSIS

As an alternative to experiments and surveys, *content analysis* is a research method whereby a researcher seeks objectively to describe the content of previously produced messages. Researchers who conduct a content analysis have no need directly to observe behavior or to question a sample of respondents. Instead, they typically study the content of books, magazines, newspapers, films, radio broadcasts, photographs, cartoons, letters, verbal dyadic interaction, political propaganda, or music.

In 1993, for example, Gray Cavender and Lisa Bond-Maupin[1] performed a content analysis of the *America's Most Wanted* and *Unsolved Mysteries* television shows that aired during the first five months of 1989. They selected a random sample of 16 episodes, which contained a total of 77 vignettes or descriptions of criminal events and participants. Using appropriate coding sheets, the researchers gathered data on the characteristics of the featured crimes, offenders, and victims; how the shows depict the crime and participants (such as the apparent motivation and dangerousness of the offenders and vulnerability of the victims); how the shows depict the relative safety of people and places; what the audience should do about crime; and information about the cinematic techniques used.

The researchers found that the two shows' depictions of crime did not reflect what is known about actual crime in the United States through official statistics, but that they were consistent with fictional television crime drama. Shows such as *America's Most Wanted* and *Unsolved Mysteries* are often referred to as "reality programs," mixing fact and fiction by taking true crime stories and presenting these as entertainment. The construction of the vignettes—with reenactments complete with professional actors, creative camera angles, music, and narration—follow the format of television drama and sometimes that of horror movies. The shows are designed to encourage the audience to feel the victims' dread and terror. The authors conclude that one of the messages conveyed by these shows is that the modern world is filled with random and terrifying danger that potentially awaits the audience. The shows then offer viewers the chance to escape the exaggerated sense of fear and

---

[1]Cavender, Gray, and Lisa Bond-Maupin. (1993). "Fear and loathing on reality television: An analysis of America's Most Wanted and Unsolved Mysteries." *Sociological Inquiry,* 63(3): 305–317.

helplessness by seizing control and actively participating in the surveillance and capture of dangerous predators.

PARTICIPANT OBSERVATION

Another widely used research method is *participant observation,* whereby a researcher "participates in the daily life of the people under study, either openly in the role of researcher or covertly in some disguised role, observing things that happen, listening to what is said, and questioning people, over some length of time."[2]

The particular strength of participant observation is its ability to provide a *complete* form of information about a situation or a series of events. The participant observer is able to determine the meaning of social situations, not from the viewpoint of outsiders, but as defined by the group members themselves.

There are many examples of participant observation in criminal justice and related fields, most involving researchers who have some level of involvement in group life but are primarily and openly there to observe. For example, Martin Sanchez Jankowski spent more than 10 years conducting a participant observation study of 37 gangs in three U.S. cities. In his 1991 book *Islands in the Street: Gangs and American Urban Society,* Jankowski describes how he not only observed but participated in gang activities, spending months at a time with a particular gang. According to his agreement with each gang, he did not participate in illegal activities but otherwise did essentially everything they did: "I ate where they ate, I slept where they slept, I stayed with their families, I traveled where they went, and in certain situations where I could not remain neutral, I fought with them" (p. 13). Among the conclusions drawn from his research are that, contrary to popular opinion, the vast majority of gang members are intelligent, free of sadistic or other psychological disorders, are not lazy, and share many of the goals and values of mainstream Americans.

MAJOR DATA SOURCES IN CRIMINOLOGY AND CRIMINAL JUSTICE[3]

SURVEYS

While all of the previously described methods are used, most of the data in criminology and criminal justice is produced by surveys. The largest and most prominent of these is the National Crime Victimization Survey (NCVS) conducted since 1972 by the U.S. Department of Justice, Bureau of Justice Statistics. For this survey, a nationwide representative sample of approximately 48,000 households is selected, and interviews of all household members at least 12 years old are conducted by U.S. Census Bureau personnel. Households stay in the sample for three years, are interviewed every six months, and new households are rotated in and out of the sample on an ongoing basis.

The NCVS provides information on crimes committed against individuals and households, regardless of whether the crimes were reported to police or anyone else. The survey produces information about victim and household characteristics (such as age, sex, race, and

---

[2]Becker, Howard S. and Geer, Blanche, "Participant Observation and Interviewing: A Comparison," in William J. Filstead (ed.), *Qualitative Methodology* (Chicago: Markham, 1970), 133.

[3]A list of Internet sites containing data and research on crime and criminal justice is provided in Appendix A.

education of each resident, and total household income), offender characteristics (such as victims' perceptions of offender sex, race, age, possible intoxication, and their relationship with the offender), and characteristics of the crimes (such as type, when and where they occurred, use of weapons, and impact on victims). Crime victims also are asked about their efforts to protect themselves from crime, and their experiences with the criminal justice system. Among the products of the NCVS are estimates of crime rates that are not dependent on the criminal justice system records, changes in crime rates over time, the level of under-reporting of crime to the police, and lifetime likelihood of victimization.

While the NCVS is the largest continuous survey project in crime research, there are many others. For example, the National Youth Survey,[4] conducted by the Institute of Behavioral Science, in 1977, for example, began its study of a national sample of 1,725 people aged 11 to 17, and surveyed these same individuals again in 1984, 1987, 1990, and 1993. The respondents in this study provided information about their own criminal and delinquent behavior such as their use of illegal drugs and commission of crimes such as larceny, assault, auto theft, sexual assault, and burglary.

In addition to studying crime victimization and self-reported criminal involvement, surveys are often used to study attitudes and opinions about crime and the criminal justice system, as well as to examine theories about the causes of crime. For example, the National Opinion Survey of Crime and Justice[5] asked a national random sample of 1,005 adults their opinions about a wide range of criminal justice issues. Included in the survey were questions about the media crime coverage, fear of becoming a victim of various kinds of crime, and how people view the fairness and effectiveness of criminal justice institutions such as the police and the courts. Surveys examining criminological theories are numerous, including a 1997 study testing Michael R. Gottfredson and Travis Hirschi's general theory of crime,[6] and other studies examining how the threat of punishment deters people from committing crime.

POLICE REPORTS

Another major source of crime information is the reported Uniform Crime Reports (UCR). Since 1929, police agencies have sent information about homicide, forcible rape, robbery, aggravated assault, burglary, larceny-theft, motor vehicle theft, and arson to the UCR. The information is compiled by the FBI and is used to count crime and to track trends over time. In addition to the number of crimes reported to police, the report contains information about crimes cleared by arrest, and characteristics of arrested persons.

The data presented in the annual UCR publication *Crime in the United States* are summary measures, meaning that only total counts of crimes reported, arrests, etc. are presented for each police agency. This makes the UCR data unsuitable for studying individual crimes, offenders, or victims. To address this, the U.S. Department of Justice also

---

[4]*National Youth Survey Project.* University of Colorado, Institute of Behavioral Science, David Huizinga and Delbert S. Elliot, principal investigators.

[5]Flanagan, Timothy J., and Dennis R. Longmire. (1995). *National Opinion Survey of Crime and Justice.* ICPSR version. Huntsville, TX: Sam Houston State University, Criminal Justice Center, Survey Research Program [producer]. Ann Arbor, MI: Inter-University Consortium for Political and Social Research [distributor].

[6]Evans, T. David, Francis T. Cullen, Velmer S. Burton, Jr., R. Gregory Dunaway, and Michael L. Benson. "The social consequences of self-control: Testing the general theory of crime." *Criminology,* 35 (1997): 475–504.

provides data where individual crime incidents (not cities or counties) are the units of analysis. The Supplemental Homicide Reports (SHR) were begun in 1961, and for each individual homicide contains detailed information such as the relationship between victims and offenders, location, use of weapons, and characteristics of the victims and offenders. Like the UCR, the SHR are based on police records of crimes reported to them. This incident-based data, as opposed to the summary data of the UCR, allows the description and analysis of individual events, and the comparison of features of different events. For example, it is possible to compare whether male and female victims tend to be killed with different weapons or if they have different relationships to their assailants.

The National Incident-Based Reporting System (NIBRS) was planned in the mid-1980s as a replacement for the UCR, and is similar to the SHR but extends to all of the crimes covered in the UCR and dozens more. Due to the vastly greater volume of data required for NIBRS compared to the UCR, the transition to NIBR is still ongoing, with only a few states providing complete information to the FBI.

WHY TEST HYPOTHESES?

Social science is often referred to, quite unfairly, as the study of the obvious. However, it is desirable, if not necessary, to test hypotheses about the nature of crime and justice, even those that seem logical and self-evident. Our everyday common sense observations are generally based on narrow, often biased preconceptions and personal experiences. These can lead us to accept without criticism invalid assumptions about the characteristics of crime and criminal behavior.

To demonstrate how we can be so easily misled by our preconceptions and stereotypes, consider what we "know" about mass murderers. How many of the following characteristics seem obvious to you? How many would not be worth studying because they are so obvious?

1. Mass murderers are almost always insane. (After all, a sane person would never shoot 14 people from the top of a tower as Charles Whitman did in 1966.)
2. Mass murderers are usually loners. (The neighbors always seem to say, "He was quiet, he stayed pretty much to himself, we never really knew him.")
3. Mass murderers look different from the rest of us. (One generally imagines a glassy-eyed lunatic, as in the horror movies.)
4. Mass murderers are usually strangers to their victims, who are unlucky enough to be in the wrong place at the wrong time. (Cases like the mass murder in a Long Island commuter train in 1993 typically come to mind.)

That these conceptions about mass murderers seem so clear-cut and indisputable might explain why it took until 1985 for anyone to look systematically at the profile of the mass murderer. Compiling detailed information about 42 mass killers, Levin and Fox found that every one of these notions was incorrect.[7] In fact, mass murderers are rarely insane—they know exactly what they are doing and are not driven to kill by voices of demons. Mass murderers are usually not loners—they have friends and often wives and children who do not anticipate their actions. Mass murderers do not look any different—they are "extraordinarily

---

[7]Levin, Jack, and James Alan Fox, *Mass Murder: America's Growing Menace.* New York: Berkley, 1991.

ordinary." Finally, random shootings in a public place are the exceptions—most mass murders occur within families or among acquaintances. Therefore, as illustrated by the example of mass murderers, it is foolish to draw conclusions on the basis of common sense alone.

THE STAGES OF CRIMINAL JUSTICE RESEARCH

Systematically testing our ideas about the nature of crime and justice often demands carefully planned and executed research in which the following occur:

1. The problem to be studied is reduced to a testable hypothesis (for example, "one-parent families generate more delinquency than two-parent families").
2. An appropriate set of instruments is developed (for example, a questionnaire or an interview schedule).
3. The data are collected (that is, the researcher might go into the field and conduct a poll or a survey).
4. The data are analyzed for their bearing on the initial hypotheses.
5. Results of the analysis are interpreted and communicated to an audience (for example, by means of a lecture, journal article, or press release).

As we shall see in subsequent chapters, the material presented in this book is most closely tied to the data analysis stage of research (above), in which the data collected or gathered by the researcher are analyzed for their bearing on the initial hypotheses. It is in this stage of research that the raw data are tabulated, calculated, counted, summarized, rearranged, compared, or, in a word, *organized,* so that the accuracy or validity of the hypotheses can be tested.

USING SERIES OF NUMBERS TO DO CRIMINAL JUSTICE RESEARCH

Anyone who has conducted research knows that problems in data analysis must be confronted in the planning stages of a research project, because they have a bearing on the nature of decisions at all other stages. Such problems often affect aspects of the research design and even the types of instruments employed in collecting the data. For this reason, we constantly seek techniques or methods for enhancing the quality of data analysis.

Most researchers would agree on the importance of *measurement* in analyzing data. When some characteristic is measured, researchers are able to assign to it a series of numbers according to a set of rules.

Criminologists, criminal justice researchers, and other social scientists have developed measures of a wide range of phenomena including fear of crime, approval of capital punishment, criminal justice program quality, post-traumatic stress, offense type, perceived likelihood of committing crime, race, recidivism risk, crime seriousness, education level, hostility, impulsivity, socioeconomic status, substance abuse treatment need, and victim blame.

Numbers have at least three important functions for researchers, depending on the particular *level of measurement* that they employ. Specifically, series of numbers can be used to

1. *classify* or *categorize* at the nominal level of measurement,
2. *rank* or *order* at the ordinal level of measurement, and
3. assign a *score* at the interval level of measurement.

THE NOMINAL LEVEL

The *nominal level of measurement* involves naming or labeling, that is, of placing cases into categories and counting their frequency of occurrence. To illustrate, we might use a nominal-level measure to indicate whether each respondent is prejudiced or tolerant toward Latinos. As shown in Table 1.1, we might question the 10 probation officers and determine that 5 can be regarded as (1) prejudiced and 5 can be considered as (2) accepting.

Other nominal-level measures in criminology and criminal justice research are crime type (e.g., property, violent, drug, sex), offense history (past criminal record versus no record), race (e.g., Asian, Caucasian, African-American, Latino), status as high school graduate (did or did not graduate), gang memberships (are or are not a member), sex (male versus female), personality type (authoritarian, passive-aggressive, extrovert), and guilt (innocent or guilty of committing a crime).

When dealing with nominal data, we must keep in mind that *every case must be placed in one, and only one, category.* This requirement indicates that the categories must be nonoverlapping or *mutually exclusive.* Thus, a respondent's race classified as white cannot also be classified as black; any respondent labeled male cannot also be labeled female. The requirement also indicates that the categories must be *exhaustive*—there must be a place for every case that arises. For illustrative purposes, imagine a study in which all respondents are interviewed and categorized by race as either black or white. Where would we categorize a Chinese respondent if he or she were to appear? In this case, it might be necessary to expand the original category system to include Asians or, assuming that most respondents will be white or black, to include an "other" category in which such exceptions can be placed.

The reader should note that nominal data are not graded, ranked, or scaled for qualities such as better or worse, higher or lower, more or less. Clearly, then, a nominal measure of sex does not signify whether males are superior or inferior to females. Nominal data are merely labeled, sometimes by name (male versus female or prejudiced versus tolerant), other times by number (1 versus 2), but always for the purpose of grouping the cases into separate categories to indicate sameness or differentness with respect to a given quality or characteristic. Thus, even when a number is used to label a category (for example, 1 = white, 2 = black, 3 = other), a quantity is not implied.

THE ORDINAL LEVEL

When the researcher goes beyond this level of measurement and seeks to order his or her cases in terms of the degree to which they have any given characteristic, he or she is working at the *ordinal level of measurement.* The nature of the relationship among ordinal

TABLE 1.1	ATTITUDES OF 10 PROBATION OFFICERS TOWARD LATINOS: NOMINAL DATA

Attitude toward Latinos	Frequency
1 = Prejudiced	5
2 = Accepting	5
Total	10

categories depends on that characteristic the researcher seeks to measure. To take a familiar example, one might classify individuals with respect to socioeconomic status as lower class, middle class, or upper class. Or, rather than categorize the students in a given classroom as *either* prejudiced *or* accepting, the researcher might rank them according to their degree of prejudice against Latinos, as indicated in Table 1.2.

The ordinal level of measurement yields information about the ordering of categories, but does not indicate the *magnitude of differences* between numbers. For instance, the researcher who employs an ordinal-level measure to study prejudice toward Latinos *does not know how much more prejudiced one respondent is than another.* In the example given earlier, it is not possible to determine how much more prejudiced Joyce is than Paul or how much less prejudiced Ben is than Linda or Ernie. This is because the intervals between the points or ranks on an ordinal scale are not known or meaningful. Therefore, it is not possible to assign *scores* to cases located at points along the scale.

THE INTERVAL LEVEL

By contrast, the *interval level of measurement* not only tells us about the ordering of categories but also indicates the exact *distance* between them.[8] Interval measures use *constant units of measurement* (for example, dollars or cents, Fahrenheit or Celsius, yards or feet, minutes or seconds) that yield *equal intervals* between points on the scale.

Some variables in their natural form are interval-level (for example, how many pounds you weigh, how many siblings you have, or how many hours you listen to the radio daily). Other variables are interval-level because of the way we scale them.

By this method, an interval measure of prejudice against Latinos—such as a set of responses to a series of questions about Latinos that is scored from 0 to 100 (100 is extreme prejudice)—might yield the data shown in Table 1.3 about the 10 probation officers.

As presented in Table 1.3, we are able to order the students in terms of their prejudices and, in addition, indicate the distances separating one from another. For instance, it is possible

TABLE 1.2 ATTITUDES OF 10 PROBATION OFFICERS TOWARD LATINOS: ORDINAL DATA	
Officer	Rank
Joyce	1 = most prejudiced
Paul	2 = second
Cathy	3 = third
Mike	4 = fourth
Judy	5 = fifth
Joe	6 = sixth
Kelly	7 = seventh
Ernie	8 = eighth
Linda	9 = ninth
Ben	10 = least prejudiced

---

[8]Some researchers further distinguish between ratio and interval levels of measurement, depending on whether the zero point on the scale is real or artificial. For the vast majority of statistical techniques, however, this distinction is irrelevant.

to say that Ben is the least prejudiced member of the class, because he received the lowest score. We can say also that Ben is only slightly less prejudiced than Linda or Ernie but much less prejudiced than Joyce, Paul, Cathy, or Mike, all of whom received extremely high scores. Depending on the purpose for which the study is designed, such information might be important to determine, but is not available at the ordinal level of measurement.

TREATING SOME ORDINAL VARIABLES AS INTERVAL

As we have seen, levels of measurement vary in terms of their degree of sophistication or refinement, from simple classification (nominal), to ranking (ordinal), to scoring (interval). At this point, the distinction between the nominal and ordinal levels should be quite clear. It would be difficult to confuse the level of measurement attained by the variable "color of hair" (blond, redhead, brunette, and black), which is nominal, with that of the variable "condition of hair" (dry, normal, oily), which is ordinal.

The distinction between ordinal and interval, however, is not always clear-cut. Often times, variables that in the strictest sense are ordinal may be treated as if they were interval when the ordered categories are fairly evenly spaced.

For example, the following two variables (*rank of professor* and *attitude toward professor*) are both ordinal.

Scale value	Rank of professor	Attitude toward professor
1	Distinguished professor	Very favorable
2	Full professor	Favorable
3	Associate professor	Somewhat favorable
4	Assistant professor	Neutral
5	Instructor	Somewhat unfavorable
6	Lecturer	Unfavorable
7	Teaching assistant	Very unfavorable

The *rank-of-professor* variable could hardly be mistaken for interval. The difference between *instructor* (5) and *lecturer* (6) is minimal in terms of prestige, salary, or qualifications,

TABLE 1.3 ATTITUDES OF 10 PROBATION OFFICERS TOWARD LATINOS: INTERVAL DATA

Student	Score[a]
Joyce	98
Paul	96
Cathy	95
Mike	94
Judy	68
Joe	21
Kelly	20
Ernie	15
Linda	11
Ben	6

[a] Higher scores indicate greater prejudice against Latinos.

whereas the difference between *instructor* (5) and *assistant professor* (4) is substantial, with the latter generally requiring a doctorate and receiving a much higher salary. By contrast, the *attitude-toward-professor* variable has scale values that are roughly evenly spaced. The difference between *somewhat unfavorable* (5) and *unfavorable* (6) *appears* to be virtually the same as the difference between *somewhat unfavorable* (5) and *neutral* (4). In fact, this is true of most attitude scales ranging from *strongly agree* to *strongly disagree, very favorable* to *very unfavorable, strongly approve* to *strongly disapprove,* and the like.

Rather than split hairs, many researchers make a practical decision. Whenever possible, they choose to treat ordinal variables as interval, but only when it is reasonable to assume that the scale has roughly equal intervals. Thus, they would treat the *attitude-toward-professor* variable as if it were interval, but they would never treat the *rank-of-professor* variable as anything other than ordinal. As you will see later in the text, treating ordinal variables that have nearly evenly spaced values as if they were interval allows researchers to use more powerful statistical procedures.

FUNCTIONS OF STATISTICS

It is when researchers use numbers—they *quantify* their data at the nominal, ordinal, or interval level of measurement—that they are likely to employ statistics as a tool of (1) *description* or (2) *decision making.* Let us now take a closer look at these important functions of statistics.

DESCRIPTION

To arrive at conclusions or obtain results, a researcher often studies hundreds, thousands, or even larger numbers of persons or groups. As an extreme case, the United States Bureau of the Census conducts a complete enumeration of the U.S. population, in which millions of individuals are contacted. Despite the aid of numerous sophisticated procedures, it is always a formidable task to describe and summarize the mass of data generated from projects in research.

To take a familiar example, the examination grades of 80 students have been listed in Table 1.4. Do you see any patterns in these grades? Can you describe these grades in a few words? In a few sentences? Can you tell if they are particularly high or low on the whole?

Your answer to these questions should be no. However, using even the most basic principles of descriptive statistics, it is possible to characterize the distribution of the examination grades in Table 1.4 with a good deal of clarity and precision, so that overall tendencies or group characteristics can be quickly discovered and easily communicated to almost anyone. First, the grades can be rearranged in consecutive order (from highest to lowest) and grouped into a much smaller number of categories. As shown in Table 1.5, this *grouped frequency distribution* (to be discussed in detail in Chapter 2) presents the grades within broader categories along with the number or *frequency* (f) of students whose grades fell into these categories. It can be readily seen, for example, that 17 students received grades between 60 and 69; only 2 students received grades between 20 and 29.

Another useful procedure (explained in Chapter 2) rearranges the grades graphically. As shown in Figure 1.1, the categories of grades are placed (from 20–29 to 90–99) along one line of a graph (that is, the *horizontal base line*) and their numbers or frequencies along another line (that is, the *vertical axis*). This arrangement results in a rather easily visualized graphic representation (for example, the bar graph), in which we can see that most grades fall between 50 and 80, whereas relatively few grades are much higher or lower.

As elaborated in Chapter 3, a particularly convenient and useful statistical method—one with which you are already more or less familiar—is to ask: What is the grade of the *average* person in this group of 80 students? The arithmetic average (or *mean*), which can be obtained by adding the entire list of grades and dividing this sum by the number of students, gives us a clearer picture of the overall group tendency or class performance. The arithmetic average in this example happens to be 60.5, a rather low grade compared against the class averages with which most students may be familiar. Apparently, this group of 80 students did somewhat poorly as a whole.

Thus, with the help of statistical devices such as grouped frequency distributions, graphs, and the arithmetic average, it is possible to detect and describe patterns or tendencies in distributions of scores (for example, the grades in Table 1.4) that might otherwise have gone unnoticed by the casual observer. In the present context, then, statistics may be defined as a *set of techniques for the reduction of quantitative data (that is, a series of numbers) to a small number of more convenient and easily communicated descriptive terms.*

TABLE 1.4   EXAMINATION GRADES FOR 80 STUDENTS

72	49	81	52	31
38	81	58	68	73
43	56	45	54	40
81	60	52	52	38
79	83	63	58	59
71	89	73	77	60
65	60	69	88	75
59	52	75	70	93
90	62	91	61	53
83	32	49	39	57
39	28	67	74	61
42	39	76	68	65
58	49	72	29	70
56	48	60	36	79
72	65	40	49	37
63	72	58	62	46

TABLE 1.5   EXAMINATION GRADES FOR 80 STUDENTS: A GROUPED FREQUENCY DISTRIBUTION

Grades	f
90–99	3
80–89	7
70–79	16
60–69	17
50–59	15
40–49	11
30–39	9
20–29	2

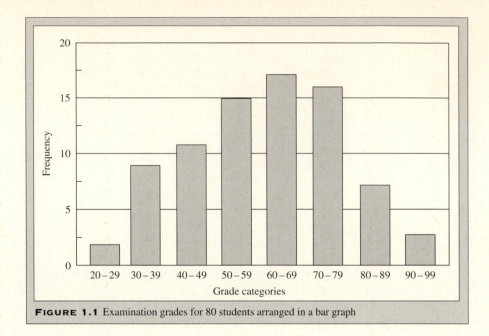

FIGURE 1.1 Examination grades for 80 students arranged in a bar graph

DECISION MAKING

For purposes of testing hypotheses, it is frequently necessary to go beyond mere description. It is often also necessary to make inferences, that is, to make decisions based on data collected on only a small portion or *sample* of the larger group we have in mind to study. Factors such as cost and time often preclude taking a complete enumeration or poll of the entire group (researchers call this larger group from which the sample was drawn a *population* or *universe*).

As we shall see in Chapter 6, every time researchers test hypotheses on a sample, they must decide whether it is indeed accurate to generalize the findings to the entire population from which they were drawn. Error inevitably results from sampling, even sampling that has been properly conceived and executed. This is the problem of generalizing or *drawing inferences* from the sample to the population.[9]

Statistics can be useful for purposes of generalizing findings, with a high degree of confidence, from small samples to larger populations. To understand better this decision-making purpose of statistics and the concept of generalizing from samples to populations,

---

[9]The concept of *sampling error* is discussed in greater detail in Chapter 6. However, to understand the inevitability of error when sampling from a larger group, you may now wish to conduct the following demonstration. Refer to Table 1.4, which contains the grades for a population of 80 students. At random (for example, by closing your eyes and pointing), select a sample of five grades from the entire list. Find the average grade by adding the five scores and dividing by 5, the total number of grades. It has already been pointed out that the average grade for the entire class of 80 students was 60.5. To what extent does your sample average differ from the class average, 60.5? Try this demonstration on several more samples of a few grades randomly selected from the larger group. With great consistency, you should find that your sample mean will almost always differ at least slightly from that obtained from the entire class of 80 students. This is what we mean by *sampling error.*

let us examine the results of a hypothetical study that was conducted to test the following hypothesis:

> *Hypothesis: Male college students are more likely than female college students to have tried marijuana.*

The researchers in this study decided to test their hypothesis at an urban university in which some 20,000 students (10,000 males and 10,000 females) were enrolled. Due to cost and time factors, they were not able to interview every student on campus, but did obtain from the registrar's office a complete listing of university students. From this list, every one hundredth student (one-half of them male, one-half of them female) was selected for the sample and subsequently interviewed by members of the research staff. The interviewers asked each of the 200 members of the sample whether he or she had ever tried marijuana and then recorded the student's gender as either male or female. After all interviews had been completed and returned to the staff office, the responses on the marijuana question were tabulated by gender and presented in Table 1.6.

Notice that results obtained from this sample of 200 students as presented in Table 1.6 are in the hypothesized direction: 35 out of 100 males reported having tried marijuana, whereas only 15 out of 100 females reported having tried marijuana. Clearly, in this small sample, males were more likely than females to have tried marijuana. For our purposes, however, the more important question is whether these gender differences in marijuana use are large enough to generalize them confidently to the much larger university population of 20,000 students. Do these results represent true population differences? Or have we obtained chance differences between males and females due strictly to sampling error—the error that occurs every time we take a small group from a larger group?

To illuminate the problem of generalizing results from samples to larger populations, imagine that the researchers had, instead, obtained the results shown in Table 1.7. Notice that these results are still in the predicted direction: 30 males as opposed to only 20 females have tried marijuana. But, are we still willing to generalize these results to the larger university population? Is it not likely that a difference of this magnitude (10 more males than females) would have happened simply by chance? Or can we confidently say that such relatively small differences reflect a real difference between males and females at that particular university?

Let us carry out the illustration a step further. Suppose that the researchers had obtained the data shown in Table 1.8. Differences between males and females shown in the table could not be much smaller and still be in the hypothesized direction: 26 males in contrast to 24 females tried marijuana—only 2 more males than females. How many of us would be willing to call *this* finding a true population difference between males and females rather than a product of chance or sampling error?

TABLE 1.6	MARIJUANA USE BY GENDER OF RESPONDENT: CASE I	

	Gender of respondent	
Marijuana use	Male	Female
Number who have tried it	35	15
Number who have not tried it	65	85
Total	100	100

TABLE 1.7 MARIJUANA USE BY GENDER OF RESPONDENT: CASE II

Marijuana use	Gender of respondent	
	Male	Female
Number who have tried it	30	20
Number who have not tried it	70	80
Total	100	100

TABLE 1.8 MARIJUANA USE BY GENDER OF RESPONDENT: CASE III

Marijuana use	Gender of respondent	
	Male	Female
Number who have tried it	26	24
Number who have not tried it	74	76
Total	100	100

Where do we draw the line? At what point does a sample difference become large enough so that we are willing to treat it as significant or real? With the aid of statistics, we can readily, and with a high degree of confidence, make such decisions about the relationship between samples and populations. To illustrate, had we used one of the statistical tests of significance discussed later in this text (for example, chi-square—see Chapter 9), we would already have known that *only those results* reported in Table 1.6 can be generalized to the population of 20,000 university students—that 35 out of 100 males but only 15 out of 100 females have tried marijuana is a finding substantial enough to be applied to the entire population with a high degree of confidence and is therefore referred to as a *statistically significant difference.* Our statistical test tells us there are only 5 chances out of 100 that we are wrong! By contrast, application of the same statistical criterion shows the results reported in Tables 1.7 and 1.8 are *statistically nonsignificant,* probably being the product of sampling error rather than real gender differences in the use of marijuana.

In the present context, then, statistics is *a set of decision-making techniques that aid researchers in drawing inferences from samples to populations and, hence, in testing hypotheses regarding the nature of social reality.*

AN IMPORTANT NOTE ABOUT ROUNDING

If you are like most students, the issue of rounding can be confusing. It is always a pleasure, of course, when an answer comes out to be a whole number because rounding is not needed. For those other times, however, when you confront a number such as 34.233333 or 7.126534, determining just how many digits to use in rounding becomes problematic.

For occasions when you need to round, the following rule can be applied: *Round a final answer to two more decimal digits than contained in the original scores.* If the original scores are all whole numbers (for example, 3, 6, 9, and 12), then round your final answer to two decimal places (for example, 4.45). If the original scores contain one decimal place (for example, 3.3, 6.0, 9.5, and 12.8), then round your answer to three decimal places (for example, 4.456). Note that a discussion of *how* to round is given in Appendix B, "A Review of Some Fundamentals of Mathematics."

Many of the problems in this book require a number of intermediate steps before arriving at the final answer. When using a calculator, it is usually not necessary to round off calculations done along the way, that is, for intermediate steps. Your calculator will often carry many more digits than you will eventually need. As a general rule for intermediate steps, therefore, do not round until it comes time to determine your final answer.

Rules of thumb, of course, must be used with some degree of good judgment. As an extreme example, you wouldn't want to round only to two decimal places in calculating the trajectory or thrust needed to send a missile to the moon; even a slight imprecision might lead to disaster. In doing problems for your statistics class, on the other hand, the precision of your answer is less important than learning the method itself. There may be times when your answer will differ slightly from that of your classmate or that contained in this book. For example, you may obtain the answer 5.55, whereas your classmate may get 5.56, yet you both may be correct. The difference is trivial and could easily have resulted from using two calculators with different memory capacities or from doing calculations in a different sequence.

In this text, we have generally followed this rule of thumb. In some illustrations, however, we rounded intermediate steps for the sake of clarity—but only to an extent that would not invalidate the final answer.

SUMMARY

This chapter linked our everyday predictions about future events with the experiences of researchers who use statistics as an aid in testing their hypotheses about the nature of crime and justice. Three levels of measurement were distinguished: the nominal level, at which data are categorized; the ordinal level, at which data are ranked; and the interval level, at which data are scored. Two major functions of statistics were identified with the data-analysis stage of social research, then briefly discussed and illustrated, namely:

1. Description (that is, the reduction of quantitative data to a small number of more convenient descriptive terms)
2. Decision making (that is, drawing inferences from samples to populations)

TERMS TO REMEMBER

Hypothesis	Level of Measurement
Variable	Nominal
Experiment	Ordinal
Survey	Interval
Content analysis	Independent variable
Participant observation	Dependent variable
Measurement	

PROBLEMS

1. A criminologist undertakes a series of studies to investigate various aspects of violence. For each of the following research situations, identify the research strategy (experiment, survey, content analysis, or participation observation) and the independent and dependent variables:

   a. Do male and female police officers describe domestic violence arrests in the same way? To find out, the researcher collected 100 arrest reports written by female officers and 100 written by males. He records and compares the language used to describe the level of violence of the alleged abuser, the level of harm to the abused, and the level of resistance to arrest.

   b. Does televised violence produce violent behavior among prisoners? To find out, researchers randomly assigned five prison cell blocks to receive uncensored programming and five cell blocks to receive programming in which all shows containing violence had been removed. They then compare the number of violent inmate confrontations in the two groups over the one-month period when subjects received different levels of violence in their television programs.

   c. Are fans more violent when their team wins or when they lose? To find out, the researcher spends his Saturdays in a sports bar featuring the local college game on several big-screen televisions. He dresses in a team hat and sweatshirt and becomes one of the crowd. At the same time, he observes and compares the number of fights that break out when the team wins versus loses.

   d. Is education level related to approval of trying as adults juveniles accused of violent crime? To find out, the researcher distributes questionnaires to a random sample of adults. Included in the questionnaires are items asking people to report their last grade of school completed and to rate on a 10-point scale their approval of trying as adults juveniles who are accused of committing murder, assault, robbery or rape.

2. Identify the level of measurement—nominal, ordinal, or interval—represented in each of the following questionnaire items:

   a. Your sex: 1 ___ Female
      2 ___ Male
   b. Your age: 1 ___ Younger than 20
      2 ___ 20–29
      3 ___ 30–39
      4 ___ 40–49
      5 ___ 50–59
      6 ___ 60–69
      7 ___ 70 or older

   c. How many people are there in your immediate family? _____

   d. Specify the highest level of education achieved by your mother:
      1 ___ None
      2 ___ Elementary school
      3 ___ Some high school
      4 ___ Graduated high school
      5 ___ Some college
      6 ___ Graduated college
      7 ___ Graduate school

   e. Your annual income from all sources: _____ (specify)

   f. Your religious preference:
      1 ___ Protestant
      2 ___ Catholic
      3 ___ Jewish
      4 ___ Other _____ (specify)

   g. The social class to which your parents belong:
      1 ___ Upper
      2 ___ Upper-middle
      3 ___ Middle-middle
      4 ___ Lower-middle
      5 ___ Lower

   h. In which of the following regions do your parents presently live?
      1 ___ Northeast
      2 ___ South
      3 ___ Midwest
      4 ___ West
      5 ___ Other _____ (specify)

   i. Indicate your political orientation by placing an "X" in the appropriate space:
      LIBERAL ___ : ___ : ___ : ___ : ___ CONSERVATIVE
              1   2   3   4   5

   j. Indicate your approval of capital punishment for convicted murderers by circling the appropriate number on the following scale:
      1   2   3   4   5
      Strongly   Strongly
      Disapprove   Approve

3. For the following items, indicate the level of measurement—nominal, ordinal, or interval:

   a. For a murder investigation, a police officer uses a tape measure to determine the distance between a witness's position and the site of the crime.

   b. The time it takes a car to travel from one mile marker to another is determined by a police officer using a stopwatch.

   c. Based on average daily population, a ranking of the "top 10" largest prisons is complied by a federal agency.

d. A legislative committee counts the number of judges, prosecutors, and defense attorneys currently employed in its state.

e. To track shoplifting losses, a store clerk takes an inventory of all items still on the shelves at the end of each month.

f. A law school dean counts the number of first-, second-, and third-year students.

g. A police officer uses a ruler to determine whether the length of a pocket knife exceeds legal limits.

h. In a criminal justice program, three college seniors are ranked first, second, and third in their class.

4. A researcher was interested in the behavior of adolescents in gangs. Specifically, he wondered how characteristics of each member's home life (parent's marital status, number of siblings, family income, etc.) influenced the leadership roles they assumed. The researcher recruited 30 gang members and asked them to record relevant aspects of their home life and their role in the gang's leadership.

a. What research strategy was used here?
b. What was the independent variable?
c. What was the dependent variable?

5. A research team was hired to determine whether a rehabilitation program reduces the likelihood that prisoners will re-offend after they are released. Four hundred inmates were declared eligible for the program, and half were randomly assigned to it while the others were kept in prisons without participating in any rehabilitative programs. All of the inmates were studied for two years after their release to see whether they were arrested again. A comparison of arrest rates was made between the rehabilitation program and the conventional prison groups.

a. What research strategy was used here?
b. What was the independent variable?
c. What was the dependent variable?

PART I
DESCRIPTION

CHAPTER 2
ORGANIZING THE DATA

CHAPTER 3
MEASURES OF CENTRAL TENDENCY

CHAPTER 4
MEASURES OF VARIABILITY

2

ORGANIZING THE DATA

- **FREQUENCY DISTRIBUTIONS OF NOMINAL DATA**
- **COMPARING DISTRIBUTIONS**
- **PROPORTIONS AND PERCENTAGES**
- **RATIOS AND RATES**
- **SIMPLE FREQUENCY DISTRIBUTIONS OF ORDINAL AND INTERVAL DATA**
- **GROUPED FREQUENCY DISTRIBUTIONS OF INTERVAL DATA**

- **CUMULATIVE DISTRIBUTIONS**
- **PERCENTILE RANKS**
- **DEALING WITH DECIMAL DATA**
- **FLEXIBLE CLASS INTERVALS**
- **CROSS-TABULATIONS**
- **GRAPHIC PRESENTATIONS**
- **SUMMARY**
- **TERMS TO REMEMBER**
- **PROBLEMS**

Collecting data entails a serious effort on the part of criminologists and criminal justice researchers who seek to increase their knowledge of crime and criminal justice issues. To interview or otherwise elicit information from judges, drug addicts, gang members, police, lawyers, middle-class Americans, or other respondents requires a degree of foresight, careful planning, and control, if not actual time spent in the field.

Data collection, however, is only the beginning as far as statistical analysis is concerned. Data collection yields the raw materials that criminal justice researchers use to analyze data, obtain results, and test hypotheses about the nature of crime and justice issues.

FREQUENCY DISTRIBUTIONS OF NOMINAL DATA

The cabinetmaker transforms raw wood into furniture; the chef converts raw food into the more palatable versions served at the dinner table. By a similar process, the criminal justice researcher—aided by "recipes" called *formulas* and *statistical techniques*—attempts to transform raw data into a meaningful and organized set of measures that can be used to test hypotheses.

What can researchers do to organize the jumble of raw numbers that they collect from their subjects? How do they go about transforming this mass of raw data into an easy-to-understand summary form? The first step is to construct a *frequency distribution* in the form of a table.

Suppose a researcher who studies victimization is interested in how people think they would respond if they were faced with different crime situations. In one experiment, the researcher presents 50 adult men with written descriptions of a hypothetical scenario where a person is walking toward his or her car and finds that a man has broken the window and is attempting to steal the car. The respondents are asked to imagine themselves in the role of the hypothetical car owner and to indicate how they would react in such a situation.

A frequency distribution of nominal data reporting the responses of the 50 men is presented in Table 2.1. Notice first that the table is headed by a number and a title that gives the reader an idea of the nature of the data presented—responses of men to hypothetical auto theft. This is a standard arrangement; every table must be clearly titled and, when presented in a series, labeled by number as well.

Frequency distributions of nominal data consist of two columns. As in Table 2.1, the left-hand column indicates which characteristic is being presented (response of person) and contains the categories of analysis (verbally confront thief, physically confront thief, withdraw and call police, shout for help). An adjacent column (headed *frequency*, or *f*) indicates the number of men in each category (25, 10, 10, and 5, respectively) as well as the total number of men (50), which can be indicated by either N = 50 or by including the word "Total" below the categories. A quick glance at the frequency distribution in Table 2.1 clearly reveals that more men believe that they would respond by either verbally or physically confronting the thief than by seeking help from the police or anyone else.

COMPARING DISTRIBUTIONS

Suppose next that the same researcher wishes to compare the responses of men and women to the hypothetical auto theft. Making comparisons between frequency distributions is a procedure often used to clarify results and add information. The particular comparison a researcher makes is determined by the question he or she seeks to answer.

In this example, the researcher decides to investigate gender differences. Are men more likely than women to seek help? To provide an answer, the researcher might present the

TABLE 2.1   RESPONSES OF MEN TO HYPOTHETICAL AUTO THEFT

Subject Response	f
Verbally confront thief	25
Physically confront thief	10
Withdraw—call police	10
Shout for help	5
	N = 50

TABLE 2.2   RESPONSES TO HYPOTHETICAL AUTO THEFT BY GENDER

Subject Response	Male	Female
Verbally confront thief	25	12
Physically confront thief	10	3
Withdraw—call police	10	25
Shout for help	5	10
Total	50	50

same scenarios and questions to a group of 50 women and then compare the results. Let us imagine that the data shown in Table 2.2 are obtained. As shown in the table, 35 out of 50 women but only 15 of the 50 men said they would either shout for help or call the police.

PROPORTIONS AND PERCENTAGES

When a researcher studies distributions of equal size, the frequency data can be used to make comparisons between the groups. Thus the numbers of men and women who would seek help can be directly compared because there are exactly 50 people of each gender in the study. In research it is relatively rare, however, to have distributions with exactly the same number of cases.

For more general use, we need a method of standardizing frequency distributions for size—a way to compare groups despite differences in total frequencies. Two of the most popular and useful methods of standardizing for size and comparing distributions are the proportion and the percentage.

The *proportion* compares the number of cases in a given category with the total size of the distribution. We can convert any frequency into a proportion P by dividing the number of cases in any given category f by the total number of cases in the distribution N:

$$P = \frac{f}{N}$$

Therefore 35 out of 50 women who said they would seek help can be expressed as the following proportion.

$$P = \frac{35}{50} = .70$$

Despite the usefulness of the proportion, many people prefer to indicate the relative size of a series of numbers in terms of the *percentage,* the frequency of occurrence of a category per 100 cases. To calculate a percentage, we simply multiply any given proportion by 100. By formula,

$$\% = (100)\,\frac{f}{N}$$

Therefore 35 out of 50 women who responded that they would seek help can be expressed as the proportion $P = 35/50 = .70$, or as a percentage $\% = (100)(35/50) = 70\%$. Thus 70% of the women in the sample said they would either shout for help or call the police.

To illustrate the utility of percentages in making comparisons between large and unequal-sized distributions, let's examine the gender of criminal justice majors at two colleges where the criminal justice programs are of very different size. Suppose, for example, that College A has 1,352 criminal justice majors, while College B has only 183.

	Criminal justice major			
Gender of	College A		College B	
student	f	%	f	%
Male	879	65	119	65
Female	473	35	64	35
Total	1352	100	183	100

TABLE 2.3   GENDER OF STUDENTS MAJORING IN CRIMINAL JUSTICE AT COLLEGES A AND B

Table 2.3 indicates both the frequencies and the percentages for criminal justice majors at colleges *A* and *B*. Notice how difficult it is to determine quickly the gender differences among criminal justice majors from the frequency data alone. By contrast, the percentages clearly reveal that females were equally represented among criminal justice majors at Colleges A and B. Specifically, 35% of the criminal justice majors at College A are females; 35% of the criminal justice majors at College B are females.

RATIOS AND RATES

A less commonly used method of standardizing for size, the *ratio,* directly compares the number of cases falling into one category (for example, males) with the number of cases falling into another category (for example, females). Thus, a ratio can be obtained in the following manner, where f_1 = frequency in any category and f_2 = frequency in any other category:

$$\text{Ratio} = \frac{f_1}{f_2}$$

If we were interested in determining the ratio of blacks to whites, we would compare the number of black respondents ($f = 150$) to the number of white respondents ($f = 100$) as $\frac{150}{100}$. By canceling common factors in the numerator and denominator, it is possible to reduce a ratio to its simplest form, for example, $\frac{150}{100} = \frac{3}{2}$. (There are 3 black respondents for every 2 white respondents.)

The researcher might increase the clarity of this ratio by giving the base (the denominator) in a more understandable form. For instance, the *sex ratio* often employed by demographers who seek to compare the number of males and females in any given population is generally given as the number of males per 100 females.

To illustrate, if the ratio of males to females is $\frac{150}{50}$, there are 150 males for 50 females (or reducing, 3 males for every 1 female). To obtain the conventional version of the sex ratio, we would multiply the previous ratio by 100:

$$\text{sex ratio} = (100)\,\frac{f\,\text{males}}{f\,\text{females}} = (100)\left(\frac{150}{50}\right) = 300$$

It then turns out that there are 300 males in the population for every 100 females.

Another kind of ratio—one that is more widely used by criminal justice researchers—is known as a rate. Criminologists and criminal justice researchers often analyze populations regarding rates of crime, recidivism, incarceration, victimization, arrest, and conviction. However, whereas most other ratios compare the number of cases in any category or subgroup with the number of cases in any other subgroup, rates indicate comparisons between the number of *actual* cases and the number of *potential* cases. For instance, to determine the recidivism rate (the rate at which offenders released from custody re-offend) for a given offender population, we might show the number of arrested persons among a population of people recently released from prison. Similarly, to ascertain the victimization rate, we might compare the number of crimes against the number of potential victims during a particular time period (such as one year). Rates are often given in terms of a base having 1,000 potential cases. Thus victimization rates are sometimes presented as the number of crimes per 1,000 citizens who are potential victims. For example, the U.S. Department of Justice presents the rape and sexual assault rate as the number of such crimes per 1,000 females aged 12 and older.[1] If 30 rapes occurred among 4,000 females aged 12 or older,

$$\text{Rape and sexual assault rate} = (1{,}000)\,\frac{f\,\text{actual cases}}{f\,\text{potential cases}} = (1{,}000)\left(\frac{30}{4{,}000}\right) = 7.5$$

It turns out there would be 7.5 rapes per every 1,000 females aged 12 or more.

There is nothing particularly special about calculating rates per potential case or per 1,000 potential cases. In fact, expressing rates per capita (i.e., per person), per 1,000, or even per million simply comes down to the decision of what would be the most convenient basis. For example, expenditures for prisons are usually expressed per inmate (as determined by average daily population of inmates in a particular prison, because prison populations can change from day to day due to factors such as transfers, releases, new commitments, and deaths). To calculate this rate, we divide the total expenditure in dollars by the average daily prison inmate population:

$$\text{Per capita (inmate) expenditure} = \frac{\text{expenditure for prison}}{\text{average number of inmates}}$$

In contrast to the previous per capita rate, homicide rates are measured as the number of murders per 100,000 residents:

$$\text{Homicide rate} = (100{,}000)\left(\frac{\text{number of homicides}}{\text{population}}\right)$$

Suppose, for example, that a state has 1,124 homicides and a population of 9,200,000. Its homicide rate (HR) would then be

$$\text{HR} = (100{,}000)\left(\frac{1{,}124}{9{,}200{,}000}\right)$$

$$= (100{,}000)\,(.000122)$$

$$= 12.2$$

Thus, there are 12.2 homicides for every 100,000 residents.

---

[1]U.S. Department of Justice, Bureau of Justice Statistics, *Violence Against Women: Estimates from the Redesigned Survey,* Special Report NCJ-15348 (Washington, D.C.: U.S. Department of Justice, August 1995).

It is important to note that we could have defined the rate as homicides per capita without multiplying the fraction (homicides over population) by the 100,000 scale factor. However, the rate of .000122 that would result, although correct, is very awkward because of its small size. So we magnify the rate to a more readable and digestible form by multiplying by 100,000 (moving the decimal point five places to the right), which then converts the per capita rate of .000122 to a per 100,000 rate of 12.2.

So far, we have discussed rates that make comparisons between different populations. For instance, we might seek to compare victimization rates between men and women, between middle-class and lower-class males, among religious groups or entire nations, and so on. Another kind of rate, *rate of change,* can be used to compare the same population at two points in time. In computing rate of change, we compare the actual change between time period 1 and time period 2 with the level at time period 1 serving as a base. Thus, a state prison population that increases from 20,000 to 30,000 between 1980 and 1990 would experience the following rate of change:

$$(100)\left(\frac{\text{time } 2f - \text{time } 1f}{\text{time } 1f}\right) = (100)\left(\frac{30,000 - 20,000}{20,000}\right) = 50\%$$

In other words, there was a population increase of 50% over the period 1980 to 1990.

Notice that a rate of change can be *negative* to indicate a decrease in size over any given period. For instance, if a population changes from 15,000 to 12,000 over a period of time, the rate of change would be

$$(100)\left(\frac{12,000 - 15,000}{15,000}\right) = -20\%$$

SIMPLE FREQUENCY DISTRIBUTIONS OF ORDINAL AND INTERVAL DATA

Because nominal data are labeled rather than graded or scaled, the categories of nominal-level distributions do not have to be listed in any particular order. Thus, the data on career preferences of criminal justice majors shown in Table 2.4 are presented in three different, yet equally acceptable arrangements.

In contrast, the categories or score values in ordinal or interval distributions represent the degree to which a particular characteristic is present. The listing of such categories or score values in simple frequency distributions must be made to reflect that order.

TABLE 2.4   DISTRIBUTION OF CAREER PREFERENCES SHOWN THREE WAYS

Career preference	f	Career preference	f	Career preference	f
Law enforcement	45	Corrections	15	Social work	15
Law	25	Law	25	Corrections	15
Corrections	15	Law enforcement	45	Law enforcement	45
Social work	15	Social work	15	Law	25
Total	100	Total	100	Total	100

For this reason, ordinal and interval categories are always arranged in order, usually from their highest to lowest values. For instance, we might list the categories of social class from upper to lower or post the results of a criminology midterm examination in consecutive order from the highest grade to the lowest grade.

Disturbing the order of ordinal and interval categories reduces the readability of the researcher's findings. This effect can be seen in Table 2.5, where both the "incorrect" and "correct" versions of a distribution of attitudes toward televised criminal trials have been presented. Which version do you find easier to follow?

GROUPED FREQUENCY DISTRIBUTIONS OF INTERVAL DATA

Interval-level scores are sometimes spread over a wide range (highest to lowest score), making the resultant simple frequency distribution long and difficult to read. When such instances occur, few cases may fall at each score value, and the group pattern becomes blurred. To illustrate, the distribution set up in Table 2.6 contains values varying from 50 to 99 and runs almost four columns in length.

In order to clarify our presentation, we might construct a *grouped frequency distribution* by condensing the separate scores into a number of smaller categories or groups, each containing more than one score value. Each category or group in a grouped distribution is known as a *class interval,* whose *size* is determined by the number of score values it contains.

The examination grades for 71 students originally presented in Table 2.6 are rearranged in a grouped frequency distribution, shown in Table 2.7. Here we find 10 class intervals, each having size 5. Thus, the highest class interval (95–99) contains the five score values 95, 96, 97, 98, and 99. Similarly, the interval 70–74 is of size 5 and contains the score values 70, 71, 72, 73, and 74.

The frequencies are next to the class intervals in Table 2.7. This column tells us the number of cases or scores in each of the categories. Thus, whereas the class interval 95–99 spans five score values (95, 96, 97, 98, and 99), it includes three scores (95, 96, and 98).

The more meaningful column, particularly if comparisons to other distributions are considered (such as the final examination scores during a different term with a different number of students), is the percentage column. This column is also called the *percentage distribution.*

TABLE 2.5   A FREQUENCY DISTRIBUTION OF ATTITUDES TOWARD TELEVISED CRIMINAL TRIALS: INCORRECT AND CORRECT PRESENTATIONS

Attitude toward televised trials	f	Attitude toward televised trials	f
Slightly favorable	9	Strongly favorable	10
Somewhat unfavorable	7	Somewhat favorable	21
Strongly favorable	10	Slightly favorable	9
Slightly unfavorable	6	Slightly unfavorable	6
Strongly unfavorable	12	Somewhat unfavorable	7
Somewhat favorable	21	Strongly unfavorable	12
Total	65	Total	65
INCORRECT		CORRECT	

TABLE 2.6   FREQUENCY DISTRIBUTION OF FINAL-EXAMINATION GRADES FOR 71 STUDENTS

Grade	f	Grade	f	Grade	f	Grade	f
99	0	85	2	71	4	57	0
98	1	84	1	70	9	56	1
97	0	83	0	69	3	55	0
96	1	82	3	68	5	54	1
95	1	81	1	67	1	53	0
94	0	80	2	66	3	52	1
93	0	79	8	65	0	51	1
92	1	78	1	64	1	50	1
91	1	77	0	63	2		$N = 71$
90	0	76	2	62	0		
89	1	75	1	61	0		
88	0	74	1	60	2		
87	1	73	1	59	3		
86	0	72	2	58	1		

TABLE 2.7   GROUPED FREQUENCY DISTRIBUTION OF FINAL-EXAMINATION GRADES FOR 71 STUDENTS

Class interval	f	%
95–99	3	4.23
90–94	2	2.82
85–89	4	5.63
80–84	7	9.86
75–79	12	16.90
70–74	17	23.94
65–69	12	16.90
60–64	5	7.04
55–59	5	7.04
50–54	4	5.63
Total	71	100

NOTE: The percentages as they appear add to only 99.99%. We write the sum as 100% instead because we know that .01% was lost in rounding.

CLASS LIMITS

Suppose you were to step on a digital bathroom scale and the number 123 appears on the display. Do you weigh exactly 123? Or isn't it more realistic to say that you weigh approximately 123? Specifically, your weight is more than 122.5 but less than 123.5, and the scale rounds to the nearest whole number. When we construct class intervals of the weight range 120–129 pounds, we must include a "fudge factor" surrounding the whole numbers. Thus, this class interval for weight is actually from 119.5 (the low end of 120) to 129.5 (the high end of 129). The actual limits for this interval are 119.5 to 129.5. Thus, in reality, anyone whose exact weight is between 119.5 and 129.5 will be included in this interval. In practical terms, anyone whose exact weight is between 119.5 and 129.5 will "tip the scale" in whole numbers from 120–129.

Each class interval has an *upper limit* and a *lower limit*. At first glance, the highest and lowest score values in any given category seem to be these limits. Thus, we might reasonably expect the upper and lower limits of the interval 60–64 to be 64 and 60, respectively. In this case, however, we would be wrong, because 64 and 60 are actually not the limits of interval 60–64.

Unlike the highest and lowest score values in an interval, *class limits* are located at the point halfway between adjacent class intervals and also serve to close the gap between them (see Figure 2.1). Thus, the upper limit of the interval 90–94 is 94.5, and the lower limit of the interval 95–99 is also 94.5. Likewise, 59.5 serves as the upper limit of the interval 55–59 and as the lower limit of the interval 60–64.

Finally, as you can see from the figure, the distance between the upper and lower limits of a class interval determines its size. That is,

$$i = U - L$$

where i = size of a class interval
U = upper limit of a class interval
L = lower limit of a class interval

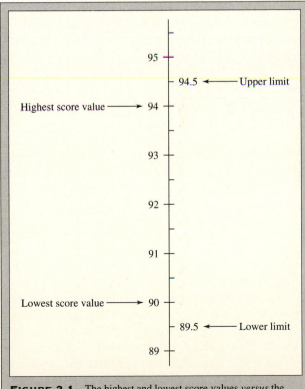

FIGURE 2.1 The highest and lowest score values *versus* the upper and lower limits of the class interval 90–94.

For example, for the interval 90–94, the size (i) is $94.5 - 89.5 = 5$. This corresponds to the value we obtain by simply counting the range of values within the interval (90, 91, 92, 93, and 94). To avoid any confusion, we recommend that you always calculate class interval size by subtracting the lower limit from the upper limit.

THE MIDPOINT

Another characteristic of any class interval is its *midpoint* (m), which we define as the middlemost score value in the class interval. A quick-and-simple method of finding a midpoint is to look for the point at which any given interval can be divided into two equal parts. Let's use some illustrations: 50 is the midpoint of the interval 48–52; 3.5 is the midpoint of the interval 2–5. The midpoint can also be computed from the lowest and highest score values in any interval. To illustrate, the midpoint of the interval 48–52 is

$$m = \frac{\text{lowest score value} + \text{highest score value}}{2} = \frac{48 + 52}{2} = 50$$

In a sense, the midpoint can be regarded as the spokesperson for all score values in a class interval. It is a single number that can be used to represent the entire class interval.

GUIDELINES FOR CONSTRUCTING CLASS INTERVALS

Constructing class intervals is just a special way of categorizing data. As discussed earlier, categories, and thus class intervals, must be mutually exclusive (nonoverlapping) and exhaustive (a place for every case).

Beginning students generally find it difficult to construct class intervals on their own. Indeed, it is a skill that develops only with practice. However, there are some general guidelines that make the task easier. Note that these are only guidelines, which, under certain circumstances, can be violated.

To present interval data in a grouped frequency distribution, the criminal justice researcher must consider the number of categories he or she wishes to employ. Texts generally advise using as few as 3 or 4 intervals to as many as 20 intervals. In this regard, it would be wise to remember that grouped frequency distributions are employed to reveal or emphasize a group pattern. Either too many or too few class intervals may blur that pattern and thereby work against the researcher who seeks to add clarity to the analysis. In addition, reducing the individual score values to an unnecessarily small number of intervals may sacrifice too much precision—precision that was originally attained by knowing the identity of individual scores in the distribution. In sum, then, the researcher generally makes a decision as to the number of intervals based on the set of data and personal objectives, factors that may vary considerably from one research situation to another.

After deciding on the number of class intervals, a researcher must then begin constructing the intervals themselves. Two basic guidelines help make this task easier and should be followed whenever possible. First, it is preferable to make the size of class intervals a whole number rather than a decimal. This tends to simplify calculations in which size is involved. Second, it is conventional to make the lowest score in a class interval some multiple of its size. Customarily, for example, exam scores are categorized as 90–99, 80–89, and so on, so that the lowest scores (for example, 80 and 90) are multiples of 10.

CUMULATIVE DISTRIBUTIONS

It is sometimes desirable to present frequencies in a cumulative fashion, especially when locating the position of one case relative to overall group performance. *Cumulative frequencies (cf)* are defined as the total number of cases having any given score *or a score that is lower*. Thus, the cumulative frequency *cf* for any category (or class interval) is obtained by adding the frequency in that category to the total frequency for all categories below it. In the case of the college board scores in Table 2.8, we see that the frequency *f* associated with the class interval 200–249 is 3. This is also the cumulative frequency for this interval, because no member of the group scored below 200. The frequency in the next class interval 250–299 is 6, and the cumulative frequency for this interval is 9 (6 + 3). Therefore, we learn that 6 students earned college board scores between 250 and 299, but that 9 students received scores of 299 *or lower*. We might continue this procedure, obtaining cumulative frequencies for all class intervals, until we arrive at the topmost entry 750–799, whose cumulative frequency (336) is equal to the total number of cases, because no member of the group scored above 799.

In addition to cumulative frequency, we can also construct a distribution that indicates *cumulative percentage (c%)*, the percentage of cases having any score or a score that is lower. To calculate the cumulative percentage, we modify the formula for percentage (%) introduced earlier in this chapter as follows:

$$c\% = (100)\frac{cf}{N}$$

where cf = cumulative frequency in any category
N = total number of cases in the distribution

TABLE 2.8 CUMULATIVE FREQUENCY (CF) DISTRIBUTION OF COLLEGE BOARD SCORES FOR 336 CRIMINAL JUSTICE STUDENTS

Class interval	f	%	cf
750–799	4	1.19	336
700–749	24	7.14	332
650–699	28	8.33	308
600–649	30	8.93	280
550–599	35	10.42	250
500–549	55	16.37	215
450–499	61	18.15	160
400–449	48	14.29	99
350–399	30	8.93	51
300–349	12	3.57	21
250–299	6	1.79	9
200–249	3	.89	3
Total	336	100	

Applying the foregoing formula to the data in Table 2.8, we find that the percent of students who scored 249 or lower was

$$c\% = (100)\left(\frac{3}{336}\right)$$

$$= (100)(.0089)$$

$$= .89$$

The percent who scored 299 or lower was

$$c\% = (100)\left(\frac{9}{336}\right)$$

$$= (100)(.0268)$$

$$= 2.68$$

The percent who scored 349 or lower was

$$c\% = (100)\left(\frac{21}{336}\right)$$

$$= (100)(.0625)$$

$$= 6.25$$

A cumulative percentage distribution based on the data in Table 2.8 is shown in Table 2.9. Note that the $c\%$ distribution can also be obtained by summing the percentage (%) distribution.

TABLE 2.9 CUMULATIVE PERCENTAGE ($c\%$) DISTRIBUTION OF COLLEGE BOARD SCORES FOR 336 STUDENTS (BASED ON TABLE 2.8)

Class interval	f	%	cf	$c\%$
750–799	4	1.19	336	100.00
700–749	24	7.14	332	98.81
650–699	28	8.33	308	91.67
600–649	30	8.93	280	83.33
550–599	35	10.42	250	74.40
500–549	55	16.37	215	63.99
450–499	61	18.15	160	47.62
400–449	48	14.29	99	29.46
350–399	30	8.93	51	15.18
300–349	12	3.57	21	6.25
250–299	6	1.79	9	2.68
200–249	3	.89	3	.89
Total	336	100		

PERCENTILE RANKS

Your statistics professor hands back the midterm exams. Knowing that a major part of your course grade depends on this test, you slowly turn over the booklet to reveal a red 77 with a circle around it. Should you quietly cheer and think about the celebration ahead? Or should you start contemplating extra-credit work you might propose to bring up your grade?

By the conventional standards that you learned in elementary and secondary school, you might immediately have translated the 77 into a C+, slightly above average. But in college, or at least in some classes, conventional standards can be tossed out the window. The score of 77 means *nothing*, without some sense of how the rest of the class performed. If most of the class scored in the 50s and 60s, then celebration can be scheduled for that evening. But if most of the class scored in the 80s and 90s, you may want to postpone the party.

To put it another way, the quality of the raw score 77 depends on how easy the test is. On a a very tough exam, a 77 might be a commendable score, whereas on a simple test, you probably should have done better. Of course, the level of difficulty of an exam can only be gauged by how the class performed as a whole, that is, on the entire distribution of scores. Thus, the only realistic way to tell if your 77 was an excellent, good, average, or poor score is to compare it against the entire distribution of scores in the class.

"How does a 77 rank in terms of the entire class?" you ask your professor. She responds that you scored the same as or better than 60% of the class, indicating that your *percentile rank* was 60%.

The percentile rank of any given score, say 77, is defined as the percentage of the cases in a distribution that falls at or below that score (for example, the percentage of the class scoring 77 or lower). Percentile ranks are simple to compute if your professor provides the entire collection of *raw* scores. For example, in the following collection of 20 scores, your 77 would be *ranked* twelfth from the bottom. Thus, your *percentile rank* would be twelfth out of 20, or 60%:

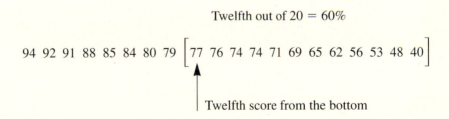

Much of the time, particularly when many numbers are involved, you may not have available the entire collection of scores that allows you to determine your ranking and percentile rank. In a large class of 80 students, for example, most professors would not wish to write on the blackboard the entire set of scores but would instead prepare a frequency distribution of class grades.

For your class of 20 students, the professor might decide to keep for herself the raw scores shown earlier and provide the class with only the following grouped frequency distribution:

Class interval	f	%	cf	c%
90–99	3	15	20	100
80–89	4	20	17	85
70–79	6	30	13	65
60–69	3	15	7	35
50–59	2	10	4	20
40–49	2	10	2	10
	$N = 20$	100		

The cumulative percentages hold the key to determining the percentile ranks. In fact, because the cumulative percentages are defined as the percentage of scores falling within or below a given class interval, the cumulative percentages are actually the percentile ranks corresponding to the upper class limits. Thus, for example, the upper limit 69.5 has a percentile rank of 35% (35% of the scores fall at or below 69.5) and the upper limit 89.5 has a percentile rank of 85% (85% of the scores lie at or below 89.5).

What about your score of 77? It does not conveniently fall at an upper class limit. You can see that your percentile rank is better than 35%, because 35% scored at or below 69.5. You also know that your percentile rank is not quite as high as 65%, because that corresponds to the upper limit 79.5. Thus, the percentile rank for 77 lies somewhere between 35% and 65%, but exactly where?

At this point, we can only estimate your percentile rank based on a process known as interpolation. Let's focus just on your class interval 70–79, which we will call the *critical interval*. The score 77 is three-quarters of the way from its lower limit 69.5 to its upper limit 79.5:

$$\frac{77 - 69.5}{79.5 - 69.5} = .75$$

Your score of 77 is three-quarters (or .75) of the way from 69.5 to 79.5, as illustrated by the following:

69.5	77	79.5
Lower limit	Your score	Upper limit

By the percentage of cases (%) for this class interval given in the earlier grouped frequency distribution, we know that 30% of the scores are between 69.5 and 79.5. We can estimate, therefore, that three-quarters of the percentage of scores in this class interval (30%) also lie at or below 77, that is, $.75 \times 30\% = 22.5\%$. By our estimate, 22.5% of the scores are between 69.5 and 77. We know already from the cumulative percentage column that 35% of the distribution is at 69.5 or below. Summing these two percentages—35% at or below 69.5 plus 22.5% between 69.5 and 77—we estimate that 57.5% of the distribution is at 77 or below. Thus, the percentile rank for your score of 77 is estimated to be 57.5%.

Note that the estimated percentile rank of 57.5% is not quite identical to the true percentile rank of 60% that we previously calculated from counting up the raw scores. This discrepancy can always be expected, because the process of interpolation is only an estimate.

The procedure just described is meant to give a conceptual understanding of the percentile rank. Its calculation from a grouped frequency distribution can also be accomplished by the following formula:

$$PR = c\%_b + \left(\frac{X - L}{i} \right)\%$$

where   PR = percentile rank
$c\%_b$ = cumulative percentage below the lower limit of the critical interval
X = raw score under consideration
L = lower limit of the critical interval
i = class interval size
% = percentage within critical interval

To illustrate the procedure for obtaining a percentile rank using the formula, let us return to the midterm score of 77. Before applying the formula, we must first locate the critical interval, that class interval in which the score of 77 appears. The critical interval for the present problem is 77–79, as demonstrated in the following:

Class interval	
90–99	
80–89	
70–79	← Class interval in which 77 occurs
60–69	
50–59	
Under 50	

There are several characteristics of the critical interval that we must determine before applying the formula for percentile rank:

1. *The lower limit of the critical interval (L).* This is the point that lies midway between the critical interval 70–79 and the class interval immediately below it, 60–69. The lower limit of 70–79 is 69.5, not the lowest score value (70).
2. *The size of the critical interval (i).* This is determined by the number of score values within the class interval 70–79. The size of the critical interval is 10, because it contains 10 score values from 70 to 79. The size of an interval is also the difference of the upper limit minus the lower limit (for example, $79.5 - 69.5 = 10$).
3. *The percentage within the critical interval (%).* We see that 30% of these exam scores fell within the class interval 70–79.
4. *The cumulative percentage below the lower limit of the critical interval ($c\%_b$).* We can read c% directly from the cumulative percentage distribution. Moving up the c% column of the table, we see that 35% of the scores fall below the critical interval. This is the cumulative percentage associated with the class interval that falls immediately below the critical interval.

We are now prepared to apply the following formula for percentile rank:

$$PR = 35.0 + \left(\frac{77 - 69.5}{10}\right)(30)$$

$$= 35.0 + \left(\frac{7.5}{10}\right)(30)$$

$$= 35.0 + 22.5$$

$$= 57.5$$

Therefore, almost 58% of the students scored at or below 77 on the exam.

As a further illustration, for obtaining percentile rank, let us find the percentile rank for a score of 619 in the SAT distribution in Table 2.9. Before applying the formula, we must first locate the critical interval, that class interval in which a score of 619 appears. As shown, the critical interval for the present problem is 600–649:

Class interval	
750–799	
700–749	
650–699	
600–649	← Class interval in which a score of 619 occurs
550–599	
500–549	
450–499	
400–449	
350–399	
300–349	
250–299	
200–249	

The following are several characteristics of the critical interval that we must determine before applying the formula for percentile rank:

1. *The lower limit of the critical interval.* The lower limit of 600–649 is 599.5, not the lowest score (600).
2. *The size of the critical interval.* The size of the critical interval is 50, because it contains 50 score values from 600–649.
3. *The percentage within the critical interval.* We see that 8.93% of these college board scores fell within the class interval, 600–649.
4. *The cumulative percentage below the lower limit of the critical interval.* Moving up the $c\%$ column of the table, we see that 74.40% of the scores fall *below* the critical interval.

We are now prepared to apply the following formula for percentile rank:

$$PR = 74.40 + \left(\frac{619 - 599.5}{50}\right)(8.93)$$

$$= 74.40 + \left(\frac{19.50}{50}\right)(8.93)$$

$$= 74.40 + (.39)(8.93)$$

$$= 74.40 + 3.48$$

$$= 77.88$$

It turns out that almost 78% received a score of 619 or below. Only 22.12% scored higher.

As another illustration, let us find the percentile rank for a score of 92 in the following distribution of scores:

Class interval	f	%	cf	$c\%$
90–99	6	12.24	49	100.00
80–89	8	16.33	43	87.76
70–79	12	24.49	35	71.43
60–69	10	20.41	23	46.94
50–59	7	14.29	13	26.53
40–49	6	12.24	6	12.24
	$N = 49$	100		

As shown in the following, the critical interval for a score of 92 is 90–99:

Class interval
90–99   ← Class interval in which 92 occurs
80–89
70–79
60–69
50–59
40–49

The following are several characteristics of the critical interval that we must determine:

1. The lower limit of the critical interval is 89.5.
2. The size of the critical interval is 10, because there are 10 score values within it from 90 to 99.
3. The percentage within the critical interval is 12.24.
4. The cumulative percentage below the lower limit of the critical interval can be found from the $c\%$ column by referring to the class interval immediately below the critical interval. The cumulative percentage associated with the class interval 80–89 is 87.76.

We are now ready to substitute in the formula for percentile rank:

$$PR = 87.76 + \left(\frac{92 - 89.5}{10}\right)(12.24)$$

$$= 87.76 + \left(\frac{2.5}{10}\right)(12.24)$$

$$= 87.76 + 3.06$$

$$= 90.82$$

Almost 91% received a score of 92 or below. Approximately 9% received a score that was higher.

There are points in a distribution of scores whose percentile ranks are so important and commonly used that they are given specific names. *Deciles* are points that divide the distribution into 10 equally sized portions. Thus, if a score is located at the first decile (percentile rank = 10), we know that 10% of the cases fall at or below it; if a score is at the second decile (percentile rank = 20), then 20% of the cases fall at or below it, and so on. *Quartiles* are points that divide the distribution into quarters. If a score is located at the first quartile (percentile rank = 25), we know that 25% of the cases fall at or below it; if a score is at the second quartile (percentile rank = 50), 50% of the cases fall at or below it; and if a score is at the third quartile (percentile rank = 75), 75% of the cases fall at or below it (see Figure 2.2). Finally, as we will encounter again in the next chapter, the *median* is the point that divides the distribution of scores in two, half above it and half

Percentile rank	Decile	Quartile
95		
90 =	9th	
85		
80 =	8th	
75 =		3rd
70 =	7th	
65		
60 =	6th	
55		
50 =	5th	2nd
45		
40 =	4th	
35		
30 =	3rd	
25 =		1st
20 =	2nd	
15		
10 =	1st	
5		

FIGURE 2.2 Scale of percentile ranks divided by deciles and quartiles

below it. Thus, the median corresponds to a percentile rank of 50, but it is also the fifth decile and second quartile.

DEALING WITH DECIMAL DATA

Not all data come in the form of whole numbers. This should not disturb us in the least, however, because the procedures we have learned and will learn in later chapters apply to decimals as well as whole numbers. So that we get used to decimal data from the start, let's consider constructing a frequency distribution of the state data on murder and non-negligent manslaughter shown in Table 2.10 (rates are shown in crimes per 100,000 population). From the raw scores, we do not get a very clear picture of nationwide patterns of murder. We are drawn to the extremes: The numbers range from a high of 19.8 in Louisiana to a low of 0.2 in North Dakota. Little else emerges until we construct a grouped frequency distribution.

Because there are only 50 cases, we would not want too many categories. An excessive number of class intervals would spread the cases too thinly. Determining the actual limits of the class intervals is the most difficult part of all. Satisfactory results come with

TABLE 2.10 STATE MURDER AND NONNEGLIGENT MANSLAUGHTER RATES

State	Rate	State	Rate
Alabama	11.9	Montana	3.3
Alaska	6.3	Nebraska	3.1
Arizona	10.5	Nevada	11.7
Arkansas	12.0	New Hampshire	1.4
California	11.8	New Jersey	5.0
Colorado	5.4	New Mexico	10.7
Connecticut	6.6	New York	11.1
Delaware	4.7	North Carolina	10.9
Florida	8.3	North Dakota	0.2
Georgia	10.0	Ohio	6.0
Hawaii	4.2	Oklahoma	6.9
Idaho	3.5	Oregon	4.9
Illinois	11.7	Pennsylvania	5.9
Indiana	7.9	Rhode Island	4.1
Iowa	1.7	South Carolina	9.6
Kansas	5.8	South Dakota	1.4
Kentucky	6.4	Tennessee	9.3
Louisiana	19.8	Texas	11.0
Maine	2.3	Utah	2.9
Maryland	11.6	Vermont	1.0
Massachusetts	3.5	Virginia	8.7
Michigan	9.8	Washington	5.5
Minnesota	3.2	West Virginia	5.4
Mississippi	15.3	Wisconsin	4.5
Missouri	10.5	Wyoming	3.4

SOURCE: *Sourcebook of Criminal Justice Statistics, 1995.* Kathleen Maguire and Ann L. Pastore, ed., U.S. Department of Justice, Bureau of Justice Statistics. (Washington, D.C.: U.S. Government Printing Office, 1996).

TABLE 2.11	Frequency distribution of state murder and non-negligent manslaughter rates

Class interval	f
18.0–20.9	1
15.0–17.9	1
12.0–14.9	1
9.0–11.9	15
6.0–8.9	8
3.0–5.9	17
0.0–2.9	7
	$N = 50$

a great deal of trial and error as well as practice. There is no "right" setup of class intervals, but those in Table 2.11 might be a good place to start.

Once we have the skeleton for the frequency distribution (its class intervals and the frequencies), the rest is fairly straightforward. Percentages, cumulative frequencies, and cumulative percentages are obtained in the usual way. For other calculations such as midpoints, however, keep in mind that these data are expressed with one decimal digit. As a consequence, this digit is important in determining the interval size or the range of score values spanned by a class interval. For example, the size of the 6.0–8.9 interval is 3.0, because it contains the score values 6.0 to 8.9 inclusive. There are 30 score values between 6.0 and 8.9, each one-tenth apart, so the size is $(30)(1/10) = 3.0$.

FLEXIBLE CLASS INTERVALS

Although we have not made a point of it earlier, you may have noticed that all the frequency distributions used so far have had class intervals all of equal size. There are occasions, however, in which this practice is not at all desirable.

The distribution of state homicide data is one such case. It seems very unbalanced to have a separate class interval for just one observation. This was necessary because the class intervals were all the same size of 3.0. We can, however, combine or collapse the upper three categories into a top class with an open upper boundary, that is, 12.0 and over. This slightly modified distribution is shown in Table 2.12.

Grouped frequency distributions can have open-ended top or bottom class intervals. The other major departure from the simple distributions provided earlier is the use of class intervals of varying size. For example, Table 2.13 presents a distribution of census data on family income for 1990, which is typical of distributions constructed with income data. Note that, whereas the class intervals containing the lower incomes have a size of $5,000, the size of the class intervals is stretched for higher-income levels. What would have been the result had a fixed class interval size of $5,000 been maintained throughout the distribution? The $25,000–$34,999 class interval would have two categories, the $35,000–$49,999 class interval would have turned into three categories, and the $50,000–$74,999 class interval would have become five categories. The effect would be

TABLE 2.12 FREQUENCY DISTRIBUTION OF STATE MURDER AND NONNEGLIGENT MANSLAUGHTER RATES

Class interval	f
12.0 and above	3
9.0–11.9	15
6.0–8.9	8
3.0–5.9	17
0.0–2.9	7
	$N = 50$

TABLE 2.13 FAMILY INCOME IN THE UNITED STATES

Income level	f (families in 1,000s)	%
$75,000 and above	8,167	12.52
$50,000–$74,999	12,080	18.52
$35,000–$49,999	13,302	20.39
$25,000–$34,999	10,716	16.43
$20,000–$24,999	5,614	8.61
$15,000–$19,999	5,232	8.02
$10,000–$14,999	4,973	7.62
$5,000–$9,999	2,781	4.26
Under $5,000	2,367	3.63
Total	65,232	100.00%

SOURCE: U.S. Bureau of the Census, *Current Population Reports*, Series P-60.

to make unnecessarily fine distinctions among the persons of higher income and to produce a needlessly lengthy frequency distribution. That is, in terms of standard of living, there is a big difference between the $5,000–$9,999 class interval and the $10,000–$14,999 class interval. In contrast, the difference between a $60,000–$64,999 category and a $65,000–$69,999 category would be relatively unimportant.

These new twists in frequency distributions should not cause you much difficulty in adapting what you have already learned in this chapter. Fortunately, the computations of cumulative distributions, percentile ranks, and the like do not change for frequency distributions with class intervals of unequal size or with unbounded top or bottom class intervals. The only modification involves calculating midpoints with unbounded top or bottom class intervals. Let's consider an example.

Table 2.14 presents data on the years in which state prisons were built across the United States. Because most states have more than one state prison, and some states have many, the total number of facilities as of 1978 (when these data were collected) stood at 521. In this frequency distribution, the class intervals broaden as the age of the institutions increases. Because less than half of the institutions were built before 1950, and even fewer predate 1925, it is unnecessary to maintain the precision of narrow class intervals for the earlier years when there are few institutions to fill them.

Calculating midpoints for most of the categories is straightforward using our midpoint formula:

$$m = \frac{\text{lowest score value} + \text{highest score value}}{2}$$

But what do we do about the last class interval (before 1875), which has no lower limit? What should we plug into the formula? Do not make the common mistake of just using zero; this would imply that there are prisons, still in use, that were constructed as early as the year 0 A.D. There are actually several reasonable solutions to guessing at the lower limit of the class interval, all of which produce similar results. The one we prefer is to assume that the bottom class interval has limits similar to the class interval just next to it. The next to last class interval (1875–1924) has a size of 50 years. If we use this size for the lowest class interval we get 1825–1874. Using 1825 and 1874 as the lowest and highest scores, respectively, gives this class interval a midpoint of 1849.5. We now have all the necessary elements to calculate any other quantity.

CROSS-TABULATIONS

Frequency distributions like those discussed so far are seen everywhere. Census Bureau publications consistently employ frequency distributions to describe characteristics of the U.S. population; presentation of the raw data—all the millions of observations—would, of course, be impossible.

We even see frequency distributions in daily newspapers; journalists, like criminal justice researchers, find tables a very convenient form of presentation. Most newspaper readers are capable of understanding basic percentages (even though they may forget how to compute them). A basic table of frequencies and percentages for some variable is usually sufficient for the level of depth and detail typically found in newspaper. Researchers, however, want to do more than just describe the distribution of some variable; they seek to explain why some individuals fall at one end of the distribution while others are at the opposite extreme.

To accomplish this objective, we need to explore tables more deeply by expanding them into two and even more dimensions. In particular, a *cross-tabulation* (or *cross-tab* for short) is a table that presents the distribution—frequencies and percents—of one

TABLE 2.14   FREQUENCY DISTRIBUTION OF STATE PRISON CONSTRUCTION

Year built	m	f	%
1970–1978	1974.0	139	26.7
1950–1969	1959.5	156	29.9
1925–1949	1937.0	125	24.0
1875–1924	1899.5	76	14.6
Before 1875	(1849.5)	25	4.8
Total		521	100

SOURCE: National Institute of Justice, *American Prisons and Jails,* Vol. III.

variable (usually the dependent variable) across the categories of one or more additional variables (usually the independent variable or variables).

In 1986, the state of Massachusetts instituted a mandatory seat belt law, calling for a $15 fine for failure to comply. To measure compliance with the law, Fox and Tracy completed a telephone survey of 997 residents of the Boston area concerning their use of seat belts and their opinions regarding the controversial law. For the primary question—the extent to which the respondent used his or her seat belt—the simple frequency distribution shown in Table 2.15 was obtained.

About half of the respondents in the survey (50.1%) stated that they wore their seat belts all the time. Two-thirds of the respondents (50.1% + 17.7% = 67.8%) stated that they wore their seat belts at least most of the time.

We are not content with just knowing the extent of seat belt compliance, however. To analyze the survey data more fully, we start by examining what types of people wear their seat belts—that is, what respondent characteristics are related to seat belt usage.

One of the more dramatic differences is between the males and females in the survey. We employed a cross-tabulation to look at the differences between the sexes in terms of seat belt use. That is, we constructed a frequency distribution of two or more variables taken simultaneously. The cross-tabulation given in Table 2.16 shows, for example, that there were 144 males who said they wore their seat belts all the time and 110 females who reported that they wore their seat belts most of the time.

The foundation for cross-tabulations was presented earlier in the chapter when the gender distributions of engineering majors across two colleges were compared.

TABLE 2.15   FREQUENCY DISTRIBUTION OF SEAT BELT USE

Use of seat belts	f	%
All the time	499	50.1
Most of the time	176	17.7
Some of the time	124	12.4
Seldom	83	8.3
Never	115	11.5
Total	997	100

TABLE 2.16   CROSS-TABULATION OF SEAT BELT USE BY GENDER

Use of seat belts	Gender of respondent		Total
	Male	Female	
All the time	144	355	499
Most of the time	66	110	176
Some of the time	58	66	124
Seldom	39	44	83
Never	60	55	115
Total	367	630	997

Cross-tabulation can be thought of as a series of frequency distributions (in this case, two of them) attached together to make one table. In this example, we have essentially a frequency distribution of seat belt use among males juxtaposed with a comparable frequency distribution of seat belt use for females.

As with one-variable frequency distributions, percentages give the results fuller meaning than frequencies alone. If we retain the same procedure as before, that is, dividing each frequency (f) by the sample size (N),

$$\% = (100)\frac{f}{N}$$

we obtain the percentage results for the two variables jointly, as shown in Table 2.17. For example, the percentage of the sample that is female and wears seat belts all the time is obtained from dividing the number of female "all-the-time" wearers by the number of respondents in the sample overall:

$$(100)\left(\frac{355}{997}\right) = (100)(.356) = 35.6\%$$

Thus, 35.6% of the sample consists of females who wear seat belts all the time (see Table 2.17).

Frequency distributions of each variable separately can be found along the margins of a two-way cross-tabulation. These are called *marginal distributions*. That is, the right margin provides a frequency and percent distribution for seat belt use identical to what we had in Table 2.15. Because the seat belt variable is placed along the rows of the cross-tabulation, the frequencies and percents for seat belt use form the row totals. Likewise, the marginal distribution of gender is found in the bottom margin of the cross-tabulation. These frequencies and percents for males and females are the column totals, because gender is the variable heading the columns.

TABLE 2.17   CROSS-TABULATION OF SEAT BELT USE BY GENDER WITH TOTAL PERCENTS

	Gender of respondent			
Use of seat belts	Male	Female	Total	
All the time	144	355	499	Row marginal
	14.4%	35.6%	50.1%	(row totals)
Most of the time	66	110	176	
	6.6%	11.0%	17.7%	
Some of the time	58	66	124	
	5.8%	6.6%	12.4%	
Seldom	39	44	83	
	3.9%	4.4%	8.3%	
Never	60	55	115	
	6.0%	5.5%	11.5%	
Total	367	630	997	
	36.8%	63.2%	100.0%	

Column marginal
(column totals)

Total sample size

The percentages in Table 2.17 are called *total percents* (total%) because they are obtained by dividing each frequency by the total sample size:

$$\text{total\%} = (100)\frac{f}{N_{\text{total}}}$$

For instance, 14.4% of the sample consists of males who wear their seat belt all the time. Similarly, 11.0% of the sample consists of females who wear their seat belt most of the time.

There is, however, something very unsettling about these percentages. For example, the small value of the percentage of "never-wearer" males (6.0%) is ambiguous. It could reflect a low prevalence or representation of males, a low prevalence of seat belt usage in the sample overall, a low rate of seat belt use among males specifically, or even a low prevalence of males among never-wearers.

There are other approaches to calculating percentages that might resolve this ambiguity. One alternative would divide the number of male never-wearers by the number of never-wearers in the sample, the number of male seldom-wearers by the number of seldom-wearers, etc., and do the comparable calculations for the females. In other words, we divide the frequencies in each row by the number of cases in that row (see Table 2.18). These percents are called *row percents*:

$$\text{row\%} = (100)\frac{f}{N_{\text{row}}}$$

TABLE 2.18   CROSS-TABULATION OF SEAT BELT USE BY GENDER WITH ROW PERCENTS

	Gender of respondent		
Use of seat belts	Male	Female	Total
All the time	144	355	499
	28.9%	71.1%	100.0%
Most of the time	66	110	176
	37.5%	62.5%	100.0%
Some of the time	58	66	124
	46.8%	53.2%	100.0%
Seldom	39	44	83
	47.0%	53.0%	100.0%
Never	60	55	115
	52.2%	47.8%	100.0%
Total	367	630	997
	36.8%	63.2%	100.0%

For example, the percentage of always-users who are female is derived from dividing the number of female all-the-time-wearers by the number of all-the-time-wearers overall:

$$(100)\left(\frac{355}{499}\right) = (100)(.711) = 71.1\%$$

Thus, we find that 71.1% of the all-the-time users in the sample are females.

Row percentages give the distribution of the column variable for each value of the row variable. Thus, these percentages represent the gender distribution within each level of seat belt use. Also, row percentages sum to 100% across each row, including the column marginal in the bottom of the cross-tabulation.

Conversely, one could calculate percentages in the other direction. *Column percents* (column%) are obtained by dividing each frequency by the number of cases in that column:

$$\text{col } \% = (100)\frac{f}{N_{\text{column}}}$$

The percentage of females who always wear a seat belt is obtained, for example, by dividing the number of female all-the-time wearers by the number of females overall:

$$(100)\left(\frac{355}{630}\right) = (100)(.563) = 56.3\%$$

Thus, 56.3% of the females in the study said that they always wear a seat belt.

Column percents for our cross-tabulation are presented in Table 2.19. Note that the percentages here sum to 100% along each column. Thus, the percentages reflect the seat belt use distribution for each gender separately as well as overall.

TABLE 2.19   CROSS-TABULATION OF SEAT BELT USE BY GENDER WITH COLUMN PERCENTS

Use of seat belts	Gender of respondent		Total
	Male	Female	
All the time	144	355	499
	39.2%	56.3%	50.1%
Most of the time	66	110	176
	18.0%	17.5%	17.7%
Some of the time	58	66	124
	15.8%	10.5%	12.4%
Seldom	39	44	83
	10.6%	7.0%	8.3%
Never	60	55	115
	16.3%	8.7%	11.5%
Total	367	630	997
	100.0%	100.0%	100.0%

CHOOSING AMONG TOTAL, ROW, AND COLUMN PERCENTS

We now have three sets of percentages—total, row, and column percents. You might wonder which are correct? In a mathematical sense, all are correct, that is, these were calculated in the correct way. But in terms of substantive meaning, certain percentages may be misleading or even useless.

First, as we noted previously, the total percents are sometimes ambiguous in their meaning, as in our cross-tabulation of seat belt use by gender. Next, according to the row percents, females predominate in every row, except for the "Never" subgroup in which the genders are nearly equal. What does this imply? Can we draw any conclusions, such as suggesting that males don't drive as much and consequently don't show up in any great proportions in any seat belt usage level? Obviously, this inference would be farfetched. The low representation of males in almost every category of use is simply a consequence of the low percentage of males in the sample in general (36.8%). Thus, that 71.1% of the all-the-time seat belt group are female seems a lot less overwhelming when we take into account that 63.2% of the total sample are female.

For our purposes, the most informative percentages are the column percents. We are interested in comparing males and females in terms of seat belt usage. That is, we want to know what percentage of the females wear their seat belts frequently compared to males. For example, 39.2% of the males say they always wear their belts compared to 56.3% of the females. Conversely, 16.3% of the males reported that they never wear a seat belt compared to only 8.7% of the females.

Fortunately, there is a rule of thumb to guide our choice between row and column percentages: *If the independent variable is on the rows, use row percents; if the independent variable is on the columns, use column percents.* In our example we are concerned with the influence the respondent's gender has on seat belt behavior; gender is the independent variable. Because it is given on the columns, we should use column percents.

Another way of stating this rule may be more meaningful: If we wish to compare rows in a cross-tabulation, we need to use row percents; column percents are required for comparing columns. Again, in our example, we want to compare the males to the females in terms of seat belt use. Gender is the column variable, and the column percents provide the seat belt distributions for the males and the females separately. Thus, these column percents should be used for making the gender comparison.

In certain cases, it may not be easy to tell which is the independent variable. For example, in the cross-tabulation of husband and wives' illegal drug use history (Table 2.20), neither variable can clearly be said to be the result of the other. (Note: The figures in each cell of the table represent frequency, row percent, column percent, and total percent, respectively.) To some extent, the drug use of husband and wife may effect each other reciprocally, and in many cases may have occurred long before the couple ever met. Similarity (or even dissimilarity) in drug use may have been part of the attraction.

With the data in Table 2.20, we could compute the percentage of husbands and wives who have both used illegal drugs (70 out of 100, row percent = 70.0); or we could compute the percentage of wives who have used drugs who are married to husbands who have also used drugs (70 out of 110, column percent = 63.6). Both would be meaningful depending on the researcher's particular interest. However, for cases like this in which there is no one variable that can be singled out as the cause of the other, total percents (which implicate neither one as being the independent variable) are frequently used. For Table 2.20, in 36.8% of the marriages, both partners have used illegal drugs at some point in their lives (70 out of 190),

TABLE 2.20   CROSS-TABULATION OF HUSBAND'S ILLEGAL DRUG USE BY WIFE'S ILLEGAL DRUG USE: FREQUENCY AND ROW, COLUMN, AND TOTAL PERCENTS

Frequency Row % Column % Total %	Wife has ever used illegal drugs		
	Yes	No	Total
Husband has ever used illegal drugs			
Yes	70	30	100
	70.0%	30.0%	52.6%
	63.6%	37.5%	
	36.8%	15.8%	
No	40	50	90
	44.4%	55.6%	47.4%
	36.4%	62.5%	
	21.1%	26.3%	
	110	80	190
	57.9%	42.1%	100.0%

and in 26.3%, both partners have never done so. Overall, in 63.1% of the marriages studied (36.8% + 26.3%), the husband and wife are the same in terms of having used illegal drugs.

The choices among total, row, and column percentages are as follows:

1. If the independent variable is on the rows, use row percents.
2. If the independent variable is on the columns, use column percents.
3. If there is no clear-cut independent variable, use total, row, or column percents, whichever is most meaningful for the particular research focus.

GRAPHIC PRESENTATIONS

Columns of numbers have been known to evoke fear, anxiety, boredom, apathy, and misunderstanding. Whereas some people seem to tune out statistical information presented in tabular form, they may pay close attention to the same data presented in graphic or picture form. As a result, many commercial researchers and popular authors prefer to use graphs as opposed to tables. For similar reasons, criminal justice researchers often use visual aids such as pie charts, bar graphs, frequency polygons, line charts, and maps in an effort to increase the readability of their findings.

PIE CHARTS

The *pie chart,* a circular graph whose pieces add up to 100%, is one of the simplest methods of graphical presentation. Pie charts are particularly useful for showing the differences in frequencies or percentages among categories of a nominal-level variable. To illustrate, Figure 2.3 presents the distribution of marital status of prisoners under sentences of death in the United States as of the last day of 1995.[2] Notice 50.3% were single (never married), 25.6% were married, 21.6% were divorced or separated, and 2.5% were widowed.

[2]U.S. Department of Justice, Bureau of Justice Statistics. *Capital Punishment in 1995,* bulletin NCJ-162043. Washington, D.C.: U.S. Government Printing Office, 1996.

In many instances, a researcher may want to direct attention to one particular category in a pie chart. In this case, a researcher may wish to highlight the married group. To highlight this aspect of the pie chart, we can "explode" (move slightly outward) the section of the pie that is most noteworthy, as in Figure 2.4.

BAR GRAPHS

The pie chart provides a quick and easy illustration of data that can be divided into a few categories only. (In fact, some computer graphics software packages limit the number of possible pie sections.) By comparison, the *bar graph* (or *histogram*) can accommodate any number of categories at any level of measurement and, therefore, is far more widely used in social research.

Figure 2.5 illustrates a bar graph of the frequency distribution of seat belt use presented in Table 2.15. The bar graph is constructed following the standard arrangement: A horizontal

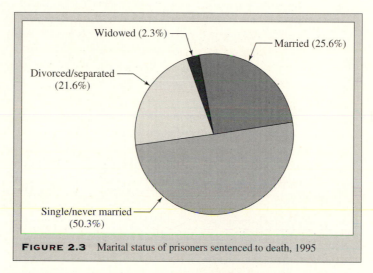

FIGURE 2.3 Marital status of prisoners sentenced to death, 1995

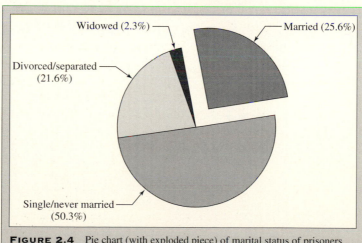

FIGURE 2.4 Pie chart (with exploded piece) of marital status of prisoners sentenced to death, 1995

base line (or x axis) along which the score values or categories (in this case, the levels of seat belt use) are marked off; and a vertical line (y axis) along the left side of the figure that displays the frequencies for each score value or category. (For grouped data, either the midpoints of the class intervals or the interval ranges themselves are arranged along the base line.) As we see in Figure 2.5, the taller the bar, the greater the frequency of the category.

Although many researchers prefer vertical bar graphs of frequencies, both graphs of percentages and horizontal bar graphs are often used. Figure 2.6, for example, shows a vertical bar graph of the percentage distribution of seat belt use. Note that the graph is identical to the frequency bar graph except for the scale used along the y axis (percentages rather than frequencies). Next, a horizontal bar graph of these same data is shown in Figure 2.7. There is no real difference between graphing horizontally or vertically; the choice often comes down to a practical decision about which will fit better on the page. Generally, a bar graph with numerous categories will be displayed best in horizontal form.

Many older statistics books dictated that bar graphs of ordinal or interval data should use bars that are joined to one another (such as Figure 1.1), and those of nominal data should use bars separated by space so that no order is implied. The use of computer graphics has changed that. Computer graphics software generally does not make such a distinction; many of these software packages routinely use separated bars. Thus, whereas nominal data must be graphed with separated bars, ordinal or interval data may be displayed with joined or disjoined bars.

Bar graphs can display the effect of one variable on another. For example, Figure 2.8 shows the seat belt use distribution by gender from the data in Table 2.16. It now makes a big difference whether we graph frequencies or percentages. The graph in Figure 2.8 is distorted because there are more females than males in the sample. As a result, most of the female bars are taller than the comparable male bars, blurring the effect of gender on

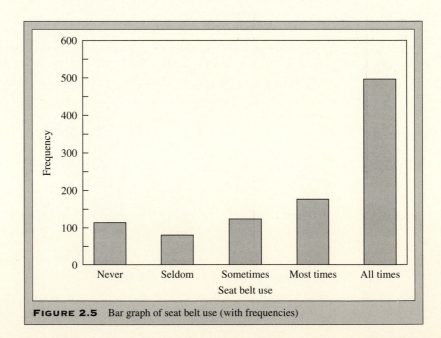

FIGURE 2.5   Bar graph of seat belt use (with frequencies)

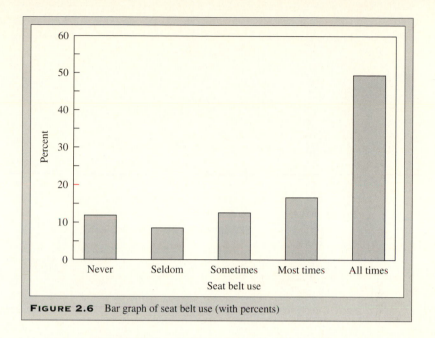

FIGURE 2.6   Bar graph of seat belt use (with percents)

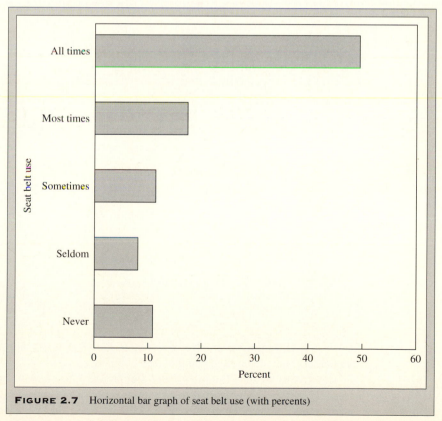

FIGURE 2.7   Horizontal bar graph of seat belt use (with percents)

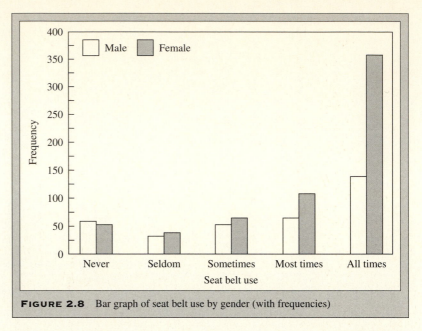

Figure 2.8 Bar graph of seat belt use by gender (with frequencies)

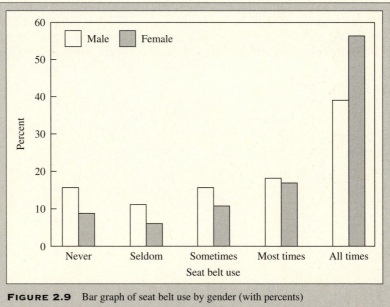

Figure 2.9 Bar graph of seat belt use by gender (with percents)

seat belt use. We get a better depiction instead by graphing the column percents from Table 2.19. Thus, the bar graph in Figure 2.9 allows us to see not only the distribution of seat belt use, but also how it is influenced by gender.

Bar graphs are also used to graph volumes and rates across population sub-groups or across time, rather than just frequency and percent distributions. For example, aggravated assault rates (number of assaults per 1,000 persons) derived from the National Crime Victimization Survey (NCVS) for the years 1992–1994 are shown by the age of the vic-

TABLE 2.21	AGGRAVATED ASSAULT RATE PER 1,000 PERSONS, BY AGE GROUP
Victim's age	Rate
12–14	21.1
15–17	28.9
18–21	29.3
22–24	22.9
25–29	16.7
30–34	11.0
35–39	9.2
40–49	8.3
50–64	3.4
65 or older	1.2

SOURCE: U.S. Department of Justice, Bureau of Justice Statistics, *Age Patterns of Victims of Serious Crimes,* Special Report NCJ-162031 (Washington, D.C.: U.S. Department of Justice, July 1997).

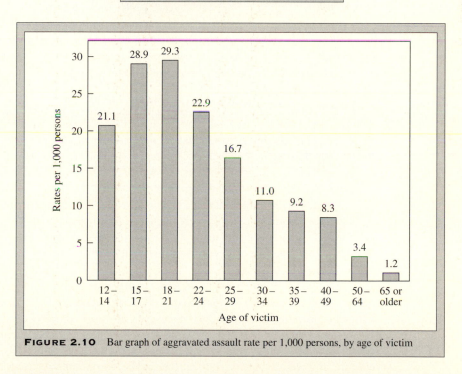

FIGURE 2.10   Bar graph of aggravated assault rate per 1,000 persons, by age of victim

tim in Table 2.21. A bar graph of these same data is presented as Figure 2.10. These rates are obtained by dividing the number of assaults suffered by victims in each age group by the number of persons in that age group and then multiplying by 1,000. To enhance the readability of the graph, we have labeled each bar with its value.

As we did with the bar graph showing seat belt use by gender (Figure 2.8), we can also add a gender dimension to the graph of aggravated assault by age. Table 2.22 presents

TABLE 2.22   AGGRAVATED ASSAULT RATE PER 1,000 PERSONS, BY AGE GROUP AND GENDER

	Rates per 1,000 persons	
Victim's age	Male	Female
12 to 14	26.4	15.5
15 to 17	39.1	18.2
18 to 21	39.5	19.1
22 to 24	31.2	14.6
25 to 29	21.1	12.3
30 to 34	12.3	9.7
35 to 39	12.8	5.5
40 to 49	11.6	5.1
50 to 64	4.4	2.5
65 or older	1.9	0.7

SOURCE: U.S. Department of Justice, Bureau of Justice Statistics, *Age Patterns of Victims of Serious Crimes,* Special Report NCJ-162031 (Washington, D.C.: U.S. Department of Justice, July 1997).

aggravated assault rates per 1,000 persons in separate age and gender categories. These same data are displayed in bar graph form in Figure 2.11.

FREQUENCY POLYGONS

Another commonly employed graphic method is the *frequency polygon.* Although the frequency polygon can accommodate a wide variety of categories, it tends to stress *continuity* along a scale rather than *differentness* and, therefore, is particularly useful for depicting ordinal and interval data. This is because frequencies are indicated by a series of points placed over the score values or midpoints of each class interval. Adjacent points are connected with a straight line, which is dropped to the base line at either end. The height of each point or dot indicates frequency of occurrence.

Table 2.23 shows a frequency distribution of the number of state and federal prisons in each of the 50 states. A frequency polygon for this distribution is then presented in Figure 2.12.

Note that the frequencies of the class intervals are plotted above their midpoints; the points are connected by straight lines, which are dropped to the horizontal base line at both ends, forming a polygon.

In order to graph cumulative frequencies (or cumulative percentages), it is possible to construct a *cumulative frequency polygon.* As shown in Figure 2.13, cumulative frequencies are arranged along the vertical line of the graph and are indicated by the height of points above the horizontal base line. Unlike a regular frequency polygon, however, the straight line connecting all points in the cumulative frequency polygon cannot be dropped back to the base line, because the cumulative frequencies being represented are a product of successive additions. Any given cumulative frequency is never less (and is usually more) than the preceding cumulative frequency. Also unlike a regular frequency polygon, the points in a cumulative graph are plotted above the upper limits of class intervals rather

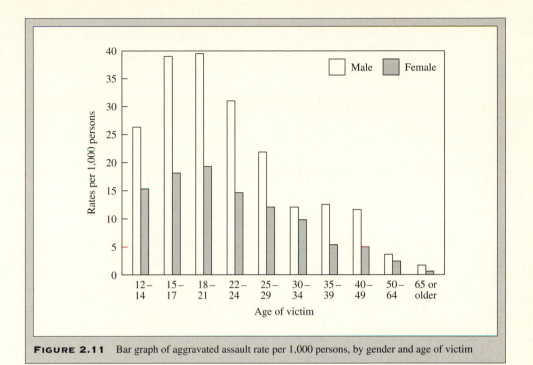

FIGURE 2.11   Bar graph of aggravated assault rate per 1,000 persons, by gender and age of victim

TABLE 2.23   GROUPED FREQUENCY DISTRIBUTION OF NUMBER OF STATE AND FEDERAL CORRECTIONAL FACILITIES IN EACH STATE, 1995

Number of prisons in state:

Class interval	f
1–10	17
11–20	8
21–30	12
31–40	4
41–50	3
51–60	0
61–70	1
71–80	1
81–90	0
91–100	3
101–110	1

SOURCE: U.S. Department of Justice, Bureau of Justice Statistics, *Correctional Populations in the United States, 1995,* Report NCJ-163916 (Washington, D.C.: U.S. Department of Justice, June 1997).

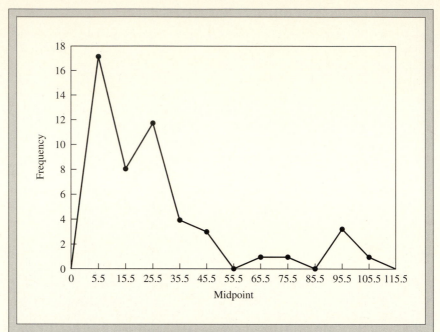

Figure 2.12 Frequency polygon for distribution of number of state and federal prisons in each state, 1995

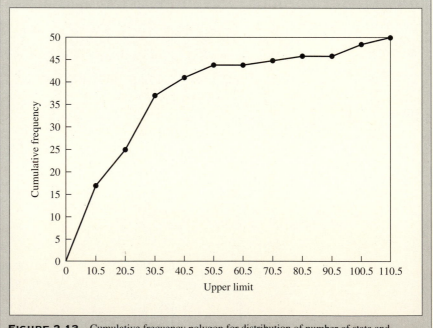

Figure 2.13 Cumulative frequency polygon for distribution of number of state and federal prisons in each state, 1995

than at their midpoints. This is because cumulative frequency represents the total number of cases *both within and below* a particular class interval.

THE SHAPE OF A FREQUENCY DISTRIBUTION

Frequency polygons can help us to visualize the variety of shapes and forms taken by frequency distributions. Some distributions are *symmetrical*—folding the curve at the center creates two identical halves. Therefore, such distributions contain the same number of extreme score values in both directions, high and low. Other distributions are said to be *skewed* and have more extreme cases in one direction than the other.

There is considerable variation among symmetrical distributions. For instance, they can differ markedly in terms of *peakedness* (or *kurtosis*). Some symmetrical distributions, as in Figure 2.14(a), are quite peaked or tall (called *leptokurtic*); others, as in Figure 2.14(b), are rather flat (called *platykurtic*); still others are neither very peaked nor very flat (called *mesokurtic*). One kind of mesokurtic symmetrical distribution, as shown in Figure 2.14(c), the *normal curve,* has special significance for social research and will be discussed in some detail in Chapter 5.

There is a variety of skewed or asymmetrical distributions. When skewness exists so that scores pile up in one direction, the distribution will have a pronounced "tail." The position of this tail indicates where the relatively few extreme scores are located and determines the *direction* of skewness.

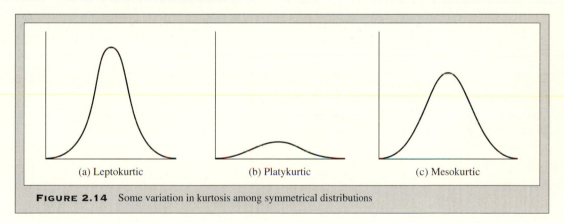

| (a) Leptokurtic | (b) Platykurtic | (c) Mesokurtic |

FIGURE 2.14 Some variation in kurtosis among symmetrical distributions

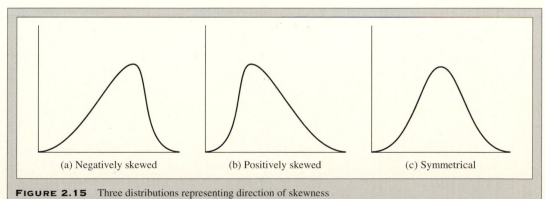

| (a) Negatively skewed | (b) Positively skewed | (c) Symmetrical |

FIGURE 2.15 Three distributions representing direction of skewness

Distribution (a) in Figure 2.15 is *negatively skewed* (skewed to the left), because it has a much longer tail on the left than the right. This distribution shows that most respondents received high scores, but only a few obtained low scores. If this were the distribution of grades on a final examination, we could say that most students did quite well and a few did poorly.

Next, look at distribution (b), whose tail is situated to the right. Because skewness is indicated by the direction of the elongated tail, we can say that the distribution is *positively skewed* (skewed to the right). The final examination grades for the students in this hypothetical classroom would be quite low, except for a few who did well.

Finally, let us examine distribution (c), which contains two identical tails. In such a case, there is the same number of extreme scores in both directions. The distribution is not at all skewed, but is perfectly symmetrical. If this were the distribution of grades on the final examination, we would have a large number of more or less average students and few students receiving very high and low grades.

LINE CHARTS

We saw previously that bar graphs could be used to display frequencies and percents from a distribution of scores as well as volumes and rates across groups, areas, or time. Frequency polygons can similarly be modified to display volumes and rates between groups or across time, although this method uses a *line chart*. In other words, frequency polygons show the *frequency* distribution of a set of scores on a single variable, whereas line charts display changes in a variable or variables between groups or over time.

In a line chart, the amount or rate of some variable is plotted and then these points are connected by line segments. Figure 2.16, for example, shows in line chart form the aggravated assault rates by age of victim that were previously displayed in a bar graph. As you can see by comparing Figures 2.16 and 2.10, it makes little difference which method is employed.

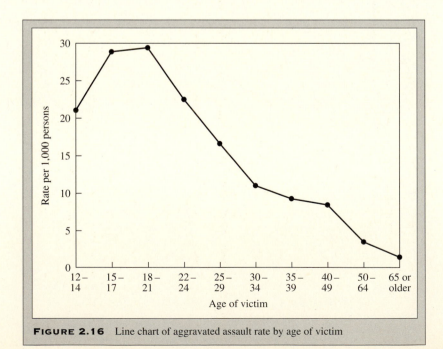

FIGURE 2.16 Line chart of aggravated assault rate by age of victim

Whereas subgroup comparisons (such as the victimization rates by age group) are plotted either with bars or lines, time trend data are far more customarily depicted with line charts. Figure 2.17, for example, shows the U.S. homicide rate (the number of homicides reported to the police per 100,000 residents) from 1950–1996, as listed in Table 2.24. Again, the graph proves to be far more revealing than the list of data. In the graph, we can clearly see a sharp and sudden upturn in the rate of homicides in the mid-1960s, an upward trend that continued until 1980, a downturn until the mid-1980s, a resurgence in the late 1980s and another downturn in the 1990s. It is incumbent on the researcher, of course, to attempt an explanation for these trends. Among those reasons advanced in the literature were changes in racial violence, a rise in drug use, changes in criminal sentencing practices, changes in the size of the adolescent population, and access to firearms.

MAPS

At one time, researchers relied almost exclusively on pie charts, bar graphs, frequency polygons, and line charts. In recent years, however, as graphics software for the computer has matured, researchers have begun to employ other forms of graphic presentation. One type in particular—the *map*—has become quite popular in conjunction with the greater use of data collected and published by the government (for example, census data).

The map offers an unparalleled method for exploring geographical patterns in data. For example, a three-category frequency distribution of homicide rates is displayed in Figure 2.18. Each state is shaded according to its category membership in the frequency distribution. The tendency for rates of homicide to be greater as one moves south is immediately apparent.

Rates were used in Figure 2.18; however, any measure (rates, percentages, frequencies, proportions, or ratios) can be employed if it suits the purpose. For example, the map in

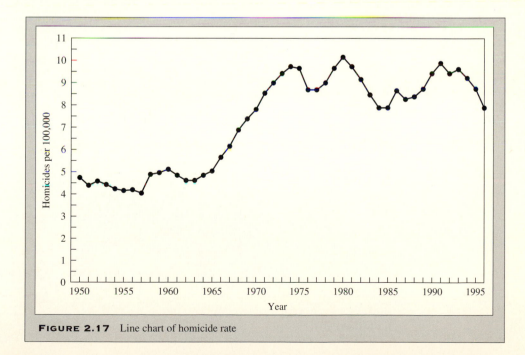

FIGURE 2.17 Line chart of homicide rate

TABLE 2.24   U.S. HOMICIDE RATE

Year	Homicide rate	Year	Homicide rate
1950	4.6	1974	9.8
1951	4.4	1975	9.6
1952	4.6	1976	8.8
1953	4.5	1977	8.8
1954	4.2	1978	9.0
1955	4.1	1979	9.7
1956	4.1	1980	10.2
1957	4.0	1981	9.8
1958	4.8	1982	9.1
1959	4.9	1983	8.3
1960	5.1	1984	7.9
1961	4.8	1985	7.9
1962	4.6	1986	8.6
1963	4.6	1987	8.3
1964	4.9	1988	8.4
1965	5.1	1989	8.7
1966	5.6	1990	9.4
1967	6.2	1991	9.8
1968	6.9	1992	9.3
1969	7.3	1993	9.5
1970	7.9	1994	9.0
1971	8.6	1995	8.2
1972	9.0	1996	7.4
1973	9.4		

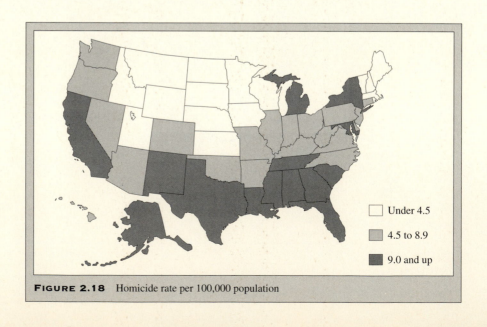

Under 4.5
4.5 to 8.9
9.0 and up

FIGURE 2.18   Homicide rate per 100,000 population

Figure 2.19 shows geographic patterns in the ratio of clients to providers in drug and/or alcohol treatment units throughout the United States. We can see in this map that the ratio of clients to providers generally is lower in the North-Central states, and higher in the Western, Southern, and Eastern States.

Both of the maps discussed thus far use hatch patterns (or shadings) to indicate levels of a variable. Another type of map known as a dot-density map is particularly well suited for displaying frequency or count data. In Figure 2.20, for example, we show variations in the size of state populations using a dot for each 10,000 persons. The density, or

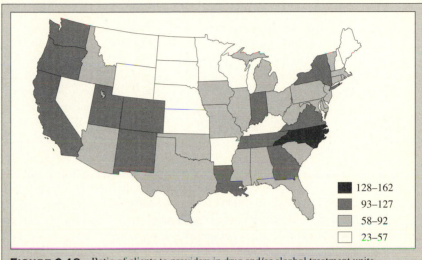

128–162
93–127
58–92
23–57

FIGURE 2.19   Ratio of clients to providers in drug and/or alcohol treatment units

Source: U.S. Department of Health and Human Services, Substance Abuse and Mental Health Services Administration, *Overview of the FY 1994 National Drug and Alcoholism Treatment Unit Survey* (NDATUS): Data From 1993 and 1980–1993. Advance Report Number 9-Rev1 (Rockville, MD: U.S. Department of Health and Human Services, May 1995).

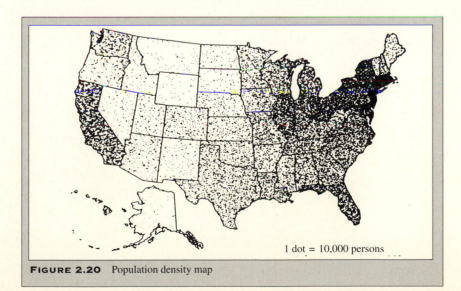

1 dot = 10,000 persons

FIGURE 2.20   Population density map

darkness, of the cluster of dots reflects the density of the population. Thus, states such as Montana, Wyoming, and Alaska can be seen to be sparsely populated, whereas states like California, Florida, and New York are heavily populated. Also, the entire northeastern megalopolis from Boston to Washington, D.C., is almost entirely blackened with dots.

In producing dot-density maps, the computer spreads the dots for a particular state in a random fashion. Thus, uneven distributions of population within a state like New York are not well represented. A dot-density map of zip code areas or counties, however, could produce a more accurate depiction of population density.

SUMMARY

In this chapter, we introduced some of the basic techniques used by the criminal justice researcher to organize the jumble of raw numbers that he or she collects. Frequency distributions and methods for comparing such distributions of nominal data (proportions, percentages, ratios, and rates) were discussed and illustrated. With respect to ordinal and interval data, the characteristics of simple, grouped, and cumulative frequency (and percent) distributions were examined. The procedure for obtaining the percentile rank of a raw score was then presented.

Also in this chapter, we extended frequency and percent distributions to cross-tabulations of two variables. There are three possible ways to determine percentages for cross-tabulations: row percents, column percents, and total percents. The choice between row and column percents depends on the placement of the independent variable within the cross-tabulation. Total percents are occasionally used instead, but only when neither the row nor column variable can be identified as independent.

Graphic presentations of data can also be used to increase the readability of research findings. Our discussion of graphic presentations included pie charts, bar graphs, frequency polygons, line charts, and maps. Pie charts provide a simple illustration of data, which are divisible into a few categories. Bar graphs are more widely used, because they can accommodate any number of categories. Frequency polygons also accommodate a wide range of categories, but are especially useful for ordinal and interval data, because they stress continuity along a scale. Among its many applications, line charts are particularly useful for tracing trends over time. Finally, maps are used for displaying geographical patterns in data.

TERMS TO REMEMBER

Frequency distribution	Median
Percentage distribution	Cross-tabulation
Proportion	Total percent
Percentage	Row percent
Ratio	Column percent
Rate	Pie chart
Grouped frequency distribution	Bar graph (histogram)
Class interval	Frequency polygon
Class limit	Cumulative frequency polygon
Map	Kurtosis
Midpoint	

TERMS TO REMEMBER (CONT.)

Cumulative frequency

Cumulative percentage

Percentile rank

Deciles

Quartiles

Skewness

Negatively skewed distribution

Positively skewed distribution

Line chart

PROBLEMS

1. From the following table representing fear of crime for 173 television viewers and 183 nonviewers, find (a) the percent of nonviewers who are highly fearful, (b) the percent of viewers who have low fear, (c) the proportion of viewers who have high fear, and (d) the proportion of nonviewers who have low fear.

	Viewing status	
Fear of Crime	Nonviewers	Viewers
Low	93	46
High	90	127
	183	173

2. From the following table representing family structure for black and white children in a particular community, find (a) the percent of delinquent children having two-parent families, (b) the percent of nondelinquent children having two-parent families, (c) the proportion of delinquent children having two-parent families, and (d) the proportion of nondelinquent children having two-parent families.

FAMILY STRUCTURE FOR DELINQUENT
AND NONDELINQUENT CHILDREN

Family structure	Delinquent	Nondelinquent
One parent	53	59
Two parent	60	167
Total	113	226

3. In a group of 4 high-risk offenders and 24 low-risk offenders, what is the ratio of low- to high-risk offenders?

4. In a group of 125 male and 80 female boot camp prison inmates, what is the gender ratio?

5. In a group of 15 defense attorneys and 20 prosecutors, what is the ratio of defense to prosecution attorneys?

6. If 300 rapes occur among 3,500 women, what is the rape rate (per 1,000 women)?

7. What is the rate of change for a probation population that increased from 15,000 in 1985 to 25,000 in 1995?

8. A class of 40 police cadets took a test consisting of 12 difficult problems. Convert the following distribution of scores (number of correct answers) into a grouped frequency distribution containing four class intervals, and (a) determine the size of class intervals, (b) indicate the upper and lower limits of each class interval, (c) identify the midpoint of each class interval, (d) find the percentage for each class interval, (e) find the cumulative frequency for each class interval, and (f) find the cumulative percentage for each class interval.

Score value	f
12	3
11	4
10	4
9	5
8	6
7	5
6	4
5	3
4	2
3	1
2	1
1	2
	$N = 40$

9. Convert the following distribution of scores into a grouped frequency distribution containing five class intervals, and (a) determine the size of class intervals, (b) indicate the upper and lower limits of each class interval, (c) identify the midpoint of each class interval, (d) find the percentage for each class interval, (e) find the cumulative frequency for each class interval, and (f) find the cumulative percentage for each class interval.

Score value	f
100	4
99	6
98	7
97	9
96	12
95	10
94	6
93	5
92	3
91	2
	$N = 64$

10. In the following distribution of scores on a promotional exam, find the percentile rank for (a) a score of 75 (passing) and (b) a score of 52.

Class interval	f	cf
90–99	6	48
80–89	9	42
70–79	10	33
60–69	10	23
50–59	8	13
40–49	5	5
	$N = 48$	

11. A group of 56 DEA agents went to the firing range to practice. Each agent was allowed 50 shots at their targets. In the following distribution of "hits," find the percentile rank for (a) a score of 36 and (b) a score of 18.

Class interval	f
40–44	5
35–39	5
30–34	8
25–29	9
20–24	10
15–19	8
10–14	6
5–9	5
	$N = 56$

12. For the family income distribution in Table 2.13, determine the percentile rank for a family earning $12,000.

13. The following is a cross-tabulation by social class of whether respondents have or have not been crime victims for a sample of 240 heads of households:

	Crime victim		
Social class	Yes	No	Total
Lower class	62	18	80
Middle class	47	63	110
Upper class	11	39	50
Total	120	120	240

a. Which is the independent variable and which is the dependent variable?
b. Compute row percents for the cross-tabulation.
c. What percent of the sample are nonvictims?
d. What percent of the sample are victims?
e. What percent of the lower-class respondents are nonvictims?
f. What percent of the middle-class respondents are victims?
g. Which social class has the greatest tendency to be victimized?

h. Which social class has the greatest tendency to be nonvictims?
i. What can be concluded about the relationship between social class and crime victimization?

14. The following is a cross-tabulation of the number of youths in juvenile detention who were predicted by staff to be violent on nonviolent, by the number who were actually violent or nonviolent subsequent to their release:

	Predicted violent	Predicted nonviolent	Total
Actual Violent	52	52	104
Actual Nonviolent	404	3,638	4,042
Total	456	3,690	4,146

a. Which is the independent variable and which is the dependent variable?
b. Compute column percents for the cross-tabulation.
c. What percent of the sample was actually violent after release from juvenile detention?
d. What percent of the sample was predicted violent?
e. What percent of youths predicted to be violent were actually violent?
f. What percent of youths predicted to be nonviolent were actually violent?
g. Of those youths who were actually violent, what percent had been predicted to be violent?
h. Of those youths who were actually nonviolent, what percent had been predicted to be violent?
i. What can be concluded about the accuracy of predictions of whether youths will be violent after their release from detention?

15. The probation sentences of five individuals are 2, 2, 4, 5, and 7 years. Present a simple frequency distribution, including cumulative percentages.

16. A researcher is interested in studying the number of violent crimes committed against homeless people in large urban areas. She selected 30 cities with populations over 500,000 and calculated a homeless murder rate (HMR) as follows:

$$HMR = 100,000 \left(\frac{\text{number of murders of homeless people}}{\text{homeless population}} \right)$$

Thus the HMR represents the number of murders per 1,000 homeless people. Here are her results (the different cities have each been assigned a number).

City	HMR	City	HMR
1	.83	16	.54
2	.62	17	.98
3	1.04	18	1.28
4	.44	19	.42
5	.52	20	.40
6	.81	21	.38
7	.39	22	.76
8	1.11	23	.89
9	.22	24	.23
10	.90	25	.55
11	1.01	26	.96
12	.74	27	.32
13	.35	28	.88
14	1.22	29	.63
15	.47	30	.58

a. Construct a grouped frequency distribution of the data presented. Use three class intervals with a class size of four, with 1.45 as the upper limit of the highest class interval. Calculate percentages, cumulative frequencies, and cumulative percentages.
b. What are the upper and lower limits of the lowest class interval?
c. What are the upper and lower limits of the second highest class interval?
d. What is the midpoint of the highest class interval?
e. Using your grouped distribution, estimate the percentage of cities that had HMRs at or below 1. Do you arrive at a different result if you use the raw data to answer the question? Why or why not?

17. Use pie charts to depict the following information:

(a)

Race of men executed in the U.S. in 1995	f	%
White	33	59
Black	22	39
Asian	1	2
Total	56	100

(b)

Age of murder victims under age 18	%
less than 1 year	12.6
1–4 years	19.7
5–14 years	21.8
15–17 years	45.9
Total	100

(c)

Victim-offender relationship	%
Intimate	29
Other relative	9
Acquaintance/friend	40
Stranger	23

18. Depict the following data in bar graphs:

(a)

State Executions in 1995	
Texas	19
Missouri	6
Virginia	5
Florida	3
Arkansas	2
Louisiana	1

(b)

Year	Prisoners per 100,000 population
1980	139
1981	154
1982	171
1983	179
1984	188
1985	202
1986	217
1987	231
1988	247
1989	276
1990	297
1991	313
1992	332
1993	359
1994	389
1995	411

19. Draw a cumulative frequency polygon to represent the following grades on a final exam:

Class interval	f	cf
90–99	3	27
80–89	6	24
70–79	12	18
60–69	4	6
50–59	2	2
	$N = 27$	

20. Display the following suicide rates (per 100,000) both as a bar graph and as a line chart.

Age	Suicide rate
15–24	13.1
25–34	15.7
35–44	15.2
45–54	16.4
55–64	17.0
65–74	19.7
75–84	25.2
85+	20.8

21. Create a grouped frequency distribution, with four categories, using the following data. Then, using your grouped frequency distribution and a blank map of the United States, display the data on the number of bombing incidents reported to or investigated by the Bureau of Alcohol, Tobacco, and Firearms.

BOMBING INCIDENTS REPORTED TO OR INVESTIGATED BY THE BUREAU OF ALCOHOL, TABACCO AND FIREARMS

Jurisdiction	
Alabama	16
Alaska	4
Arizona	132
Arkansas	4
California	418
Colorado	43
Connecticut	15
Delaware	2
District of Columbia	2
Florida	277
Georgia	21
Hawaii	4
Idaho	7
Illinois	188
Indiana	26
Iowa	47
Kansas	15
Kentucky	43
Louisiana	25
Maine	11
Maryland	55
Massachusetts	15
Michigan	105
Minnesota	60
Mississippi	9
Missouri	39
Montana	10
Nebraska	9
Nevada	29
New Hampshire	7
New Jersey	39
New Mexico	29
New York	88
North Carolina	13
North Dakota	18
Ohio	125
Oklahoma	31
Oregon	50
Pennsylvania	59
Rhode Island	2
South Carolina	10
South Dakota	6
Tennessee	34
Texas	108
Utah	22
Vermont	5
Virginia	46
Washington	65
West Virginia	7
Wisconsin	30
Wyoming	11
Guam	0
Puerto Rico	2
Virgin Islands	0

CHAPTER 3

MEASURES OF CENTRAL TENDENCY

- **THE MODE**

- **THE MEDIAN**

- **THE MEAN**

- **TAKING ONE STEP AT A TIME**

- **COMPARING THE MODE, MEDIAN, AND MEAN**

- **OBTAINING THE MODE, MEDIAN, AND MEAN FROM A SIMPLE FREQUENCY DISTRIBUTION**

- **OBTAINING THE MODE, MEDIAN, AND MEAN FROM A GROUPED FREQUENCY DISTRIBUTION**

- **SUMMARY**

- **TERMS TO REMEMBER**

- **STEP-BY-STEP STUDY GUIDE: MODE, MEDIAN, AND MEAN FOR RAW SCORES**

- **PROBLEMS**

Researchers in criminology and criminal justice have used the term "average" to ask such questions as: What is the *average* age at first arrest for drug offenses? What is the *average* caseload for public defenders? What is the *average* prison sentence for convicted sex offenders? How many robberies are committed by the *average* prisoner convicted of robbery? What are the *average* monthly shoplifting losses for small retail businesses? On *average*, how many automobile accidents happen as the direct result of drug or alcohol abuse?

A useful way to describe a group as a whole is to find a single number that represents what is average or typical of that set of data. Such a value is known as a measure of *central tendency,* because it is generally located toward the middle or center of a distribution where most of the data tend to be concentrated.

What the layperson means by the term *average* is often vague and even confusing. The criminal justice researcher's conception is much more precise; it is expressed numerically as one of several different kinds of measures of average or central tendency that may take on quite different numerical values in the same set of data. Only the three best known measures of central tendency are discussed here: the mode, the median, and the mean.

THE MODE

The *mode* (Mo) is the most frequent, most typical, or most common value in a distribution. For example, there are more Protestants in the United States than people of any other religion; and so we refer to this religion as the mode. Similarly, if at a given university engineering is the most popular major, this too would represent the mode. The mode is the only measure of central tendency available for nominal-level variables, such as religion

69

and college major. It can, however, be used to describe the most common score in any distribution, regardless of the level of measurement.

To find the mode, find the score or category that occurs most often in a distribution. The mode can be easily found by inspection, rather than by computation. For instance, in the set of scores ①, 2, 3, ①, ①, 6, 5, 4, ①, 4, 4, 3, the mode is 1, because it is the number that occurs more than any other score in the set (it occurs four times). Make no mistake: The mode is *not* the frequency of the most frequent score ($f = 4$), but the value of the most frequent score ($Mo = 1$).

Some frequency distributions contain two or more modes. In the following set of data, for example, the scores 2 and 6 *both* occur most often: 6, 6, 7, 2, 6, 1, 2, 3, 2, 4. Graphically, such distributions have two points of maximum frequency, suggestive of the humps on a camel's back. These distributions are referred to as being *bimodal* in contrast to the more common *unimodal* variety, which has only a single hump or point of maximum frequency.

Figure 3.1, for example, shows the test scores on a criminal law and a criminal justice statistics final exam. The criminal law scores are unimodal, that is, the performance levels cluster around a single mode. The statistics scores, however, are bimodal, that is, the performance levels cluster around two modes. In the statistics course, apparently, there are many students who caught on, and another distinct group who did not.

THE MEDIAN

When ordinal or interval data are arranged in order of size, it becomes possible to locate the *median* (Mdn), the *middlemost* point in a distribution. Therefore, the median is regarded as the measure of central tendency that cuts the distribution into two equal parts, just as the median strip of a highway cuts it in two.

The position of the median value can be located by inspection or by the formula

$$\text{Position of median} = \frac{N + 1}{2}$$

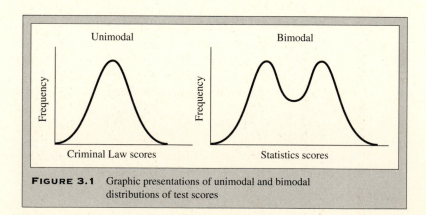

FIGURE 3.1   Graphic presentations of unimodal and bimodal distributions of test scores

If we have an odd number of cases, then the median will be the case that falls exactly in the middle of the distribution. Thus, 16 is the median value for the scores 11, 12, 13, (16), 17, 20, 25; this is the case that divides the distribution of numbers, so that there are three scores on either side of it. According to the formula $(7 + 1)/2 = 4$, we see that the median 16 is the fourth score in the distribution counting from either end.

If the number of cases is even, the median is always that *point* above which 50% of the cases fall and below which 50% of the cases fall. For an even number of cases, there will be two middle cases. To illustrate, the numbers 16 and 17 represent the middle cases for the following data: 11, 12, 13, (16), (17), 20, 25, 26. By the formula $(8 + 1)/2 = 4.5$, the median will fall midway between the fourth and fifth cases; the middlemost point in this distribution turns out to be 16.5, because it lies halfway between 16 and 17, the fourth and fifth scores in the set. Likewise, the median is 9 in the data 2, 5, (8), (10), 11, 12, again because it is located exactly midway between the two middle cases $(6 + 1)/2 = 3.5$.

Another circumstance must be explained and illustrated—we may be asked to find the median from data containing several middle scores having identical numerical values. The solution is simple—that numerical value becomes the median. Therefore, in the data 11, 12, 13, (16), (16), (16), 25, 26, 27, the median case is 16, although it occurs more than once.

Finally, if the data are not in order from low to high (or high to low), you should put them in order before trying to locate the median. Thus, in the data 3, 2, 7, the median is 3, the middle score after arranging the numbers 2, (3), 7.

THE MEAN

By far the most commonly used measure of central tendency, the arithmetic mean $\overline{X}$, is obtained by adding up a set of scores and dividing by the number of scores. Therefore, we define the mean more formally as *the sum of a set of scores divided by the total number of scores in the set.* By formula,

$$\overline{X} = \frac{\Sigma X}{N}$$

where $\overline{X}$ = mean (read as X bar)
   Σ = sum (expressed as the Greek capital letter sigma)[1]
   X = raw score in a set of scores
   N = total number of scores in a set

Using the previous formula, we learn that the mean IQ for the eight respondents listed in Table 3.1 is 108.

---

[1] The Greek capital letter sigma (Σ), called the summation sign, will be encountered many times throughout the text. It simply indicates that we must *sum* or add up what follows. In the present example, ΣX indicates adding up the raw scores. See Appendix B for a discussion of the summation sign.

TABLE 3.1   CALCULATING THE MEAN: AN ILLUSTRATION

Offender	X (IQ)	
Gene	125	
Steve	92	$\overline{X} = \dfrac{\Sigma X}{N}$
Bob	72	
Michael	126	
Joan	120	$= \dfrac{864}{8}$
Jim	99	
Jane	130	$= 108$
Mary	100	
	$\Sigma X = 864$	

Unlike the mode, the mean is not always the score that occurs most often. Unlike the median, it is not necessarily the middlemost point in a distribution. Then, what does the *mean* mean? How can it be interpreted?

As we shall see, the mean can be regarded as the "center of gravity" of a distribution. It is similar to the notion of a seesaw or a fulcrum and lever (see Figure 3.2). Four blocks of weight are placed on the lever. The block marked *11* is 7 units (inches, feet, or whatever) to the right of the fulcrum. It balances with the blocks marked *1, 2,* and *2,* which are 3, 2, and 2 units to the left of the fulcrum, respectively. In a distribution of data, the mean acts as a fulcrum: It is the point in a distribution around which the scores above it balance with those below it.

In order to understand this characteristic of the mean, we must first understand the concept of *deviation.* The deviation indicates the distance and direction of any raw score from the mean, just as we noted that a particular block is 7 units to the right of the fulcrum.

To find the deviation for a particular raw score, we simply subtract the mean from that score:

$$\text{Deviation} = X - \overline{X}$$

where X = any raw score in the distribution
         $\overline{X}$ = mean of the distribution

For the set of raw scores 9, 8, 6, 5, and 2 in Table 3.2, $\overline{X} = 6$. The raw score 9 lies exactly three raw score units above the mean of 6 (or $X - \overline{X} = 9 - 6 = +3$). Similarly, the raw score 2 lies four raw score units below the mean (or $X - \overline{X} = 2 - 6 = -4$). Thus, the greater the deviation $(X - \overline{X})$, the greater is the distance of that raw score from the mean of the distribution.

Considering the mean as a point of balance in the distribution, we can now say that the sum of the deviations that fall above the mean is equal in absolute value (ignoring the minus signs) to the sum of the deviations that fall below the mean. Let us return to the set of scores 9, 8, 6, 5, 2 in which $\overline{X} = 6$. If the mean for this distribution is the "center of gravity," then disregarding minus signs and adding together the positive deviations (deviations of raw scores 8 and 9) should equal adding together the negative deviations

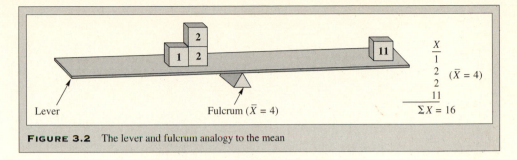

FIGURE 3.2 The lever and fulcrum analogy to the mean

TABLE 3.2 DEVIATIONS OF A SET OF RAW SCORES FROM X

X	$X - \overline{X}$	
9	+3	$\left.\begin{array}{c}\end{array}\right\} + 5$
8	+2	
6	0	$\overline{X} = 6$
5	−1	$\left.\begin{array}{c}\end{array}\right\} - 5$
2	−4	

(deviations of raw scores 5 and 2). As shown in Table 3.2, this turns out to be the case because the sum of deviations below $\overline{X}$ (−5) equals the sum of deviations above $\overline{X}$ (+5).

Taking another example, 4 is the mean for the numbers 1, 2, 3, 5, 6, and 7. We see that the sum of deviations below this score is −6, whereas the sum of deviations above it is +6. We shall return to the concept of deviation in Chapters 4 and 5.

TAKING ONE STEP AT A TIME

When you open a cookbook to find a method for making a chocolate cake, the recipe can at first appear overwhelming. But when you approach the cake "formula" step by step, you often find that it was easier than it looked. In a similar way, some of the statistical "recipes" that you will encounter later in this book can also look overwhelming, or at least very complicated. Our advice is to confront formulas step by step, that is, to perform a series of small mathematical tasks to achieve the eventual solution. Throughout this book, we will often demonstrate calculations through step-by-step illustrations. Try not to focus so much on whether there are four, six, or seven steps, but on the progression from one to another. Now let's review the steps to calculate the mode, median, and mean.

STEP-BY-STEP ILLUSTRATION
MODE, MEDIAN, AND MEAN

Suppose that a criminal justice researcher surveys a population of drug abusers to find out the average number of times they use illegal drugs each month. She collects the following responses from her first seven respondents:

$$5 \quad 10 \quad 25 \quad 15 \quad 18 \quad 2 \quad 5$$

STEP 1   Arrange the scores from highest to lowest.

$$25$$
$$18$$
$$15$$
$$10$$
$$5$$
$$5$$
$$2$$

STEP 2   Find the most frequent score.

$$Mo = 5$$

STEP 3   Find the middlemost score. Because there are seven scores (an odd number), the fourth from either end is the median.

$$Mdn = 10$$

STEP 4   Determine the sum of the scores.

$$25$$
$$18$$
$$15$$
$$10$$
$$5$$
$$5$$
$$\underline{2}$$
$$\Sigma X = 80$$

STEP 5   Determine the mean by dividing the sum by the number of scores.

$$\bar{X} = \frac{\Sigma X}{N} = \frac{80}{7} = 11.43$$

Thus the mode, median, and mean provide very different pictures of average monthly drug use. The mode suggests relatively infrequent drug use while the medium and mean indicate much more frequent use.

COMPARING THE MODE, MEDIAN, AND MEAN

The time comes when the criminal justice researcher chooses a measure of central tendency for a particular research situation. Will he or she employ the mode, the median, or the mean? The decision involves several factors, including the following:

1. Level of measurement
2. Shape or form of the distribution of data
3. Research objective

LEVEL OF MEASUREMENT

Because the mode requires only a frequency count, it can be applied to any set of data at the nominal, ordinal, or interval level of measurement. For instance, we might determine that the modal category in a nominal-level measure of religious affiliation (Protestant, Catholic, or Jewish) is Protestant, because the largest number of our respondents identify themselves as such. Similarly, we might learn that the largest number of students attending a particular university have a 2.5 grade-point average (Mo = 2.5).

The median requires an ordering of categories from highest to lowest. For this reason, it can only be obtained from ordinal or interval data, *not* from nominal data. To illustrate, we might find that the median annual income is $37,000 among police officers in a small town. The result gives us a meaningful way to examine the central tendency in our data. By contrast, it would make little sense if we were to compute the median for religious affiliation or criminal offense type (e.g., burglary, arson, murder), when ranking or scaling cannot be carried out.

The use of the mean is exclusively restricted to interval data. Applying it to ordinal or nominal data yields a meaningless result, generally not at all indicative of central tendency. What sense would it make to compute the mean for a distribution of religious affiliation or gender? Although less obvious, it is equally inappropriate to calculate a mean for data that can be ranked but not scored.

SHAPE OF THE DISTRIBUTION

The shape, or form, of a distribution is another factor that can influence the researcher's choice of a measure of central tendency. In a perfectly symmetrical unimodal distribution, the mode, median, and mean will be identical, because the point of maximum frequency (Mo) is also the middlemost score (Mdn), as well as the "center of gravity" ($\overline{X}$). As shown in Figure 3.3, the measures of central tendency will coincide at the most central point, the "peak" of the symmetrical distribution.

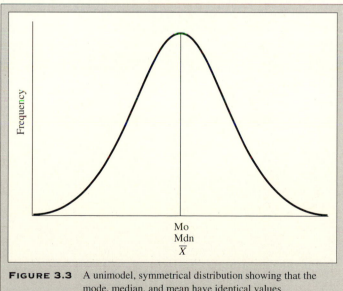

FIGURE 3.3   A unimodel, symmetrical distribution showing that the mode, median, and mean have identical values

When criminal justice researchers work with a symmetrical distribution, their choice of measure of central tendency is chiefly based on their particular research objectives and the level at which their data are measured. When they work with a skewed distribution, however, this decision is very much influenced by the shape, or form, of their data.

As shown in Figure 3.4, the mode, median, and mean do not coincide in skewed distributions, *although their relative positions remain constant*—moving away from the "peak" and toward the "tail," the order is always from mode, to median, to mean. The mode is at the peak of the curve, because this is the point where the most frequent scores occur. The mean, by contrast, is found closest to the tail, where the relatively few extreme scores are located. For this reason, the mean score in the positively skewed distribution in Figure 3.4(a) lies toward the high-score values; the mean in the negatively skewed distribution in Figure 3.4(b) falls close to the low-score values.

Whereas the mean is very much influenced by extreme scores in either direction, the median is modified little, if at all, by changes in extreme values. This is because the mean considers all of the scores in any distribution, whereas the median (by definition) is concerned only with the numerical value of the score that falls at the middlemost position in a distribution. As illustrated, changing an extreme score value from 10 in distribution *A* to 95 in distribution *B* does not at all modify the median value (Mdn = 7.5), whereas the mean shifts from 7.63 to 18.25:

| Distribution A: | 5 | 6 | 6 | 7 | 8 | 9 | 10 | 10 | Mdn = 7.5 | $\overline{X}$ = 7.63 |
| Distribution B: | 5 | 6 | 6 | 7 | 8 | 9 | 10 | 95 | Mdn = 7.5 | $\overline{X}$ = 18.25 |

In a skewed distribution, the median always falls somewhere between the mean and the mode. It is this characteristic that makes the median the most desirable measure of central tendency for describing a skewed distribution of scores. To illustrate this advantage of the median, let us turn to Table 3.3 and examine the average annual salary among legal secretaries working in a government agency. If we were public relations practitioners hired by the agency to give it a favorable public image, we would probably want to calculate the mean in order to show that the average legal secretary makes $25,000 and is relatively well paid. On the other hand, if we were union representatives seeking to upgrade

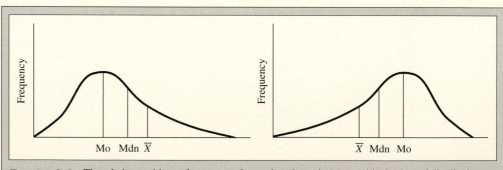

FIGURE 3.4   The relative positions of measures of central tendency in (a) a positively skewed distribution and (b) a negatively skewed distribution

salary levels, we would probably want to employ the mode to demonstrate that the average salary is only $15,000. Finally, if we were criminal justice researchers seeking to report accurately the average salary among the employees in this agency, we would wisely employ the median ($20,000), because it falls between the other measures of central tendency and, therefore, gives a more balanced picture of the salary structure. The most acceptable method would be to report all three measures of central tendency and permit the audience to interpret the results. It is unfortunately true that few researchers—let alone public relations practitioners or union representatives—report more than a single measure of central tendency. Even more unfortunate is that some reports of research fail to specify exactly which measure of central tendency—the mode, median, or mean—was used to calculate the average amount or position in a group of scores. As shown in Table 3.3, a reasonable interpretation of findings may be impossible without such information.

It was noted earlier that some frequency distributions can be characterized as being bimodal, because they contain two points of maximum frequency. To describe bimodal distributions properly, it is generally useful to identify *both* modes; important aspects of such distributions can be obscured using either the median or the mean.

Consider the situation of a criminologist who conducted personal interviews with 20 randomly selected registered voters in order to determine their support for trying juvenile felony defendants as adults. Each respondent was asked, "On a scale from 1 to 10 (1 = definitely should NOT, 10 = definitely SHOULD), rate how strongly you believe that juveniles accused of felony offenses should be tried as adults."

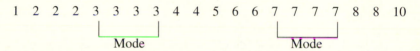

As shown, there is a wide range of responses to this question, from believing that juveniles definitely should not be tried as adults to definitely should. Most people fell somewhere between the two extremes. Using either the mean ($\overline{X} = 4.85$) or median (Mdn = 4.5), we might conclude that the average respondent felt neither in favor of nor opposed to trying juveniles as adults. Some might interpret these results as indicating that the average person is undecided. Knowing that the distribution is bimodal, however, we can see that there were

TABLE 3.3	MEASURES OF CENTRAL TEN-DENCY IN A SKEWED DISTRIBU-TION OF ANNUAL SALARIES

Salary	
$60,000	
30,000	$\overline{X}$ = $25,000
20,000	
20,000	Mdn = $20,000
15,000	
15,000	Mo = $15,000
15,000	

actually two concentrations of responses—one indicating moderate rejection of trying juveniles as adults (Mo = 3), and the other indicating moderate acceptance (Mo = 7).[2]

OBTAINING THE MODE, MEDIAN, AND MEAN FROM A SIMPLE FREQUENCY DISTRIBUTION

In the last chapter, we saw how a set of raw scores could be rearranged in the form of a simple frequency distribution, that is, a table of the frequency of occurrence of each score value. It is important to note that a simple frequency distribution does not change the data; it only shows them in a different way. Therefore, the mode, median, and mean obtained from a simple frequency distribution also do not change, but they are calculated differently.

Let's consider the following raw scores representing the age at first incarceration for a sample of prison inmates:

18 18 19 19 19 19 20 20 20 21 21 22
22 23 23 24 25 26 26 26 27 27 29 30 31

There are more respondents first incarcerated at age 19; thus Mo = 19. The middlemost score (the thirteenth from either end) is 22; thus Mdn = 22. Finally, the scores sum to 575; thus $\bar{X} = 575/25 = 23$.

These data can be rearranged as a simple frequency distribution as follows:

	X	f
	31	1
	30	1
	29	1
	28	0
	27	2
	26	3
	25	1
	24	1
	23	2
	22	2
	21	2
	20	3
Mo →	19	4
	18	2

In the case of a simple frequency distribution in which the score values and frequencies are presented in separate columns, the mode is the score value that appears most often in the frequency column of the table. Therefore, Mo = 19 in the simple frequency distribution shown previously. This agrees, of course, with the mode obtained from the raw scores.

[2] Sometimes distributions can be "almost" bimodal. For example, suppose that one more respondent recorded a 3 rather than a 2 as their indication of support for trying juveniles as adults. There would only be one real mode (Mo = 3). But because there would be almost as many 7s, 7 would almost (but not quite) be a mode as well. In such a case, it is wise to report that the distribution has two peaks, with one somewhat smaller than the other.

To find the median for this simple frequency distribution, we start by identifying the position of the median. There are 25 age-at-first-incarceration scores (as opposed to 14 score values, 18 through 31). With $N = 25$,

$$\text{Position of median} = \frac{25 + 1}{2}$$

$$= \frac{26}{2}$$

$$= 13$$

The median turns out to be the thirteenth score in this frequency distribution. To help locate the thirteenth score, we construct a cumulative frequency distribution as shown in the third column of the following table (for a small number of scores, this can be done in your head):

	X	f	cf
	31	1	25
	30	1	24
	29	1	23
	28	0	22
	27	2	22
	26	3	20
	25	1	17
	24	1	16
	23	2	15
Mdn →	22	2	13
	21	2	11
	20	3	9
	19	4	6
	18	2	2

Beginning with the lowest score value (18), we add frequencies until we reach a score value that represents the thirteenth score in the distribution. This is accomplished by searching for the smallest score value having a cumulative frequency that is at least 13.

In this distribution of age at first incarceration, the cumulative frequency for the score value 18 is 2, meaning that the two youngest ages were 18. The cumulative frequency for the score value 19 is 6, indicating that six respondents were first incarcerated by the age of 19. Continuing, we eventually see that the score value of 22 has a cumulative frequency of at least 13. Here, 13 respondents were incarcerated by the age of 22. Thus, the median, the thirteenth score, is 22, which agrees with the result obtained from raw scores. Note, finally, that the median is *not* the middlemost score *value* (there are 14 different values, and 22 is not middlemost in the column).

To obtain the mean, we first need to calculate the sum of the scores. In a simple frequency distribution, this can be done efficiently, by noting that there are, for example, two scores of 18, four scores of 19, and so on. Thus, rather than adding 18 twice and 19 four times, we can first multiply 18 by 2 and 19 by 4 *before* adding. That is, we can multiply the score values by their respective frequencies and then add the products in order to obtain the sum of scores. Just as in the raw-score formula, we divide the sum by the number of scores to determine the mean.

Thus, a more practical and less time-consuming way to compute the mean from a simple frequency distribution is provided by the following formula:

$$\overline{X} = \frac{\Sigma fX}{N}$$

where $\overline{X}$ = mean
X = a score value in the distribution
f = frequency of occurrence of X
N = total number of scores

In the following table, the third column (headed fX) contains the products of the score values multiplied by their frequencies of occurrence. Summing the fX column, we obtain $\Sigma fX = 575$.

X	f	fX
31	1	31
30	1	30
29	1	29
28	0	0
27	2	54
26	3	78
25	1	25
24	1	24
23	2	46
22	2	44
21	2	42
20	3	60
19	4	76
18	2	36
		$\Sigma fX = 575$

Thus,

$$\overline{X} = \frac{\Sigma fX}{N} = \frac{575}{25} = 23$$

This result also agrees with the mean obtained from the raw scores themselves.

OBTAINING THE MODE, MEDIAN, AND MEAN FROM A GROUPED FREQUENCY DISTRIBUTION

Sometimes you may come across a table in a published document that gives an interesting or useful grouped frequency distribution. How could you obtain the mode, median, or mean for this distribution even though the original raw scores are not accessible? Fortunately, there is a way to obtain each of our measures of central tendency when data are in the form of a grouped frequency distribution—whether you or someone else constructed the grouped distribution. We must caution, however, that because grouped frequency distributions are somewhat crude representations of the underlying raw data, the mode, median, and mean obtained from a grouped frequency distribution are only approximations of what you would get if they were calculated directly from the raw scores. For this reason, most researchers prefer to use the ungrouped formulas (using raw scores or a simple frequency distribution) whenever the raw data are available.

In order to illustrate, let's construct a grouped frequency distribution of the 25 age-at-first-incarceration scores presented in the last section. Using five class intervals each with a size of 3 years provides an easy-to-read presentation of the data.

Class interval	m	f
30–32	31	2
27–29	28	3
24–26	25	5
21–23	22	6
18–20	19	9
		$N = 25$

In a grouped frequency distribution, the mode is the midpoint of the class interval that has the greatest frequency. The highest frequency occurs in the 18–20 interval, and thus we determine that the mode is approximately 19, the midpoint of this interval. As it turns out in this case, the mode obtained from this class interval matches the actual mode from the original raw scores.

Recall in Chapter 2, we were able to approximate percentile ranks from grouped frequency distributions. By a similar method, we can now determine the median for a grouped frequency distribution from the following formula:

$$\text{Median} = L + \left(\frac{N/2 - cf_b}{f} \right)i$$

where N = number of cases in the distribution
cf_b = cumulative frequency below the lower limit of the critical interval
L = lower limit of the critical interval
f = frequency within the critical interval
i = class-interval size

STEP-BY-STEP ILLUSTRATION
MEDIAN FOR GROUPED FREQUENCY DISTRIBUTION

Let's determine the median for the grouped frequency distribution showing age at first incarceration for the 25 respondents. To locate the median of data grouped into a frequency distribution, we must first construct a cumulative frequency distribution, find the class interval containing the median (called the *critical interval*), and then interpolate.

STEP 1 Construct a cumulative frequency distribution.

Class interval	m	f	cf
30–32	31	2	25
27–29	28	3	23
24–26	25	5	20
21–23	22	6	15
18–20	19	9	9
		$N = 25$	

STEP 2 Locate the critical interval.

Starting with the interval that contains the lowest values (the youngest ages of first incarceration, 18–20), we add frequencies until arriving at that interval holding the case that divides the distribution into two equal parts, the middlemost score. Because $N = 25$, we look for the 12.5th case ($N/2 = 25/2 = 12.5$). Moving up from the lowest interval, we see that 9 of the respondents were incarcerated by the age of 20, and 15 were incarcerated by the age of 23. Thus, the middlemost case must lie in the 21–23 interval. This is the critical interval.

STEP 3 Calculate the median.

To use the formula for the median of a grouped frequency distribution, we will need the sample size ($N = 25$), the cumulative frequency below the critical interval ($cf_b = 9$), and for the critical interval itself, the frequency ($f = 6$), size ($i = 3$), and lower limit ($L = 20.5$).

$$Median = L + \left(\frac{N/2 - cf_b}{f} \right) i$$

$$= 20.5 + \left(\frac{12.5 - 9}{6} \right)(3)$$

$$= 20.5 + 1.75$$

$$= 22.25$$

Thus, we are able to estimate from the grouped frequency distribution that the median age at first incarceration was just over 22 years. This, in fact, comes quite close to the actual median of 22 obtained from the raw scores.

In order to obtain the mean from a grouped frequency distribution, the formula used for a simple frequency distribution can be modified slightly by substituting the class interval midpoints (m) in place of the score values (X). Specifically,

$$\bar{X} = \frac{\Sigma fm}{N}$$

where $\overline{X}$ = mean

m = midpoint of a class interval

f = frequency of a class interval

N = total number of scores

STEP-BY-STEP ILLUSTRATION

MEAN FOR GROUPED FREQUENCY DISTRIBUTION

Let's now determine the mean for the grouped frequency distribution of age at first incarceration.

STEP 1 Construct a column in which you multiply the midpoint by the frequency for each class interval, and then add the products.

Class interval	m	f	fm
30–32	31	2	62
27–29	28	3	84
24–26	25	5	125
21–23	22	6	132
18–20	19	9	171
			$\Sigma fm = 574$

STEP 2 Divide the sum by the number of scores.

$$\overline{X} = \frac{\Sigma fm}{N} = \frac{574}{25} = 22.96$$

Thus, the mean approximated from the grouped frequency distribution is extremely close to the actual mean of 23 obtained from the raw scores.

SUMMARY

This chapter has introduced the three best known measures of central tendency, measures of what is average or typical of a set of data. The mode was defined as the category or score that occurs most often; the median was regarded as the middlemost point in a distribution; the mean was considered as the sum of a set of scores divided by the total number of scores in a set. These measures of central tendency were compared with regard to level of measurement; shape, or form, of distribution; and research objective. We can summarize those conditions for choosing among the three measures in the following way:

Mode
   1. Level of measurement: nominal, ordinal, or interval
   2. Shape of distribution: most appropriate for bimodal
   3. Objective: fast, simple, but rough measure of central tendency

Median
1. Level of measurement: ordinal or interval
2. Shape of distribution: most appropriate for highly skewed
3. Objective: precise measure of central tendency; sometimes can be used for more advanced statistical operations or for splitting distributions into two categories (for example, high versus low)

Mean
1. Level of measurement: interval
2. Shape of distribution: most appropriate for unimodal symmetrical
3. Objective: precise measure of central tendency; often can be used for more advanced statistical operations including decision-making tests (discussed in subsequent chapters of the text)

After comparing the three measures of central tendency in terms of their application to research, we illustrated how the mode, median, and mean can be calculated for both simple and grouped frequency distributions.

TERMS TO REMEMBER

Central tendency	Median
Mode	Mean
Unimodal distribution	Deviation
Bimodal distribution	

STEP-BY-STEP STUDY GUIDE

MODE, MEDIAN, AND MEAN FOR RAW SCORES

STEP 1 Arrange the scores from highest to lowest.

STEP 2 The mode (Mo) is the most frequent score.

STEP 3 The median (Mdn) is the middlemost score in the ordered list of scores. If there is an odd number of scores, the median is the score in the exact middle of the list; if there is an even number of scores, the median is halfway between the two middlemost scores.

STEP 4 Determine the sum of the scores (ΣX).

STEP 5 Calculate the mean ($\overline{X}$) by dividing the sum by the number of scores.

$$\overline{X} = \frac{\Sigma X}{N}$$

PROBLEMS

1. The following is a list of seven Massachusetts state prisons and their security levels (pre-release is the lowest security level, maximum is highest).

Prison	Security Level
Cedar Junction	Maximum
Old Colony	Medium
Lancaster	Pre-release
Shirley-medium	Medium
Shirley-minimum	Minimum
Park Drive	Pre-release
Concord	Medium

   a. Find the modal security level.
   b. Find the median security level.
   c. Explain why it is inappropriate to calculate a mean security level.

2. The following table provides chart data for the patients in a particular prison hospital ward:

Patient	Room	Physician	Condition	Length of stay
Carter, M.	202	Pollock	Critical	8 days
Levin, J.	203	McClare	Fair	4 days
Fox, J.	203	Lench	Good	5 days
Garcia, L.	205	Lench	Fair	7 days
Arluke, A.	201	Pollock	Serious	2 days
Parodi, A.	203	McClare	Good	9 days
Stark, D.	204	Lench	Fair	5 days
Chow, F.	202	Pollock	Critical	1 day
McDevitt, J.	204	Loftus	Serious	2 days

Calculate the most appropriate measure of central tendency for each of the variables (room number, attending physician, condition, and length of hospital stay).

3. A group of high school students was surveyed about its use of various drugs, including alcohol. Asked how frequently they had gotten drunk in the previous 6 months, the students responded:

   4 2 0 2 1 3 0 1 7 5 3

Calculate (a) the median and (b) the mean for these scores.

4. A group of five convicts was given the following prison sentences (in years):

   4 5 3 3 40

   a. Find the mode.
   b. Find the median.
   c. Find the mean.
   d. Which measure provides the most accurate indication of central tendency for these scores?

5. The number of arrests for five individuals are 2, 2, 4, 5, and 7:

   a. What is the mode?
   b. What is the median?
   c. What is the mean?

6. In a study of racial composition of juries in a particular court, the number of white jurors on the last seven juries were:

   9 8 10 6 7 6 5

   a. What is the mode?
   b. What is the median?
   c. What is the mean?

7. The next jury impaneled by the court in problem #6 had 12 white jurors, resulting in the following distribution:

   9 8 10 6 7 6 5 12

   a. What is the mode?
   b. What is the median?
   c. What is the mean?

8. Six students in a sociology seminar were questioned by means of a seven-point interval-level scale regarding attitudes toward cultural diversity on campus. Their responses on the scale, from 1 being strongly unfavorable to 7 being strongly favorable, were as follows:

   5 2 6 7 4 6

   a. Find the mode.
   b. Find the median.
   c. Find the mean.
   d. Overall, how favorable toward diversity were these students?

9. Referring to the sentence lengths given in Problem 4, calculate the deviations (from the mean) for each of the five convicts. What do these deviations indicate about the sentence lengths received by the convicts?

10. Given the following heights of 10 randomly chosen parole officers, answer the following questions:

    Heights (in inches):

    60, 64, 76, 55, 70, 69, 62, 65, 66, 71

    a. What is the deviation from the mean of a height of 63 inches?
    b. What is the deviation from the mean of a height of 58 inches?
    c. What is the deviation from the mean of a height of 72 inches?

d. What is the deviation from the mean of a height of 69 inches?

11. The following scores represent the number of children born to each of 20 female prison inmates:

2 0 2 1 5 3 4 0 1 1 2 1 3 2 4 6 3 2 0 2

a. Calculate the mode, median, and mean from the scores.
b. Rearrange the scores into a simple frequency distribution and recalculate the mode, median, and mean.

12. The scores on a fear of crime survey for 30 students were arranged in the following simple frequency distribution (higher scores indicate greater fear of crime):

Fear of crime	f
7	3
6	4
5	6
4	7
3	5
2	4
1	1
	$N = 30$

Find (a) the mode, (b) the median, and (c) the mean.

13. The scores on a crime seriousness scale were obtained for 46 adults. For the following simple frequency distribution, calculate (a) the mode, (b) the median, and (c) the mean:

Score value	f
10	3
9	4
8	6
7	8
6	9
5	7
4	5
3	2
2	1
1	1
	$N = 46$

14. A criminologist is interested in the level of compliance of women ordered to perform community service as a condition of their probation. She selects a sample of nine women, each of whom were sentenced to perform 50 hours of service. She contacts each offender's work site supervisor and obtains records of the total number of hours actually completed. The results were:

Offenders's Name	Hours of Community Service
Kristiana	23
Joanna	41
Jasmine	31
Emily	14
Flora	45
Debbie	27
Marika	34
Shirley	39
Emma	25

a. What is the mean number of hours of community service performed?
b. What is the deviation from the mean of Kristiana's hours performed?
c. What is the deviation from the mean of Jasmine's hours performed?
d. What is the deviation from the mean of Emily's hours performed?

15. A reporter who covered the O.J. Simpson criminal trial gave a lecture on the advantages and disadvantages of televised trials. You stand outside the auditorium and ask people as they are leaving how they rate the lecture on a 10-point scale (1 representing "I hated it" and 10 representing "I loved it"). You collect data from 50 people, resulting in the following frequency distribution

Rating	Frequency
1	4
2	6
3	7
4	6
5	9
6	7
7	4
8	5
9	2
10	0

a. What is the mode?
b. What is the median?
c. What is the mean?

16. For the following grouped frequency distribution of scores on a contract law exam in a class of 56 students, find (a) the mode, (b) the median, and (c) the mean:

Class interval	f
90–99	16
80–89	17
70–79	15
60–69	3
50–59	2
40–49	3
	$N = 56$

17. A focus group of 10 registered voters was chosen to evaluate the performance of a senate candidate during a debate about capital punishment.

Rater	Knowledge rating	Delivery rating
A	7	5
B	8	6
C	9	5
D	3	5
E	5	6
F	8	7
G	9	6
H	4	5
I	8	6
J	7	5

a. Find the mode, the median, and the mean for the knowledge ratings.
b. Find the mode, the median, and the mean for the delivery ratings.
c. On which characteristic was the candidate rated more favorably?

18. Find the mean, median, and mode for the following set of suicide rates (number of suicides per 100,000 population), representing six large metropolitan areas:

Metropolitan area	Suicide rate
A	15
B	13
C	13
D	18
E	20
F	13

19. The following frequency distribution contains the educational levels attained by the 39 corrections officers in a small prison:

Educational level	f
Graduate school	3
Completed college	5
Some college	11
Completed high school	14
Some high school	6
	$N = 39$

Given the level at which "educational level" was measured (nominal, ordinal, or interval), calculate the measures of central tendency appropriate for describing the distribution given. (*Hint:* You should calculate only two of the measures of central tendency.)

CHAPTER 4

MEASURES OF VARIABILITY

- **THE RANGE**
- **THE MEAN DEVIATION**
- **THE VARIANCE AND STANDARD DEVIATION**
- **THE RAW-SCORE FORMULA FOR VARIANCE AND STANDARD DEVIATION**
- **THE MEANING OF THE STANDARD DEVIATION**
- **COMPARING MEASURES OF VARIABILITY**
- **OBTAINING THE VARIANCE AND STANDARD DEVIATION FROM A SIMPLE FREQUENCY DISTRIBUTION**

- **OBTAINING THE VARIANCE AND STANDARD DEVIATION FROM A GROUPED FREQUENCY DISTRIBUTION**
- **SUMMARY**
- **TERMS TO REMEMBER**
- **STEP-BY-STEP STUDY GUIDE: VARIANCE AND STANDARD DEVIATION FOR RAW SCORES**
- **PROBLEMS**

In Chapter 3, we saw that the mode, median, and mean could be used to summarize in a single number what is average or typical of a distribution. When employed alone, however, any measure of central tendency yields only an incomplete picture of a set of data and, therefore, can mislead or distort as well as clarify.

In order to illustrate this possibility, consider that Honolulu, Hawaii, and Phoenix, Arizona, have almost the same mean daily temperature of 75°. Can we, therefore, assume that the temperature is basically alike in both localities? Or is it not possible that one city is better suited for year-round swimming and other outdoor activities?

As shown in Figure 4.1, Honolulu's temperature varies only slightly throughout the year, usually ranging between 70° and 80°. By contrast, the temperature in Phoenix can differ seasonally from a low of about 40° in January to a high of over 100° in July and August. Needless to say, Phoenix's swimming pools are not overcrowded year-round.

Consider another example. Suppose that Judge A and Judge B both average (mean) 24 months in the prison sentences they hand down to defendants convicted of assault. One could easily be misled by this statistic into thinking that the two judges agree in their philosophies about proper sentencing. Suppose we learn further that Judge *A*, believing in complete equality in sentencing, gives all defendants convicted of assault 24 months, whereas Judge *B* gives anywhere from 6 months to 6 years, depending on her assessment of both the defendants'

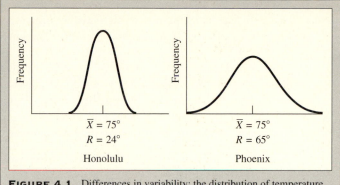

FIGURE 4.1   Differences in variability: the distribution of temperature in Honolulu and Phoenix (approximate figures)

demeanor in court and the nature of the prior criminal record. If you were an attorney maneuvering to have your client's case heard by a particular judge, which judge would you choose?

It can be seen that we need, in addition to a measure of central tendency, an index of how the scores are scattered around the center of the distribution. In a word, we need a measure of what is commonly referred to as *variability* (also known as *spread, width,* or *dispersion*). Returning to an earlier example, we might say that the distribution of temperature in Phoenix has greater variability than the distribution of temperature in Honolulu. In the same way, we can say that the distribution of sentences given by Judge *A* has less variability than the distribution of sentences given by Judge *B*. This chapter discusses only the best known measures of variability: the range, the mean deviation, the variance, and the standard deviation.

THE RANGE

To get a quick but rough measure of variability, we might find what is known as the *range* (*R*), the difference between the highest and lowest scores in a distribution. For instance, if Honolulu's hottest temperature of the year was 89° and its coldest temperature of the year was 65°, then the range of temperature in Honolulu would be 24° (89 − 65 = 24). If Phoenix's hottest day was 106° and its coldest day 41°, the range of temperature in Phoenix would be 65° (106 − 41 = 65). By formula,

$$R = H - L$$

where R = range
H = highest score in a distribution
L = lowest score in a distribution

The advantage of the range—its quick-and-easy computation—is also its most important disadvantage. That is, the range is totally dependent on only two score values, the largest and smallest cases in a given set of data. As a result, the range usually gives merely a crude index of the variability of a distribution.

In a particular week, for example, probation officer A received eight new offenders ages 18, 18, 19, 19, 20, 20, 22, and 23. Probation officer B also received eight new offenders, ages 18, 18, 19, 19, 20, 20, 22, and 43. Officer A comments that his offenders range in age from 18 to 23. Officer B responds that he has a much older caseload, ranging in age from 18 to 43. With the exception of one offender, however, the two groups are identical in age distribution. The range is clearly affected by just one case, and can provide a misleading or distorted picture of the variability within the whole group. Any measure that is so strongly affected by just one score may not give a precise indication of variability and, for most purposes, should be considered only a preliminary or rough index.

THE MEAN DEVIATION

In the previous chapter, the concept of deviation was defined as the distance of any given raw score from its mean. To find a deviation, we were told to subtract the mean from any raw score $(X - \overline{X})$. If we now wish to obtain a measure of variability that takes into account every score in a distribution (rather than only two score values), we might take the absolute deviation (or distance) of each score from the mean of the distribution $|X - \overline{X}|$, add these deviations,[1] and then divide this sum by the number of scores. The result would be the *mean deviation*. By formula,

$$\text{MD} = \frac{\Sigma |X - \overline{X}|}{N}$$

where
$$\text{MD} = \text{mean deviation}$$
$$\Sigma |X - \overline{X}| = \text{sum of the absolute deviations}$$
$$\text{(disregarding plus and minus signs)}$$
$$N = \text{total number of scores}$$

It is critical to note that to obtain $\Sigma |X - \overline{X}|$, we *must* ignore plus and minus signs and add absolute values. This is true because the sum of actual deviations $\Sigma (X - \overline{X})$, the deviations using signs to show direction whether above or below the mean, is always zero. Plus and minus deviations cancel themselves out and therefore cannot be used to describe or compare the variability of distributions. By contrast, the sum of absolute deviations tends to become larger as the variability of a distribution increases.

STEP-BY-STEP ILLUSTRATION
MEAN DEVIATION

We can now illustrate the step-by-step procedure for computing the mean deviation by considering the set of scores 9, 8, 6, 4, 2, and 1, representing the number of months of probation that six offenders received as sentences for possession of marijuana.

---

[1] The vertical bars around $X - \overline{X}$ represent an absolute value. An absolute value of a quantity or number is its value without regard for any negative sign. Thus, for example, $|3|$ and $|-3|$ both equal 3.

STEP 1 Find the mean for the distribution.

$$
\begin{array}{c}
X \\
\hline
9 \\
8 \\
6 \\
4 \\
2 \\
1 \\
\hline
\Sigma X = 30
\end{array}
\qquad
\begin{aligned}
\overline{X} &= \frac{\Sigma X}{N} \\[1em]
&= \frac{30}{6} \\[1em]
&= 5
\end{aligned}
$$

STEP 2 Subtract the mean from each raw score, take absolute values (ignore the signs), and add these absolute deviations.

X	$X - \overline{X}$	$\lvert X - \overline{X}\rvert$
9	+4	4
8	+3	3
6	+1	1
4	−1	1
2	−3	3
1	−4	4
$\Sigma X = 30$	0	$\Sigma\lvert X - \overline{X}\rvert = 16$

STEP 3 Divide $\Sigma\lvert X - \overline{X}\rvert$ by N to adjust for the number of cases involved.

$$
\begin{aligned}
\text{MD} &= \frac{\Sigma\lvert X - \overline{X}\rvert}{N} \\[1em]
&= \frac{16}{6} \\[1em]
&= 2.67
\end{aligned}
$$

Following this procedure, we see that the mean deviation is 2.67 for the set of scores 9, 8, 6, 4, 2, and 1. This indicates that, on the average, length of probation sentence deviates from the mean by 2.67 months.

To understand better the utility of the mean deviation, let us turn to distributions of fines for minor traffic offenses, (a), (b), and (c) in Table 4.1. Notice first that the mean of each distribution is 40. Note also that there seem to be important differences in variability among the distributions—differences that can be detected with the help of the range and the mean deviation.

Let us first examine income distribution (a), in which all fines are exactly alike. Because all scores in this distribution take on identical numerical values (40), we can say that distribution (a) has no variability at all. Everyone was fined the same amount on that day.

As a result, the range is 0, and there is absolutely no deviation from the mean (MD = 0). Distributions (b) and (c) do contain variability. More specifically, distribution (b) has a range of 6 and a mean deviation of 1.71; distribution (c) has a range of 30 and a mean deviation of 8.57. We can therefore say that distribution (b) contains less variability than distribution (c)—the fines in distribution (b) are more alike than the fines in distribution (c).

TABLE 4.1   VARIABILITY IN DISTRIBUTIONS OF TRAFFIC OFFENSE FINES WITH THE SAME MEAN ($40)

Distribution (a)		Distribution (b)		Distribution (c)	
X	$\lvert X - \overline{X} \rvert$	X	$\lvert X - \overline{X} \rvert$	X	$\lvert X - \overline{X} \rvert$
$40	0	$43	+3	$55	+15
40	0	42	+2	50	+10
40	0	41	+1	45	+5
40	0	40	0	40	0
40	0	39	−1	35	−5
40	0	38	−2	30	−10
40	0	37	−3	25	−15
	$\Sigma \lvert X - \overline{X} \rvert = 0$		$\Sigma \lvert X - \overline{X} \rvert = 12$		$\Sigma \lvert X - \overline{X} \rvert = 60$
	$\overline{X} = \$40$		$\overline{X} = \$40$		$\overline{X} = \$40$
	$R = \$0$		$R = \$6$		$R = \$30$
	MD = $0		MD = $1.71		MD = $8.57
No variability		Some variability		Most variability	

THE VARIANCE AND STANDARD DEVIATION

For reasons that will soon become apparent, the mean deviation is no longer widely used by criminal justice researchers; it has been largely abandoned as a measure of variability in favor of its more effective "first cousins," the *variance* and *standard deviation*. As we shall see, however, the mean deviation cannot be regarded as a waste of time, for, if nothing else, it provides us with a sound basis for understanding the nature of the standard deviation.

In a previous discussion, we learned that the mean deviation avoids the problem of negative numbers that cancel out positive numbers by ignoring plus and minus signs and summing the absolute deviations from the mean. This procedure for creating a measure of variability has the distinct disadvantage that such absolute values are not always useful in more advanced statistical analyses (because they cannot easily be manipulated algebraically).

To overcome this problem and obtain a measure of variability that is more amenable to advanced statistical procedures, we might square the actual deviations from the mean and add them together $\Sigma(X - \overline{X})^2$. As illustrated in Table 4.2, using the length of probation data, this procedure would get rid of minus signs, since squared numbers are always positive.

Having added the squared deviations from the mean, we might divide this sum by N in order to control for the number of scores involved. This is the mean of the squared deviations, but it is better known as the *variance*. (*Note:* You may recall that a similar procedure was followed to get the mean deviation when we divided the sum of absolute deviations by N.) Symbolized by s^2, the variance is

$$s^2 = \frac{\Sigma(X - \overline{X})^2}{N}$$

where s^2 = variance
$\Sigma(X - \overline{X})^2$ = sum of the squared deviations from the mean
N = total number of scores

Continuing with the illustration in Table 4.2, we see that the variance is

$$s^2 = \frac{\Sigma(X - \overline{X})^2}{N}$$

$$= \frac{52}{6}$$

$$= 8.67$$

The advantage of the variance over the mean deviation, besides the problematic nature of absolute values, is that it gives appropriately greater emphasis to extreme scores. That is, it is more sensitive to the degree of deviation in the distribution. To illustrate, Figure 4.2

TABLE 4.2   SQUARING DEVIATIONS TO ELIMINATE NEGATIVE NUMBERS

X	$X - \overline{X}$	$(X - \overline{X})^2$
9	+4	16
8	+3	9
6	+1	1
4	−1	1
2	−3	9
1	−4	16
	−0	$\Sigma(X - \overline{X})^2 = 52$

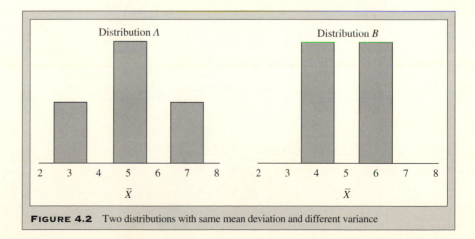

FIGURE 4.2   Two distributions with same mean deviation and different variance

shows the following two distributions, *A* and *B*, which have the same mean deviation. Distribution *B* is more compact, however, which is ignored by the mean deviation (two deviations of 1 are equivalent to one deviation of 2). The variance, on the other hand, gives greater weight to the extremes by squaring the deviations. That is, one deviation of 2 becomes more formidable after squaring ($2^2 = 4$) than two deviations of 1 ($1^2 + 1^2 = 2$).

	Distribution *A*			Distribution *B*	
X	$\lvert X - \bar{X} \rvert$	$(X - \bar{X})^2$	X	$\lvert X - \bar{X} \rvert$	$(X - \bar{X})^2$
3	2	4	4	1	1
5	0	0	4	1	1
5	0	0	6	1	1
7	2	4	6	1	1
	$\bar{X} = 5$			$\bar{X} = 5$	
	$MD = 1$			$MD = 1$	
	$s^2 = 2$			$s^2 = 1$	

One further problem arises, however. As a direct result of having squared the deviations, the unit of measurement is altered, making the variance rather difficult to interpret. The variance is 8.67, but 8.67 of what? The variance is expressed as the square of whatever unit expresses our data. If the data were IQ scores, the variance would be in $(IQ)^2$ units. If the data were prison sentence lengths in months, the variance would be expressed in months squared.

In order to put the measure of variability into the right perspective—that is, to return to our original unit of measurement—we take the square root of the variance. This gives us the *standard deviation,* a measure of variability we obtain by summing the squared deviations from the mean, dividing by *N*, and then taking the square root. Symbolized by *s*, the standard deviation is

$$s = \sqrt{\frac{\Sigma(X - \bar{X})^2}{N}}$$

where

s = standard deviation

$\Sigma(X - \bar{X})^2$ = sum of the squared deviations from the mean

N = the total number of scores

STEP-BY-STEP ILLUSTRATION

STANDARD DEVIATION

To summarize, the procedure for computing the standard deviation does not differ much from the method we learned earlier to obtain the mean deviation. With reference to the months of probation data, the following steps are carried out:

STEP 1   Find the mean for the distribution.

X
9
8
6
4
2
1
$\Sigma X = 30$

$$\overline{X} = \frac{\Sigma X}{N}$$

$$= \frac{30}{6}$$

$$= 5$$

STEP 2   Subtract the mean from each raw score to get the deviation.

X	$X - \overline{X}$
9	$+4$
8	$+3$
6	$+1$
4	-1
2	-3
1	-4

STEP 3   Square each deviation before adding the squared deviations together.

X	$X - \overline{X}$	$(X - \overline{X})^2$
9	$+4$	16
8	$+3$	9
6	$+1$	1
4	-1	1
2	-3	9
1	-4	16
		$\Sigma(X - \overline{X})^2 = 52$

STEP 4   Divide by N and get the square root of the result.

$$s = \sqrt{\frac{\Sigma(X - \overline{X})^2}{N}}$$

$$= \sqrt{\frac{52}{6}}$$

$$= \sqrt{8.67}$$

$$= 2.94$$

We can now say that the standard deviation is 2.94 months for the six probationers.

On average, that is, the scores in this distribution deviate from the mean by nearly three months. For example, the 2 in this distribution is below the mean, but only by an average amount.

THE RAW-SCORE FORMULA FOR VARIANCE AND STANDARD DEVIATION

Until now, we have used the deviation to obtain the variance and standard deviation. There is an easier method for computing these statistics, especially with the help of a calculator. This method works directly with the raw scores. The raw-score formulas for variance and standard deviation are

$$s^2 = \frac{\Sigma X^2}{N} - \overline{X}^2$$

$$s = \sqrt{\frac{\Sigma X^2}{N} - \overline{X}^2}$$

where ΣX^2 = the sum of the squared raw scores. (*Important:* Each raw score is *first* squared and then these squared raw scores are summed.)
N = total number of scores
$\overline{X}^2$ = mean squared

STEP-BY-STEP ILLUSTRATION
VARIANCE AND STANDARD DEVIATION USING RAW SCORES

The step-by-step procedure for computing s^2 and s by the raw-score method can be illustrated by returning to the months of probation data: 9, 8, 6, 4, 2, and 1.

STEP 1   Square each raw score before adding the squared raw scores together.

X	X^2
9	81
8	64
6	36
4	16
2	4
1	1
	$\Sigma X^2 = 202$

STEP 2   Obtain the mean and square it.

X
9
8
6
4
2
1

$$\overline{X} = \frac{\Sigma X}{N} = \frac{30}{6} = 5$$

$$\overline{X}^2 = 25$$

$$\Sigma X = 30$$

STEP 3   Insert the results from Steps 1 and 2 into the formulas.

$$s^2 = \frac{\Sigma X^2}{N} - \overline{X}^2$$

$$= \frac{202}{6} - 25$$

$$= 33.67 - 25$$

$$= 8.67$$

$$s = \sqrt{\frac{\Sigma X^2}{N} - \overline{X}^2}$$

$$= \sqrt{\frac{202}{6} - 25}$$

$$= \sqrt{8.67}$$

$$= 2.94$$

As Step 3 shows, applying the raw-score formulas to the months of probation data yields exactly the same results as the original method, which worked with deviations.

THE MEANING OF THE STANDARD DEVIATION

We noted earlier that the standard deviation is more interpretable than the variance because it is in the correct unit of measurement. Even so, the series of steps required to compute the standard deviation can leave the reader with an uneasy feeling as to the meaning of his or her result. For example, suppose we learn that $s = 4$ in a particular distribution of scores. What is indicated by this number? Exactly what can we say now about that distribution that we could not have said before?

Chapter 5 will seek to clarify the full meaning of the standard deviation. For now, we note briefly that the standard deviation (like the mean deviation before it) represents the average variability in a distribution, because it measures the average of deviations from the mean. The procedures of squaring and taking the square root also enter the picture but chiefly to eliminate minus signs and return to the more convenient unit of measurement, the raw-score unit.

We note also that the greater the variability around the mean of a distribution, the larger the standard deviation. Thus, $s = 4.5$ indicates greater variability than $s = 2.5$. For instance, the distribution of daily temperatures in Phoenix, Arizona, has a larger standard deviation than does the distribution of temperatures for the same period in Honolulu, Hawaii.

Let's also reconsider the case of prison sentencing that we encountered earlier to see the importance of variance and standard deviation for understanding and interpreting distributions. Table 4.3 displays the sentences given two sets of six defendants in robbery trials by the respective judges. Note first the advantage of the standard deviation over the variance. Even though they are equal in their abilities to measure variability or dispersion, the standard deviation has a more tangible interpretation. In this case, the standard deviation is expressed in terms of months—something that has meaning to us. The variance, however, is stated in terms of months squared, which renders the variance more difficult to understand.

Returning to a comparison of the two judges, we see that Judge A has a larger mean yet a smaller variance and standard deviation than Judge B. One might say, at least on the basis of these data alone, that Judge A is harsher but fairer, and Judge B is more lenient but inconsistent. For an attorney, your best bet might be Judge A. Even though you can expect a longer sentence (because of the higher mean), you may not want to risk the severe sentences that Judge B has been known to give.

Now let's add another piece to the puzzle. The highly variable sentences of Judge B are not so unreasonable as they may seem. The long sentences were given to offenders with long criminal records and the short sentences to first-and second-time offenders. (We will consider techniques for measuring the sources of variability in later chapters.) As an attorney, your preference for a judge would depend, therefore, on the criminal history of your client. If he had a history of minor offenses or no criminal history at all, you would prefer Judge B, because you would expect a shorter sentence from her than from Judge A, who now seems rather inflexible. On the other hand, if representing a repeat offender, you would prefer Judge A, because she seems to focus less on the background of the offender than on the current charge.

TABLE 4.3   SENTENCES FOR ROBBERY BY TWO JUDGES

Judge A	Judge B
34	26
30	43
31	22
33	35
36	20
34	34
$\overline{X} = 33.0$	$\overline{X} = 30.0$
$s^2 = 4.0$	$s^2 = 65.0$
$s = 2.0$	$s = 8.1$

Thus, the standard deviation is a useful device for measuring the degree of variability in a distribution or for comparing the variability in different distributions. It is also employed, and quite frequently, for calibrating the relative standing of individual scores within a distribution. The standard deviation in this sense is a standard against which we assess the placement of one score (such as your examination score) within the whole distribution (such as the examination scores of the entire class).

To understand this meaning of the standard deviation, consider first an analogy to the placement of a plant in a room. If we wish to discuss the distance of a plant from a living room wall, we might think in terms of feet as a unit of measurement of distance (for example, "The plant in the living room is located a distance of 5 ft from this wall"). But how do we measure the width of a base line of a frequency polygon that contains the scores of a group of respondents arranged from low to high (in ascending order)? As a related matter, how do we come up with a method to find the distance between any raw score and its mean—a standardized method that permits comparisons between raw scores in the same distribution as well as between different distributions? If we were talking about plants, we might find that one plant is 5 ft from the living room wall, and another plant is 10 ft from the kitchen wall. In the concept of feet, we have a standard unit of measurement and, therefore, we can make such comparisons in a meaningful way. But how about comparing raw scores? For instance, can we always compare 85 on an English exam with 80 in German? Which grade is really higher? A little thought will show that it depends on how the other students in each class performed.

One method for giving a rough indicator of the width of a base line is the range, because it gives the distance between the highest and lowest scores along the base line. But the range cannot be effectively used to locate a score relative to its mean, because—aside from its other weaknesses—the range covers the entire width of the base line. By contrast, the size of the standard deviation is smaller than that of the range and usually covers far less than the entire width of the base line.

Just as we "lay off" a carpet in feet or yards, so we might lay off the base line in units of standard deviation. For instance, we might add the standard deviation to the value of the mean in order to find which raw score is located exactly one standard deviation from the mean. As shown in Figure 4.3, therefore, if $\overline{X} = 80$ and $s = 5$, then the raw score 85 lies exactly one standard deviation *above* the mean ($80 + 5 = 85$), a distance of $+1s$. This direction is *plus* because all deviations above the mean are positive; all deviations below the mean are *minus,* or negative.

We continue laying off the base line by adding the value of the standard deviation to the raw score 85. This procedure gives us the raw score 90, which lies exactly two standard deviations above the mean ($85 + 5 = 90$). Likewise, we add the standard deviation to the raw score 90 and obtain 95, which represents the raw score falling exactly three standard deviations from the mean: We subtract 5 from 80, 5 from 75, and 5 from 70 to obtain $-1s$, $-2s$, and $-3s$.

The process of laying off the base line in units of standard deviation is in many respects similar to measuring the distance between a plant and the wall in units of feet. However, the analogy breaks down in at least one important respect: Whereas feet and yards are of constant size (1 ft always equals 12 in.; 1 yd always equals 3 ft), the value of the standard deviation varies from distribution to distribution. Otherwise, we could not use the standard deviation as previously illustrated to compare the variability of distributions (for example, the judges in Table 4.3). For this reason, we must calculate the size of the standard deviation for any

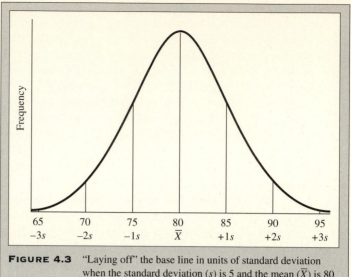

FIGURE 4.3   "Laying off" the base line in units of standard deviation when the standard deviation (s) is 5 and the mean ($\overline{X}$) is 80

distribution with which we happen to be working. Also as a result, it is usually more difficult to understand the standard deviation as opposed to feet or yards as a unit of measurement.

As we will see in detail in the next chapter, the standard deviation has a very important meaning for interpreting scores in what we call the normal distribution. Actually, unless a distribution is highly skewed, approximately two-thirds of its scores fall within one standard deviation above and below the mean. Sometimes this range is called the *normal range* because it contains cases that are considered close to the norm. For example, a child whose reading score falls precisely at the mean is, in a strict sense, average; but children whose reading speeds are close to the mean in either direction (more specifically, within one standard deviation of the mean) also are regarded as being within the normal range. Thus if the mean reading speed is 120 words per minute with a standard deviation of 25 words per minute, then the normal range may be defined as 95–145 words per minute, and approximately two-thirds of children read at a speed that lies within the normal range (see Figure 4.4). We will return to this concept of the standard deviation in Chapter 5.

COMPARING MEASURES OF VARIABILITY

The range is regarded generally as a preliminary or rough index of the variability of a distribution. It is quick and simple to obtain but not very reliable, and it can be applied to interval or ordinal data.

The range does serve a useful purpose in connection with computations of the standard deviation. As illustrated in Figure 4.3, six standard deviations cover almost the entire distance from the highest to lowest score in a distribution ($-3s$ to $+3s$). This fact alone gives us a convenient method for estimating (but not computing) the standard deviation. Generally, the size of the standard deviation is approximately one-sixth of the size of the range. For instance, if the range is 36, then the standard deviation might be expected to fall close to 6; if the range is 6, the standard deviation will likely be close to 1.

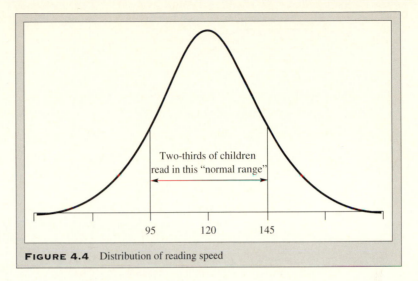

FIGURE 4.4   Distribution of reading speed

This rule can take on considerable importance for the reader who wishes to find out whether her or his result is anywhere in the vicinity of being correct. To take an extreme case, if $R = 10$ and our calculated $s = 12$, we have made some sort of an error, because the standard deviation cannot be larger than the range. A note of caution: The one-sixth rule applies when we have a large number of scores. For a small number of cases, there will generally be a smaller number of standard deviations to cover the range of a distribution.

Whereas the range is calculated from only two score values, both the standard deviation and the mean deviation take into account every score value in a distribution. Despite its relative stability, however, the mean deviation is no longer widely used in criminal justice research, because it cannot be employed in many advanced statistical analyses. By contrast, the standard deviation employs the mathematically acceptable procedure of clearing the signs (by squaring deviations) rather than ignoring them. As a result, the standard deviation has become the initial step for obtaining certain other statistical measures, especially in the context of statistical decision making. We shall be exploring this characteristic of the standard deviation in detail in subsequent chapters.

Despite its usefulness as a reliable measure of variability, the standard deviation also has its drawbacks. As compared with other measures of variability, the standard deviation tends to be difficult and time consuming to calculate. However, this disadvantage is being more and more overcome by the increasing use of high-speed and computers to perform statistical analyses. The standard deviation (like the mean deviation) also has the characteristic of being an interval-level measure and, therefore, cannot be used with nominal or ordinal data—the type of data with which many researchers often work.

OBTAINING THE VARIANCE AND STANDARD DEVIATION FROM A SIMPLE FREQUENCY DISTRIBUTION

In the last chapter, we saw how measures of central tendency could be calculated from a set of scores rearranged in the form of a simple frequency distribution. The variance and standard deviation can be obtained in a similar fashion.

Let's return to the following raw scores representing the age at first incarceration of a sample of 25 prison inmates:

18   18   19   19   19   19   20   20   20   21   21   22
22   23   23   24   25   26   26   26   27   27   29   30   31

Calculated from these raw scores, the variance $s^2 = 14.56$ and the standard deviation $s = 3.82$. These data can be rearranged as a simple frequency distribution as follows:

X	f
31	1
30	1
29	1
28	0
27	2
26	3
25	1
24	1
23	2
22	2
21	2
20	3
19	4
18	2

To obtain the variance and standard deviation from a simple frequency distribution, we apply the following formulas:

$$s^2 = \frac{\Sigma f X^2}{N} - \overline{X}^2$$

$$s = \sqrt{\frac{\Sigma f X^2}{N} - \overline{X}^2}$$

where X = score value
f = score frequency
N = number of cases
$\overline{X}$ = mean of the simple frequency distribution

STEP-BY-STEP ILLUSTRATION
VARIANCE AND STANDARD DEVIATION OF A SIMPLE FREQUENCY DISTRIBUTION

In order to obtain the variance and standard deviation, we must first calculate the mean using the steps outlined in the previous chapter.

STEP 1 Multiply each score value (X) by its frequency (f) to obtain the fX products, and then sum the fX column.

X	f	fX
31	1	31
30	1	30
29	0	0
28	1	29
27	2	54
26	3	78
25	1	25
24	1	24
23	2	46
22	2	44
21	2	42
20	3	60
19	4	76
18	2	36
		$\Sigma fX = 575$

STEP 2 Square each score value (X^2) and multiply by its frequency (f) to obtain the fX^2 products, and then sum the fX^2 column.

X	f	fX	fX^2
31	1	31	961
30	1	30	900
29	1	29	841
28	0	0	0
27	2	54	1,458
26	3	78	2,028
25	1	25	625
24	1	24	576
23	2	46	1,058
22	2	44	968
21	2	42	882
20	3	60	1,200
19	4	76	1,444
18	2	36	648
			$\Sigma fX^2 = 13,589$

STEP 3 Obtain the mean and square it.

$$\bar{X} = \frac{\Sigma fX}{N} = \frac{575}{25} = 23$$

$$\bar{X}^2 = (23)^2 = 529$$

STEP 4 Calculate the variance using the results from the previous steps.

$$s^2 = \frac{\Sigma f X^2}{N} - \overline{X}^2$$

$$= \frac{13{,}589}{25} - 529$$

$$= 543.56 - 529$$

$$= 14.56$$

STEP 5 Calculate the standard deviation (the square root of the variance).

$$s = \sqrt{\frac{\Sigma f X^2}{N} - \overline{X}^2}$$

$$= \sqrt{\frac{13{,}589}{25} - 529}$$

$$= \sqrt{543.56 - 529}$$

$$= \sqrt{14.56}$$

$$= 3.82$$

Finally, note that the variance and standard deviation calculated from the simple frequency distribution are identical to the values obtained from the raw scores.

OBTAINING THE VARIANCE AND STANDARD DEVIATION FROM A GROUPED FREQUENCY DISTRIBUTION

As in the case of finding the mean for a grouped frequency distribution, formulas for the variance and standard deviation of a grouped frequency distribution can be obtained by replacing the score values (X) by class-interval midpoints (m) in the two formulas for a simple frequency distribution. Specifically, for a grouped frequency distribution,

$$s^2 = \frac{\Sigma f m^2}{N} - \overline{X}^2$$

$$s = \sqrt{\frac{\Sigma f m^2}{N} - \overline{X}^2}$$

where m = midpoint of a class interval
 f = frequency within a class interval
 N = number of cases
 $\overline{X}$ = mean of the grouped frequency distribution

Note that the mean calculated for the grouped frequency distribution is used in the formulas for $\overline{X}$. Recall that because grouped frequency distributions are crude representations of the underlying raw scores, the variance and standard deviation calculated from a grouped frequency distribution are only approximations of what you would get if they were calculated from the raw scores.

STEP-BY-STEP ILLUSTRATION
VARIANCE AND STANDARD DEVIATION OF A GROUPED FREQUENCY DISTRIBUTION

Let's return to the five-category grouped frequency distribution of the 25 age-at-first-incarceration scores used in the previous chapter.

Class interval	m	f
30–32	31	2
27–29	28	3
24–26	25	5
21–23	22	6
18–20	19	9
		$N = 25$

STEP 1 Multiply each midpoint (m) by the frequency (f) in the class interval to obtain the fm products, and then sum the fm column.

Class interval	m	f	fm
30–32	31	2	62
27–29	28	3	84
24–26	25	5	125
21–23	22	6	132
18–20	19	9	171
			$\Sigma fm = 574$

STEP 2 Square each midpoint (m^2) and multiply by the frequency (f) of the class interval to obtain the fm^2 products, and then sum the fm^2 column.

Class interval	m	f	fm	fm^2
30–32	31	2	62	1,922
27–29	28	3	84	2,352
24–26	25	5	125	3,125
21–23	22	6	132	2,904
18–20	19	9	171	3,249
				$\Sigma fm^2 = 13,552$

STEP 3   Obtain the mean and square it.

$$\bar{X} = \frac{\Sigma fm}{N} = \frac{574}{25} = 22.96$$

$$\bar{X}^2 = (22.96)^2 = 527.16$$

STEP 4   Calculate the variance using the results from the previous steps.

$$s^2 = \frac{\Sigma fm^2}{N} - \bar{X}^2$$

$$= \frac{13,552}{25} - 527.16$$

$$= 542.08 - 527.16$$

$$= 14.92$$

STEP 5   Calculate the standard deviation (the square root of the variance).

$$s = \sqrt{\frac{\Sigma fX^2}{N} - \bar{X}^2}$$

$$= \sqrt{\frac{13,552}{25} - 527.16}$$

$$= \sqrt{542.08 - 527.16}$$

$$= \sqrt{14.92}$$

$$= 3.86$$

Thus, the variance ($s^2 = 14.92$) and standard deviation ($s = 3.86$) approximated from the grouped frequency distribution are almost identical to the actual variance ($s^2 = 14.56$) and standard deviation ($s = 3.82$) obtained from the raw scores.

SUMMARY

In this chapter, we have been introduced to the range, the mean deviation, the variance, and the standard deviation—four measures of variability or the way scores are scattered around the center of a distribution. The range was regarded as a quick but very rough indicator of variability, which can be found easily by taking the difference between the highest and lowest scores in a distribution. The mean deviation—the sum of the absolute deviations divided by N—was treated as a mathematically inadequate measure of variability but a sound basis for understanding the variance, the mean of the squared deviations from the mean. In the standard deviation (the square root of the variance), we have a reliable, interval-level measure of variability, which can be utilized for more advanced descriptive and decision-making statistical operations. The full meaning of the standard deviation will be explored in subsequent discussions of the normal curve and generalizations from samples to populations.

TERMS TO REMEMBER

Variability	Variance
Range	Standard deviation
Mean deviation	

STEP-BY-STEP STUDY GUIDE

VARIANCE AND STANDARD DEVIATION FOR RAW SCORES

STEP 1 Square each raw score and then sum (ΣX^2).

STEP 2 Obtain the mean and then square it ($\overline{X}^2$).

STEP 3 Calculate the variance and then the standard deviation.

$$s^2 = \frac{\Sigma X^2}{N} - \overline{X}^2$$

$$s = \sqrt{\frac{\Sigma X^2}{N} - \overline{X}^2}$$

PROBLEMS

1. Two students in a forensic psychology class compared their scores on a series of five quizzes:

Student A	Student B
4	6
9	5
3	7
8	5
9	6

Considering the concepts of both central tendency and variability, find (a) which student tended to perform better on the quizzes and (b) which student tended to perform more consistently on the quizzes.

2. The following are the weeks in drug rehabilitation programs for six parolees.

1 3 3 4 3 4

a. Calculate the range of weeks.
b. Calculate the mean deviation.

c. Calculate the standard deviation using the deviations from the mean.
d. Calculate the standard deviation using the raw-score formula.

3. On a scale designed to measure attitude toward racial segregation, two college classes scored as follows:

Class A	Class B
4	4
6	3
2	2
1	1
1	4
1	2

Compare the variability of attitudes toward racial segregation among the members of the two classes by calculating for each class (a) the range, (b) the mean deviation, and (c) the standard deviation. Which class has greater variability of attitude scores?

4. The number of prior arrests for a group of individuals at their parole hearings are 0, 2, 2, 3, 4, 5, and 12. Compute the (a) range, (b) mean deviation, (c) variance, and (d) standard deviation.

5. At the end of their shift, a group of police officers recorded the number of traffic citations they issued that day: 4, 5, 8, 7, 9, 8, 7, 3, 6, 7. Calculate the range, the mean deviation, the variance, and the standard deviation of tickets issued.

6. High school students were surveyed about their use of various drugs, including alcohol. Asked how frequently they had been drunk in the previous 6 months, the students responded:

   4   2   0   2   1   3   0   1   7   5   3

   Calculate the (a) range, (b) mean deviation, and (c) variance and standard deviation for these self-report scores.

7. On a measure of authoritarianism (higher scores reflect greater tendency toward prejudice, ethnocentrism, and submission to authority), seven students scored as follows:

   1   6   6   3   7   4   10

   Calculate the (a) range, (b) mean deviation, and (c) variance and standard deviation for these authoritarianism scores.

8. On a 20-item measure of self-esteem (higher scores reflect greater self-esteem), five teenagers scored as follows:

   16   5   18   9   11

   Calculate the (a) range, (b) mean deviation, and (c) variance and standard deviation for these self-esteem scores.

9. Find the standard deviation for the following frequency distribution of the daily average number of hours that high school students said they spend "hanging out" with their friends:

X	f
5	3
4	5
3	6
2	2
1	2
	$N = 18$

10. Find the variance and standard deviation for the following frequency distribution of attitudes toward capital punishment held by 25 college students (seven-point scale; higher score indicates more favorable attitude toward capital punishment):

X	f
7	2
6	3
5	5
4	7
3	4
2	3
1	1
	$N = 25$

11. Find the variance and standard deviation for the following frequency distribution of scores made on a statistics exam:

X	f
10	2
9	5
8	8
7	7
6	4
5	3
	$N = 29$

12. For the following grouped frequency distribution of civil service exam scores, find the variance and standard deviation:

Class interval	f
90–99	6
80–89	8
70–79	4
60–69	3
50–59	2
	$N = 23$

13. Twenty-five judges from superior courts, drug courts, and traffic courts were monitored to determine the number of decisions handed down during a particular week. For the following grouped frequency distribution, find the variance and standard deviation:

Class interval	f
20–24	2
15–19	4
10–14	8
5–9	5
0–4	6
	$N = 25$

14. For the following grouped frequency distribution of criminal justice program prestige scores, calculate the variance and standard deviation:

Class interval	f
70–84	3
55–69	9
40–54	14
25–39	16
10–24	8
	$N = 50$

15. In the previous chapter, you were asked to find the mode, median, and mean for the following set of suicide rates (number of suicides per 100,000 population), rounded to the nearest whole number, representing six large metropolitan areas. Now, determine the range, mean deviation, standard deviation, and variance:

Metropolitan area	Suicide rate
A	15
B	13
C	13
D	18
E	20
F	13

16. Find the standard deviation and variance for the following frequency distribution of hours 40 Texas border patrol officers spent in a particular week filling in their daily logbook.

X	f
10	1
9	0
8	2
7	4
6	7
5	11
4	5
3	3
2	4
1	2
0	1
	$N = 40$

17. IQ scores are standardized to have a mean of 100 and a standard deviation of 15. Using the idea of "laying off" the base line in units of standard deviation introduced in this chapter, find the IQ scores that are located one standard deviation above and one standard deviation below the mean.

PART II
FROM DESCRIPTION TO DECISION MAKING

CHAPTER 5
PROBABILITY AND THE NORMAL CURVE

CHAPTER 6
SAMPLES AND POPULATIONS

PROBABILITY AND THE NORMAL CURVE

- **RULES OF PROBABILITY**

- **PROBABILITY DISTRIBUTIONS**

- **THE NORMAL CURVE AS A PROBABILITY DISTRIBUTION**

- **CHARACTERISTICS OF THE NORMAL CURVE**

- **THE MODEL AND THE REALITY OF THE NORMAL CURVE**

- **THE AREA UNDER THE NORMAL CURVE**

- **STANDARD SCORES AND THE NORMAL CURVE**

- **FINDING PROBABILITY UNDER THE NORMAL CURVE**

- **OBTAINING PERCENTILE RANKS FROM THE NORMAL CURVE**

- **SUMMARY**

- **TERMS TO REMEMBER**

- **STEP-BY-STEP STUDY GUIDE: PROBABILITY UNDER THE NORMAL CURVE**

- **STEP-BY-STEP STUDY GUIDE: PERCENTILE RANKS FROM THE NORMAL CURVE**

- **PROBLEMS**

In Part One, we focused on ways to describe variables. In particular, we began to explore variables by concentrating on their distributions—by categorizing data and graphing frequencies. This permitted us to see patterns and trends, to see the most frequent occurrences and the most extreme. We further summarized these distributions by computing measures of central tendency and variability.

Up until now, our interpretations and conclusions about variables have come solely from what we observed. We collected information about a variable and then described what we obtained using a variety of statistical measures, such as percentages and means. From this point on, our approach will be somewhat different. We will first suggest certain theories, propositions, or hypotheses about variables, which will then be tested using the data we observe.

The cornerstone of *decision making*—the process of testing hypotheses through analysis of data—is probability. Probability is a difficult concept to grasp, yet we use it quite frequently. We ask such questions as: "How likely is it that I will get an A on this exam?" "How likely is it that this marriage will last?" "If I draw a card, what is the chance that it will be smaller than a 5?" "What is the chance that this team will win the series?" "How likely is it that a police officer will make an arrest on a domestic disturbance call?" "How likely is it that the defense will win in a criminal trial?" "How likely is it that an offender released from prison will eventually return to prison for new offenses?" In everyday conversation, we answer these questions with vague responses such as "probably," "pretty good chance," or "unlikely." With probability, we offer far more precise answers, such as "There is an 80 percent chance of the eventual reincarceration of a released prisoners."

In mathematical terms, probability (P) varies from 0 to 1.0, although sometimes a percentage rather than a decimal is used to express the level of probability. For example, a .50 probability (or 5 chances out of 10) is sometimes called a 50% chance. Although percentages may be used more in everyday language, the decimal form is more appropriate for statistical use.

A zero probability implies that something is impossible; probabilities near zero, such as .05 or .10, imply very unlikely occurrences. At the other extreme, a probability of 1.0 constitutes certainty, and high probabilities such as .90, .95, or .99 signify very probable or likely outcomes.

Some probabilities are easy to calculate: Most people know that the probability of getting heads on a coin flip is .50. However, more complex situations involve the application of various basic rules of probability. Just as we had to learn basic arithmetic operations, so we must learn a few basic operations that will permit us to calculate more complex and interesting probabilities.

RULES OF PROBABILITY

The term *probability* refers to the relative likelihood of occurrence of any given outcome or event, that is, *the probability associated with an event is the number of times that event can occur relative to the total number of times any event can occur:*

$$\text{Probability of an outcome or event} = \frac{\text{Number of times the outcome or event can occur}}{\text{Total number of times any outcome or event can occur}}$$

For example, if a room contains three men and seven women, the probability that the next person coming out of the room is a man would be 3 in 10:

$$\text{Probability of a man coming out next} = \frac{\text{number of men in the room}}{\text{total number of men and women in the room}} = \frac{3}{10} = .30$$

In the same way, the probability of drawing a single card (let us say, the ace of spades) from a shuffled pack of 52 cards is 1 in 52, because the outcome, the ace of spades, can occur only once out of the total number of times any outcome can occur, 52 cards. The probability of drawing any spade would be 13 out of 52, or $^{13}\!/_{52} = \frac{1}{4} = .25$, because the complete deck of 52 cards includes 13 spades.

The probability of an event not occurring, known as the *converse rule* of probability, is 1 minus the probability of that event occurring. Thus, the probability of not drawing a spade is $1 - .25 = .75$.

For another example, suppose that the recidivism rate for rapists is 65%. In other words, a rapist released from prison has a .65 probability of being rearrested. The converse is nonrecidivism. The probability that a discharged rapist does not recidivate is $1 - .65 = .35$.

An important characteristic of probability is found in the *addition rule,* which states that *the probability of obtaining any one of several different and distinct outcomes equals the sum of their separate probabilities.* Suppose, for example, that we wish to find the probability of drawing the ace of spades, the queen of diamonds, *or* the king of hearts in a single draw from a well-shuffled pack of 52 cards. By adding their separate probabilities ($\frac{1}{52} + \frac{1}{52} + \frac{1}{52}$), we learn that the probability of obtaining any one of these cards in a single draw is equal to $\frac{3}{52}$ ($P = .06$). In other words, we have 6 chances in 100 to obtain the ace of spades, the queen of diamonds, or the king of hearts in a single draw (see Figure 5.1).

As another example of adding probabilities, suppose that a defendant in a criminal trial has a .42 probability of being convicted as charged, a .26 probability of being convicted of a lesser charge, and a .32 chance of being found not guilty. The chance of a conviction on *any* charge is $.42 + .26 = .68$. Note also that this answer agrees with the converse rule by which the probability of being found guilty (the converse of not guilty) is $1 - .32 = .68$.

The addition rule always assumes that the outcomes being considered are *mutually exclusive*—that is, no two outcomes can occur simultaneously. For instance, no single card from a deck of 52 cards can be a spade, a diamond, *and* a heart at the same time. Similarly, a coin that is flipped just one time cannot possibly land both on its head *and* its tail.

Probability of getting the ace of spades	$\frac{1}{52}$
Probability of getting the queen of diamonds	$\frac{1}{52}$
Probability of getting the king of hearts	$+\ \frac{1}{52}$
Probability of getting either the ace of spades, the queen of diamonds, or the king of hearts	$\frac{3}{52}$ ($P = .06$)

FIGURE 5.1   The probability of obtaining either the ace of spades, queen of diamonds, or king of hearts in a single draw: an example of the addition rule

Assuming mutually exclusive outcomes, we can say that the probability associated with all possible outcomes of an event always equals 1. This indicates that some outcome must occur. If not heads, then tails; if not an ace, then a king, queen, jack, ten, and so on. In the flip of a coin, the probability of getting heads is equal to ½ ($P = .50$). Of course, the probability of getting tails is also ½ ($P = .50$). Adding together the probabilities for all possible outcomes, then, we learn that the probability of getting either heads or tails is equal to 1 (½ + ½ = 1).

Another important property of probability occurs in the *multiplication rule,* which focuses on the problem of obtaining two or more outcomes in combination. The *multiplication rule* states that *the probability of obtaining a combination of independent outcomes equals the product of their separate probabilities.* The assumption of *independent outcomes* means that the occurrence of one does not change the likelihood of the other. Rather than *either . . . or,* the multiplication rule is addressed to *and.*

For example, what is the probability of getting heads on both of two coin flips—that is, heads on the first and heads on the second flip? (We refer here to flipping two different coins at the same time, but all the results we obtain apply equally to two successive flips of the same coin.) Because the two outcomes (results of the flips) are independent of one another, the outcome of the first flip does not influence the outcome of the other flip. On the first flip, the probability of obtaining a head is ½ ($P = .50$); on the second flip, the probability is also ½ ($P = .50$) regardless of the outcome of the first coin flip. Because of independence, the probability of heads on both is the probability of heads on each multiplied together (see Figure 5.2). That is,

$$P(\text{heads on both coins}) = P(\text{heads on flip 1})\, P(\text{heads on flip 2})$$

$$= \left(\frac{1}{2}\right)\left(\frac{1}{2}\right)$$

$$= \frac{1}{4}$$

$$= .25$$

Suppose that a prosecutor is working on two cases, a robbery trial and a kidnapping trial. From previous experience, she feels that she has a .80 chance of getting a conviction

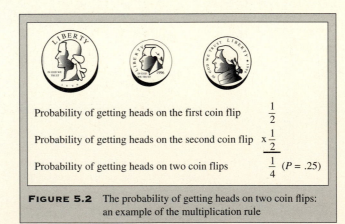

Probability of getting heads on the first coin flip	$\frac{1}{2}$
Probability of getting heads on the second coin flip	x $\frac{1}{2}$
Probability of getting heads on two coin flips	$\frac{1}{4}$ ($P = .25$)

FIGURE 5.2   The probability of getting heads on two coin flips: an example of the multiplication rule

on the robbery and a .70 chance of a conviction on the kidnapping. Thus, the probability that she will get convictions on *both* cases is (.80)(.70) = .56 (slightly better than half).

PROBABILITY DISTRIBUTIONS

In the previous section, we encountered distributions of data in which frequencies and percentages associated with particular values were determined. For example, Table 2.8 showed the frequency distribution of college board scores of 336 students. The possible values of the scores were represented by the categories, and the frequencies and percents represent the relative occurrences of the scores among the group.

A *probability distribution* is directly analogous to a frequency distribution, except that it is based on theory (probability theory) rather than on what is observed in the real world (empirical data). In a probability distribution, we specify the possible values of a variable and calculate the probabilities associated with each. The probabilities represent the likelihood of each value, directly analogous to the percentages in a frequency distribution.

Suppose we were again to flip two coins and let X represent the number of heads we obtain. The variable X has three possible values, 0, 1, and 2, according to whether we obtain zero, one, or two heads. Zero heads ($X = 0$) has a probability of

$$P(0 \text{ heads}) = P(\text{tails on flip 1})P(\text{tails on flip 2})$$

$$= (.50)(.50) = .25$$

We multiply the probability of getting tails on the coins because the flips of the two coins are independent.

Similarly, for two heads ($X = 2$),

$$P(2 \text{ heads}) = P(\text{heads on flip 1})P(\text{heads on flip 2})$$

$$= (.50)(.50) = .25$$

Determining the probability of heads on one of two flips ($X = 1$) requires an additional consideration. There are two ways to obtain one flip of heads: (1) heads on flip 1 and tails on flip 2 (HT); or (2) tails on flip 1 and heads on flip 2 (TH). Because these two possible outcomes are mutually exclusive (they cannot both occur), we may add their respective probabilities. That is,

$$P(1 \text{ heads}) = P(\text{HT or TH})$$

$$= P(\text{HT}) + P(\text{TH})$$

As before, the individual coin flips are independent. Thus, we can multiply the probability of a head times the probability of a tail to get the probability of first a head then a tail, $P(\text{HT})$; and we can also multiply the probability of a tail times the probability of a head to obtain the probability of first a tail and then a head, $P(\text{TH})$. That is,

$$P(\text{HT}) + P(\text{TH}) = P(\text{H})P(\text{T}) + P(\text{T})P(\text{H})$$

$$= (.50)(.50) + (.50)(.50)$$

$$= .25 + .25$$

$$= .50$$

The complete probability distribution for variable *X* is summarized in Table 5.1. Note that the probabilities sum to 1.00. The distribution can be plotted much the way we did with frequency distributions in Chapter 2. A bar graph of a probability distribution places the values of the variable along the horizontal base line, and the probabilities along the vertical axis (see Figure 5.3). We see that the distribution is symmetric, as one would expect of coins that favor neither of their sides.

THE DIFFERENCE BETWEEN PROBABILITY DISTRIBUTIONS AND FREQUENCY DISTRIBUTIONS

It is important to be clear on the difference between frequency distributions, like those we saw in Chapter 2, and probability distributions. Look again at Figure 5.2, which shows the probability distribution of the number of heads in two flips of a coin. This is a perfectly symmetrical distribution, with the probability of two heads equal to .25, identical to the probability of no heads. Furthermore, it shows that the probability of one head out of

TABLE 5.1	PROBABILITY DISTRIBUTION FOR NUMBER OF HEADS IN TWO FLIPS
X	Probability (*P*)
0	.25
1	.50
2	.25
Total	1.00

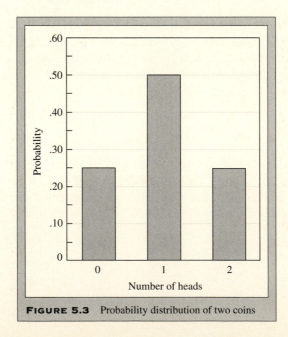

FIGURE 5.3   Probability distribution of two coins

two is .50. This distribution is based on probability theory. It describes what *should* happen when we flip two coins.

Now let's observe some data. Flip two coins and record the number of heads. Repeat this nine more times. How many times did you get zero heads, one head, and two heads? Our own results of a sample of 10 flips of a pair of coins are shown in Table 5.2.

This is a frequency distribution, not a probability distribution. It is based on actual observations of flipping two coins 10 times. Although the percentages (30%, 60%, and 10%) may seem like probabilities, they are not. The percentage distribution does not equal the probability distribution given earlier in Table 5.1. A probability distribution is theoretical or ideal: It portrays what the percentages should be in a perfect world. Unfortunately, we did not get a perfect outcome—there were more zero-head outcomes, that two-head outcomes, for instance. The problem is that just about anything can happen in only 10 sets of flips. In fact, we could have obtained even more skewed results than these.

Imagine if we were to repeat our flips of two coins many more times. The results of our flipping the two coins 1,000 times are shown in the frequency distribution in Table 5.3.

This frequency distribution (with $N = 1,000$) looks a lot better. Why is that? Was our luck just better this time than when we flipped the coins 10 times? In a sense, it is a matter of luck, but not completely. As we said previously, with only 10 sets of flips almost anything can happen—you could even get a streak of zero heads. But when we run our experiment for 1,000 pairs of flips, things even out over the long run. There will have been streaks of zero heads, but so too will there have been streaks of one head and two heads. As we approach an infinite number of flips of the two coins, the laws of probability become apparent. Our luck, if you want to call it that, evens out.

TABLE 5.2   FREQUENCY DISTRIBUTION OF 10 FLIPS OF TWO COINS

Number of heads	f	%
0	3	30.0
1	6	60.0
2	1	10.0
Total	10	100.0

TABLE 5.3   FREQUENCY DISTRIBUTION OF 1,000 FLIPS OF TWO COINS

Number of heads	f	%
0	253	25.3
1	499	49.9
2	248	24.8
Total	1,000	100.0

A probability distribution is essentially a frequency distribution for an infinite number of flips. Thus, we may never observe this distribution of infinite flips, but we know it looks like Figure 5.3.

MEAN AND STANDARD DEVIATION OF A PROBABILITY DISTRIBUTION

Returning to the frequency distribution in Table 5.2 for 10 flips of two coins, let's compute the mean number of heads (using the formula for a simple frequency distribution):

$$\overline{X} = \frac{\Sigma fX}{N}$$

$$= \frac{(3)(0) + (6)(1) + (1)(2)}{10}$$

$$= .8$$

This is low. The probability distribution of the two coin flips shown in Figure 5.3 clearly suggests that the average should be 1.00. That is, for the flip of two coins, in the long run you should expect to average one head. Note, however, that the frequency distribution $N = 1,000$ seems to be more in line with this expectation. For Table 5.3,

$$\overline{X} = \frac{\Sigma fX}{N}$$

$$= \frac{(253)(0) + (499)(1) + (248)(2)}{1,000}$$

$$= .995$$

Again, our "luck" averages out in the long run.

As you might suspect, a probability distribution has a mean. (Because the mean of a probability distribution is the value we expect to average in the long run, it is sometimes called an *expected value*.) For our case of the number of heads in two coin flips, the mean is 1. We use the Greek letter μ (*mu*) for the mean of a probability distribution (here $\mu = 1$) in order to distinguish it from $\overline{X}$, the mean of a frequency distribution $\overline{X}$ is something we calculate from a set of observed data and their frequencies. On the other hand, the mean of a probability distribution (μ) is a quantity that comes from our theory of what the distribution should look like.

A probability distribution also has a standard deviation, symbolized by σ (*sigma*), the Greek letter equivalent of s. Up to this point, we have used s to signify standard deviation generally. But from here on, s will represent the standard deviation of a set of observed data obtained from research, and σ shall represent the standard deviation of a theoretical distribution that is not observed directly. Similarly, s^2 will denote the variance of a set of observed data, and σ^2 will be the variance of a theoretical distribution. We will encounter μ, σ, and σ^2 often in chapters to come, and it is important to keep in mind the difference between $\overline{X}$, s, and s^2 (summary measures of observed data) on the one hand, and μ, σ, and σ^2 (characteristics of theoretical distributions) on the other.

THE NORMAL CURVE AS A PROBABILITY DISTRIBUTION

Previously, we saw that frequency distributions can take a variety of shapes or forms. Some are perfectly symmetrical or free of skewness; others are skewed either negatively or positively; still others have more than one hump; and so on. This is true as well for probability distributions.

Within this great diversity, there is one probability distribution with which many students are already familiar, if only from being graded on "the curve." This distribution, commonly known as the *normal curve,* is a theoretical or ideal model that was obtained from a mathematical equation, rather than from actually conducting research and gathering data. However, the usefulness of the normal curve for the researcher can be seen in its applications to actual research situations.

As we will see, for example, the normal curve can be used for describing distributions of scores, interpreting the standard deviation, and making statements of probability. In subsequent chapters, we will see that the normal curve is an essential ingredient of statistical decision making, whereby the researcher generalizes her or his results from samples to populations. Before proceeding to a discussion of techniques of decision making, it is first necessary to gain an understanding of the properties of the normal curve.

CHARACTERISTICS OF THE NORMAL CURVE

How can the normal curve be characterized? What are the properties that distinguish it from other distributions? As indicated in Figure 5.4, the normal curve is a type of smooth, symmetrical curve whose shape reminds many individuals of a bell and is thus widely known as the bell-shaped curve. Perhaps the most outstanding feature of the normal curve is its *symmetry:* If we were to fold the curve at its highest point at the center, we would create two equal halves, each the mirror image of the other.

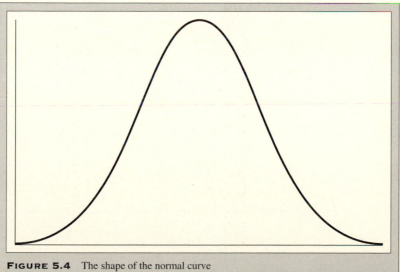

FIGURE 5.4   The shape of the normal curve

In addition, the normal curve is unimodal, having only one peak or point of maximum frequency—that point in the middle of the curve at which the mean, median, and mode coincide (the student may recall that the mean, median, and mode occur at different points in a skewed distribution—see Chapter 3). From the rounded central peak of the normal distribution, the curve falls off gradually at both tails, extending indefinitely in either direction and getting closer and closer to the base line without actually reaching it.

THE MODEL AND THE REALITY OF THE NORMAL CURVE

Because it is a probability distribution, the normal curve is a theoretical ideal. We might ask then: To what extent do distributions of actual data (that is, the data collected by researchers in the course of doing research) closely resemble or approximate the form of the normal curve? For illustrative purposes, let us imagine that all social, psychological, criminilogical, and physical phenomena were normally distributed. What would this hypothetical world be like?

So far as physical human characteristics are concerned, most adults would fall within the 5 to 6 ft range of height, with far fewer being either very short (less than 5 ft) or very tall (more than 6 ft). As shown in Figure 5.5, IQ would be equally predictable—the greatest proportion of IQ scores would fall between 85 and 115. We would see a gradual falling off of scores at either end with few "geniuses" who score higher than 145 and equally few who score lower than 55. Likewise, relatively few individuals would be regarded as either excellent or extremely inept lawyers, while the majority would be regarded as adequate or average. Finally, even the pattern of wear resulting from the flow of traffic in doorways would resemble the normal distribution—most wear would take place in the center of the doorway, whereas gradually decreasing amounts of wear would occur at either side.

Some readers have, by this time, noticed that the hypothetical world of the normal curve does not differ radically from the real world. Characteristics such as height, IQ, political orientation, and wear in doorways do, in fact, seem to approximate the theoretical

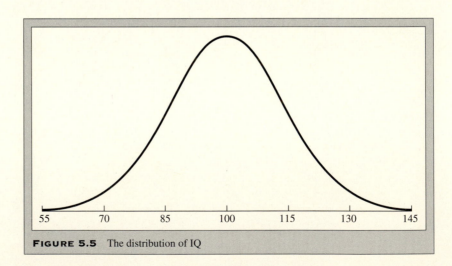

FIGURE 5.5 The distribution of IQ

normal distribution. Because so many phenomena have this characteristic—because it occurs so frequently in nature (and for other reasons that will soon become apparent)—researchers in many fields have made extensive use of the normal curve by applying it to the data that they collect and analyze.

But it should be noted that many variables in criminal justice and criminology (as elsewhere) simply do not conform to the theoretical notion of the normal distribution. Many distributions are skewed; others have more than one peak; some are symmetrical but not bell-shaped. As a concrete example, let us consider the distribution of wealth throughout the world. It is well known that the "have-nots" greatly outnumber the "haves." Thus, as shown in Figure 5.6, the distribution of wealth (as indicated by per capita income) is extremely skewed, so that a small proportion of the world's population receives a large proportion of the world's income. A criminologist (relying on, for example, relative deprivation or conflict theory) would argue that this heavily skewed income distribution is one of the main forces behind widespread criminal behavior. Likewise, population specialists tell us that the United States is steadily becoming a land of the young and the old: The baby boomers are heading toward middle age and older, and there is a large surge in the proportion of the population under 10 years old. The large number of young people is of concern to criminologists and criminal justice professionals. Since most crime is committed by people between the ages of 15 and 30, we would expect that as the number of people in this age group grows, crime rates will increase.

Where we have good reason to expect radical departures from normality—as in the case of age and income—the normal curve cannot be used as a model of the data we have obtained. Thus, it cannot be applied at will to all of the distributions encountered by the

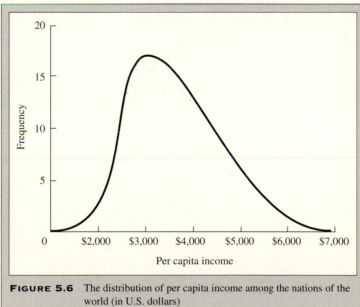

FIGURE 5.6 The distribution of per capita income among the nations of the world (in U.S. dollars)

researcher but must be used with a good deal of discretion. Fortunately, statisticians know that many phenomena of interest to the social researcher take the form of the normal curve.

THE AREA UNDER THE NORMAL CURVE

It is important to keep in mind that the normal curve is an ideal or theoretical distribution (that is, a probability distribution). Therefore, we denote its mean by μ and its standard deviation by σ. The mean of the normal distribution is at its exact center (see Figure 5.7). The standard deviation (σ) is the distance between the mean (μ) and the point on the base line just below where the reversed S-shaped portion of the curve shifts direction.

In order to employ the normal distribution in solving problems, we must acquaint our-selves with the *area under the normal curve: the area that lies between the curve and the base line containing 100% or all of the cases in any given normal distribution.* Figure 5.7 illustrates this characteristic.

We could enclose a portion of this total area by drawing lines from any two points on the base line up to the curve. For instance, using the mean as a point of departure, we could draw one line at the mean (μ) and another line at the point that is 1σ (1 standard deviation distance) above the mean. As illustrated in Figure 5.8, this shaded portion of the normal curve includes 34.13% of the total frequency.

In the same way, we can say that 47.72% of the cases under the normal curve lie between the mean and 2σ above the mean, and that 49.87% lie between the mean and 3σ above the mean (see Figure 5.9).

As we shall see, *a constant proportion of the total area under the normal curve will lie between the mean and any given distance from the mean as measured in sigma units.* This is true regardless of the mean and standard deviation of the particular distribution and

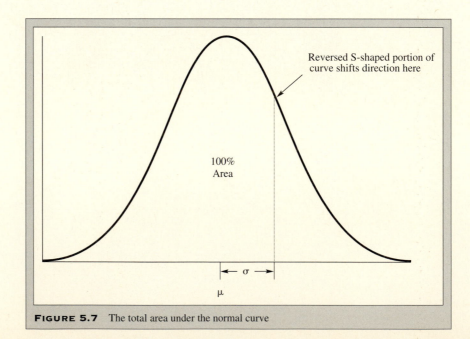

FIGURE 5.7   The total area under the normal curve

applies universally to all data that are normally distributed. Thus, the area under the normal curve between the mean and the point 1σ above the mean *always* turns out to include 34.13% of the total cases, whether we are discussing the distribution of height, intelligence, law school grades, or the pattern of wear in a doorway. The basic requirement, in each case, is only that we are working with a *normal* distribution of scores.

The symmetrical nature of the normal curve leads us to make another important point—namely, that *any given sigma distance above the mean contains the identical proportion of*

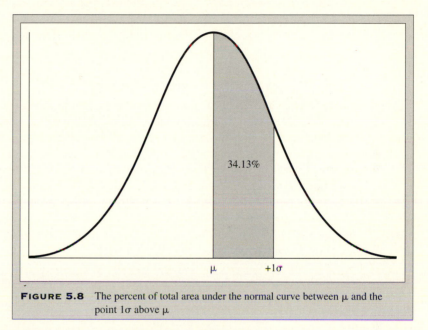

34.13%

μ   +1σ

FIGURE 5.8 The percent of total area under the normal curve between μ and the point 1σ above μ

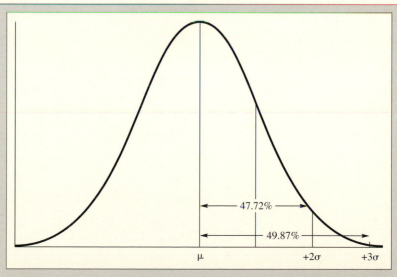

47.72%

49.87%

μ   +2σ   +3σ

FIGURE 5.9 The percent of total area under the normal curve between μ and the points that are 2σ and 3σ from μ

cases as the same sigma distance below the mean. Thus, if 34.13% of the total area lies between the mean and 1σ *above* the mean, then 34.13% of the total area also lies between the mean and 1σ *below* the mean; if 47.72% lies between the mean and 2σ *above* the mean, then 47.72% lies between the mean and 2σ *below* the mean; if 49.87% lies between the mean and 3σ *above* the mean, then 49.87% also lies between the mean and 3σ *below* the mean. In other words, as illustrated in Figure 5.10, 68.26% of the total area of the normal curve (34.13% + 34.13%) falls between −1σ and +1σ from the mean; 95.44% of the area (47.72% + 47.72%) falls between −2σ and +2σ from the mean; and 99.74%, or almost all, of the cases (49.87% + 49.87%) falls between −3σ and +3σ from the mean. It can be said, then, that six standard deviations include practically all of the cases (more than 99%) under any normal distribution.

CLARIFYING THE STANDARD DEVIATION

An important function of the normal curve is to help interpret and clarify the meaning of the standard deviation. To understand how this function is carried out, let us examine what some researchers tell us about gender differences in IQ. Despite the claims of male chauvinists, there is evidence that both males and females have mean IQ scores of approximately 100. Let us also say these IQ scores differ markedly in terms of variability around the mean. In particular, let us suppose hypothetically that male IQs have greater *heterogeneity* than female IQs; that is, the distribution of male IQs contains a much larger percent of extreme scores representing very bright as well as very dull individuals, whereas the distribution of female IQs has a larger percent of scores located closer to the average, the point of maximum frequency at the center.

Because the standard deviation is a measure of variation, these gender differences in variability should be reflected in the sigma value of each distribution of IQ scores. Thus, we might find that the standard deviation is 15 for male IQs, but only 10 for female IQs.

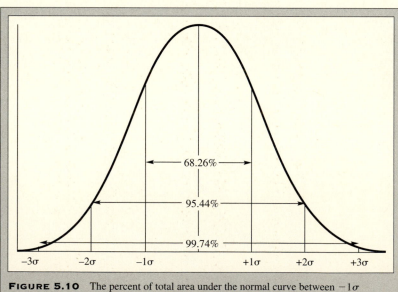

FIGURE 5.10   The percent of total area under the normal curve between −1σ and +1σ, −2σ and +2σ, and −3σ and +3σ

Knowing the standard deviation of each set of IQ scores and assuming that each set is normally distributed, we could then estimate and compare the percent of males and females having any given range of IQ scores.

For instance, measuring the base line of the distribution of male IQ in standard deviation units, we would know that 68.26% of male IQ scores fall between -1σ and $+1\sigma$ from the mean. Because the standard deviation is always given in raw-score units and $\sigma = 15$, we would also know that these are points on the distribution at which IQ scores of 115 and 85 are located ($\mu - \sigma = 100 - 15 = 85$ and $\mu + \sigma = 100 + 15 = 115$). Thus, 68.26% of the males would have IQ scores that fall between 85 and 115.

Moving away from the mean and farther out from these points, we would find, as illustrated in Figure 5.11, that 99.74%, or practically all, of the males have IQ scores between 55 and 145 (between -3σ and $+3\sigma$).

In the same manner, looking next at the distribution of female IQ scores as depicted in Figure 5.12 we see that 99.74% of these cases would fall between scores of 70 and 130 (between -3σ and $+3\sigma$). In contrast to males, then, the distribution of female IQ scores could be regarded as being relatively homogeneous, having a smaller proportion of extreme scores in either direction. This difference is reflected in the comparative size of each standard deviation and in the proportion of IQ scores falling between -3σ and $+3\sigma$ from the mean.

USING TABLE A

In discussing the normal distribution, we have so far treated only those distances from the mean that are exact multiples of the standard deviation. That is, they were precisely one, two, or three standard deviations either above or below the mean. The question now arises: What must we do to determine the percent of cases for distances lying between any two score values? For instance, suppose we wish to determine the percent of total frequency that falls between the mean and, say, a raw score located 1.40σ above the mean. As illus-

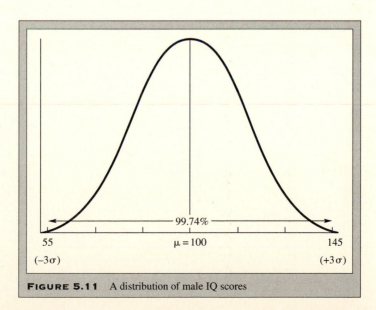

99.74%

55           $\mu = 100$ 145

(-3σ) $(+3\sigma)$

FIGURE 5.11   A distribution of male IQ scores

trated in Figure 5.13 a raw score 1.40σ above the mean is obviously greater than 1σ but less than 2σ from the mean. Thus, we know this distance from the mean would include more than 34.13% but less than 47.72% of the total area under the normal curve.

To determine the exact percentage within this interval, we must employ Table A in Appendix C. This shows the percent under the normal curve (1) between the mean and various sigma distances from the mean (in column b) and (2) at or beyond various scores

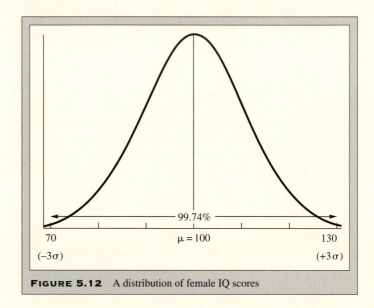

FIGURE 5.12   A distribution of female IQ scores

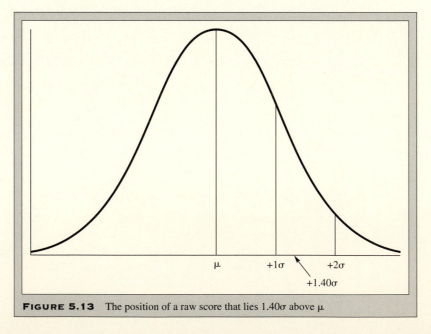

FIGURE 5.13   The position of a raw score that lies 1.40σ above μ

toward either tail of the distribution (in column c). These sigma distances (from .00 to 4.00) are labeled z in the lefthand column (column a) of Table A and have been given two decimal places.

Notice that the symmetry of the normal curve makes it possible to give percentages for only one side of the mean, that is, only one-half of the curve (50%). Values in Table A represent either side. The following is a portion of Table A:

(a)	(b)	(c)
	Area between	Area
z	mean and z	beyond z
.00	.00	50.00
.01	.40	49.60
.02	.80	49.20
.03	1.20	48.80
.04	1.60	48.40
.05	1.99	48.01
.06	2.39	47.61
.07	2.79	47.21
.08	3.19	46.81
.09	3.59	46.41

When learning to use and understand Table A, we might first attempt to locate the percent of cases between a sigma distance of 1.00 and the mean (the reason being that we already know that 34.13% of the total area falls between these points on the base line). Looking at column b of Table A, we see it indeed indicates that exactly 34.13% of the total frequency falls between the mean and a sigma distance of 1.00. Likewise, we see that the area between the mean and the sigma distance 2.00 includes exactly 47.72% of the total area under the curve.

But what about finding the percent of cases between the mean and a sigma distance of 1.40? This was the problem in Figure 5.13, which necessitated the use of the table in the first place. The entry in column b corresponding to a sigma distance of 1.40 includes 41.92% of the total area under the curve. Finally, how do we determine the percent of cases at or beyond 1.40 standard deviations from the mean? Without a table to help us, we might locate the percentage in this area under the normal curve by simply subtracting our earlier answer from 50%, because this is the total area lying on either side of the mean. However, this has already been done in column c of Table A, where we see that exactly 8.08% $(50 - 41.92 = 8.08)$ of the cases fall at or above the score that is 1.40 standard deviations from the mean.

STANDARD SCORES AND THE NORMAL CURVE

We are now prepared to find the percent of the total area under the normal curve associated with any given sigma distance from the mean. However, at least one more important question remains to be answered: How do we determine the sigma distance of any given raw score? That is, how do we go about translating our raw score—the score that we originally collected from our respondents—into units of standard deviation? If we wished to translate feet into yards, we would simply divide the number of feet by 3, because there are 3 ft in a yard. Likewise, if we were translating minutes into hours, we would divide the number of minutes by 60, because there are 60 min in every hour. In precisely the same manner, we can translate any given raw score into sigma units by dividing the distance of the raw score from the mean by the standard deviation. To illustrate, let us imagine a raw score of 6 from a distribution in which μ is 3 and σ is 2. Taking the difference between the raw score and the mean and obtaining a deviation $(6 - 3)$, we see that a raw score of 6 is 3 raw-score units above the mean. Dividing this raw-score distance by $\sigma = 2$, we see that this raw score is 1.5 (one and one-half) standard deviations above the mean. In other words, the sigma distance of a raw score of 6 *in this particular distribution* is 1.5 standard deviations above the mean. We should note that regardless of the measurement situation, there are always 3 ft in a yard and 60 min in an hour. The constancy that marks these other standard measures is not shared by the standard deviation. It changes from one distribution to another. For this reason, we must know the standard deviation of a distribution by calculating it, estimating it, or being given it by someone else before we are able to translate any particular raw score into units of standard deviation.

The process that we have just illustrated—that of finding sigma distance from the mean—yields a value called a *z score* or *standard score,* which indicates the *direction and degree that any given raw score deviates from the mean of a distribution on a scale of sigma units* (notice that the left-hand column of Table A in Appendix C is labeled *z*). Thus, a *z* score of $+1.4$ indicates that the raw score lies 1.4σ (or almost $1\frac{1}{2}\sigma$) *above* the mean, whereas a *z* score of -2.1 means that the raw score falls slightly more than 2σ *below* the mean (see Figure 5.14).

We obtain a *z* score by finding the deviation $(X - \mu)$, which gives the distance of the raw score from the mean, and then dividing this raw-score deviation by the standard deviation.

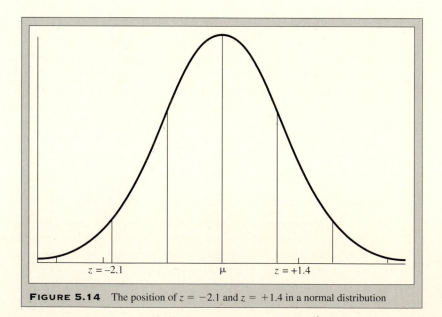

FIGURE 5.14   The position of $z = -2.1$ and $z = +1.4$ in a normal distribution

Computed by formula,

$$z = \frac{X - \mu}{\sigma}$$

where μ = mean of a distribution
          σ = standard deviation of a distribution
          z = standard score

As an example, suppose we are studying the distribution of annual income for guards in a large security company in which the mean annual income is $14,000 and the standard deviation is $1,500.[1] Assuming the distribution of annual income is normally distributed, we can translate the raw score from this distribution, $16,000, into a standard score in the following manner:

$$z = \frac{16,000 - 14,000}{1,500} = +1.33$$

Thus, an annual income of $16,000 is 1.33 standard deviations above the mean annual income of $14,000 (see Figure 5.15).

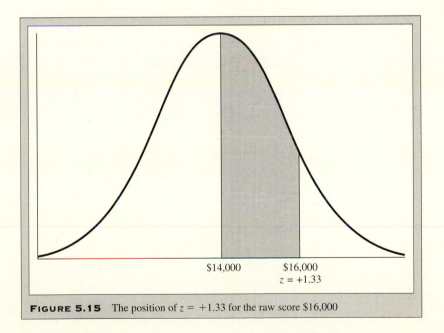

$14,000 $16,000
              $z = +1.33$

FIGURE 5.15   The position of $z = +1.33$ for the raw score $16,000

[1]It was pointed out earlier that income distributions are generally skewed by the presence of a few very wealthy persons. Nevertheless, among a group of people whose incomes are constrained (such as security guards), it is common to find a fairly normal distribution of the salary data.

As another example, suppose we are working with a normal distribution of scores representing satisfaction with local police among a group of project tenants (higher scores indicate greater satisfaction with police).

Let us say this distribution has a mean of 10 and a standard deviation of 3. To determine how many standard deviations a score of 3 lies from the mean of 10, we obtain the difference between this score and the mean, that is,

$$X - \mu = 3 - 10$$
$$= -7$$

We then divide by the standard deviation:

$$z = \frac{X - \mu}{\sigma}$$
$$= -\frac{7}{3}$$
$$= -2.33$$

Thus, as shown in Figure 5.16, a raw score of 3 in this distribution of scores falls 2.33 standard deviations below the mean.

Note: If we know a z score and seek to obtain its raw-score equivalent, we use the formula

$$X = z\sigma + \mu$$

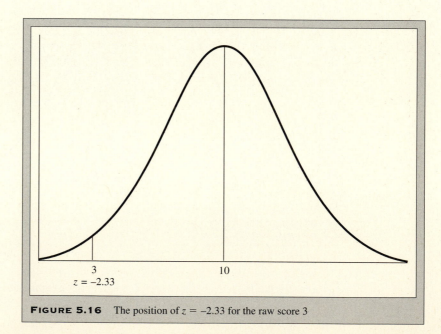

3
$z = -2.33$

10

FIGURE 5.16   The position of $z = -2.33$ for the raw score 3

For the present example,

$$X = (-2.33)(3) + 10$$
$$= -7 + 10$$
$$= 3$$

FINDING PROBABILITY UNDER THE NORMAL CURVE

As we shall now see, the normal curve can be used in conjunction with z scores and Table A to determine the probability of obtaining any raw score in a distribution. In the present context, the normal curve is a distribution in which it is possible to determine probabilities associated with various points along its base line. As noted earlier, the normal curve is a *probability distribution* in which the total area under the curve equals 100%—it contains a central area surrounding the mean, where scores occur most frequently, and smaller areas toward either end, where there is a gradual flattening out and thus a smaller proportion of extremely high and low scores. In probability terms, then, we can say that probability decreases as we travel along the base line away from the mean in either direction. Thus, to say that 68.26% of the total frequency under the normal curve falls between -1σ and $+1\sigma$ from the mean is to say that the probability is approximately 68 in 100 that any given raw score will fall within this interval. Similarly, to say that 95.44% of the total frequency under the normal curve falls between -2σ and $+2\sigma$ from the mean is also to say that the probability is approximately 95 in 100 that any raw score will fall within this interval, and so on.

This is precisely the same concept of probability or *relative frequency* that we saw in operation when drawing a single card from an entire pack of cards or flipping a coin. Note, however, that the probabilities associated with areas under the normal curve are always given relative to 100%, which is the entire area under the curve (for example, 68 in 100, 95 in 100, 99 in 100, and so on).

STEP-BY-STEP ILLUSTRATION

PROBABILITY UNDER THE NORMAL CURVE

To apply the concept of probability in relation to the normal distribution, let us return to an earlier example. We were then asked to translate into its z-score equivalent a raw score from a company's distribution of annual salary for security guards, which we assumed approximated a normal curve. This distribution of income had a mean of $14,000 with a standard deviation of $1,500.

By applying the z-score formula, we learned earlier that an annual income of $16,000 was 1.33 σ above the mean $14,000, that is,

$$z = \frac{16,000 - 14,000}{1,500} = +1.33$$

Let us now determine the probability of obtaining a score that lies between $14,000, the mean, and $16,000. In other words, what is the probability of randomly choosing, in just one attempt, a security guard whose annual income falls between $14,000 and $16,000? The problem is graphically illustrated in Figure 5.17 (we are solving for the shaded area under the curve) and can be solved in two steps using the z-score formula and Table A in Appendix C.

STEP 1　Translate the raw score ($16,000) into a z score.

$$z = \frac{X - \mu}{\sigma}$$

$$= \frac{16,000 - 14,000}{1,500}$$

$$= +1.33$$

Thus, a raw score, $16,000 is located 1.33σ above the mean.

STEP 2　Using Table A, find the percent of total frequency under the curve falling between the z score (z = +1.33) and the mean.

In column b of Table A, we find that 40.82% of the security guards earn between $14,000 and $16,000 (see Figure 5.18). Thus, by moving the decimal two places to the left, we see that the probability (rounded off) is 41 in 100. More precisely, $P = .4082$ that we would obtain an individual whose annual income lies between these figures.

In the previous example, we were asked to determine the probability associated with the distance between the mean and a particular sigma distance from it. Many times, however, we may wish to find the percent of area that lies at or *beyond* a particular raw score toward either tail of the distribution or to find the probability of obtaining these scores. For

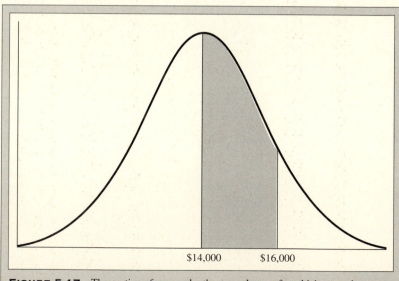

FIGURE 5.17　The portion of area under the normal curve for which we seek to determine probability of occurrence

instance, in the present case, we might wish to learn the probability of obtaining an annual income of $16,000 or *greater.*

This problem can be illustrated graphically, as shown in Figure 5.19 (we are solving for the shaded area under the curve). In this case, we would follow Steps 1 and 2, thus obtaining the z score and finding the percent under the normal curve between $14,000 and a $z = 1.33$ (from Table A). In the present case, however, we must go a step beyond

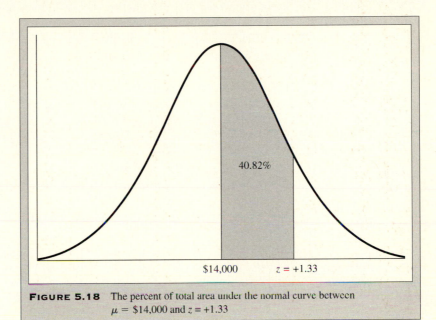

FIGURE 5.18   The percent of total area under the normal curve between
$\mu = \$14,000$ and $z = +1.33$

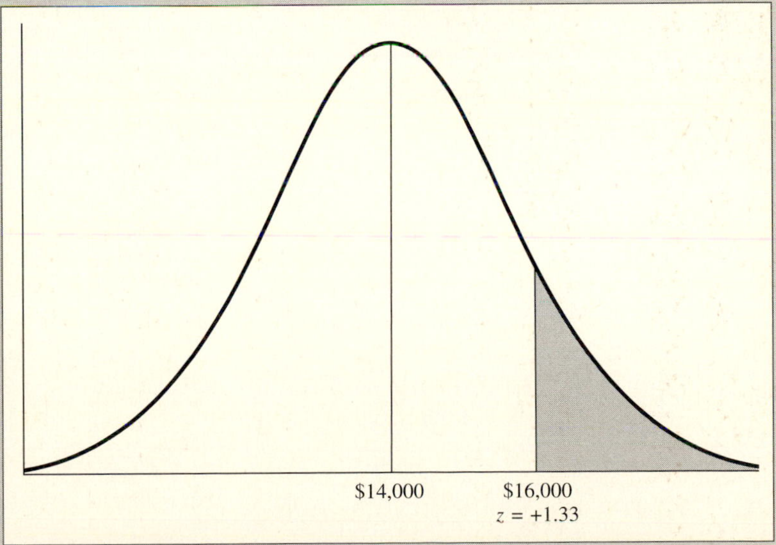

FIGURE 5.19   The portion of total area under the normal curve for which we seek to determine probability of occurrence

and *subtract* the percentage obtained in Table A from 50%—that percent of the total area lying on either side of the mean. Fortunately, column c of Table A has already done this for us.

Therefore, subtracting 40.82% from 50% or simply looking in column c of Table A, we learn that slightly more than 9% (9.18%) fall *at* or *beyond* $16,000. In probability terms, we can say (by moving the decimal two places to the left) there are only slightly more than 9 chances in 100 ($P = .0918$) that we would find a security guard in this company whose income was $16,000 or greater.

It was noted earlier that any given sigma distance above the mean contains the identical proportion of cases as the same sigma distance below the mean. For this reason, our procedure in finding probabilities associated with points below the mean is identical to that followed in the previous examples.

For instance, the percent of total area between the z score -1.33 ($12,000) and the mean is identical to the percent between the z score $+1.33$ ($16,000) and the mean. Therefore, we know that $P = .4082$ of obtaining a security guard whose income falls between $12,000 and $14,000. Likewise, the percent of total frequency at or beyond -1.33 ($12,000 or less) equals that at or beyond $+1.33$ ($16,000 or more). Thus, we know $P = .0918$ that we shall obtain a security guard from the company with an annual income of $12,000 or less.

We can use the addition rule to find the probability of obtaining more than a single portion of the area under the normal curve. For instance, we have already determined that $P = .09$ for incomes of $12,000 or less and for incomes of $16,000 or more. To find the probability of obtaining *either* $12,000 or less *or* $16,000 or more, we simply add their separate probabilities as follows:

$$P = .0918 + .0918$$

$$= .1836$$

In a similar way, we can find the probability of obtaining a security guard whose income falls between $12,000 and $16,000 by adding the probabilities associated with z scores of 1.33 on either side of the mean. Therefore,

$$P = .4082 + .4082$$

$$= .8164$$

Notice that .8164 + .1836 equals 1.00, representing all possible outcomes under the normal curve.

The application of the multiplication rule to the normal curve can be illustrated by finding the probability of obtaining four security guards whose incomes are $16,000 or greater. We already know that $P = .0918$ associated with finding a single security guard whose income is at least $16,000. Therefore,

$$P = (.0918)(.0918)(.0918)(.0918)$$

$$= (.0918)^4$$

$$= .00007$$

Applying the multiplication rule, we see that the probability of randomly selecting four security guards with incomes of $16,000 or more is only 7 chances in 100,000.

OBTAINING PERCENTILE RANKS FROM THE NORMAL CURVE

In Chapter 2, we used the process of interpolation to estimate percentile ranks for frequency distributions. For example, we are able to estimate the percentile rank for an SAT score of 619 based on a specific set of scores of 336 test takers.

For variables like SAT scores, which closely resemble a normal distribution in shape, we can utilize z scores and the areas under the normal curve given in Table A to find percentile ranks. Whereas the interpolation method presented in Chapter 2 provided only approximations of percentile ranks, the approach introduced here will provide exact values but only for truly normally distributed data. That is, the accuracy of results from applying Table A to real-life problems will be only as good as the closeness of the data to a true normal curve.

Let us suppose that you wanted to determine, based on a normal curve, the percentile rank for an SAT score of 619. The SAT scores come in standardized form so that they have a mean (μ) of 500 and a standard deviation (σ) of 100 for the entire population of thousands of test takers across the country. As shown in Figure 5.20, the percentile rank for a score of 619 will be the percent of the area under the curve to the left of 619.

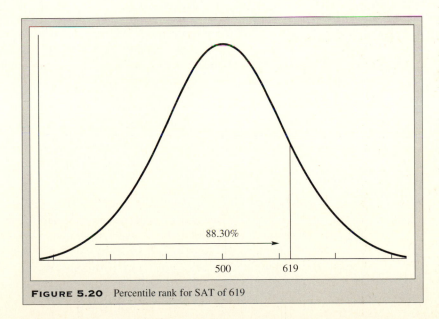

FIGURE 5.20   Percentile rank for SAT of 619

In terms of standard deviation units,

$$z = \frac{X - \mu}{\sigma} = \frac{619 - 500}{100} = 1.19$$

Thus, a score of 619 is $+1.19\sigma$ away from the population mean of the normal distribution of SAT scores. Consulting column b of Table A for a z score of 1.19, we find that 38.30% of the area lies between this point and the mean. Combining this percentage with the 50% that falls to the left of the mean, we determine that 88.30% of the distribution lies below 619. We conclude, therefore, that 619 has a percentile rank of 88.30%, or rounded off to 88%.

Before moving ahead, it will be instructive to compare the percentile rank for a 619 SAT score obtained in Chapter 2 by interpolating within a frequency distribution of 336 SAT scores (percentile rank = 77.88%) to that obtained here based on the normal distribution (percentile rank = 88.30%). The discrepancy between these two calculations is because the interpolation was based on an observed sample distribution of 336 cases, which was close to but not exactly normal and which had a sample mean and standard deviation close to but not precisely 500 and 100, respectively. In contrast, when using the normal-curve approach for finding percentile ranks, we make the assumption that the 619 score was part of a truly normal distribution with a population mean of 500 and a population standard deviation of 100. It is encouraging, however, that the percentile rank computed from a sample of 336 cases is fairly close to that determined from a theoretical normal curve.

STEP-BY-STEP ILLUSTRATION

PERCENTILE RANK FOR SCORE ABOVE THE MEAN

Suppose we wanted to find the percentile rank for a serial murderer who scored 109 on the Wechsler IQ test. Knowing that this standardized test is scaled in the population to have a mean (μ) of 100 and a standard deviation (σ) of 15, we can obtain the percentile rank using the following steps (see Figure 5.21):

STEP 1   Convert the raw score into standard deviation units using the z-score formula.

$$z = \frac{X - \mu}{\sigma} = \frac{109 - 100}{15} = .60$$

STEP 2   Using Table A, determine the percent of area at or below the z score.
From column b of Table A, we determine that 22.57% of the distribution lies between a z of .60 and the mean. Because percentile ranks are defined as the percentage at or below a given score, we must add the 50% corresponding to the left side of the distribution below the mean. As shown in Figure 5.21, a total of 72.57% lies at or below a z score of .60, that is, at or below an IQ of 109. Thus, the percentile rank for 109 is 72.57%.

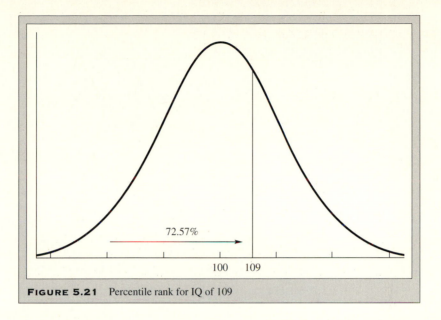

72.57%

100 109

FIGURE 5.21 Percentile rank for IQ of 109

STEP-BY-STEP ILLUSTRATION

PERCENTILE RANK FOR SCORE BELOW THE MEAN

As shown in the next illustration, we must modify the procedure only slightly to find percentile ranks for scores that are below the mean. Applying the step-by-step procedure, let's obtain the percentile rank for an IQ of 90.

STEP 1 Convert the raw score into standard deviation units using the z-score formula.

$$z = \frac{X - \mu}{\sigma} = \frac{90 - 100}{15} = -.67$$

STEP 2 Using Table A, determine the percent of area at or below the z score.

Because the score falls below the mean (see Figure 5.22), column c of Table A directly provides the desired percentage. Even though z is negative (as it always is for scores less than the mean), we enter Table A for the z value of .67, ignoring the sign. Column c indicates that 25.14% of the area falls in the left tail at or below a z score of $-.67$. Thus, the percentile rank for an IQ of 90 is 25.14% (which is just about the first quartile).

In sum, percentile ranks for normal distributions can be obtained by using Table A, along with the formula for z. It is strongly advised, moreover, that you always graph these problems as we have done before attempting the calculations. In fact, we strongly urge you always to use drawings whenever doing any normal curve problem. Only by drawing the normal curve and indicating the values that are given (raw scores, means, and percentages), can you make certain of which side of the curve to use, whether z is

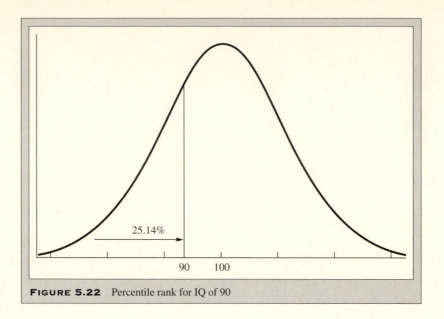

FIGURE 5.22 Percentile rank for IQ of 90

negative or positive, which column of Table A to use, and whether to add or subtract percentages.

SUMMARY

In this chapter, we discussed the concept of probability, which is the foundation for decision making in statistics. Probability is defined as the number of times an event can occur relative to the total number of times any event can occur. Probabilities range from zero (an impossible event) to one (a certainty). The converse, addition, and multiplication rules of probability were also discussed. Finally, the concept of a probability distribution as a theoretical ideal was introduced and compared to the frequency distributions presented earlier in this text. Properties of the theoretical normal distribution were discussed in the context of real-world problems of social research. Thus, it was shown that the area under the normal curve can be used to interpret the standard deviation and make statements of probability. The importance of the normal distribution will become more apparent in subsequent chapters.

TERMS TO REMEMBER

Probability
Converse rule
Addition rule
Mutually exclusive outcomes
Multiplication rule

Independent outcomes
Normal curve
Area under the normal curve
z score (standard score)

STEP-BY-STEP STUDY GUIDE
PROBABILITY UNDER THE NORMAL CURVE

STEP 1   Convert the raw score into standard deviation units.

$$z = \frac{X - \mu}{\sigma}$$

STEP 2   Using Table A, find the percentage of total frequency (or area) under the curve using column b or c as appropriate.

STEP-BY-STEP STUDY GUIDE
PERCENTILE RANKS FROM THE NORMAL CURVE

STEP 1   Convert the raw score into standard deviation units.

$$z = \frac{X - \mu}{\sigma}$$

STEP 2   Using Table A, determine the area at or below the z score. If z is positive, use the percentage area from the mean to the z score found in column b of the table and then add 50%. If z is negative, use the percentage area to the left of the z score found in column c.

PROBLEMS

1. The following students are enrolled in a course in constitutional law. They are listed along with their year in school and whether or not they are majoring in criminal justice.

Student	Year	Criminal Justice major
1	Sophomore	Yes
2	Senior	No
3	Junior	Yes
4	Freshman	No
5	Freshman	Yes
6	Sophomore	Yes
7	Sophomore	Yes
8	Junior	No
9	Sophomore	Yes
10	Sophomore	No

What is the probability of selecting at random from this class

a. a sophomore?
b. a student majoring in criminal justice?
c. a freshman or a sophomore?
d. not a freshman?

2. Suppose that 20% of men ($P = .20$) and 15% of women ($P = .15$) are carriers of a particular genetic trait. This trait can only be inherited by a child if both parents are carriers. What is the probability that a child is born with this genetic trait?

3. A student taking a midterm exam in a private security course comes to two questions pertaining to a class that he missed, and so he decides to take a random guess on both questions. One of the questions is True/False and the other is multiple choice with five possible answers. What is the probability of guessing

a. the correct answer to the True/False question?
b. the correct answer to the multiple-choice question?
c. the correct answers to both the True/False and the multiple-choice questions?
d. the incorrect answers to both the True/False and the multiple-choice questions?
e. the correct answer to the True/False question and the incorrect answer to the multiple-choice question?

f. the incorrect answer to the True/False question and the correct answer to the multiple-choice question?

4. Suppose that you purchase a lottery ticket that contains two numbers and a letter, such as

$$3 \quad 7 \quad P$$

a. What is the probability that you match the first digit?
b. What is the probability that you match the second digit?
c. What is the probability that you do not match the first digit?
d. What is the probability that you match both the first and second digits?
e. What is the probability that you match the letter?
f. What is the probability of a perfect match (both digits and the letter)?

5. A particular community wants to address the problem of racial conflict in the local high school. The mayor decides to set up a three-person commission of residents to advise him. In order to be completely fair in the selection process, the mayor decides to choose the commission members at random, designating the first selection as the chair. The racial/ethnic composition of the community is 50% white, 30% black, and 20% Latino. What is the probability that

a. the chair is a white resident?
b. the chair is a black resident?
c. the chair is white or Latino?
d. all three commission members are black?

6. Drawing one card at random from a standard deck of 52 cards, what is the probability of drawing.

a. the eight of diamonds?
b. the eight of diamonds or the eight of hearts?
c. an eight?
d. a red card?
e. a picture card (jack, queen, or king)?
f. from six through nine, inclusive?
g. an odd-numbered card?

7. Drawing one card from one standard deck of 52 cards and a second card from another standard deck of 52 cards, what is the probability that

a. both cards are red?
b. neither card is red?
c. the cards are different colors?
d. both cards are aces?
e. both cards are jacks or higher (jack, queen, king, or ace)?

8. Research has shown that in general, about 6 out of 10 people released from prison return within three years. What is the probability that

a. a particular offender released from prison will remain free for more that three years?
b. two offenders released on the same day will both return to prison within three years?

9. Suppose that 2% of convicted felons are in fact innocent.

a. If a person is convicted of a felony, what is the probability that he is guilty?
b. If two people are convicted of felonies, what is the probability that both are guilty?
c. If three people are convicted of felonies, what is the probability that all three are guilty?
d. If four people are convicted of felonies, what is the probability that all four are guilty?

10. Under any normal distribution of scores, what percentage of the total area falls

a. between the mean (μ) and a score value that lies one standard deviation (1σ) above the mean?
b. between a score value that lies one standard deviation below the mean and a score value that lies one standard deviation above the mean?
c. between the mean and a score value that lies $+2\sigma$ above the mean?
d. between a score value that lies -2σ below the mean and a score value that lies $+2\sigma$ above the mean?

11. The Scholastic Aptitude Test (SAT) is standardized to be normally distributed with a mean $\mu = 500$ and a standard deviation $\sigma = 100$. What percentage of SAT scores falls

a. between 500 and 600?
b. between 400 and 600?
c. between 500 and 700?
d. between 300 and 700?
e. above 600?
f. below 300?

12. For the SAT, determine the z score (that is, the number of standard deviations and the direction) that each of the following scores falls from the mean:

a. 500
b. 400
c. 650
d. 575
e. 750
f. 380

13. Using the z scores calculated in problem 12 and Table A, what is the percentage of SAT scores that falls

    a. 500 or above?
    b. 400 or below?
    c. between 500 and 650?
    d. 575 or above?
    e. between 250 and 750?
    f. 380 or above? (*Hint:* 50% of the area falls on either side of the curve.)

14. IQ scores are normally distributed with a mean $\mu = 100$ and a standard deviation $\sigma = 15$. Based on this distribution, determine

    a. the percentage of IQ scores between 100 and 120.
    b. the probability of selecting a person at random having an IQ between 100 and 120.
    c. the percentage of IQ scores between 88 and 100.
    d. the probability of selecting a person at random having an IQ between 88 and 100.
    e. the percentage of IQ scores that are 110 or above.
    f. The probability of selecting a person at random having an IQ of 110 or above.
    g. the probability of selecting two people at random both having an IQ of 110 or above.
    h. the percentile rank corresponding to an IQ score of 125.

15. Suppose that at a large district court, legal secretaries are paid by the hour. Data from the personnel office shows that the distribution of hourly wages paid to legal secretaries is approximately normal with a mean of $12 and a standard deviation of $2.50. Determine

    a. the percentage of legal secretaries earning an hourly wage of $15 or more.
    b. the probability of randomly selecting from personnel files a legal secretary who earns an hourly wage of $15 or more.
    c. the percentage of legal secretaries who earn between $10 and $12 per hour.
    d. the probability of randomly selecting from personnel files a legal secretary who earns between $10 and $12 per hour.
    e. the percentage of legal secretaries who earn an hourly wage of $11 or less.
    f. the probability of randomly selecting from personnel files a legal secretary who earns an hourly wage of $11 or less.
    g. the probability of randomly selecting from personnel files a legal secretary whose hourly wage is extreme in either direction—either $10 or less or $14 or more.
    h. the probability of randomly selecting from personnel files two legal secretaries whose hourly wages are less than average (mean).
    i. the probability of randomly selecting from personnel files two legal secretaries whose hourly wages are $13.50 or more.

16. A police detective was interested in studying the amount of time spent interrogating criminal suspects. Collecting data from police reports on all of the interrogations she and her colleagues performed over the past five years, she found that the lengths of time were normally distributed with a mean length of 106 minutes and a standard deviation of 8 minutes. Determine

    a. the percentage of interrogations that last two hours or more.
    b. the probability that a particular interrogation lasted two hours or more.
    c. the probability that two interrogations lasted two hours or more.

17. Examination of court records in a particular state shows that the mean prison sentence length for first-offense drug dealers is 26 months, and there is a 2-month standard deviation from this norm. The records also reveal that sentence lengths are approximately normally distributed.

    a. What percentage of first-time drug dealers receive sentences of 23 or fewer months?
    b. A defense attorney was concerned that his client received a particularly harsh sentence of 30 months. What is the percentile rank of this offender's sentence? How likely is it for the sentence lengths to be 30 months or more?
    c. Another defense attorney is pleased that her client received a sentence of 18 months. What is the percentile rank of this sentence length? How likely is it that a person would receive a sentence of 18 or fewer months?

18. A major automobile company specializing in providing cruisers to police departments claims that its new model has an average mpg (miles per gallon) rating of 25 mpg. Company officials concede that some cars vary based on a variety of factors, and that the mpg performances have a standard deviation of 4 mpg. You and your staff are employed by the state police to test drive new models of cruisers. Randomly selecting five cruisers from the assembly line, your staff finds them to have a poor mpg performance defined as 20 mpg or below.

a. Assuming the company's claim to be true ($\mu = 25$ and $\sigma = 4$), what is the probability that a single cruiser selected randomly performs poorly (mpg of 20 or below)?

b. Assuming the company's claim to be true ($\mu = 25$ and $\sigma = 4$), what is the probability that five cruisers selected randomly all perform poorly (mpg of 20 or below)?

c. Given the poor performance that your group observed with the five test cruisers, what conclusion can you draw about the company's mpg claim?

19. Assume that scores among Asian-Americans on an alienation scale are normally distributed with a mean $\mu = 22$ and a standard deviation $\sigma = 2.5$ (higher scores reflect greater feelings of alienation). Based on this distribution, determine

a. the probability of an Asian-American having an alienation score between 22 and 25.

b. the probability of an Asian-American having an alienation score of 25 or more.

20. Among the parole officers in a particular state, the mean number of sick days per year is $\mu = 3.5$ with a standard deviation $\sigma = 1.2$. Assuming absences among state parole officers are normally distributed, determine

a. the probability that a particular officer missed between 3.5 and 5 days.

b. the probability that a particular officer missed 5 or more days.

c. the probability that three officers all missed 5 or more days.

SAMPLES AND POPULATIONS

- **SAMPLING METHODS**

- **SAMPLING ERROR**

- **SAMPLING DISTRIBUTION OF MEANS**

- **STANDARD ERROR OF THE MEAN**

- **CONFIDENCE INTERVALS**

- **THE *t* DISTRIBUTION**

- **ESTIMATING PROPORTIONS**

- **SUMMARY**

- **TERMS TO REMEMBER**

- **STEP-BY-STEP STUDY GUIDE: CONFIDENCE INTERVAL FOR THE MEAN USING *z***

- **STEP-BY-STEP STUDY GUIDE: CONFIDENCE INTERVAL FOR THE MEAN USING *t***

- **STEP-BY-STEP STUDY GUIDE: CONFIDENCE INTERVAL FOR THE PROPORTION**

- **PROBLEMS**

Criminologists and criminal justice researchers generally seek to draw conclusions about large numbers of individuals. For instance, he or she might be interested in the 280 million inhabitants of the United States, 1,000 members of a particular police union, the 10,000 African-Americans who are living in a southern town, or the 45,000 individuals under probation supervision in a particular state.

Until this point, we have been pretending that the researcher investigates the entire group that he or she tries to understand. Known as a *population* or *universe,* this group consists of a set of individuals who share at least one characteristic, whether common citizenship, membership in a police union, ethnicity, or the like. Thus we might speak about the population of the United States, the population of police union members, the population of African-Americans residing in a particular town, or the population of people with drunk driving convictions.

Because criminal justice researchers operate with limited time, energy, and economic resources, they rarely study each and every member of a given population. Instead, researchers study only a *sample*—a smaller number of individuals from the population. Through the sampling process, researchers seek to generalize from a sample (a small group) to the entire population from which it was taken (a larger group).

In recent years, for example, sampling techniques have allowed political pollsters to make fairly accurate predictions of election results based on samples of only a few hundred registered voters. For this reason, candidates for major political offices routinely monitor the effectiveness of their campaign strategy by examining sample surveys of voter opinion.

Sampling is an integral part of everyday life. How else would we gain much information about other people than by sampling those around us? For example, we might casually discuss political issues with other students to find out where students generally stand with respect to their political opinions; we might attempt to determine how our classmates are studying for a particular examination by contacting only a few members of the class beforehand; we might even invest in the stock market after finding that a small sample of our associates have made money through investments.

SAMPLING METHODS

The criminal justice researcher's methods of sampling are usually more thoughtful and scientific than those of everyday life. He or she is primarily concerned with whether sample members are representative enough of the entire population to permit making accurate generalizations about that population. In order to make such inferences, the researcher selects an appropriate sampling method according to whether or not each and every member of the population has an equal chance of being drawn into the sample. If every population member is given an equal chance of sample selection, a *random* sampling method is being used; otherwise, a *nonrandom* type is employed.

NONRANDOM SAMPLES

The most popular nonrandom sampling method, *accidental* or convenience sampling, differs least from our everyday sampling procedures, because it is based exclusively on what is convenient for the researcher. That is, the researcher simply includes the most convenient cases in his or her sample and excludes the inconvenient cases. Most students can recall at least a few instances when an instructor, who was doing research, has asked all students in the class to take part in an experiment or to fill out a questionnaire. The popularity of this form of accidental sampling in psychology has provoked some observers to view psychology as "the science of the college sophomore," because so many college students are the subjects for research.

A new form of accidental sampling makes use of the telephone's "900" numbers to solicit public opinion on a wide variety of issues, both trivial and serious. Most of the time, these polls are presented with a disclaimer about their unscientific basis. Clearly, it is difficult to generalize from a sample of volunteer respondents who have paid to register their point of view (sometimes more than once).

Another nonrandom type is *quota* sampling. In this sampling procedure, diverse characteristics of a population, such as age, gender, social class, or ethnicity, are sampled in the proportions that they occupy in the population. Suppose, for instance, that we were asked to draw a quota sample from the employees at a large federal criminal justice agency, where 42% were females and 58% were males. Using this method, interviewers were given a quota of employees to locate, so that 42% of the sample was female and 58% was male. The same percentages are included in the sample as are represented in the population from which the sample was drawn. If the total sample size is 200, then 84 female employees and 116 male employees are selected. Although gender may be properly represented in this sample, other characteristics such as age or race may not be. The inadequacy of quota sampling is precisely its lack of control over factors other than those set by quota.

A third variety of nonrandom sample is known as *judgment* or *purposive* sampling. In this type of sampling, logic, common sense, or sound judgment can be used to select a sample that is representative of a larger population. For instance, to draw a judgment sample of magazines that reflect middle-class values, we might, on an intuitive level, select *Reader's Digest, People,* or *Parade,* because articles from these titles *seem* to depict what most middle-class Americans desire (for example, the fulfillment of the American dream, economic success, and the like). In a similar way, those state districts that have traditionally voted for the winning candidates for state office might be polled in an effort to predict the outcome of a current state election.

RANDOM SAMPLES

As previously noted, random sampling gives each and every member of the population an equal chance of being selected for the sample.[1] This characteristic of random sampling indicates that every member of the population must be identified before the random sample is drawn, a requirement usually fulfilled by obtaining a list that includes every population member. A little thought will suggest that getting such a complete list of the population members is not always an easy task, especially if one is studying a large and diverse population. To take a relatively easy example, where could we get a *complete* list of students currently enrolled in a large university? Those researchers who have tried will attest to its difficulty. For a more laborious assignment, try finding a list of every resident in a large city. How can we be certain of identifying everyone, even those residents who do not wish to be identified?

The basic type of random sample, *simple random* sampling, can be obtained by a process not unlike that of the now familiar technique of putting everyone's name on separate slips of paper and, while blindfolded, drawing only a few names from a hat. This procedure ideally gives every population member an equal chance for sample selection since one, and only one, slip per person is included. For several reasons (including the fact that researchers would need an extremely large hat), researchers attempting to take a random sample usually do not draw names from a hat. Instead, they use a *table of random numbers* such as Table H in Appendix C. A portion of a table of random numbers is reproduced here:

		Column number																				
		1	2	3	4	5	6	7	8	9	10	11	12	13	14	15	16	17	18	19	20
Row number	1	2	3	1	5	7	5	4	8	5	9	0	1	8	3	7	2	5	9	9	3
	2	6	2	4	9	7	0	8	8	6	9	5	2	3	0	3	6	7	4	4	0
	3	0	4	5	5	5	0	4	3	1	0	5	3	7	4	3	5	0	8	9	0
	4	1	1	8	3	7	4	4	1	0	9	6	2	2	1	3	4	3	1	4	8
	5	1	6	0	3	5	0	3	2	4	0	4	3	6	2	2	2	3	5	0	0

A table of random numbers is constructed so as to generate a series of numbers having no particular pattern or order. As a result, the process of using a table of random numbers yields a representative sample similar to that produced by putting slips of paper in a hat and drawing names while blindfolded.

---

[1] Sometimes certain groups in a population are oversampled by giving their members a larger chance of selection. This inequality is compensated for in data analysis, however, and the sample is still considered random.

To draw a simple random sample by means of a table of random numbers, the criminal justice researcher first obtains a list of the population and assigns a unique identifying number to each member. For instance, if she is conducting research on the 500 students enrolled in Introduction to Criminology, she might secure a list of students from the instructor and give each student a number from 001 to 500. Having prepared the list, she proceeds to draw the members of her sample from a table of random numbers. Let us say the researcher seeks to draw a sample of 50 students to represent the 500 members of a class population. She might enter the random numbers table at any number (with eyes closed, for example) and move in any direction, taking appropriate numbers until she has selected the 50 sample members. Looking at the earlier portion of the random numbers table, we might arbitrarily start at the intersection of column 1 and row 3, moving from left to right to take every number that comes up between 001 and 500. The first numbers to appear at column 1 and row 3 are 0, 4, and 5. Therefore, student number 045 is the first population member chosen for the sample. Continuing from left to right, we see that 4, 3, and 1 come up next, so that student number 431 is selected. This process is continued until all 50 sample members have been taken. A note to the student: In using the table of random numbers, always disregard numbers that come up a second time or are higher than needed.

All random sample methods are actually variations of the simple random sampling procedure just illustrated. For instance, with *systematic* sampling, a table of random numbers is not required, because a list of population members is sampled by fixed intervals. By employing systematic sampling, then, every *n*th member of a population is included in a sample of that population. To illustrate, in drawing a sample from the population of 10,000 public housing tenants, we might arrange a list of tenants, then beginning at a random place, take every tenth name on the list, and come up with a sample of 1,000 tenants.

The advantage of systematic sampling is that a table of random numbers is not required. As a result, this method is less time-consuming than the simple random procedure, especially for sampling from large populations. On the negative side, taking a systematic sample assumes that position on a list of population members does not influence randomness. If this assumption is not taken seriously, the result may be to overselect certain population members, while underselecting others. This can happen, for instance, when houses are systematically sampled from a list in which corner houses (which are generally more expensive than other houses on the block) occupy a fixed position, or when the names in a telephone directory are sampled by fixed intervals so that names associated with certain ethnic ties are underselected.

Another variation on simple random sampling, the *stratified* sample, involves dividing the population into more homogeneous subgroups or *strata* from which simple random samples are then taken. Suppose, for instance, we wish to study the acceptance of capital punishment among the population of a certain city. Because attitudes toward capital punishment vary by religion and socioeconomic status, we might stratify our population on these variables, thereby forming more homogeneous subgroups with respect to acceptance of capital punishment. More specifically, say, we could identify Catholics, Protestants, and Jews as well as upper-class, middle-class, and lower-class members of the population. Our stratification procedure might yield the following subgroups or strata:

upper-class Protestants

middle-class Protestants

lower-class Protestants

upper-class Catholics

middle-class Catholics

lower-class Catholics

upper-class Jews

middle-class Jews

lower-class Jews

Having identified our strata, we proceed to take a simple random sample from each subgroup or stratum (for example, from lower-class Protestants, from middle-class Catholics, and so on), until we have sampled the entire population. That is, each stratum is treated for sampling purposes as a complete population, and simple random sampling is applied. Specifically, each member of a stratum is given an identifying number, listed, and sampled by means of a table of random numbers. As a final step in the procedure, the selected members of each subgroup or stratum are combined in order to produce a sample of the entire population.

Stratification is based on the idea that a homogeneous group requires a smaller sample than does a heterogeneous group. For instance, studying individuals who are walking on a downtown street probably requires a larger sample than studying individuals living in a middle-class suburb. One can usually find individuals walking downtown who have any combination of characteristics. By contrast, persons living in a middle-class suburb are generally more alike with respect to education, income, political orientation, family size, and attitude toward work, to mention only a few characteristics.

On the surface, stratified random samples bear a striking resemblance to the nonrandom quota method previously discussed, because both procedures usually require the inclusion of sample characteristics in the exact proportions that they contribute to the population. Therefore, if 32% of our population is made up of middle-class Protestants, then exactly 32% of our sample must be drawn from middle-class Protestants; in the same way, if 11% of our population consists of lower-class Jews, then 11% of our sample must be similarly constituted, and so on. In the context of stratified sampling, an exception arises when a particular stratum is disproportionately well represented in the sample, making possible a more intensive subanalysis of that group. Such an occasion might arise, for example, when African-Americans, who constitute a small proportion of a given population, are oversampled in an effort to examine their characteristics more closely.

Despite their surface similarities, quota and stratified samples are essentially different. Whereas members of quota samples are taken by whatever method is chosen by the investigator, members of stratified samples are always selected on a *random* basis, generally by means of a table of random numbers applied to a complete list of the population members.

Before leaving the topic of sampling methods, let us examine the nature of an especially popular form of random sampling known as the *cluster* or *multistage* sampling method. Such samplings are frequently used to minimize the costs of large surveys, which require interviewers to travel to many scattered localities. Employing the cluster method, at least two levels of sampling are put into operation:

1. The *primary sampling unit* or cluster, which is a well-delineated area that includes characteristics found in the entire population (for example, a city, census tract, city block, and so on)
2. The sample members within each cluster

For illustrative purposes, imagine that we wanted to interview a representative sample of individuals living in a large area of the city. Drawing a simple random, systematic, or stratified sample of respondents scattered over a wide area would entail a good deal of traveling, not to mention time and money. By means of multistage sampling, however, we would limit our interviewing to those individuals who are located within relatively few clusters. We might begin, for example, by treating the city block as our primary sampling unit or cluster. We might proceed, then, by obtaining a list of all city blocks within the area, from which we take a simple random sample of blocks. Having drawn our sample of city blocks, we might select the individual respondents (or households) on each block by the same simple random method. More specifically, all individuals (or households) on each of the selected blocks are listed and, with the help of a table of random numbers, a sample of respondents from each block is chosen. Using the cluster method, any given interviewer locates one of the selected city blocks and contacts more than one respondent who lives there.

On a much wider scale, the same cluster procedure can be applied to nationwide surveys by treating counties or cities as the primary sampling units initially selected and by interviewing a simple random sample of each of the chosen counties or cities. In this way, interviewers need not cover each and every county or city, but only a much smaller number of such areas that have been randomly selected for inclusion.

SAMPLING ERROR

Throughout the remainder of the text, we will be careful to distinguish between the characteristics of the samples we study and populations to which we hope to generalize. To make this distinction in our statistical procedures, we can therefore no longer use the same symbols to signify the mean and the standard deviation of both sample and population. Instead, we must employ different symbols, depending on whether we are referring to sample or population characteristics. We will always symbolize the mean of a *sample* as $\overline{X}$ and the mean of a *population* as μ. The standard deviation of a *sample* will be symbolized as s and the standard deviation of its *population* as σ. Because population distributions are rarely ever observed in full, just as with probability distributions, it is little wonder we use the symbols μ and σ for both the population and the probability distributions.

The criminal justice researcher typically tries to obtain a sample that is representative of the larger population in which he or she has an interest. Because random samples give every population member the same chance for sample selection, they are in the long run more representative of population characteristics than unscientific methods. As discussed briefly in Chapter 1, however, by chance alone, we can *always* expect some difference between a sample, random or otherwise, and the population from which it is drawn. A sample mean ($\overline{X}$) will almost never be exactly the same as the population mean (μ); a sample standard deviation (s) will hardly ever be exactly the same as the population standard deviation (σ). Known as *sampling error,* this difference results regardless of how well the sampling plan has been designed and carried out, under the researcher's best intentions, in which no cheating occurs and no mistakes have been made.

Even though the term *sampling error* may seem strange, you are probably more familiar with the concept than you realize. Recall that election polls, for example, typically generalize from a relatively small sample to the entire population of voters. When reporting the results, pollsters generally provide a margin of error. You might read that the Gallup or Roper organization predicts that candidate X will receive 56% of the vote, with a ±4% margin of error. In other words, the pollsters feel confident that somewhere between 52% (56% − 4%) and 60% (56% + 4%) of the vote will go candidate X's way. *Why can't they simply say that the vote will be precisely 56%?* The reason for the pollsters' uncertainty about the exact vote is because of the effect of sampling error. By the time you finish this chapter, not only will you understand this effect, but you will also be able to calculate the margin of error involved when you generalize from a sample to a population.

Table 6.1 illustrates the operation of sampling error. The table contains the population of 20 final examination grades and three samples A, B, and C drawn at random from this population (each taken with the aid of a table of random numbers). As expected, there are differences among the sample means, and none of them equals the population mean ($\mu = 71.55$).

SAMPLING DISTRIBUTION OF MEANS

Given the presence of sampling error, the student may wonder how it is possible *ever* to generalize from a sample to a larger population. To come up with a reasonable answer, let us consider the work of a hypothetical criminologist studying public interest in televised news coverage of criminal trials. This criminologist was afforded an interesting research opportunity during the O.J. Simpson trial. A television news programming director commissioned this person to examine the extent of the public's viewing of prime-time news coverage during the night the verdict was announced. Rather than attempt to study the millions of U.S. residents whose households contain television, he selected 200 such individuals at random from the entire population. The criminologist interviewed each of the 200 individuals and asked them how many minutes they viewed television news coverage of the O.J. Simpson

TABLE 6.1   A POPULATION AND THREE RANDOM SAMPLES OF FINAL EXAMINATION GRADES

Population			Sample A	Sample B	Sample C
70	80	93	96	40	72
86	85	90	99	86	96
56	52	67	56	56	49
40	78	57	52	67	56
89	49	48	303	249	273
99	72	30			
96	94	1,431	$\overline{X} = 75.75$	$\overline{X} = 62.25$	$\overline{X} = 68.25$
	$\mu = 71.55$				

criminal trial between 7 and 11 pm the night the verdict was revealed. He found that in his sample of 200 randomly selected individuals, the minutes viewing O.J. Simpson trial coverage during this four-hour time period ranged from 0 to 240 minutes, with a mean of 101.5 minutes (see Figure 6.1).

It turns out that this hypothetical criminologist is mildly eccentric. He has a notable fondness—or rather, compulsion—for drawing samples from populations. So intense is his enthusiasm for sampling that he continues to draw many additional 200-person samples and to calculate the average (mean) time spent viewing O.J. Simpson criminal trial verdict coverage for the people in each of these samples. Our eccentric criminologist continues this procedure until he has drawn 100 samples containing 200 people *each*. In the process of drawing 100 random samples, he actually studies 20,000 people (200 × 100 = 20,000).

Let us assume, as shown in Figure 6.2, that among the entire population of individuals in America, the average (mean) viewing of the O.J. Simpson trial news broadcasts is 99.75 minutes. Also as illustrated in Figure 6.2, let us suppose that the samples taken by our eccentric researcher yield means that range between 92 and 109 minutes. In line with our previous discussion, this could easily happen simply on the basis of sampling error.

Frequency distributions of *raw scores* can be obtained from both samples and populations. In a similar way, we can construct a *sampling distribution of means,* a frequency distribution of a large number of random sample *means* that have been drawn from the same population. Table 6.2 presents the 100 sample means collected by our eccentric researcher in the form of a sampling distribution. As when working with a distribution of raw scores, the means in Table 6.2 have been arranged in consecutive order from high to low and their frequency of occurrence indicated in an adjacent column.

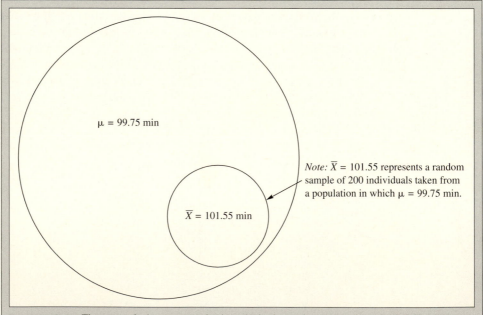

FIGURE 6.1 The mean of minutes spent viewing televised news broadcasts about the O.J. Simpson criminal trial verdict for a random sample selected from the hypothetical population

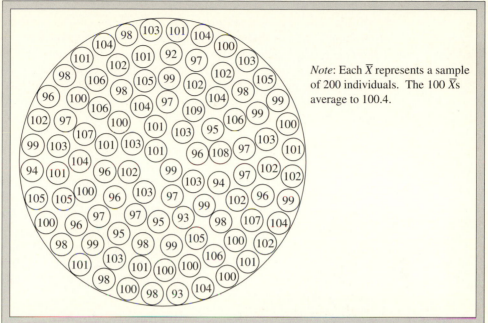

Note: Each $\overline{X}$ represents a sample of 200 individuals. The 100 $\overline{X}$s average to 100.4.

FIGURE 6.2   The mean of minutes spent viewing televised news broadcasts about the O.J. Simpson criminal trial verdict for 100 random samples selected from a hypothetical population in which $\mu = 99.75$ minutes

TABLE 6.2   OBSERVED SAMPLING DISTRIBUTION OF MEANS (TELEVISED NEWS VIEWING TIME) FOR 100 SAMPLES

Mean	f	
109	1	
108	1	
107	2	
106	4	
105	5	
104	7	
103	9	
102	9	
101	11	
100	11	Mean of 100 sample means = 100
99	9	
98	9	
97	8	
96	6	
95	3	
94	2	
93	2	
92	1	
	$N = 100$	

CHARACTERISTICS OF A SAMPLING DISTRIBUTION OF MEANS

Until this point, we have not directly come to grips with the problem of generalizing from samples to populations. The theoretical model known as the *sampling distribution of means* (approximated by the 100 sample means obtained by our eccentric criminologist) has certain properties, which give to it an important role in the sampling process. Before moving on to the procedure for making generalizations from samples to populations, we must first examine the characteristics of a sampling distribution of means:

1. *The sampling distribution of means approximates a normal curve.* This is true of all sampling distributions of means regardless of the shape of the distribution of raw scores in the population from which the means are drawn, as long as the sample size is reasonably large (over 30). If the raw data are normally distributed to begin with, then the distribution of sample means is normal regardless of sample size.
2. *The mean of a sampling distribution of means (the mean of means) is equal to the true population mean.* If we take a large number of random sample means from the same population and find the mean of all sample means, we will have the value of the true population mean. Therefore, the mean of the sampling distribution of means is the same as the mean of the population from which it was drawn. They can be regarded as interchangeable values.
3. *The standard deviation of a sampling distribution of means is smaller than the standard deviation of the population.* The sample mean is more stable than the scores that comprise it.

This last characteristic of a sampling distribution of means is at the core of our ability to make reliable inferences from samples to populations. As a concrete example from everyday life, consider how you might compensate for a digital bathroom scale that tends to give you different readings of your weight, even when you immediately step back on it. Obviously, your actual weight doesn't change, but the scale says otherwise. More likely, the scale is very sensitive to where your feet are placed or how your body is postured. The best approach to determining your weight, therefore, might be to weigh yourself four times and take the mean. Remember, the mean weight will be more reliable than any of the individual readings that go into it.

Let's now return to the eccentric criminologist and his interest in people's viewing of televised news broadcasts about the O.J. Simpson criminal trial verdict. As illustrated in Figure 6.3, the variability of a sampling distribution is always smaller than the variability in either the entire population or any one sample. Figure 6.3(a) shows the population distribution of viewing time with a mean (μ) of 99.75 (ordinarily we would not have this information). The distribution is skewed to the right: More people spent less than the mean of 99.75 minutes viewing news coverage of the O.J. Simpson trial on this particular night, but a few in the right tail of the distribution seemed unable to tear themselves away for even a moment. Figure 6.3(b) shows the distribution of viewing time within one particular sample of 200 individuals. Note that it is similar in shape and somewhat close in mean ($\overline{X} = 102$) to the population distribution. Figure 6.3(c) shows the sampling distribution of means (the means from our eccentric researcher's 100 samples). It appears fairly normal rather than skewed, has a mean (100.4) almost equal to the population mean, and has far less variabil-

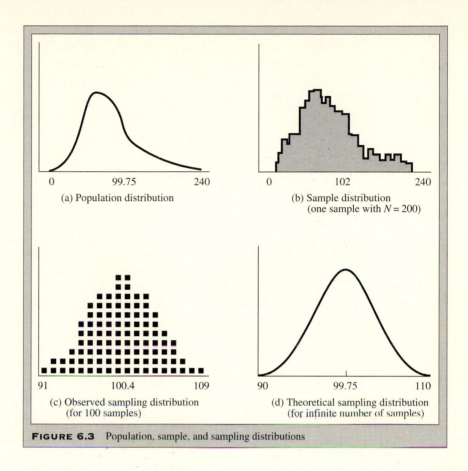

FIGURE 6.3   Population, sample, and sampling distributions

ity than either the population distribution in (a) or the sample distribution in (b), which can be seen by comparing the base-line values. Had the eccentric criminologist continued forever to take samples of 200 individuals, a graph of the means of these samples would look like a normal curve, as in Figure 6.3(d). This is the true sampling distribution.

Let's think about the diminished variability of a sampling distribution in another way. In the population, there are some individuals who spent little time watching the trial coverage, for less than 30 minutes, for example. How likely would it be to get a sample of 200 individuals with a mean of under 30 minutes? Given that $\mu = 99.75$, it would be virtually impossible. We would have to obtain by random draw a huge number of O.J. trialphobics and very few O.J. trialaholics. The laws of chance make it highly unlikely that this would occur.

THE SAMPLING DISTRIBUTION OF MEANS AS A NORMAL CURVE

As indicated in Chapter 5, if we define probability in terms of the likelihood of occurrence, then the normal curve can be regarded as a probability distribution (we can say that probability decreases as we travel along the base line away from the mean in either direction).

With this notion, we can find the probability of obtaining various raw scores in a distribution, given a certain mean and standard deviation. For instance, to find the probability associated with obtaining an annual income between $14,000 and $16,000 in a population having a mean income of $14,000 and a standard deviation of $1,500, we translate the raw score $16,000 into a *z* score (+1.33) and go to Table A in Appendix C to get the percent of the distribution falling between the *z* score 1.33 and the mean. This area contains 40.82% of the raw scores. Thus, *P* = .41 rounded off that we will find an individual whose annual income lies between $14,000 and $16,000. If we want the probability of finding someone whose income is $16,000 or more, we must go to column c of Table A, which subtracts the percent obtained in column b of Table A, from 50%—that percentage of the area that lies on either side of the mean. From column c of Table A, we learn that 9.18% falls at or beyond $16,000. Therefore, moving the decimal two places to the left, we can say *P* = .09 (9 chances in 100) that we would find an individual whose income is $16,000 or greater.

In the present context, we are no longer interested in obtaining probabilities associated with a distribution of *raw scores*. Instead, we find ourselves working with a distribution of *sample means,* which have been drawn from the total population of scores, and we wish to make probability statements about those sample means.

As illustrated in Figure 6.4, because the sampling distribution of means takes the form of the normal curve, we can say that probability decreases as we move farther away from the mean of means (true population mean). This makes sense because the sampling distribution is a product of chance differences among sample means (sampling error). For this reason, we would expect by chance and chance alone that most sample means will fall close to the value of the true population mean, and relatively few sample means will fall far from it.

It is critical that we distinguish clearly between the standard deviation of raw scores in the population (σ) and the standard deviation of the sampling distribution of sample means. For this reason, we denote the standard deviation of the sampling distribution

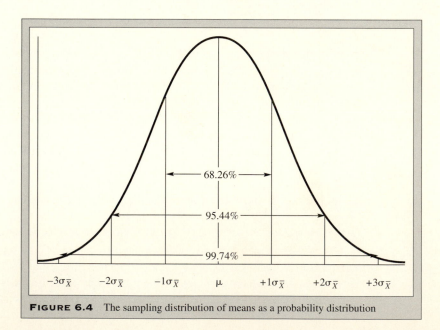

FIGURE 6.4   The sampling distribution of means as a probability distribution

by $\sigma_{\bar{X}}$. The use of the Greek letter σ reminds us that the sampling distribution is an unobserved or theoretical probability distribution, and the subscript $\bar{X}$ signifies that this is the standard deviation among all possible sample means.

Figure 6.4 indicates that about 68% of the sample means in a sampling distribution fall between $-1\sigma_{\bar{X}}$ and $+1\sigma_{\bar{X}}$ from the mean of means (true population mean). In probability terms, we can say that $P = .68$ of any given sample mean falling within this interval. In the same way, we can say the probability is about .95 (95 chances out of 100) that any sample mean falls between $-2\sigma_{\bar{X}}$ and $+2\sigma_{\bar{X}}$ from the mean of means, and so on.

Because the sampling distribution takes the form of the normal curve, we are also able to use z scores and Table A to get the probability of obtaining any sample mean, not just those that are exact multiples of the standard deviation. Given a mean of means (μ) and standard deviation of the sampling distribution ($\sigma_{\bar{X}}$), the process is identical to that used in the previous chapter for a distribution of raw scores. Only the names have been changed.

Imagine, for example, that a certain university claims its recent graduates earn an average (μ) annual income of \$20,000. We have reason to question the legitimacy of this claim and decide to test it out on a random sample of 100 new alumni. In the process, we get a sample mean of only \$18,500. We now ask: How probable is it that we would get a sample mean of \$18,500 or less if the true population mean is actually \$20,000? Has the university told the truth? Or is this only an attempt to propagandize to the public in order to increase enrollments or endowments? Figure 6.5 illustrates the area for which we seek a solution. Because the sample size is fairly large ($N = 100$), the sampling distribution of means is approximately normal, even if the distribution of incomes of the individual alumni is not.

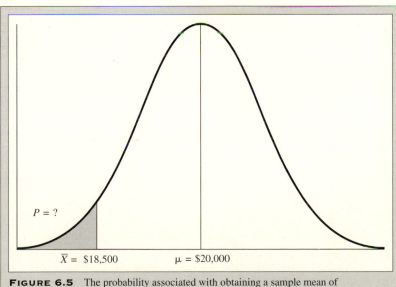

$P = ?$

$\bar{X} = \$18,500$ $\mu = \$20,000$

FIGURE 6.5   The probability associated with obtaining a sample mean of \$18,500 or less if the true population mean is \$20,000 and the standard deviation is \$700

To locate a sample mean in the sampling distribution in terms of the number of standard deviations it falls from the center, we obtain the z score:

$$z = \frac{\overline{X} - \mu}{\sigma_{\overline{X}}}$$

where $\overline{X}$ = sample mean in the distribution
μ = mean of means (equal to the university's claim as to the true population mean)
$\sigma_{\overline{X}}$ = standard deviation of the sampling distribution of means

Suppose we know hypothetically that the standard deviation of the sampling distribution is $700. Following the standard procedure, we translate the sample mean $18,500 into a z score as follows:

$$z = \frac{18,500 - 20,000}{700} = -2.14$$

The result of the previous procedure is to tell us that a sample mean of $18,500 lies exactly 2.14 standard deviations below the claimed true population mean of $20,000. Going to column b of Table A in Appendix C, we see that 48.38% of the sample means fall between $18,500 and $20,000. Column c of Table A gives us the percent of the distribution that represents sample means of $18,500 or less, if the true population mean is $20,000. This figure is 1.62%. Therefore, the probability is .02 rounded off (2 chances out of 100) of getting a sample mean of $18,500 or less, when the true population mean is $20,000. With such a small probability of being wrong, we can say with some confidence that the true population mean is *not* actually $20,000. It is doubtful whether the university's report of alumni annual income represents anything but bad propaganda.

STANDARD ERROR OF THE MEAN

Up until now, we have pretended that the criminal justice researcher actually has first-hand information about the sampling distribution of means. We have acted as though he or she, like the eccentric researcher, really has collected data on a large number of sample means, which were randomly drawn from some population. If so, it would be a simple enough task to make generalizations about the population, because the mean of means takes on a value that is equal to the true population mean.

In actual practice, the criminal justice researcher rarely collects data on more than one or two samples, from which he or she still expects to generalize to an entire population. Drawing a sampling distribution of means requires the same effort as it might take to study each and every population member. As a result, the researcher does not have actual knowledge as to the mean of means or the standard deviation of the sampling distribution. However, the standard deviation of a theoretical sampling distribution (the distribution that would exist in theory if the means of all possible samples were obtained) can be derived. This quantity—known as the *standard error of the mean* ($\sigma_{\overline{X}}$)—is obtained by dividing the population standard deviation by the square root of the sample size. That is,

$$\sigma_{\bar{X}} = \frac{\sigma}{\sqrt{N}}$$

To illustrate, the IQ test is standardized to have a population mean (μ) of 100 and a population standard deviation (σ) of 15. If one were to take a sample size of 10, the sample mean would be subject to a standard error of

$$\sigma_{\bar{X}} = \frac{15}{\sqrt{10}}$$

$$= \frac{15}{3.1623}$$

$$= 4.74$$

Thus, whereas the population of IQ scores has a standard deviation $\sigma = 15$, the sampling distribution of the sample mean for $N = 10$ has a standard error (theoretical standard deviation) $\sigma_{\bar{X}} = 4.74$.

As previously noted, the criminal justice researcher who investigates only one or two samples cannot know the mean of means, the value of which equals the true population mean. He or she only has the obtained sample mean, which differs from the true population mean as the result of sampling error. But have we not come full circle to our original position? How is it possible to estimate the true population mean from a single sample mean, especially in light of such inevitable differences between samples and populations?

We have, in fact, traveled quite some distance from our original position. Having discussed the nature of the sampling distribution of means, we are now prepared to estimate the value of a population mean. With the aid of the standard error of the mean, we can find *the range of mean values within which our true population mean is likely to fall. We can also estimate the probability that our population mean actually falls within that range of mean values.* This is the concept of the *confidence interval.*

CONFIDENCE INTERVALS

In order to explore the procedure for finding a *confidence interval,* let us continue with the case of IQ scores. Suppose that the dean of a certain law school wants to estimate the mean IQ of her student body without having to go through the time and expense of administering tests to all 1,000 students. Instead, she selects 25 students at random and gives them the test. She finds that the mean for her sample is 105. She also realizes that because this value of $\bar{X}$ comes from a sample rather than the entire population of students, she cannot be sure that $\bar{X}$ is actually reflective of the student population. As we have already seen, after all, sampling error is the inevitable product of only taking a portion of the population.

We do know, however, that 68.26% of all random sample means in the sampling distribution of means will fall between -1 and standard error and $+1$ standard error from the true population mean. In our case (with IQ scores for which $\sigma = 15$), we have a standard error of

$$\sigma_{\overline{X}} = \frac{\sigma}{\sqrt{N}}$$

$$= \frac{15}{\sqrt{25}}$$

$$= \frac{15}{5}$$

$$= 3$$

Therefore, using 105 as an *estimate* of the mean for all students (an estimate of the true population mean), we can establish a range within which there are 68 chances out of 100 (rounded off) that the true population mean will fall. Known as the *68% confidence interval,* this range of mean IQs is graphically illustrated in Figure 6.6.

The 68% confidence interval can be obtained in the following manner:

$$68\% \text{ confidence interval} = \overline{X} \pm \sigma_{\overline{X}}$$

where $\overline{X}$ = sample mean
$\sigma_{\overline{X}}$ = standard error of the sample mean

By applying this formula to the problem at hand,

$$68\% \text{ confidence interval} = 105 \pm 3$$

$$= 102 \text{ to } 108$$

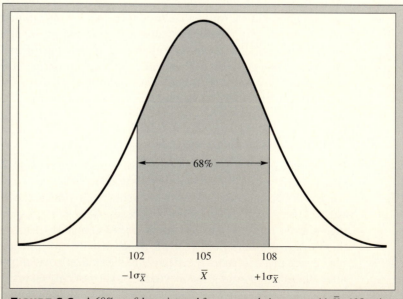

FIGURE 6.6   A 68% confidence interval for true population mean with $\overline{X} = 105$ and $\sigma_{\overline{X}} = 3$

The dean can therefore conclude with 68% confidence that the mean IQ for the entire school (μ) is 105, give or take 3. In other words, there are 68 chances out of 100 ($P = .68$) that the true population mean lies within the range 102 to 108. This estimate is made despite sampling error, but with a ±3 margin of error and at a specified probability level (68%), known as the *level of confidence.*

Confidence intervals can technically be constructed for any level of probability. Criminal justice researchers are not confident enough to estimate a population mean knowing there are only 68 chances out of 100 of being correct (68 out of every 100 sample means fall within the interval between 102 and 108). As a result, it has become a matter of convention to use a *wider,* less precise confidence interval having a *better probability* of making an accurate or true estimate of the population mean. Such a standard is found in the *95% confidence interval,* whereby the population mean is estimated, knowing there are 95 chances out of 100 of being right; there are 5 chances out of 100 of being wrong (95 out of every 100 sample means fall within the interval). Even when using the 95% confidence interval, however, it must always be kept firmly in mind that the researcher's sample mean could be one of those five sample means that fall outside of the established interval. In statistical decision making, one never knows for certain.

How do we go about finding the 95% confidence interval? We already know that 95.44% of the sample means in a sampling distribution lie between $-2\sigma_{\bar{X}}$ and $+2\sigma_{\bar{X}}$ from the mean of means. Going to Table A, we can make the statement that 1.96 standard errors in both directions cover exactly 95% of the sample means (47.50% on either side of the mean of means). In order to find the 95% confidence interval, we must first multiply the standard error of the mean by 1.96 (the interval is 1.96 units of $\sigma_{\bar{X}}$ in either direction from the mean). Therefore,

$$95\% \text{ confidence interval} = \bar{X} \pm 1.96\sigma_{\bar{X}}$$

where $\bar{X}$ = sample mean
$\sigma_{\bar{X}}$ = standard error of the sample mean

If we apply the 95% confidence interval to our estimate of the mean IQ of a student body, we see

$$95\% \text{ confidence interval} = 105 \pm (1.96)(3)$$
$$= 105 \pm 5.88$$
$$= 99.12 \text{ to } 110.88$$

Therefore, the dean can be 95% confident that the population mean lies in the interval 99.12 to 110.88. Note that if asked whether her students are above the norm in IQ (the norm is 100), she could not quite conclude that to be the case with 95% confidence. This is because the true population mean of 100 is within the 95% realm of possibilities based on these results. However, given the 68% confidence interval (102 to 108), the dean could assert with 68% confidence that students at her school average above the norm in IQ.

An even more stringent confidence interval is the *99% confidence interval.* From Table A in Appendix C, we see that the z score 2.58 represents 49.50% of the area on either side of the curve. Doubling this amount yields 99% of the area under the curve; 99% of the sample means fall into that interval. In probability terms, 99 out of every 100 sample means fall between $-2.58\sigma_{\bar{X}}$ and $+2.58\sigma_{\bar{X}}$ from the mean. Conversely, only 1 out of every 100 means falls outside of the interval. By formula,

$$99\% \text{ confidence interval} = \bar{X} \pm 2.58\sigma_{\bar{X}}$$

where $\bar{X}$ = sample mean
$\sigma_{\bar{X}}$ = standard error of the sample mean

With regard to estimating the mean IQ for the population of students,

$$99\% \text{ confidence interval} = 105 \pm (2.58)(3)$$
$$= 105 \pm 7.74$$
$$= 97.26 \text{ to } 112.74$$

Consequently, based on the sample of 25 students, the dean can infer with 99% confidence that the mean IQ for the entire school is between 97.26 and 112.74.

Note that the 99% confidence interval consists of a wider band (97.26 to 112.74) than does the 95% confidence interval (99.12 to 110.88). The 99% interval encompasses more of the total area under the normal curve and therefore a larger number of sample means. This wider band of mean scores gives us greater confidence that we have accurately estimated the true population mean. Only a single sample mean in every 100 lies outside of the interval. On the other hand, by increasing our level of confidence from 95% to 99%, we have also sacrificed a degree of precision in pinpointing the population mean. Holding sample size constant, the social researcher must choose between greater precision or greater confidence that he or she is correct.

The precision of an estimate is determined by the *margin of error,* obtained by multiplying the standard error by the z score representing a desired level of confidence. This is the extent to which the sample mean is expected to vary from the population mean due to sampling error alone.

Figure 6.7 compares confidence intervals for the 68%, the 95%, and the 99% levels of confidence. The greater the level of confidence that the interval includes the true population mean, the larger the z score, the larger the margin of error, and the wider the confidence interval.

STEP-BY-STEP ILLUSTRATION
95% CONFIDENCE INTERVAL USING Z

Let's summarize the method for finding the 95% confidence interval using a step-by-step illustration. Suppose that a certain automobile company wishes to determine the expected miles per gallon for one of its new police cruisers. Based on years of experi-

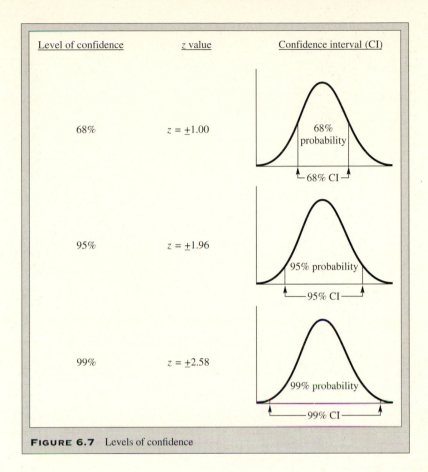

Level of confidence	z value	Confidence interval (CI)
68%	$z = \pm1.00$	68% probability / 68% CI
95%	$z = \pm1.96$	95% probability / 95% CI
99%	$z = \pm2.58$	99% probability / 99% CI

FIGURE 6.7   Levels of confidence

ence with cruisers, the company statistician realizes that not all are equal, and that a standard deviation of 4 miles per gallon ($\sigma = 4$) is to be expected due to variations in parts and workmanship. In order to estimate the mean miles per gallon for the new model, he test runs a random sample of 100 cruisers off the assembly line and obtains a sample mean of 26 miles per gallon.

We follow these steps for obtaining a 95% confidence interval for the mean miles per gallon for all cruisers of this model.

STEP 1   Obtain the mean for a random sample (in this problem, it is given).

$$N = 100, \qquad \bar{X} = 26$$

STEP 2   Calculate the standard error of the mean.

$$\sigma_{\bar{X}} = \frac{\sigma}{\sqrt{N}}$$

$$= \frac{4}{\sqrt{100}}$$

$$= \frac{4}{10}$$

$$= .4$$

STEP 3   Compute the margin of error by multiplying the standard error of the mean by 1.96, the value of z for a 95% confidence interval.

$$\text{Margin of error} = 1.96\sigma_{\bar{X}}$$

$$= (1.96)(.4)$$

$$= .78$$

STEP 4   Add and subtract the margin of error from the sample mean to find the range of mean scores within which the population mean is expected, with 95% confidence, to fall.

$$95\% \text{ confidence interval} = \bar{X} \pm 1.96\sigma_{\bar{X}}$$

$$= 26 \pm .78$$

$$= 25.22 \text{ to } 26.78$$

Thus, the statistician can be 95% confident that the true mean miles per gallon for this model (μ) is between 25.22 and 26.78.

STEP-BY-STEP ILLUSTRATION
99% CONFIDENCE INTERVAL USING z

Reporting these data to his superiors, the statistician is informed that 95% confidence is not confident enough for their needs. To be 99% confident, the statistician need not collect more data but only perform some additional calculations for a 99% confidence interval using a different value of z.

STEP 1   Obtain the mean for a random sample (this is the same as with the 95% confidence interval).

$$N = 100, \qquad \bar{X} = 26$$

STEP 2   Calculate the standard error of the mean (this is the same as with the 95% confidence interval).

$$\sigma_{\bar{X}} = \frac{\sigma}{\sqrt{N}}$$

$$= \frac{4}{\sqrt{100}}$$

$$= \frac{4}{10}$$

$$= .4$$

STEP 3   Compute the margin of error by multiplying the standard error of the mean by 2.58, the value of z for a 99% confidence interval (we begin to see a change from the 95% confidence interval).

$$\text{Margin of error} = 2.58\sigma_{\bar{X}}$$

$$= (2.58)(.4)$$

$$= 1.03$$

STEP 4 Add and subtract the margin of error from the sample mean to find the range of mean scores within which the population mean is expected, with 99% confidence, to fall.

$$99\% \text{ confidence interval} = \bar{X} \pm 2.58\sigma_{\bar{X}}$$

$$= 26 \pm 1.03$$

$$= 24.97 \; to \; 27.03$$

Thus, the statistician is 99% confident that the true mean miles per gallon for this model (μ) is between 24.97 and 27.03. Reporting this with 99% certainty to his superiors, they complain that the interval is now wider than it was before and that the estimate is less precise. He explains to them that the greater the level of confidence, the larger the interval, so that 99% of the possible sample means are encompassed rather than just 95%. They are still not pleased, so the statistician decides to go back and increase the sample size, which will decrease the standard error and, as a result, will narrow the confidence intervals.

THE *t* DISTRIBUTION

Thus far, we have only dealt with situations in which the standard error of the mean was known or could be calculated from the population standard deviation by the formula

$$\sigma_{\bar{X}} = \frac{\sigma}{\sqrt{N}}$$

If you think about it realistically, it makes little sense that we would know the standard deviation of our variable in the population (σ) but not know and need to estimate the population mean (μ). Indeed, there are very few cases when the population standard deviation (and thus the standard error of the mean $\sigma_{\bar{X}}$) is known. In certain areas of education and psychology, the standard deviations for standardized scales such as the SAT and IQ scores are determined by design of the test. Usually, however, we need to estimate not only the population mean from a sample but also the standard error from the same sample.

To obtain an *estimate* of the standard error of the mean, one might be tempted simply to substitute the sample standard deviation (s) for the population standard deviation (σ) in the previous standard error formula. This, however, would have the tendency to underestimate the size of the true standard error ever so slightly. This problem arises because the sample standard deviation tends to be a bit smaller than the population standard deviation.

Recall from Chapter 3 that the mean is the point of balance within a distribution of scores; the mean is the point in a distribution around which the scores above it perfectly balance with those below it, as in the lever and fulcrum analogy in Figure 3.2. As a result, the sum of squared deviations (and, therefore, the variance and standard deviation) computed around the mean is smaller than from any other point of comparison.

Thus, for a given sample drawn from a population, the sample variance and standard deviation (s^2 and s) are smaller when computed from the sample mean than they would be if one actually knew and used the population mean (μ) in place of the sample mean. In a sense, the sample mean is custom tailored to the sample, whereas the population mean is off the rack; it fits the sample data fairly well but not perfectly like the sample mean does. Thus, the sample variance and the standard deviation are slightly biased estimates (tend to be too small) of the population variance and standard deviation.

It is necessary, therefore, to let out the seam a bit, that is, to inflate the sample variance and standard deviation slightly in order to produce more accurate estimates of the population variance and population standard deviation. To do so, we divide by $N - 1$ rather than N. That is, unbiased estimates of the population variance and the population standard deviation are given by

$$\hat{\sigma}^2 = \frac{\Sigma\,(X - \bar{X})^2}{N - 1}$$

and

$$\hat{\sigma} = \sqrt{\frac{\Sigma\,(X - \bar{X})^2}{N - 1}}$$

The caret over the Greek letter σ indicates that it is an unbiased sample estimate of this population value.[2] Note that in large samples, this correction is trivial (s^2 and s are almost equivalent to $\hat{\sigma}^2$ and $\hat{\sigma}$). This should be the case because in large samples the sample mean tends to be a very reliable (close) estimate of the population mean.

The distinction between the sample variance and standard deviation using the sample size N as the denominator versus the sample estimate of the population variance and standard deviation using $N - 1$ as the denominator may be small computationally but is important theoretically. That is, it makes little difference in terms of the final numerical result whether we divide by N or $N - 1$, especially if the sample size N is fairly large. Still, there are two very different purposes for calculating the variance and standard deviation: (1) to describe the extent of variability within a sample of cases or respondents and (2) to make an inference or generalize about the extent of variability within the larger population of cases from which a sample was drawn. It is likely that an example would be helpful right about now.

Suppose that an elementary school teacher is piloting a new language-based math curriculum that teaches math skills through word problems and logical reasoning rather than through rote memorization of math facts. Just before the end of the school year, she administers a math test to her class of 25 pupils to determine the extent to which they have learned the material using the novel teaching strategy. Her interest lies not only in the average performance of the class (mean score), but also in whether the new approach tends to be easy for some pupils but difficult for others (standard deviation). In fact, she suspects that the curriculum may be a good one, but not for all kinds of learners. She calculates the

---

[2] Alternatively, $\hat{\sigma}^2$ and $\hat{\sigma}$ can be calculated from s^2 and s by multiplying by a bias correction factor, $N/(N - 1)$. Specifically,

$$\hat{\sigma}^2 = s^2\,\frac{N}{N - 1} \qquad \text{and} \qquad \hat{\sigma} = s\,\sqrt{\frac{N}{N - 1}}$$

sample variance (and standard deviation) using the N denominator because her sole interest is in her particular class of pupils. She has no desire to generalize to pupils elsewhere.

As it turns out, this same class of students had been identified by the curriculum design company as a "test case." Because it would not be feasible to assemble a truly random selection of fourth-graders from around the country into the same classroom, this particular class was viewed as "fairly representative" of fourth-graders. The designers' interest extends well beyond the walls of this particular classroom, of course. Their interest is in using this sample of 25 fourth-graders to estimate the central tendency and variability in the overall population (that is, to generalize to all fourth-graders were they to have had this curriculum). The sample mean test score for the class could be used to generalize to the population mean, but the sample variance and standard deviation would have to be adjusted slightly. Specifically, using $N - 1$ in the denominator provides an unbiased or fair estimate of the variability that would exist in the entire population of fourth-graders.

At this point, we have only passing interest in estimating the population standard deviation. Our primary interest here is in estimating the standard error of the mean based on a sample of N scores. The same correction procedure applies, nevertheless. That is, an unbiased estimate of the standard error of the mean is given by replacing σ by s and N by $N - 1$,

$$s_{\bar{X}} = \frac{s}{\sqrt{N - 1}}$$

where s is the sample standard deviation, as obtained in Chapter 4, from a distribution of raw scores or from a frequency distribution. Technically, the unbiased estimate of the standard error should be symbolized by $\hat{\sigma}_{\bar{X}}$ rather than $s_{\bar{X}}$. However, for the sake of simplicity, $s_{\bar{X}}$ can be used without any confusion as the unbiased estimate of the standard error.

One more problem arises when we estimate the standard error of the mean. The sampling distribution of means is no longer quite normal if we do not know the population standard deviation. That is, the ratio

$$\frac{\bar{X} - \mu}{s_{\bar{X}}}$$

with an estimated standard error in the denominator, does not quite follow the z or normal distribution. The fact that we estimate the standard error from sample data adds an extra amount of uncertainty in the distribution of sample means, beyond that which arises due to sampling variability alone. In particular, the sampling distribution of means when we estimate the standard error is a bit wider (more dispersed) than a normal distribution, because of this added source of variability (that is, the uncertainty in estimating the standard error of the mean). The ratio

$$t = \frac{\bar{X} - \mu}{s_{\bar{X}}}$$

follows what is known as the *t* distribution, and thus it is called the *t ratio*. There is actually a whole family of *t* distributions (see Figure 6.8). A concept known as *degrees of freedom* (which we will encounter often in later chapters) is used to determine which of the *t* distributions applies in a particular instance. The degrees of freedom indicate how close the *t* distribution comes to approximating the normal curve.[3] When estimating a population mean, the degrees of freedom are one less than the sample size; that is,

$$df = N - 1$$

The greater the degrees of freedom, the larger the sample size, and the closer the *t* distribution gets to the normal distribution. This makes good sense, because the extent of uncertainty that causes us to use a *t* ratio rather than a *z* score diminishes as the sample size gets larger. In other words, the quality or reliability of our estimate of the standard error of the mean increases as our sample size increases, and so the *t* ratio approaches a *z* score. Recall that the only difference between the *t* ratio and the *z* score is that the former uses an estimate of the standard error based on sample data. We repeat for the sake of emphasis that as the sample size and thus the degrees of freedom increase, the *t* distribution becomes a better approximation of the normal or *z* distribution.

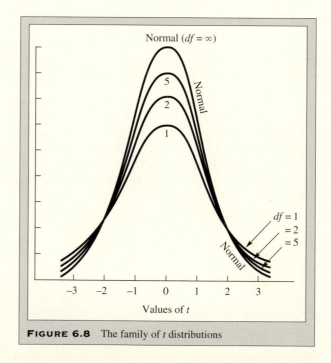

FIGURE 6.8 The family of *t* distributions

[3]Another way to look at the concept of degrees of freedom is a bit more subtle. Degrees of freedom are the number of observations that is free rather than fixed. When calculating the sample variance for use in determining the estimate of the standard error ($s_{\bar{x}}$), we really do not have N free observations. Because the sample mean is an element in calculating the sample standard deviation, this must be considered a fixed quantity. Then once we have all but the last observation ($N - 1$ of them), the last observation is predetermined. For example, for the set of data 2, 3, and 7, we take as given that the mean is 4 when we calculate the sample standard deviation. If someone told you that the mean of three cases was 4 and that two of the cases were 2 and 3, you would then know that the last case had to be 7. This is because for the mean of three observations to be 4, $\Sigma X = 12$.

When dealing with the *t* distribution, we use Table B rather than Table A. Unlike Table A, for which we had to search out values of *z* corresponding to 95% and 99% areas under the curve, Table B is calibrated for special areas. More precisely, Table B is calibrated for various levels of the Greek letter α (alpha). The alpha value represents the area in the tails of the *t* distribution. Thus, the alpha value is *one minus the level of confidence.* That is,

$$\alpha = 1 - \text{level of confidence}$$

For example, for a 95% level of confidence, $\alpha = .05$. For a 99% level of confidence, $\alpha = .01$.

We enter Table B with two pieces of information: (1) the degrees of freedom (which, for estimating a sample mean, is $N - 1$) and (2) the alpha value, the area in the tails of the distribution. For example, if we wanted to construct a 95% confidence interval with a sample size of 20, we would have 19 degrees of freedom (df $= 20 - 1 = 19$), $\alpha = .05$ area combined in the two tails, and, as a result, a *t* value from Table B of 2.093.

What would one do, however, for larger samples for which the degrees of freedom may not appear in Table B? For instance, a sample size of 50 produces 49 degrees of freedom. The *t* value for 49 degrees of freedom and $\alpha = .05$ is somewhere between 2.021 (for 40 df) and 2.000 (for 60 df). Given that these two values of *t* are so close, it makes little practical difference what we decide on for a compromise value. However, to be on the safe side, it is recommended that one go with the more modest degrees of freedom (40) and thus the larger value of *t* (2.021).

The reason *t* is not tabulated for all degrees of freedom over 30 is that they become so close that it would be like splitting hairs. Note that the values of *t* get smaller and tend to converge as the degrees of freedom increase. For example, the *t* values for $\alpha = .05$ begin at 12.706 for 1 df, decrease quickly to just under 3.0 for 4 df, gradually approach a value of 2.000 for 60 df, and finally approach a limit of 1.960 for infinity degrees of freedom (that is, an infinitely large sample). This limit of 1.960 is also the .05 value for *z* we found earlier from Table A. Again, we see that the *t* distribution approaches the *z* or normal distribution as the sample size increases.

Thus, for cases in which the standard error of the mean is estimated, we can construct confidence intervals using an appropriate table value of *t* as follows:

$$\text{confidence interval} = \overline{X} \pm ts_{\overline{X}}$$

STEP-BY-STEP ILLUSTRATION

CONFIDENCE INTERVAL USING *t*

With a step-by-step example, let's see how the use of the *t* distribution translates into constructing confidence intervals. Suppose that a criminal justice researcher wanted to examine the number of security cameras in the stores of a large shopping mall. He selected a random sample of 10 stores and counted the number of security cameras in each store:

X	X_1
1	1
5	2
2	2
3	4
4	3

STEP 1   Find the mean of the sample.

$$
\begin{array}{c}
X \\
\hline
1 \\
5 \\
2 \\
3 \\
4 \\
1 \\
2 \\
2 \\
4 \\
3 \\
\hline
\end{array}
$$

$$\Sigma X = 27$$

STEP 2   Obtain the standard deviation of the sample (we will use the formula for raw scores).

X	X^2
1	1
5	25
2	4
3	9
4	16
1	1
2	4
2	4
4	16
3	9

$$\Sigma X^2 = 89$$

$$s = \sqrt{\frac{\Sigma X^2}{N} - \bar{X}^2}$$

$$= \sqrt{\frac{89}{10} - (2.7)^2}$$

$$= \sqrt{8.9 - 7.29}$$

$$= \sqrt{1.61}$$

$$= 1.2689$$

STEP 3   Obtain the estimated standard error of the mean.

$$s_{\bar{X}} = \frac{s}{\sqrt{N - 1}}$$

$$= \frac{1.2689}{\sqrt{10 - 1}}$$

$$= \frac{1.2689}{3}$$

$$= .423$$

STEP 4   Determine the value of t from Table B.

$$df = N - 1 = 10 - 1 = 9$$

$$\alpha = .05$$

Thus,

$$t = 2.262$$

STEP 5   Obtain the margin of error by multiplying the standard error of the mean by 2.262.

$$\text{Margin of error} = ts_{\bar{X}}$$

$$= (2.262)(.423)$$

$$= .96$$

STEP 6   Add and subtract this product from the sample mean in order to find the interval within which we are 95% confident the population mean falls:

$$95\% \text{ confidence interval} = \bar{X} \pm ts_{\bar{X}}$$

$$= 2.7 \pm .96$$

$$= 1.74 \text{ to } 3.66$$

Thus, we can be 95% certain that the mean number of security cameras per store is between 1.74 and 3.66.

In order to construct a 99% confidence interval, Steps 1 through 3 would remain the same. Next, with df = 9 and $\alpha = .01$ (that is, $1 - .99 = .01$), from Table B, we find $t = 3.250$. The 99% confidence interval is then

$$99\% \text{ confidence interval} = \bar{X} \pm ts_{\bar{X}}$$

$$= 2.7 \pm (3.250)(.423)$$

$$= 2.7 \pm 1.37$$

$$= 1.33 \text{ to } 4.07$$

Thus, we can be 99% confident that the population mean (mean number of security cameras per store) is between 1.34 and 4.06. This interval is somewhat wider than the 95% interval (1.75 to 3.65), but for this trade-off, we gain greater confidence in our estimate.

ESTIMATING PROPORTIONS

Thus far, we have focused on procedures for estimating population means. The researcher often seeks to come up with an estimate of a population *proportion* strictly on the basis of a proportion obtained in a random sample. A familiar circumstance is the pollster whose data suggest that a certain proportion of the vote will go to a particular political issue or candidate for office. When a pollster reports that 45% of the vote will be in favor of a certain candidate, he does so with the realization that he is less than 100% certain. In general, he is 95% or 99% confident that his estimated proportion falls within the range of proportions (for example, between 40% and 50%).

We estimate proportions by the procedure that we have just used to estimate means. All statistics—including means and proportions—have their sampling distributions, and the sampling distribution of a proportion is normal. Just as we found earlier the standard error of the mean, we can now find the *standard error of the proportion*. By formula,

$$s_P = \sqrt{\frac{P(1 - P)}{N}}$$

where s_P = standard error of the proportion (an estimate of the standard deviation
of the sampling distribution of proportions)
P = sample proportion
N = total number in the sample

For illustrative purposes, let us say 45% of a random sample of 100 college students report they are in favor of the legalization of all drugs. The standard error of the proportion would be

$$s_P = \sqrt{\frac{(.45)(.55)}{100}}$$

$$= \sqrt{\frac{.2475}{100}}$$

$$= \sqrt{.0025}$$

$$= .05$$

The t distribution was used previously for constructing confidence intervals for the population mean when *both* the population mean (μ) and the population standard deviation (σ) were unknown and had to be estimated. When dealing with proportions, however, only *one* quantity is unknown: We estimate the population proportion (π, the Greek letter *pi*) by the sample proportion P. Consequently, we use the z distribution for constructing confidence intervals for the population proportion (π) (with z = 1.96 for a 95% confidence interval and z = 2.58 for a 99% confidence interval) rather than the t distribution.

To find the 95% confidence interval for the population proportion, we multiply the standard error of the proportion by 1.96 and add and subtract this product to and from the sample proportion:

95% confidence interval = $P \pm 1.96s_P$

where P = sample proportion
s_P = standard error of the proportion

If we seek to estimate the proportion of college students in favor of the legalization of drugs,

95% confidence interval = $.45 \pm (1.96)(.05)$

$$= .45 \pm .098$$

$$= .35 \text{ to } .55$$

We are 95% confident that the true population proportion is neither smaller than .35 nor larger than .55. More specifically, somewhere between 35% and 55% of this population of college students are in favor of the legalization of all drugs. There is a 5% chance we are wrong; 5 times out of 100 such confidence intervals will not contain the true population proportion.

STEP-BY-STEP ILLUSTRATION
CONFIDENCE INTERVAL FOR PROPORTIONS

One of the most common applications of confidence intervals for proportions arises in election polling. Polling organizations routinely report not only the proportion (or percentage) of a sample of respondents planning to vote for a particular candidate, but also the margin of error—that is, z times the standard error.

Suppose that a polling organization contacted 400 members of a local chapter of a large police union and asked them whether they intended to vote for candidate A or candidate B in a union leader election. Suppose that 60% reported their intention to vote for candidate A. Let us now derive the standard error, margin of error, and 95% confidence interval for the proportion indicating a preference for candidate A.

STEP 1 Obtain the standard error of the proportion.

$$
\begin{aligned}
s_P &= \sqrt{\frac{P(1 - P)}{N}} \\
&= \sqrt{\frac{(.60)(1 - .60)}{400}} \\
&= \sqrt{\frac{.24}{400}} \\
&= \sqrt{.0006} \\
&= .0245
\end{aligned}
$$

STEP 2 Multiply the standard error of the proportion by 1.96 to obtain the margin of error.

$$
\begin{aligned}
\text{Margin of error} &= (1.96)s_P \\
&= (1.96)(.0245) \\
&= .0480
\end{aligned}
$$

STEP 3 Add and subtract the margin of error to find the confidence interval

$$
\begin{aligned}
95\% \text{ confidence interval} &= P \pm (1.96)s_P \\
&= .60 \pm .0480 \\
&= .5520 \text{ to } .6480
\end{aligned}
$$

Thus, with a sample size of 400, the poll has a margin of error of ±4.8%, or about 5%. Given the resulting confidence interval (roughly, 55% to 65%), candidate A can feel fairly secure about her prospects for the election as a leader of the union.

SUMMARY

This chapter has explored the key concepts and procedures related to generalizing from samples to populations. Both random and nonrandom sampling methods were presented. It was pointed out that sampling error—the inevitable difference between samples and populations—occurs despite a well-designed and well-executed sampling plan. As a result of sampling error, we can discuss the characteristics of the sampling distribution of means, a distribution that forms a normal curve and whose standard deviation can be estimated with the aid of the standard error of the mean. Armed with such information, we can construct confidence intervals for means (or proportions) within which we have confidence (95% or 99%) that the true population mean (or proportion) actually falls. In this way, we are able to make generalizations from a sample to a population.

This chapter also introduced the t distribution for instances when the population standard deviation (σ) is unknown and must be estimated from sample data. The t distribution will play a major role in hypothesis tests presented in the next chapter.

TERMS TO REMEMBER

Population (universe)	Random sample
Sample	Simple random sample
Nonrandom sample	Systematic sample
Accidental	Stratified sample
Quota	Cluster or multistage sample
Judgment or purposive	Table of random numbers
Primary sampling unit	99% confidence interval
Sampling error	Margin of error
Sampling distribution of means	t distribution
Standard error of the mean	Degrees of freedom
Confidence interval	Alpha (α)
Level of confidence	Standard error of the proportion
95% confidence interval	

STEP-BY-STEP STUDY GUIDE
CONFIDENCE INTERVAL FOR THE MEAN USING *z*

STEP 1   Obtain the sample mean.

$$\overline{X} = \frac{\Sigma X}{N}$$

STEP 2   Compute the standard error of the mean.

$$\sigma_{\bar{X}} = \frac{\sigma}{\sqrt{N}}$$

STEP 3   Obtain the margin of error by multiplying the standard error of the mean by the appropriate z value from Table A (or from the bottom row of Table B).

$$\text{Margin of error} = z\sigma_{\bar{X}}$$

STEP 4   Add and subtract the margin of error from the sample mean to obtain the desired confidence interval.

$$\text{Confidence interval} = \bar{X} \pm z\sigma_{\bar{X}}$$

STEP-BY-STEP STUDY GUIDE

CONFIDENCE INTERVAL FOR THE MEAN USING t

STEP 1   Obtain the sample mean.

$$\bar{X} = \frac{\Sigma X}{N}$$

STEP 2   Calculate the standard deviation.

$$s = \sqrt{\frac{\Sigma X^2}{N} - \bar{X}^2}$$

STEP 3   Compute the standard error of the mean.

$$s_{\bar{X}} = \frac{s}{\sqrt{N-1}}$$

STEP 4   Determine the degrees of freedom.

$$df = N - 1$$

STEP 5   Obtain the margin of error by multiplying the standard error of the mean by the appropriate t value from Table B, depending on the level of confidence and degrees of freedom.

$$\text{Margin of error} = ts_{\bar{X}}$$

STEP 6   Add and subtract the margin of error from the sample mean to obtain the desired confidence interval.

$$\text{Confidence interval} = \bar{X} \pm ts_{\bar{X}}$$

STEP-BY-STEP STUDY GUIDE

CONFIDENCE INTERVAL FOR THE PROPORTION

STEP 1   Obtain the sample proportion P.

$$P = \frac{f}{N}$$

STEP 2   Calculate the standard error of the proportion.

$$s_P = \sqrt{\frac{P(1 - P)}{N}}$$

STEP 3   Compute the margin of error by multiplying the standard error of the proportion by the appropriate z value from Table A, depending on the level of confidence.

$$\text{Margin of error} = zs_P$$

STEP 4   Add and subtract the margin of error from the sample proportion to obtain the desired confidence interval.

$$\text{Confidence interval} = P \pm zs_P$$

PROBLEMS

1. Suppose that the population standard deviation (σ) for a normally distributed standardized test of achievement is known to be 7.20. What would the standard error of the sample mean ($\sigma_{\bar{x}}$) be if we were to draw a random sample of 16 test scores?

2. Suppose that the random sample in Problem 1 yielded these observed scores:

6	5	6	12	5	10	11	13
12	10	9	20	23	20	28	18

   a. Find the 95% confidence interval for the mean.
   b. Find the 99% confidence interval for the mean.

3. Now suppose that we did not feel comfortable assuming that $\sigma = 7.20$. Using the scores in Problem 2:

   a. estimate the standard error of the sample mean ($s_{\bar{x}}$)
   b. find the 95% confidence interval for the mean.
   c. find the 99% confidence interval for the mean.

4. Estimate the standard error of the mean with the following sample of 30 responses on a seven-point scale, measuring whether an extremist hate group should be given a permit to demonstrate (1 = strongly oppose through 7 = strongly favor):

3	5	1	4
3	3	6	6
2	3	3	1
1	2	2	1
5	2	1	3
4	3	1	4
5	2	2	3
3	4		

5. With the sample mean in Problem 4, find: (a) the 95% confidence interval and (b) the 99% confidence interval.

6. A researcher was interested in examining the number of questions asked by students during a criminal justice statistics course. She unobtrusively observes one month of lectures, and records the following number of questions asked by each of 20 randomly selected students:

6 10 12 5 4 3 6 7 9 5 7 8 8 10 13 3 4 8 9 10

   a. Calculate the mean for this sample.
   b. Calculate the standard deviation for this sample.
   c. Estimate the standard error of the mean.
   d. Using a 99% confidence level, what is the value of t?

e. Construct a 99% confidence interval for the mean number of questions asked by the students.

7. Estimate the standard error of the mean with the following sample of 34 scores on a 10-item objective test of knowledge about civil trial procedures:

10	1	4	8
10	7	5	5
5	6	6	10
7	6	3	8
5	7	4	7
4	6	5	5
6	5	6	4
7	3	5	4
8	5		

8. With the sample mean in Problem 7, find: (a) the 95% confidence interval and (b) the 99% confidence interval.

9. Estimate the standard error of the mean with the following sample of 32 scores representing the number of hours that students had studied for a midterm exam:

4	4	3	2
5	6	6	6
1	7	1	1
7	5	8	7
7	8	8	8
8	4	2	5
6	3	5	2
6	6	4	5

10. With the sample mean in Problem 9, find: (a) the 95% confidence interval and (b) the 99% confidence interval.

11. To determine students' opinions about campus security at a particular college, an 11-point attitude scale was administered to a random sample of 40 students. This survey yielded a sample mean of 6 (the higher the score, the higher the perceived level of effectiveness of campus security measures) and a standard deviation of 1.5.

a. Estimate the standard error of the mean.
b. Find the 95% confidence interval for the population mean.
c. Find the 99% confidence interval for the population mean.

12. A researcher is interested in estimating the average age when cigarette smokers first began to smoke. Taking a random sample of 25 smokers, she determines a sample mean of 16.8 years and a sample standard deviation of 1.5 years. Construct a 95%

confidence interval to estimate the population mean age of onset of smoking.

13. A corrections researcher is examining prison health care costs and wants to determine how long inmates survive once diagnosed with a particular form of cancer. Using data collected on a group of 20 patients with the disease, she observes an average survival time (time until death) of 38 months with a standard deviation of 9 months. Using a 95% level of confidence, estimate the population mean survival time.

14. A local police department attempted to estimate the average rate of speed (μ) of vehicles along a strip of Main Street. With hidden radar, the speed of a random selection of 25 vehicles was measured, which yielded a sample mean of 42 mph and a standard deviation of 6 mph.

a. Estimate the standard error of the mean.
b. Find the 95% confidence interval for the population mean.
c. Find the 99% confidence interval for the population mean.

15. In order to estimate the proportion of students on a particular campus who favor a campus-wide ban on alcohol, a researcher interviewed a random sample of 50 students from the college population. She found that 36% of the sample favored banning alcohol (sample proportion = .36). With this information, (a) find the standard error of the proportion and (b) find a 95% confidence interval for the population proportion.

16. A polling organization interviewed by phone 400 randomly selected adults in New York City about their opinion on random drug testing for taxi drivers and found that 38% favored such a regulation.

a. Find the standard error of the proportion.
b. Find the 95% confidence interval for the population proportion.
c. Find the 99% confidence interval for the population proportion.

17. A major research organization conducted a national survey to determine what percent of Americans feel that they are more or less likely to become a crime victim now than they were five years ago. Asking 1,200 randomly selected respondents if their feeling of safety had improved over the past five years, 45% reported that they feel less safe.

a. Find the standard error of the proportion.
b. Find the 95% confidence interval for the population proportion.

c. Find the 99% confidence interval for the population proportion.

18. A director of campus security wants to estimate the proportion of college seniors that have had something stolen from them while students at Hypothetical University. In a phone survey of a random sample of 120 seniors, 74 said they have had something stolen.

   a. Find the standard error of the proportion.
   b. Find the 95% confidence interval for the population proportion.
   c. Find the 99% confidence interval for the population proportion.

19. A referendum, if passed, would provide state funds for after-school sports and music programs. The programs are intended to help decrease a growing juvenile violence rate. A pollster surveyed a random sample of 500 registered voters and found that 54% intended to vote for the bill. Using a 95% confidence interval, determine whether the pollster is justified in predicting that the referendum will pass.

20. A researcher sought to estimate the average number of informants that rookie police officers cultivated during their first year on the force. After questioning a random sample of 50 police officers completing their first year, he finds a sample mean of 3 and a sample standard deviation of 1. Construct a 95% confidence interval to estimate the mean number of informants cultivated by the entire population of rookie police officers during their first year on the force.

21. An administrator of a large criminal justice program wanted to estimate the average number of books required by instructors. Using bookstore data, she drew a random sample of 25 courses for which she obtained a sample mean of 2.8 books and a sample standard deviation of .4. Construct a 99% confidence interval to estimate the mean number of books assigned by instructors on campus.

PART III

DECISION MAKING

CHAPTER 7
TESTING DIFFERENCES BETWEEN MEANS

CHAPTER 8
ANALYSIS OF VARIANCE

CHAPTER 9
NONPARAMETRIC TESTS OF SIGNIFICANCE

CHAPTER 10
CORRELATION

CHAPTER 11
REGRESSION ANALYSIS

CHAPTER 12
NONPARAMETRIC MEASURES OF CORRELATION

CHAPTER 13
APPLYING STATISTICAL PROCEDURES TO RESEARCH

CHAPTER

7

TESTING DIFFERENCES BETWEEN MEANS

- **THE NULL HYPOTHESIS: NO DIFFERENCE BETWEEN MEANS**

- **THE RESEARCH HYPOTHESIS: A DIFFERENCE BETWEEN MEANS**

- **SAMPLING DISTRIBUTION OF DIFFERENCES BETWEEN MEANS**

- **TESTING HYPOTHESES WITH THE DISTRIBUTION OF DIFFERENCES BETWEEN MEANS**

- **LEVELS OF SIGNIFICANCE**

- **STANDARD ERROR OF THE DIFFERENCE BETWEEN MEANS**

- **TESTING THE DIFFERENCE BETWEEN MEANS**

- **COMPARING THE SAME SAMPLE MEASURED TWICE**

- **TWO SAMPLE TESTS OF PROPORTIONS**

- **ONE-TAILED TESTS**

- **REQUIREMENTS FOR TESTING THE DIFFERENCE BETWEEN MEANS**

- **SUMMARY**

- **TERMS TO REMEMBER**

- **STEP-BY-STEP STUDY GUIDE: TEST OF DIFFERENCES BETWEEN MEANS FOR INDEPENDENT GROUPS**

- **STEP-BY-STEP STUDY GUIDE: TEST OF DIFFERENCES BETWEEN PROPORTIONS**

- **STEP-BY-STEP STUDY GUIDE: TEST OF DIFFERENCES BETWEEN MEANS FOR THE SAME SAMPLE MEASURED TWICE**

- **PROBLEMS**

In Chapter 6, we saw that a population mean or proportion can be estimated from the information we gain from a single sample. For instance, we might estimate the level of anomie in a certain city, the proportion of businesses who hire private security, or the mean attitude toward community registration of convicted sex offenders.

Although the descriptive, fact-gathering approach of estimating means and proportions has obvious importance, it *does not* constitute the primary decision-making goal or activity of research. Quite to the contrary, most criminal justice researchers are preoccupied with the task of *testing hypotheses* about the differences between two or more samples.

When testing differences between samples, criminal justice researchers ask such questions as: Do political conservatives approve of longer prison sentences for violent criminals than do political liberals? Do female prosecutors have higher conviction rates than male prosecutors? Do offenders who have completed drug rehabilitation programs have lower recidivism rates than offenders who have not had any drug rehabilitation programming? Do urban police have higher death rates than rural police? Note that each research question involves making a comparison between two groups: conservatives versus liberals, male versus female lawyers, offenders who have versus have not completed a drug rehabilitation program, urban versus rural police.

Take a more concrete example. Suppose that a researcher interested in crime victim recovery wanted to evaluate crime victim counseling services provided by the courts in his city. He selects 10 crime victims and randomly assigns five to the "treatment" group where they receive the counseling services provided by the court, and five victims to the "control" group where they do not receive counseling.

Suppose further that following the time in which the treatment group receives counseling, all 10 of the victims are administered the same questionnaire assessing their levels of anxiety. The sample mean score for the five subjects in the control group was 82, and the sample mean for the treatment group was 77 (higher scores indicate higher anxiety). Is the victim counseling provided by the court effective in reducing anxiety? Perhaps. Perhaps not. It is impossible to draw any firm conclusions until we know more about the data.

Let us say just for a moment that the sets of anxiety scores for the two groups of crime victims were as follows:

Control	Treatment
82	78
83	77
82	76
80	78
83	76
Mean = 82	Mean = 77

In the Control group, the recall scores are consistently in the low 80s, so we would have a good deal of confidence that the population mean would be close to the sample mean of 82. Similarly, we would say with confidence that the population mean for the treatment group is likely near the sample mean of 77. Given the homogeneity of the scores and thus the sample means, we could probably conclude that the difference between sample means is more than just a result of pure chance or sampling error. In fact, the counseling received by the individuals in the treatment group does appear to reduce anxiety.

Now suppose instead that the following sets of scores produced the two sample means 82 and 77. It is clear that in both groups, there is wide variability or spread among the anxiety scores. As a result, both sample means are relatively unstable estimates of their respective population means. Given the heterogeneity of the sample scores and the unreliability of the sample means, we therefore could not conclude that the difference between sample means is anything more than a result of pure chance or sampling error. In fact, there is not enough evidence to conclude that the victim counseling services affects anxiety.

Control	Treatment
90	70
98	90
63	91
74	56
85	78
Mean = 82	Mean = 77

THE NULL HYPOTHESIS: NO DIFFERENCE BETWEEN MEANS

It has become conventional in statistical analysis to set out testing the *null hypothesis*—the hypothesis that says two samples have been drawn from equivalent populations. According to the null hypothesis, any observed difference between samples is regarded as a chance occurrence resulting from sampling error alone. Therefore, an obtained difference between two sample means does not represent a true difference between their population means.

In the present context, the null hypothesis can be symbolized as

$$\mu_1 = \mu_2$$

where μ_1 = mean of the first population
        μ_2 = mean of the second population

Let us examine null hypotheses for the research questions posed earlier:

1. Conservatives are no more or less likely than liberals to approve of longer prison sentences.
2. Male and female prosecutors have the same conviction rate.
3. Drug rehabilitation program graduates have the same recidivism rates as offenders who do not go through such programs.
4. Urban and rural police have the same death rates.

It should be noted that the null hypothesis does not deny the possibility of obtaining differences between *sample* means. On the contrary, it seeks to explain such differences between sample means by attributing them to the operation of sampling error. In accordance with the null hypothesis, for example, if we find that a *sample* of female parole officers earns less money ($\overline{X}$ = $32,000) than a *sample* of male parole officers ($\overline{X}$ = $33,000), we do not, on that basis, conclude that the population of female probation officers earns less money than the population of male probation officers. Instead, we treat our obtained sample difference ($33,000 − $32,000 = $1,000) as a product of sampling error—the difference that inevitably results from the process of sampling from a given population. As we shall see later, this aspect of the null hypothesis provides an important link with sampling theory.

To conclude that sampling error is responsible for our obtained difference between sample means is to *accept* the null hypothesis. The use of the term *accept* does not imply that we have proven the population means are equal ($\mu_1 = \mu_2$) or even that we believe it. Technically, we are merely unable to reject the null hypothesis due to lack of contradictory evidence. For the sake of simplicity, the phrase *accept the null hypothesis* will be used throughout the text when we are unable to reject it.

THE RESEARCH HYPOTHESIS: A DIFFERENCE BETWEEN MEANS

The null hypothesis is generally (although not necessarily) set up with the hope of nullifying it. This makes sense, for most criminal justice researchers seek to establish relationships between variables. That is, they are often more interested in finding differences than in determining that differences do not exist. Differences between groups—whether expected on theoretical or empirical grounds—often provide the rationale for research.

If we reject the null hypothesis, if we find our hypothesis of no difference between means probably does not hold, we automatically accept the *research hypothesis* that a true population difference does exist. This is often the hoped-for result in criminal justice research. The research hypothesis says that the two samples have been taken from populations having different means. It says that the obtained difference between sample means is too large to be accounted for by sampling error.

The research hypothesis for mean differences is symbolized by

$$\mu_1 \neq \mu_2$$

where μ_1 = mean of the first population
        μ_2 = mean of the second population

Note: $\neq$ is read *does not equal.*

The following research hypotheses can be specified for the research questions posed earlier:

1. Conservatives differ from liberals in approval of longer prison sentences.
2. Male and female prosecutors do not have the same conviction rates.
3. Drug rehabilitation program graduates do not have the same recidivism rates as offenders who do not go through such programs.
4. Urban and rural police have different death rates.

SAMPLING DISTRIBUTION OF DIFFERENCES BETWEEN MEANS

In the preceding chapter, we saw that the 100 means from the 100 samples drawn by our eccentric criminologist could be plotted in the form of a sampling distribution of means. In a similar way, let us now imagine that the same criminologist studies not one but two samples at a time in order to make comparisons between them.

Suppose, for example, that our eccentric criminologist is interested in people's attitudes toward criminal justice punishment. Specifically, he wants to assess whether people are lenient in their attitudes toward punishing convicted offenders, and to examine whether there is a relationship between gender and leniency.

To test for gender differences, he first constructs a multi-item scale, which includes several questions about approval of capital punishment, mandatory sentences (including "three-strikes" legislation), trying juveniles as adults, the use of parole, and opinions about appropriate prison sentence lengths for various crimes. His leniency scale ranges from a minimum of 1 (not at all lenient, or punitive) to a maximum of 100 (extremely lenient). Next, he selects a random sample of 30 females and a random sample of 30 males from the student directory, and administers his questionnaire to all 60 students. As graphically illustrated in Figure 7.1, our eccentric researcher finds his sample of females is more lenient ($\overline{X} = 58.0$) than his sample of males ($\overline{X} = 54.0$).

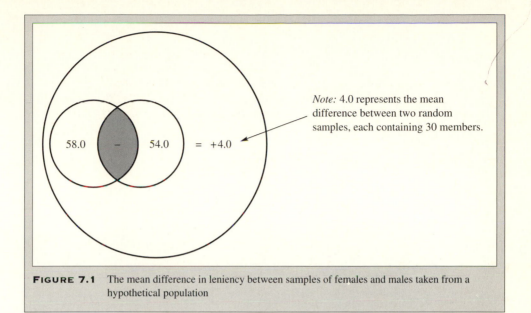

Note: 4.0 represents the mean difference between two random samples, each containing 30 members.

FIGURE 7.1 The mean difference in leniency between samples of females and males taken from a hypothetical population

Before our eccentric researcher concludes that women are actually more lenient than men, he might ask: In light of sampling error, can we expect a difference between 58.0 and 54.0 (58.0 − 54.0 = +4.0) strictly on the basis of chance and chance alone? Based solely on the luck of the draw, could the female sample have been comprised of more lenient people than the male sample? Must we accept the null hypothesis of no population difference, or is the obtained sample difference +4.0 large enough to indicate a true population difference between females and males with respect to their criminal justice punishment attitudes?

In Chapter 2, we were introduced to frequency distributions of raw scores from a given population. In Chapter 6, we saw it was possible to construct a sampling distribution of mean scores, a frequency distribution of sample means. In addressing ourselves to the question at hand, we must now take the notion of frequency distribution a step further and examine the nature of a *sampling distribution of differences between means,* that is, a frequency distribution of a large number of *differences* between sample means that have been randomly drawn from a given population.

To illustrate the sampling distribution of differences between means, let us return to the compulsive activities of our eccentric researcher whose passion for drawing random samples has once again led him to continue the sampling process beyond its ordinary limits. Rather than draw a single sample of 30 females and a single sample of 30 males, he studies 70 *pairs* of such samples (70 pairs of samples, *each* containing 30 females and 30 males), feeling fortunate that he teaches at a large school.

For each pair of samples, the eccentric researcher administers the same scale of leniency. He then calculates a sample mean for each female sample and a sample mean for each male sample. Thus, he has a female mean and a male mean for each of his 70 pairs of samples.

Next, he derives a difference-between-means score by subtracting the mean score for males from the mean score for females for each pair of samples. For example, his first comparison produced a difference between means of +4.0. His second pair of means

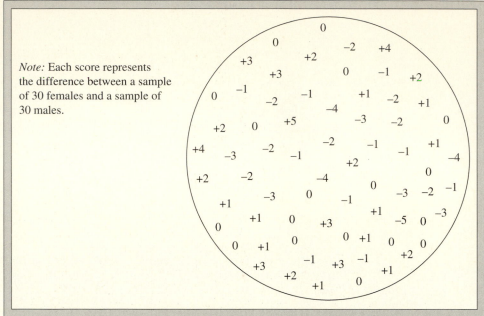

Note: Each score represents the difference between a sample of 30 females and a sample of 30 males.

FIGURE 7.2   Seventy mean difference scores representing differences in leniency between samples of females and males taken at random from a hypothetical population

might be 57.0 for the female sample and 56.0 for the male sample, yielding a difference-between-means score of +1.0. Likewise, the third pair of samples may have produced a mean of 60.0 for the females and a mean of 64.0 for the males, and the difference between means would be −4.0. Obviously, the larger the difference score, the more the two samples of respondents differ with respect to leniency. Note that we always subtract the second sample mean from the first sample mean (in the present case, we subtract the mean score for the male sample from the mean score for the female sample). The 70 difference-between-means scores derived by our eccentric researcher have been illustrated in Figure 7.2.

Let us suppose that we know that the populations of females and males do not differ at all with respect to leniency in criminal justice punishment attitudes. Let us say for the sake of argument that $\mu = 57.0$ in both the female and male populations. If we assume the null hypothesis is correct, and that females and males are identical in this respect, we can use the 70 mean differences obtained by our eccentric researcher to illustrate the sampling distribution of differences between means. This is true because the sampling distribution of differences between means makes the assumption that all sample pairs differ only by virtue of sampling error and not as a function of true population differences.

The 70 scores representing differences between means shown in Figure 7.2 have been rearranged in Table 7.1 as a *sampling distribution of differences between means*. Like the scores in other types of frequency distributions, these have been arranged in consecutive order from high to low, and frequency of occurrence is indicated in an adjacent column.

TABLE 7.1   SAMPLING DISTRIBUTION OF DIFFERENCES FOR 70 PAIRS OF RANDOM SAMPLES

Mean difference[a]	f
+5	1
+4	2
+3	5
+2	7
+1	10
0	18
−1	10
−2	8
−3	5
−4	3
−5	1
	$N = 70$

[a]These difference scores include fractional values (for example, −5 includes the values −5.0 through −5.9).

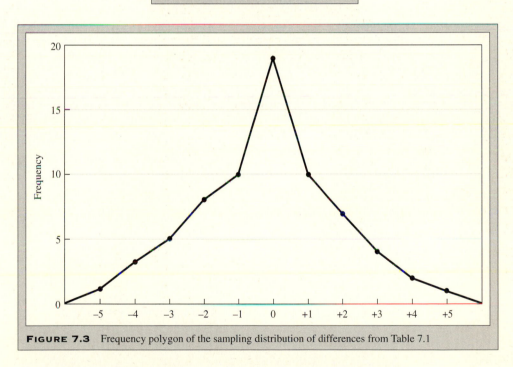

FIGURE 7.3   Frequency polygon of the sampling distribution of differences from Table 7.1

To depict the key properties of a sampling distribution of differences between means, the frequency distribution from Table 7.1 has been graphically presented in Figure 7.3. As illustrated therein, we see that the *sampling distribution of differences between means approximates a normal curve whose mean (mean of differences between means) is zero.*[1] This

---

[1]This assumes we have drawn large random samples from a given population of raw scores.

makes sense because the positive and negative differences between means in the distribution tend to cancel out one another (for every negative value, there tends to be a positive value of equal distance from the mean).

As a normal curve, most of the differences between sample means in this distribution fall close to zero—its middlemost point; there are relatively few differences between means having extreme values in either direction from the mean of these differences. This is to be expected, because the entire distribution of differences between means is a product of sampling error rather than actual population differences between females and males. In other words, if the actual mean difference between the populations of females and males is zero, we also expect the mean of the sampling distribution of differences between sample means to be zero.

TESTING HYPOTHESES WITH THE DISTRIBUTION OF DIFFERENCES BETWEEN MEANS

In earlier chapters, we learned to make probability statements regarding the occurrence of both raw scores and sample means. In the present case, we seek to make statements of probability about the difference scores in the sampling distribution of differences between means. As pointed out earlier, this sampling distribution takes the form of the normal curve and, therefore, can be regarded as a probability distribution. We can say that probability decreases as we move farther and farther from the mean of differences (zero). More specifically, as illustrated in Figure 7.4, we see that 68.26% of the mean differences fall between $+1\sigma_{\overline{X}_1-\overline{X}_2}$ and $-1\sigma_{\overline{X}_1-\overline{X}_2}$ from zero. (The notation $\sigma_{\overline{X}_1-\overline{X}_2}$ represents the standard deviation of the differences between $\overline{X}_1$ and $\overline{X}_2$.) In probability terms, this indicates $P = .68$ that any difference between sample means falls within this interval. Similarly, we can say the probability is roughly .95 (95 chances in 100) that any sample mean difference falls between $-2\sigma_{\overline{X}_1-\overline{X}_2}$ and $+2\sigma_{\overline{X}_1-\overline{X}_2}$ from a mean difference of zero, and so on.

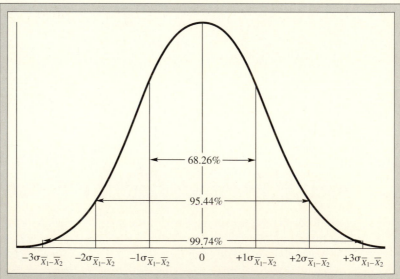

FIGURE 7.4 The sampling distribution of differences between means as a probability distribution

The sampling distribution of differences provides a sound basis for testing hypotheses about the difference between two sample means. Unlike the eccentric researcher who compulsively takes pairs of samples, one after another, most normal researchers would study only one pair of samples to make inferences on the basis of just one difference between means.

Suppose, for instance, that a normal criminologist wanted to test the eccentric criminologists's hypothesis, or at least a variation of it, in a realistic way. She is interested in the relationship between gender and criminal justice attitudes, and decides to examine gender differences in leniency or punitiveness of attitudes regarding criminal justice punishment among criminal justice professionals.

She randomly selects 30 female and 30 male probation officers and administers the eccentric researcher's leniency scale to all 60 officers. She obtains mean leniency scores of 45 for the female probation officers and 40 for the male probation officers. The researcher's reasoning then goes like this: If the obtained difference between means of 5 $(45 - 40 = 5)$ lies so far from a difference of zero that it has only a small probability of occurrence in the sampling distribution of differences between means, we reject the null hypothesis—the hypothesis that says the obtained difference between means is a result of sampling error. If, on the other hand, our sample mean difference falls so close to zero that its *probability* of occurrence is large, we must accept the null hypothesis and treat our obtained difference between means merely as a result of sampling error.

Therefore, we seek to determine how far our obtained difference between means (in this case, 5) lies from a mean difference of zero. In so doing, we must first translate our obtained difference into units of standard deviation.

Recall that we translate *raw scores* into units of standard deviation by the formula

$$z = \frac{X - \mu}{\sigma}$$

where X = raw score

μ = mean of the distribution of raw scores

σ = standard deviation of the distribution of raw scores

Likewise, we translate the *mean scores* in a distribution of sample means into units of standard deviation by the formula

$$z = \frac{\bar{X} - \mu}{\sigma_{\bar{X}}}$$

where $\bar{X}$ = sample mean

μ = population mean (mean of means)

$\sigma_{\bar{X}}$ = standard error of the mean (standard deviation of the distribution of means)

In the present context, we similarly seek to translate our sample mean difference $(\bar{X}_1 - \bar{X}_2)$ into units of standard deviation by the formula

$$z = \frac{(\bar{X}_1 - \bar{X}_2) - 0}{\sigma_{\bar{X}_1 - \bar{X}_2}}$$

where $\overline{X}_1$ = mean of the first sample
           $\overline{X}_2$ = mean of the second sample
           0 = zero, the value of the mean of the sampling distribution of
           differences between means (we assume that $\mu_1 - \mu_2 = 0$)
$\sigma_{\overline{X}_1 - \overline{X}_2}$ = standard deviation of the sampling distribution of differences
           between means

Because the value of the mean of the distribution of differences between means is
assumed to be zero, we can drop it from the z-score formula without altering our result.
Therefore,

$$z = \frac{\overline{X}_1 - \overline{X}_2}{\sigma_{\overline{X}_1 - \overline{X}_2}}$$

With regard to leniency between the female and male probation officer samples, we
must translate our obtained difference between means into its z-score equivalent. If the
standard deviation of the sampling distribution of differences between means $\sigma_{\overline{X}_1 - \overline{X}_2}$ is 2
(more on how to get this number later), we obtain the following z score:

$$z = \frac{45 - 40}{2}$$

$$= \frac{5}{2}$$

$$= +2.5$$

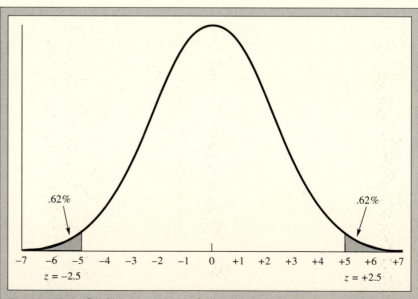

FIGURE 7.5   Graphic representation of the percent of total area in the distribution of
differences between $z = -2.5$ and $z = +2.5$

Thus, a difference of 5 between the means for the two samples falls 2.5 standard deviations from a mean difference of zero in the distribution of differences between means.

What is the probability that a difference of 5 or more between sample means can happen strictly on the basis of sampling error? Going to column c of Table A in Appendix C, we learn that $z = 2.5$ cuts off 0.62% of the area in each tail, or 1.24% in total (see Figure 7.5). Rounding off, $P = .01$ that the mean difference of 5 (or greater than 5) between samples can happen strictly on the basis of sampling error. That is, a mean difference of 5 or more occurs by sampling error (and therefore appears in the sampling distribution) *only once* in every 100 mean differences. Knowing this, would we not consider rejecting the null hypothesis and accepting the research hypothesis that a population difference actually exists between male and female probation officers with respect to the leniency of their attitudes regarding criminal justice punishment? One chance out of 100 represents pretty good odds.

Given that situation, most of us would choose to reject the null hypothesis, even though we might be wrong in doing so (don't forget that 1 chance out of 100 still remains). However, the decision is not always so clear-cut. Suppose, for example, we learn our difference between means happens by sampling error 10 ($P = .10$), 15 ($P = .15$), or 20 ($P = .20$) times out of 100. Do we still reject the null hypothesis? Or do we play it safe and attribute our obtained difference to sampling error?

We need a consistent cutoff point for deciding whether a difference between two sample means is so large that it can no longer be attributed to sampling error. We need a method for determining when our results show a *statistically significant difference*.

LEVELS OF SIGNIFICANCE

To establish whether our obtained sample difference is statistically significant—the result of a real population difference and not just sampling error—it is customary to set up a *level of significance,* which we denote by the Greek letter α (alpha). The alpha value is the level of probability at which the null hypothesis can be rejected with confidence, and the research hypothesis can be accepted with confidence. Accordingly, we decide to reject the null hypothesis if the probability is very small (for example, less than 5 chances out of 100) that the sample difference is a product of sampling error. Conventionally, we symbolize this small probability by $P < .05$.

It is a matter of convention to use the $\alpha = .05$ *level of significance.* That is, we are willing to reject the null hypothesis if an obtained sample difference occurs by chance less then 5 times out of 100. The .05 significance level has been graphically depicted in Figure 7.6. As shown, the .05 level of significance is found in the small areas of the tails of the distribution of mean differences. These are the areas under the curve that represent a distance of plus or minus 1.96 standard deviations from a mean difference of zero. In this case (with an $\alpha = .05$ level of significance), the z scores 1.96 are called *critical values;* if we obtain a z score that exceeds 1.96 (that is, $z > 1.96$ or $z < -1.96$), it is called statistically significant. The shaded regions in Figure 7.6 are called the *critical* or *rejection regions,* because a z score within these areas leads us to reject the null hypothesis (the top portion of the figure shows the critical regions for a .05 level of significance).

To understand better why this particular point in the sampling distribution represents the .05 level of significance, we might turn to column c of Table A in Appendix C to determine the percent of total frequency associated with 1.96 standard deviations from

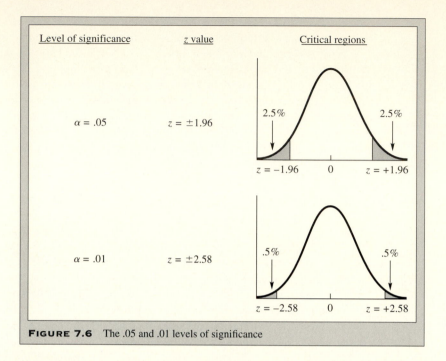

FIGURE 7.6   The .05 and .01 levels of significance

the mean. We see that 1.96 standard deviations in *either* direction represent 2.5% of the differences in sample means. In other words, 95% of these differences fall between $-1.96\ \sigma_{\bar{X}_1-\bar{X}_2}$ and $+1.96\ \sigma_{\bar{X}_1-\bar{X}_2}$ from a mean difference of zero; only 5% fall at or beyond this point (2.5% + 2.5% = 5%).

Significance levels can be set up for any degree of probability. For instance, a more stringent level is the *.01 level of significance,* whereby the null hypothesis is rejected if there is less than 1 chance out of 100 that the obtained sample difference could occur by sampling error. The .01 level of significance is represented by the area that lies 2.58 standard deviations in both directions from a mean difference of zero (see Figure 7.6).

Levels of significance do not give us an *absolute* statement as to the correctness of the null hypothesis. Whenever we decide to reject the null hypothesis at a certain level of significance, we open ourselves to the chance of making the wrong decision. Rejecting the null hypothesis when we should have accepted it is known as *Type I error* (see Figure 7.7). A Type I error can only arise when we reject the null hypothesis, and its probability varies according to the level of significance we choose. For example, if we reject the null hypothesis at the .05 level of significance and conclude that there are gender differences in criminal justice punishment attitudes, then there are 5 chances out of 100 we are wrong. In other words, $P = .05$ that we have committed Type I error, and that gender actually has no effect at all. Likewise, if we choose the $\alpha = .01$ level of significance, there is only 1 chance out of 100 ($P = .01$) of making the wrong decision regarding the difference between genders. Obviously, the more stringent our level of significance (the farther out in the tail it lies), the less likely we are to make Type I error. To take an extreme example, setting up a .001 sig-

	DECISION	
	Accept null hypothesis	Reject null hypothesis
Null hypothesis is true	Correct decision	Type I error $P(\text{Type I error}) = \alpha$
Null hypothesis is false	Type II error $P(\text{Type II error}) = \beta$	Correct decision

REALITY

FIGURE 7.7   Type I and Type II errors

nificance level means that Type I error occurs only 1 time in every 1,000. The probability of Type I error is symbolized by α.

The farther out in the tail of the curve our critical value falls, however, the greater the risk of making another kind of error known as *Type II error.* This is the error of accepting the null hypothesis when we should have rejected it. Type II error indicates that our research hypothesis may still be correct, despite the decision to reject it and accept the null hypothesis. One method for reducing the risk of committing Type II error is to increase the size of the samples, so that a true population difference is more likely to be represented. The probability of Type II error is denoted by β (beta).

We can never be certain that we have not made a wrong decision with respect to the null hypothesis, for we examine only differences between sample means, not between means of the complete population. As long as we do not have knowledge of true population means, we take the risk of making either a Type I or a Type II error, depending on our decision. This is the risk of statistical decision making that the criminal justice researcher must be willing to take.

CHOOSING A LEVEL OF SIGNIFICANCE

We have seen that the probabilities of Type I error and Type II error are inversely related: The larger one error is, the smaller the other. In practice, a researcher does not have actual control of the likelihood of Type II error (β) directly. That is, she or he cannot set the probability of a Type II error to whatever level is desired. On the other hand, the chance of a Type I error is a quantity directly controlled by the researcher, because it is precisely the level of significance (α) he or she chooses for the hypothesis test. Of course, the larger the chosen level of significance (say, .05 or even .10), the larger the chance of Type I error and the smaller the chance of Type II error. The smaller the chosen significance level (say, .01 or even .001), the smaller the chance of Type I error, but the greater the likelihood of Type II error.

We predetermine our level of significance for a hypothesis test on the basis of which type of error (Type I or Type II) is more costly or damaging and therefore riskier. If in a particular instance it would be far worse to reject a true null hypothesis (Type I error) than to accept a false null hypothesis (Type II error), we should opt for a small level of significance (for example, $\alpha = .01$ or $.001$) to minimize the risk of Type I error, even at the expense of increasing the chance of Type II error. If, however, it is believed that Type II error would be worse, we would set a large significance level ($\alpha = .05$ or $.10$) in order to produce a lower chance of Type II error, that is, a lower beta value.

Suppose, for example, a researcher were doing research on gender differences in SAT performance for which she administered an SAT to a sample of males and a sample of females. Before deciding upon a level of significance, she should pause and ask: Which is worse—claiming that there is a true gender difference on the basis of results distorted by excessive sampling error (Type I error) or not claiming a difference when there is in fact one between the population of males and the population of females? In this instance, a Type I error would probably be far more damaging—could even be used as a basis for discriminating unfairly against women—and so she should elect a small alpha value (say, .01).

Let's consider a reverse situation—one in which Type II error is far more worrisome. Suppose a researcher is testing the effects of marijuana smoking on SAT performance, and he compares a sample of smokers with a sample of nonsmokers. If there was even a modest indication that marijuana smoking affected one's performance, this information should be disseminated. We would not want a researcher to accept the null hypothesis of no population difference between smokers and nonsmokers in spite of an observed difference in sample means just because the difference was not quite significant. This Type II error could have a serious impact on public health and safety. A Type I error, by which the researcher was misled to believe marijuana smoking altered performance when the sample difference was only due to chance, would certainly not be as problematic. Given this situation, the researcher would be advised to select a large alpha level (like .10) to avoid the risk of a serious Type II error. That is, he should be less stringent in rejecting the null hypothesis.

WHAT IS THE DIFFERENCE BETWEEN P AND α?

The difference between P and α can be a bit confusing. To avoid confusion, let's compare the two quantities directly. Put simply, P is the exact probability that the null hypothesis is true in light of the sample data; the alpha value is the threshold below which is considered so small that we decide to reject the null hypothesis. That is, we reject the null hypothesis if the P value is less than the alpha value and otherwise accept it.

In testing hypotheses, a researcher decides ahead of time on the alpha value. This choice is made on the basis of weighing the implications of Type I and Type II errors, or is simply made by custom—that is, $\alpha = .05$. The alpha value refers to the size of the tail regions under the curve (of z, for example) that will lead us to reject the null hypothesis. That is, alpha is the area to the right of the tabled critical value of $+z$ and to the left of the tabled value of $-z$. With $\alpha = .05$, these regions are to the right of $z = +1.96$ and to the left of -1.96 (see Figure 7.8). (With the t distribution, the critical values depend also on the degrees of freedom.) Thus, alpha represents the chance of Type I error that we are willing to tolerate.

In contrast, P is the actual probability that the null hypothesis is true. If this probability is small enough (that is, if the null hypothesis is very unlikely), we tend to reject the null hypothesis. Unlike the alpha value, which is determined by the researcher in advance, the P value is determined by the data themselves—specifically by the computed value of the test statistic, such as the z score—and is not set by the researcher. The P value is the area to the right of the calculated $+z$ on the positive side plus the area to the left of the calculated $-z$ on the negative side. Thus, if after data collection, a z score of 2.12 is obtained, we learn from column c of Table A that $P = .034$ (.017 in each tail). If this were the result, we would conclude that $P < .05$, and so we would reject the null hypothesis (see Figure 7.8).

In practice, one does not regularly look up the actual value of P, as we just did from Table A. One only needs to look at whether the calculated z value exceeds the critical value for the chosen α level. Note that the quickest way to determine the critical value for z is to look at the bottom row of the t table. That is, with infinity degrees of freedom, t is equal to z.

If the calculated z exceeds the critical value, we simply say $P < .05$ (if .05 were the significance level preselected) and that the results are statistically significant at the .05 level. If the calculated z does not exceed the critical value, we would say the result (or difference)

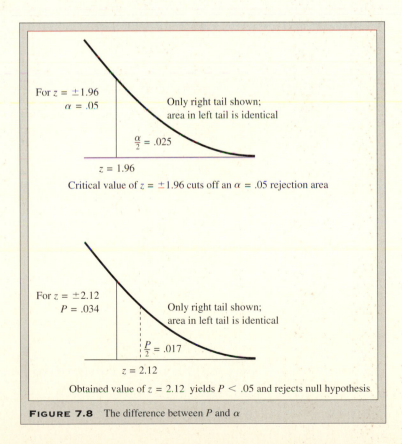

For $z = \pm 1.96$
$\alpha = .05$

Only right tail shown; area in left tail is identical

$\frac{\alpha}{2} = .025$

$z = 1.96$

Critical value of $z = \pm 1.96$ cuts off an $\alpha = .05$ rejection area

For $z = \pm 2.12$
$P = .034$

Only right tail shown; area in left tail is identical

$\frac{P}{2} = .017$

$z = 2.12$

Obtained value of $z = 2.12$ yields $P < .05$ and rejects null hypothesis

FIGURE 7.8   The difference between P and α

was not significant. In other words, one does not need to determine the actual value of P to make a decision on the hypothesis. With most statistical software currently available, the exact P values are automatically calculated from elaborate formulas. Therefore, in the future, we may see more people giving the actual P value rather than just saying $P < .05$.

STANDARD ERROR OF THE DIFFERENCE BETWEEN MEANS

We rarely have firsthand knowledge of the standard deviation of the distribution of mean differences. And just as in the case of the sampling distribution of means (Chapter 6), it would be a major effort if we were actually to draw a large number of sample pairs to calculate it. Yet this standard deviation plays an important role in the method for testing hypotheses about mean differences and, therefore, cannot be ignored.[2]

Fortunately, we do have a simple method whereby the standard deviation of the distribution of differences can be estimated on the basis of just two samples that we actually draw. The sample estimate of the standard deviation of the sampling distribution of differences between means, referred to as the *standard error of the difference between means* and symbolized by $s_{\overline{X}_1 - \overline{X}_2}$, is

$$s_{\overline{X}_1 - \overline{X}_2} = \sqrt{\left(\frac{N_1 s_1{}^2 + N_2 s_2{}^2}{N_1 + N_2 - 2}\right)\left(\frac{N_1 + N_2}{N_1 N_2}\right)}$$

where $s_1{}^2$ and $s_2{}^2$ are the variances of the two samples first introduced in Chapter 4:

$$s_1{}^2 = \frac{\Sigma X_1{}^2}{N_1} - \overline{X}_1{}^2$$

$$s_2{}^2 = \frac{\Sigma X_2{}^2}{N_2} - \overline{X}_2{}^2$$

The formula for $s_{\overline{X}_1 - \overline{X}_2}$ combines information from the two samples. Thus, the variance for each sample in addition to the respective sample sizes goes into our estimate of how different $\overline{X}_1$ and $\overline{X}_2$ can be due to sampling error alone. A large difference between $\overline{X}_1$ and $\overline{X}_2$ can result if (1) one mean is very small; (2) one mean is very large; or (3) one mean is moderately small while the other is moderately large. The likelihood of any of these conditions occurring is dictated by the variances and sample sizes present in the respective samples.

---

[2] In the last chapter, it was pointed out that the true population standard deviation (σ) and standard error ($\sigma_{\overline{X}}$) are rarely known. Also in the two sample cases, the true standard error of the difference is generally unknown. However, for the rare situation in which the standard errors of both sample means are known, the true standard error of the difference between means is

$$\sigma_{\overline{X}_1 - \overline{X}_2} = \sqrt{\sigma_{\overline{X}_1}{}^2 + \sigma_{\overline{X}_2}{}^2} = \sqrt{\frac{\sigma_1{}^2}{N_1} + \frac{\sigma_2{}^2}{N_2}}$$

TESTING THE DIFFERENCE BETWEEN MEANS

Suppose that we obtained the following data for a sample of 25 liberals and 35 conservatives on the leniency scale:

Liberals	Conservatives
$N_1 = 25$	$N_2 = 35$
$\overline{X}_1 = 60$	$\overline{X}_2 = 49$
$s_1 = 12$	$s_2 = 14$

From this information, we can calculate the estimate of the standard error of the difference between means:

$$s_{\overline{X}_1 - \overline{X}_2} = \sqrt{\left(\frac{N_1 s_1^2 + N_2 s_2^2}{N_1 + N_2 - 2}\right)\left(\frac{N_1 + N_2}{N_1 N_2}\right)}$$

$$= \sqrt{\left[\frac{(25)(12)^2 + (35)(14)^2}{25 + 35 - 2}\right]\left(\frac{25 + 35}{(25)(35)}\right)}$$

$$= \sqrt{\left(\frac{3{,}600 + 6{,}860}{58}\right)\left(\frac{60}{875}\right)}$$

$$= \sqrt{(180.3448)(.0686)}$$

$$= \sqrt{12.3717}$$

$$= 3.52$$

The standard error of the difference between means (our estimate of the standard deviation of the theoretical sampling distribution of differences between means) turns out to be 3.52. If we were testing the difference in leniency between liberals (mean of 60) and conservatives (mean of 49), we could use our standard error result to translate the difference between sample means into a t ratio:

$$t = \frac{\overline{X}_1 - \overline{X}_2}{s_{\overline{X}_1 - \overline{X}_2}}$$

Here,

$$t = \frac{60 - 49}{3.52}$$

$$= \frac{11}{3.52}$$

$$= 3.12$$

We use t rather than z because we do not know the true population standard deviations for liberals and conservatives. Because we are estimating both σ_1 and σ_2 from s_1 and s_2, respectively, we compensate by using the wider t distribution, with degrees of freedom $N_1 + N_2 - 2$. For each population standard deviation that we estimate, we lose one degree of freedom from the total number of cases. Here, we have 60 cases from which we subtract 2 to obtain the 58 degrees of freedom.

Turning to Table B in Appendix C, we use the critical value for 40 degrees of freedom, the next lowest to 58, which is not given explicitly. Our calculated t value of 3.12 exceeds all the standard critical points, except that for the .001 level. Therefore, we could reject the null hypothesis at the .10, .05, or .01 level, whichever we had established for the alpha value at the start of our study. Had a .001 alpha value been established for whatever reason (there would seem little justification for choosing such a stringent test in this instance), we would have to accept the null hypothesis despite the large t value. Our chance of a Type II error would run quite high as a consequence.

STEP-BY-STEP ILLUSTRATION

TEST OF DIFFERENCE BETWEEN MEANS

To provide a step-by-step illustration of the foregoing procedure for testing a difference between two sample means, let us say we wanted to test the null hypothesis at the $\alpha = .05$ significance level that females are no more or less lenient toward offenders than males ($\mu_1 = \mu_2$). Our research hypothesis is that females differ from males with respect to leniency ($\mu_1 \neq \mu_2$). To test this hypothesis, let us say we gave a measure of leniency (for example, the Leniency Scale) to a random sample of 35 females and a random sample of 35 males, and obtained the following scores of leniency for each sample (X = scores ranging from 1 representing low leniency to 5 representing high leniency):

Males ($N = 35$)		Females ($N = 35$)	
X_1	$X_1{}^2$	X_2	$X_2{}^2$
1	1	1	1
1	1	1	1
1	1	2	4
2	4	1	1
1	1	1	1
1	1	1	1
3	9	3	9
3	9	1	1
1	1	1	1
1	1	2	4
2	4	4	16
1	1	1	1
2	4	1	1
1	1	1	1

(continued)

(*continued*)

Males ($N = 35$)		Females ($N = 35$)	
X_1	$X_1{}^2$	X_2	$X_2{}^2$
1	1	1	1
1	1	5	25
1	1	1	1
2	4	2	4
4	16	2	4
5	25	1	1
1	1	1	1
1	1	1	1
2	4	1	1
1	1	2	4
2	4	3	9
1	1	1	1
2	4	1	1
1	1	1	1
1	1	2	4
1	1	2	4
1	1	2	4
3	9	1	1
3	9	1	1
1	1	1	1
4	16	1	1
$\Sigma X_1 = 60$	$\Sigma X_1{}^2 = 142$	$\Sigma X_2 = 54$	$\Sigma X_2{}^2 = 114$

STEP 1 Find the mean for each sample.

$$\overline{X}_1 = \frac{\Sigma X_1}{N_1} \qquad \overline{X}_2 = \frac{\Sigma X_2}{N_2}$$

$$= \frac{60}{35} \qquad\qquad = \frac{54}{35}$$

$$= 1.71 \qquad\qquad = 1.54$$

STEP 2 Find the variance for each sample.

$$s_1{}^2 = \frac{\Sigma X_1{}^2}{N_1} - \overline{X}_1{}^2 \qquad s_2{}^2 = \frac{\Sigma X_2{}^2}{N_2} - \overline{X}_2{}^2$$

$$= \frac{142}{35} - 2.92 \qquad\quad = \frac{114}{35} - 2.37$$

$$= 4.06 - 2.92 \qquad\quad = 3.26 - 2.37$$

$$= 1.14 \qquad\qquad\quad = .89$$

STEP 3 Find the standard error of the difference between means.

$$s_{\overline{X}_1 - \overline{X}_2} = \sqrt{\left(\frac{N_1 s_1{}^2 + N_2 s_2{}^2}{N_1 + N_2 - 2}\right)\left(\frac{N_1 + N_2}{N_1 N_2}\right)}$$

$$= \sqrt{\left[\frac{(35)(1.14) + (35)(.89)}{35 + 35 - 2}\right]\left[\frac{35 + 35}{(35)(35)}\right]}$$

$$= \sqrt{\left(\frac{39.90 + 31.15}{68}\right)\left(\frac{70}{1,225}\right)}$$

$$= \sqrt{\left(\frac{71.05}{68}\right)\left(\frac{70}{1,225}\right)}$$

$$= \sqrt{(1.0449)(.0571)}$$

$$= \sqrt{.0597}$$

$$= .24$$

STEP 4 Compute the t value from the difference between means and the standard error of the difference.

$$t = \frac{\overline{X}_1 - \overline{X}_2}{s_{\overline{X}_1 - \overline{X}_2}}$$

$$= \frac{1.71 - 1.54}{.24}$$

$$= \frac{.17}{.24}$$

$$= .71$$

STEP 5 Determine table critical value for t.

$$df = N_1 + N_2 - 2 = 35 + 35 - 2 = 68$$

Use next lowest value, 60, to find

$$\alpha = .05$$

$$\text{table } t = 2.00$$

STEP 6 Compare calculated and table t values. The calculated t (.71) does not exceed the table t (2.00) in either the positive or negative direction, so we accept the null hypothesis of no difference in population means.

Thus, even though the sample means were not equal, they were not sufficiently different to conclude that females in the population are any more or less lenient than males in the population. Of course, we could be wrong and be committing a Type II error (accepting a false null hypothesis), in that there could in fact be a difference between population means. But these sample results are not disparate enough ($\overline{X}_1 - \overline{X}_2$ is not large enough), nor are the sample sizes large enough to allow us to infer that the sample difference would hold in the population.

THE ASSUMPTION OF EQUAL VARIANCES

The formula for the estimated standard error of the difference betwee
discussed pools together or combines variance information from bo/
so, it is assumed that the population variances are the same for the
$\sigma_1^2 = \sigma_2^2$). Of course, because we do not know the two population vari..
judge on the basis of the two sample variances (s_1^2 and s_2^2) whether the assumption or eq
population variances is at all plausible.

There is an alternative formula for estimating the standard error of the difference
between means in the face of unequal population variances. In practice, however, instances
in which such a formula are needed are rare. Specifically, the standard error formula presented appears to give valid results except in the very extreme case in which both (1) the
sample variances are wildly different (for example, when one sample variance is many times
the other), and (2) the sample sizes are very dissimilar. For all practical purposes, therefore,
the formula for the standard error of the difference between means provided here can be used
in almost all research situations.

COMPARING THE SAME SAMPLE MEASURED TWICE

So far, we have discussed making comparisons between two *independently* drawn samples (for example, males versus females, blacks versus whites, or liberals versus conservatives). Before leaving this topic, we must now introduce a final variation of the two
mean comparison referred to as a *before–after* or *panel* design: the case of a *single* sample measured at two different points in time (time 1 versus time 2). For example, a
researcher may seek to measure hostility in a single sample of children both before and
after they watch a certain television program. In the same way, we might want to measure
differences in attitudes toward capital punishment before and after a highly publicized
murder trial.

Keep in mind the important distinction between studying the same sample on two
different occasions versus sampling from the same population on two different occasions.
The *t* test of difference between means for the same sample measured twice generally
assumes that the same people are examined repeatedly—in other words, each respondent
is compared to himself or herself at another point in time.

For example, a polling organization might interview the sample of 1,000 adults one
week before and one week after the trial to measure changes in attitudes over time.
Because the same sample is measured twice, the *t* test of difference between means for
the same sample measured twice is appropriate.

Suppose, instead, that this polling organization administered the same survey instru-
ment to one sample of 1,000 adults before the trial and to a different sample of 1,000
adults after the trial. Even though the research looks at changes in attitudes over time, the
two samples would have been chosen independently—that is, the selection of respondents
after the trial would not have depended in any way on who was selected before the trial.
Although the same population would have been sampled twice, the particular people
interviewed would be different, and thus the *t* test of difference between means for independent groups would apply.

STEP-BY-STEP ILLUSTRATION

TEST OF DIFFERENCE BETWEEN MEANS FOR SAME SAMPLE MEASURED TWICE

To provide a step-by-step illustration of a before–after comparison, let us suppose that we wish to evaluate the effectiveness of a treatment program for men who are convicted of battering their wives or girlfriends. Specifically, corrections officials are interested in examining the effectiveness of a two-month anger management program in reducing levels of hostility toward women. In this case, then, μ_1 is the mean score of hostility toward women at time 1 (*before* the treatment program), and μ_2 is the mean score on the hostility scale at time 2 (*after* the program). Therefore

Null hypothesis: $(\mu_1 = \mu_2)$	The degree of hostility does not differ before and after the program.
Research hypothesis: $(\mu_1 \neq \mu_2)$	The degree of hostility differs before and after the program.

To examine the program's impact, a random sample of six of the men selected for the program are administered a questionnaire (the Hostility Toward Women Scale) before they participate in the program, and again one month after they have completed the program. The research team obtained the following Hostility Toward Women Scale scores from the pre- and post-program administrations of the questionnaire:

Program participant	Before program (X_1)	After program (X_2)	Difference $(D = X_1 - X_2)$	(Difference)² (D^2)
Jeffrey	2	1	1	1
Bill	1	2	−1	1
George	3	1	2	4
Leon	3	1	2	4
Mitchell	1	2	−1	1
Myron	4	1	3	9
	$\Sigma X_1 = 14$	$\Sigma X_2 = 8$		$\Sigma D^2 = 20$

As the table shows, making a before–after comparison focuses our attention on the *difference* between time 1 and time 2, as reflected in the formula to obtain the standard deviation (for the distribution of before–after difference scores):

$$s_D = \sqrt{\frac{\Sigma D^2}{N} - (\overline{X}_1 - \overline{X}_2)^2}$$

where s_D = standard deviation of the distribution of before–after difference scores
   D = after raw score subtracted from before raw score
   N = number of cases or respondents in sample

STEP 1 Find the mean for each point in time.

$$\overline{X}_1 = \frac{\Sigma X_1}{N} \qquad \overline{X}_2 = \frac{\Sigma X_2}{N}$$

$$= \frac{14}{6} \qquad\qquad = \frac{8}{6}$$

$$= 2.23 \qquad\qquad = 1.33$$

STEP 2 Find the standard deviation for the difference between time 1 and time 2.

$$s_D = \sqrt{\frac{\Sigma D^2}{N} - (\overline{X}_1 - \overline{X}_2)^2}$$

$$= \sqrt{\frac{20}{6} - (2.33 - 1.33)^2}$$

$$= \sqrt{\frac{20}{6} - (1.00)^2}$$

$$= \sqrt{3.33 - 1.00}$$

$$= \sqrt{2.33}$$

$$= 1.53$$

STEP 3 Find the standard error of the mean difference.

$$s_{\overline{D}} = \frac{s_D}{\sqrt{N-1}}$$

$$= \frac{1.53}{\sqrt{6-1}}$$

$$= \frac{1.53}{2.24}$$

$$= .68$$

STEP 4 Translate the sample mean difference into units of standard error of the mean difference.

$$t = \frac{\overline{X}_1 - \overline{X}_2}{s_{\overline{D}}}$$

$$= \frac{2.33 - 1.33}{.68}$$

$$= \frac{1.00}{.68}$$

$$= 1.47$$

STEP 5   Find the number of degrees of freedom.

$$\text{df} = N - 1$$
$$= 6 - 1$$
$$= 5$$

Note: N refers to the total number of *cases,* not the number of scores, for which there are two per case or respondent.

STEP 6   Compare the obtained t ratio with the appropriate t ratio in Table B.

$$\text{obtained } t = 1.47$$

$$\text{table } t = 2.571$$

$$\text{df} = 5$$

$$\alpha = .05$$

In order to reject the null hypothesis at the .05 significance level with 5 degrees of freedom, we must obtain a calculated t ratio of at least 2.571. Because our t ratio is only 1.47—less than the required table value—we accept the null hypothesis and reject the research hypothesis. The obtained sample difference in hostility scores before and after the program was probably the result of sampling error.

Two Sample Tests of Proportions

In the previous chapter, we learned how to construct confidence intervals for means and for proportions using the notion of the standard error of the mean and of the proportion. In this chapter, we shifted attention to the difference between samples and employed a standard error of the difference between means. It would seem logical also to consider the sampling distribution of the difference between proportions.

The important role of testing the difference between proportions goes far beyond simply a desire to have our presentation symmetrical and complete. So many important measures used in criminology and criminal justice are cast in terms of proportions. We are often interested in knowing if two groups (for example, males/females, whites/blacks, northerners/southerners, etc.) differ in the percentage who favor some criminal justice policy, who have some characteristic or attribute, or who succeed on some test.

Fortunately, the logic of testing the difference between two proportions is the same as for testing the difference between means. The only change is in the symbols and formulas used for calculating sample proportions and the standard error of the difference. As before, our statistic (z) is the difference between sample statistics divided by the standard error of the difference.

Rather than the z formula we used for testing the difference between means (with known σ_1 and σ_2), we use

$$z = \frac{P_1 - P_2}{s_{P_1 - P_2}}$$

where P_1 and P_2 are the respective sample proportions. The standard error of the difference in proportions is given by

$$s_{P_1 - P_2} = \sqrt{P^*(1 - P^*)\left(\frac{N_1 + N_2}{N_1 N_2}\right)}$$

where P^* is the combined sample proportion,

$$P^* = \frac{N_1 P_1 + N_2 P_2}{N_1 + N_2}$$

STEP-BY-STEP ILLUSTRATION
TEST OF DIFFERENCE BETWEEN PROPORTIONS

We will describe the necessary steps for this test by illustration. A criminal justice researcher is interested in the characteristics of people who drive under the influence of alcohol. In particular, she is interested in whether men admit to drunk driving more or less often than women do. She takes a sample of 200 males and 200 females over age 21 and asks them to fill out a questionnaire. Early in the questionnaire, respondents are asked whether they have ever consumed alcohol. Respondents saying they have not are eliminated from the samples but are not replaced by someone else. Consequently, the final sample sizes for the analysis are less than 200 each. The following hypotheses address the population proportions of men who say they have driven a car while under the influence of alcohol (π_1), and the proportion of women who say they have done so (π_2):

Null hypothesis: The proportion of men and women who say they have driven
($\pi_1 = \pi_2$)   *under the influence of alcohol is equal.*

Research hypothesis: The proportion of men and women who say they have driven
($\pi_1 \neq \pi_2$)   *under the influence of alcohol is not equal.*

The researcher obtains the following data:

	Male	Female	Total
Sample size (N)	180	150	330
Driven under the influence (f)	81	48	129
Proportion who have driven under the influence (P)	0.45	0.32	0.39

STEP 1 Compute the two sample proportions and the combined sample proportion.

$$P_1 = \frac{f_1}{N_1} = \frac{81}{180} = .45$$

$$P_2 = \frac{f_2}{N_2} = \frac{48}{150} = .32$$

$$P^* = \frac{N_1 P_1 + N_2 P_2}{N_1 + N_2}$$

$$= \frac{(180)(.45) + (150)(.32)}{180 + 150}$$

$$= \frac{81 + 48}{180 + 150}$$

$$= \frac{129}{330}$$

$$= .39$$

STEP 2 Compute the standard error of the difference.

$$s_{P_1 - P_2} = \sqrt{P^*(1 - P^*)\left(\frac{N_1 + N_2}{N_1 N_2}\right)}$$

$$= \sqrt{(.39)(1 - .39)\left[\frac{180 + 150}{(180)(150)}\right]}$$

$$= \sqrt{(.39)(.61)\left(\frac{330}{27,000}\right)}$$

$$= \sqrt{\frac{78.507}{27,000}}$$

$$= \sqrt{.002908}$$

$$= .0539$$

STEP 3   Translate the difference between proportions into units of the standard error of the difference.

$$z = \frac{P_1 - P_2}{s_{P_1 - P_2}}$$

$$= \frac{.45 - .32}{.0539}$$

$$= 2.41$$

STEP 4   Compare the obtained z value with the critical value in Table A (or from the bottom row of Table B).

For $\alpha = .05$, the critical value of $z = 1.96$. Because the obtained $z = 2.41$, we reject the null hypothesis. Because the difference between sample proportions was statistically significant, the criminal justice researcher was able to conclude that, according to self-reports, men and women drive under the influence of alcohol at different rates.

ONE-TAILED TESTS

The tests of significance covered thus far are known as *two-tailed tests:* We can reject the null hypothesis at both tails of the sampling distribution. A very large t ratio in *either* the positive or negative direction leads to rejecting the null hypothesis. A *one-tailed test,* in contrast, rejects the null hypothesis at only one tail of the sampling distribution.

Many statistics texts, particularly older editions, stress both one- and two-tailed tests. The one-tailed test has been deemphasized in recent years because statistical software packages (for example, *SPSS*) routinely produce two-tailed significance tests as part of their standard output.

Still, there are some occasions in which a one-tailed test is appropriate. We will briefly discuss the differences between one-and two-tailed tests for those instances. It should be emphasized, however, that the only changes are in the way the hypotheses are stated and the place where the t table is entered; fortunately, none of the formulas presented thus far changes in any way.

Suppose that in a neighborhood with very high rates of juvenile crime, community leaders have created new crime prevention programs for youth that focus on providing remedial academic programs for high school freshmen. The community leaders' hope is that improved skill levels will reduce high school drop-out rates, which in turn are expected to reduce crime rates.

A team of criminal justice researchers is enlisted to help evaluate the program. One part of their evaluation is an examination of the program's effectiveness in improving math skills. The researchers decide to use a before–after design in which nine youngsters targeted for remediation are administered a math test, and then are given a similar test 6 months later following participation in the remedial math program. The approach discussed earlier (two-tailed test) would have us set up our hypotheses as follows:

Null hypothesis: *Math ability does not differ before and after remediation.*
$(\mu_1 = \mu_2)$

Research hypothesis: *Math ability differs before and after remediation.*
$(\mu_1 \neq \mu_2)$

The research hypothesis covers two possible results—that the students do far better (the mean score on the post-test is higher than on the pretest) and that they do far worse (the post-test mean is lower than the pretest mean). However, in evaluating whether the remedial program is worthwhile (that is, produces a significant improvement in math skills), the researcher would not be excited by a significant reduction in performance.

A one-tailed test is appropriate when a researcher is only concerned with a change (for a sample tested twice) or difference (between two independent samples) in one pre-specified direction, or when a researcher anticipates the *direction* of the change or difference. For example, an attempt to show that black defendants receive harsher sentences (mean sentence) than whites would indicate the need for a one-tailed test. If, however, a researcher is just looking for differences in sentencing by race, whether it is blacks or whites who get harsher sentences, he or she would instead use a two-tailed test.

In our example of remedial education, the following hypotheses for a one-tailed test would be appropriate:

Null hypothesis:　　　　*Math ability does not improve after remediation.*
$(\mu_1 \geq \mu_2)$

Research hypothesis:　　*Math ability improves after remediation.*
$(\mu_1 < \mu_2)$

Note carefully the difference in these hypotheses from those stated earlier. The null hypothesis includes the entire sampling distribution to the right of the critical value; the research hypothesis only includes a change in one direction. This translates into a critical region on the distribution of t with only one tail. Moreover, the tail is larger than with a two-tailed test, because the entire area (for example, $\alpha = .05$) is loaded into one tail

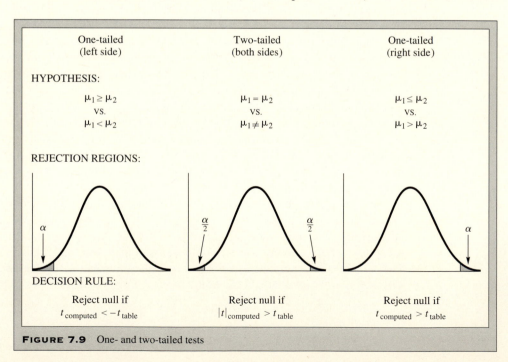

	One-tailed (left side)	Two-tailed (both sides)	One-tailed (right side)

HYPOTHESIS:

	$\mu_1 \geq \mu_2$	$\mu_1 = \mu_2$	$\mu_1 \leq \mu_2$
	VS.	VS.	VS.
	$\mu_1 < \mu_2$	$\mu_1 \neq \mu_2$	$\mu_1 > \mu_2$

REJECTION REGIONS:

DECISION RULE:

	Reject null if	Reject null if	Reject null if
	$t_{\text{computed}} < -t_{\text{table}}$	$\lvert t \rvert_{\text{computed}} > t_{\text{table}}$	$t_{\text{computed}} > t_{\text{table}}$

FIGURE 7.9　One- and two-tailed tests

rather than divided into the two sides. As a consequence the table value of t that permits the rejection of the null hypothesis is somewhat lower and easier to achieve. However, any t value in the opposite direction—no matter how extreme—would not allow rejection of the null hypothesis.

The differences between two-tailed and one-tailed tests are summarized in Figure 7.9. As a general rule, to construct a one-tailed test from two-tailed probabilities, simply use a table value with twice the area of the two-tailed test. Thus, for example, the critical value for a two-tailed test with $\alpha = .10$ is identical to that for a one-tailed test with $\alpha = .05$. For convenience, however, a separate table of one-tailed critical values for t is given in Table C.

STEP-BY-STEP ILLUSTRATION
ONE-TAILED TEST OF MEANS FOR SAME SAMPLE MEASURED TWICE

Note as we carry out our example that the mechanics for calculating t are unchanged when we employ a one-tailed rejection region. Suppose the before and after math scores for a sample of nine remedial students are as follows:

Student	Before (X_1)	After (X_2)	Difference $(D = X_1 - X_2)$	(Difference)^2 (D^2)
1	58	66	-8	64
2	63	68	-5	25
3	66	72	-6	36
4	70	76	-6	36
5	63	78	-15	225
6	51	56	-5	25
7	44	69	-25	625
8	58	55	3	9
9	50	55	-5	25
	$\Sigma X_1 = 523$	$\Sigma X_2 = 595$		$\Sigma D^2 = 1{,}070$

We can compute the t value exactly as we did in the previous section.

STEP 1   Find the mean for both the before and the after tests.

$$\overline{X}_1 = \frac{\Sigma X_1}{N} \qquad \overline{X}_2 = \frac{\Sigma X_2}{N}$$

$$= \frac{523}{9} \qquad = \frac{595}{9}$$

$$= 58.11 \qquad = 66.11$$

STEP 2   Find the standard deviation of the differences.

$$s_D = \sqrt{\frac{\Sigma D^2}{N} - (\overline{X}_1 - \overline{X}_2)^2}$$

$$= \sqrt{\frac{1{,}070}{9} - (58.11 - 66.11)^2}$$

$$= \sqrt{118.89 - 64}$$

$$= \sqrt{54.89}$$

$$= 7.41$$

STEP 3 Find the standard error of the difference between means.

$$s_{\bar{D}} = \frac{s_D}{\sqrt{N-1}}$$

$$= \frac{7.41}{\sqrt{9-1}}$$

$$= \frac{7.41}{2.83}$$

$$= 2.62$$

STEP 4 Translate the sample mean difference into units of the standard error of the difference.

$$t = \frac{\bar{X}_2 - \bar{X}_2}{s_{\bar{D}}}$$

$$= \frac{58.11 - 66.11}{2.62}$$

$$= \frac{-8.00}{2.62}$$

$$= -3.05$$

STEP 5 Find the degrees of freedom.

$$df = N - 1$$

$$= 9 - 1$$

$$= 8$$

STEP 6 Compare the obtained t ratio with the critical value from Table C.

$$\text{obtained } t = -3.05$$

$$\text{table } t = -1.86$$

$$\alpha = .05$$

Because we hypothesized that the post-test mean should be higher than the pretest mean, t should be negative. Therefore, we use the negative critical value. The obtained t

(-3.05) is more extreme in the negative direction than the critical value (-1.86), so we reject the null hypothesis. Thus, the remedial math program has produced a statistically significant improvement in math ability.

All the tests of sample differences that we have presented in this chapter can be modified into one-tailed tests. If the researcher who tested for differences in proportions of males and females who have driven while under the influence of alcohol had anticipated that the proportion for males would be larger, a one-tailed test could have been employed.

By the same token, the t test of difference in mean leniency between males and females discussed earlier could have been structured as a one-tailed test, if the researcher's theory suggested, for example, that men would be more lenient on the average. Changing to a one-tailed test only affects the hypotheses and the critical value of t, but not any of the calculations. The null hypothesis would instead be that men (group 1) are no more lenient than females (group 2), or symbolically ($\mu_1 \le \mu_2$), and the research hypothesis would be that men are more lenient ($\mu_1 > \mu_2$). With a .05 level of significance and again using 60 degrees of freedom in lieu of the actual 68, we obtain now from Table C a critical value $t = 1.67$. Locating the entire .05 rejection region into one tail lessens somewhat the size of t needed for significance (from 2.00 to 1.67), but still the calculated t ratio ($t = +0.71$, the same as before) is not nearly significant.

STEP-BY-STEP ILLUSTRATION

INDEPENDENT GROUPS, ONE-TAILED TEST

A professor who teaches a writing-intensive course required for all first-year criminal justice majors wants to determine whether students who attended private/sectarian schools are better prepared in English than students who attended public high schools. The professor decides to test her hypothesis concerning English preparedness using her class of 72 students.

During the first week of class, the professor gives a test covering grammar and vocabulary; she also asks on the test which type of high school the student had attended— private/sectarian or public. The professor learns that there are 22 private/sectarian school graduates and 50 public school graduates in her class. She then calculates descriptive statistics separately for the two groups:

Private/sectarian school	Public school
$N_1 = 22$	$N_2 = 50$
$\overline{X}_1 = 85$	$\overline{X}_2 = 82$
$s_1 = 6$	$s_2 = 8$

Because she anticipated that the graduates of private/sectarian high schools would score better on the test, the professor set up her hypotheses as follows:

Null hypothesis: *English preparedness is not greater among private/sectarian*
($\mu_1 \le \mu_2$) *high school graduates than among public high school*
  graduates.

Research hypothesis: English preparedness is greater among private/sectarian
$(\mu_1 > \mu_2)$ high school graduates than among public high school
graduates.

STEP 1   Obtain the sample means (these are given as 85 and 82, respectively).

$$\overline{X}_1 = \frac{\Sigma X_1}{N_1} = 85$$

$$\overline{X}_2 = \frac{\Sigma X_2}{N_2} = 82$$

STEP 2   Obtain sample standard deviations (the sample standard deviations are given as 6 and 8, respectively).

$$s_1 = \sqrt{\frac{\Sigma X_1^2}{N_1} - \overline{X}_1^2} = 6$$

$$s_2 = \sqrt{\frac{\Sigma X_2^2}{N_2} - \overline{X}_2^2} = 8$$

STEP 3   Calculate the standard error of the difference between means.

$$s_{\overline{X}_1 - \overline{X}_2} = \sqrt{\left(\frac{N_1 s_1^2 + N_2 s_2^2}{N_1 + N_2 - 2}\right)\left(\frac{N_1 + N_2}{N_1 N_2}\right)}$$

$$= \sqrt{\left[\frac{(22)(6)^2 + (50)(8)^2}{22 + 50 - 2}\right]\left[\frac{22 + 50}{(22)(50)}\right]}$$

$$= \sqrt{\left[\frac{(22)(36) + (50)(64)}{70}\right]\left(\frac{72}{1,100}\right)}$$

$$= \sqrt{\left(\frac{3,992}{70}\right)\left(\frac{72}{1,100}\right)}$$

$$= \sqrt{3.7328}$$

$$= 1.93$$

STEP 4   Translate the sample mean difference into units of the standard error of the difference.

$$t = \frac{\overline{X}_1 - \overline{X}_2}{s_{\overline{X}_1 - \overline{X}_2}}$$

$$= \frac{85 - 82}{1.93}$$

$$= \frac{3}{1.93}$$

$$= 1.55$$

STEP 5   Determine the degrees of freedom.

$$df = N_1 + N_2 - 2$$

$$= 22 + 50 - 2$$

$$= 70$$

STEP 6   Compare the obtained t ratio with the appropriate t ratio in Table C.

$$\text{obtained } t = 1.55$$

$$\text{table } t = 1.671$$

$$df = 70$$

$$\alpha = .05$$

Because the calculated t (1.55) does not exceed the table value (1.671), the professor cannot reject the null hypothesis. Therefore, although the difference between sample means was consistent with the professor's expectations (85 versus 82), the difference was not larger than she could have observed by chance alone. Furthermore, using a one-tailed test with the entire 5% critical region on one side of the sampling distribution made it easier to find a significant difference by lowering the critical value. Still, the results obtained by the professor were not quite statistically significant.

REQUIREMENTS FOR TESTING THE DIFFERENCE BETWEEN MEANS

As we shall see throughout the remainder of this text, every statistical test should be used only if the criminal justice researcher has at least considered certain requirements, conditions, or assumptions. Employing a test inappropriately may confuse an issue and mislead the investigator. As a result, the following requirements should be kept firmly in mind when considering the appropriateness of the z score or t ratio as a test of significance:

1. *A comparison between two means.* The z score and t ratio are employed to make comparisons between two means from independent samples or from a single sample measured twice (repeated measures).
2. *Interval data.* The assumption is that we have scores at the interval level of measurement. Therefore, we cannot use the z score or t ratio for ranked data or data that can only be categorized at the nominal level of measurement (see Chapter 1).
3. *Random sampling.* We should have drawn our samples on a random basis from a population of scores.
4. *A normal distribution.* The t ratio for small samples requires that the sample characteristic we have measured be normally distributed in the underlying population (the t ratio for

large samples is not much affected by failure to meet this assumption). Often, we cannot be certain that normality exists. Having no reason to believe otherwise, many researchers pragmatically assume their sample characteristic to be normally distributed. However, if the researcher has reason to suspect that normality cannot be assumed, and the sample size is not large, he or she is best advised that the *t* ratio may be an inappropriate test.

5. *Equal variances.* The *t* ratio for independent samples assumes that the population variances are equal. The sample variances, of course, may differ as a result of sampling. A moderate difference between the sample variances does not invalidate the results of the *t* ratio. But when this difference in sample variances is extreme (for example, when one sample variance is 10 times larger than the other), the *t* ratio presented here may not be appropriate. An adjusted formula for unequal variances does exist but is beyond the scope of this text.

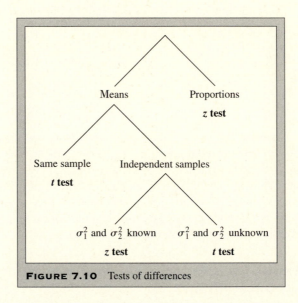

FIGURE 7.10   Tests of differences

SUMMARY

This chapter has focused on testing hypotheses about differences between sample means and proportions (see Figure 7.10). Relating to this purpose, the sampling distribution of differences as a probability distribution was described and illustrated. With the aid of this distribution and the standard error of the difference, a probability statement about a mean difference could be made and, on that basis, a null hypothesis rejected or accepted at a specified level of significance. In addition, we saw that a *t* ratio (and degrees of freedom) could be used to test hypotheses about differences between two independent samples and for a single sample measured at two points in time. The appropriateness of the *t* ratio depends on certain requirements such as (1) making a comparison between two means, (2) interval data, (3) random sampling, (4) a normal distribution, and (5) equal variances. A test of the difference between proportions was also presented. Finally, we showed how one-tailed tests could be used when the direction of the difference between means or proportions can be anticipated in advance.

TERMS TO REMEMBER

Null hypothesis	Type I error
Research hypothesis	Type II error
Sampling distribution of differences between means	Standard error of the difference between means
Level of significance	Statistically significant difference
.05 level of significance	Two-tailed test
.01 level of significance	One-tailed test
t ratio	

STEP-BY-STEP STUDY GUIDE

TEST OF DIFFERENCES BETWEEN MEANS FOR INDEPENDENT GROUPS

STEP 1 Obtain the mean for both groups.

$$\overline{X}_1 = \frac{\Sigma X_1}{N_1}$$

$$\overline{X}_2 = \frac{\Sigma X_2}{N_2}$$

STEP 2 Calculate the variance for both groups.

$$s_1^2 = \frac{\Sigma X_1^2}{N_1} - \overline{X}_1^2$$

$$s_2^2 = \frac{\Sigma X_2^2}{N_2} - \overline{X}_2^2$$

STEP 3 Obtain the standard error of the difference between means.

$$s_{\overline{X}_1 - \overline{X}_2} = \sqrt{\left(\frac{N_1 s_1^2 + N_2 s_2^2}{N_1 + N_2 - 2}\right)\left(\frac{N_1 + N_2}{N_1 N_2}\right)}$$

STEP 4 Compute the t ratio by dividing the mean difference by the standard error of the difference.

$$t = \frac{\overline{X}_1 - \overline{X}_2}{s_{\overline{X}_1 - \overline{X}_2}}$$

STEP 5 Calculate the degrees of freedom.

$$df = N_1 + N_2 - 2$$

STEP 6 Compare the obtained t ratio to the critical value from Table B or C. If the obtained value exceeds the critical value, then reject the null hypothesis of no difference; otherwise, accept the null hypothesis.

STEP-BY-STEP STUDY GUIDE

TEST OF DIFFERENCES BETWEEN MEANS FOR THE SAME SAMPLE MEASURED TWICE

STEP 1　Obtain the mean for both points in time.

$$\bar{X}_1 = \frac{\Sigma X_1}{N_1}$$

$$\bar{X}_2 = \frac{\Sigma X_2}{N_2}$$

STEP 2　Calculate the standard deviation of the difference ($D = X_1 - X_2$) between time 1 and time 2.

$$s_D = \sqrt{\frac{\Sigma D^2}{N} - (\bar{X}_1 - \bar{X}_2)^2}$$

STEP 3　Obtain the standard error of the mean difference.

$$s_{\bar{D}} = \frac{s_D}{\sqrt{N-1}}$$

STEP 4　Compute the t ratio by dividing the mean difference by the standard error of the mean difference.

$$t = \frac{\bar{X}_1 - \bar{X}_2}{s_{\bar{D}}}$$

STEP 5　Calculate the degrees of freedom.

$$df = N - 1$$

STEP 6　Compare the obtained t ratio to the critical value from the Table B or C. If the obtained value exceeds the critical value, then reject the null hypothesis of no difference; otherwise, accept the null hypothesis.

STEP-BY-STEP STUDY GUIDE

TEST OF DIFFERENCES BETWEEN PROPORTIONS

STEP 1　Obtain the proportions from both groups and the combined sample proportion.

$$P_1 = \frac{f_1}{N_1}$$

$$P_2 = \frac{f_2}{N_2}$$

$$P* = \frac{N_1 P_1 + N_2 P_2}{N_1 + N_2}$$

STEP 2   Compute the standard error of the difference.

$$s_{P_1 - P_2} = \sqrt{P*(1 - P*)\left(\frac{N_1 + N_2}{N_1 N_2}\right)}$$

STEP 3   Calculate the t ratio by dividing the difference between proportions by the standard error of the difference.

$$z = \frac{P_1 - P_2}{s_{P_1 - P_2}}$$

STEP 4   Compare the obtained z value to the critical value from Table A (or from the bottom row of Table B or C). If the obtained value exceeds the critical value, reject the null hypothesis of no difference; otherwise, accept the null hypothesis.

PROBLEMS

1. The Scholastic Aptitude Test (SAT) is standardized to have a population mean $\mu = 500$ and a population standard deviation $\sigma = 100$. Suppose that a researcher gives the SAT to a random sample of 50 males and 50 females, yielding sample means of 511 and 541, respectively. Based on these sample sizes, the researcher has already calculated the true standard deviation of the sampling distribution of the difference between means $\sigma_{\bar{X}_1 - \bar{X}_2}$ to be 20. Based on the areas under the normal curve given in Table A, find the probability of obtaining a sample mean for females that is at least 30 points higher than the sample mean for males.

2. Two groups of subjects participated in an experiment designed to test the effect of frustration on aggression. The experimental group of 40 subjects received a frustrating puzzle to solve, whereas the control group of 40 subjects received an easy, nonfrustrating version of the same puzzle. Level of aggression was then measured for both groups. Whereas the experimental group (frustration) had a mean aggression score $\bar{X}_1 = 4.0$ and a standard deviation of $s_1 = 2.0$, the control group (no frustration) had a mean aggression score $\bar{X}_2 = 3.0$ and a standard deviation of $s_2 = 1.5$ (higher mean scores indicate greater aggression). Using these results, test the null hypothesis of no difference with respect to aggression between the frustration and no-frustration conditions. What does the outcome of this test indicate?

3. Two groups of students took quizzes in statistics. Only one group was given formal course preparation for the quiz; the other group read the required text but never attended lectures on the material. The first group (attendance at lectures) received quiz scores of 2, 2, 3, and 4; the second group (no attendance at lectures) received quiz scores of 1, 1, 2, and 3. Test the null hypothesis of no difference with respect to quiz scores between students in attendance at lectures and students not in attendance at lectures. What do your results indicate?

4. A criminologist was interested in whether there was any disparity in sentencing based on the race of the defendant. She selected at random 18 burglary convictions and compared the prison terms given to the 10 whites and 8 blacks sampled. The sentence lengths (in years) are shown below for the white and black offenders. Using these data, test the null hypothesis that whites and blacks convicted of burglary in this jurisdiction do not differ with respect to prison sentence length.

Whites	Blacks
3	4
5	8
4	7
7	3
4	5
5	4
6	5
4	4
3	
2	

5. In a field experiment on the effects of community crime prevention efforts on fear of crime, residents of one large condominium complex were encouraged to

participate in a variety of efforts: Monthly condo association meetings were held to discuss effective crime prevention strategies, signs were posted stating that the complex was part of a neighborhood crime watch, and parking lot lighting was improved. In a physically identical complex several blocks away, none of these measures were taken. After six months, five condominium owners in each complex were randomly chosen and were given a fear-of-crime questionnaire. Crime occurring in both complexes was tracked and found to be identical, so differences in fear of crime could not be attributed to differences in actual crime. Using the following data, test the null hypothesis that the community crime prevention program had no impact on residents' feelings of safety from crime. Higher scores indicate feelings of greater safety.

Program	Control
15	8
17	7
14	9
11	12
13	14

6. A researcher rode along with patrol officers for several weeks and recorded the number of minutes police officers spent interviewing witnesses at a variety of crime scenes. Using the following numbers of minutes that male and female officers spent interviewing witnesses, test the null hypothesis that there are no gender differences in time spent:

Males	Females
8	15
11	19
13	13
4	11
2	18

7. A legal researcher was interested in sex differences in the willingness of prosecutors to plea bargain. She recorded the number of cases plea bargained out of their last 10 cases for a sample of eight female and seven male prosecutors. Test the null hypothesis that male and female prosecutors do not differ in their plea bargaining of cases. What do your results indicate?

Females	Males
8	1
3	5
1	8
7	3
7	2
6	1
8	2
5	

8. A personnel consultant was hired to study the influence of sick-pay benefits on absenteeism among security guards. She randomly selected samples of part-time guards who do not get paid when out sick and full-time guards who are paid when out sick. Using the following data on the number of days absent during a one-year period, test the null hypothesis that part-time and full-time security guards do not differ in absenteeism. What do your results indicate?

Part-time	Full-time
1	2
1	2
2	4
3	2
3	2

9. A psychologist asked to provide expert testimony in a criminal trial examined whether crime witnesses of different races make different age estimates of offenders. To find out, he showed samples of African-Americans and Caucasians a videotape of actors portraying an armed robbery. After seeing the tape, the subjects were asked to estimate the age of the robber. Using the age estimates below, test for the significance of the difference between means.

African-Americans	Caucasians
18	17
23	11
12	12
14	16
18	14
16	12
15	12

10. One of the goals of a boot camp prison program is to improve the self-esteem of offenders. Offenders in this program were given a self-esteem questionnaire during the first and last weeks of their stay at the boot camp. Test for the significance of the differences in the before–after scores on the self-esteem scale of a random sample of five boot camp graduates.

Inmate	Before	After
A	18	39
B	15	30
C	10	21
D	12	10
E	9	20

11. Even in the darkest areas of human behavior, we tend to imitate our heroes. A suicidologist studied the incidence of suicide in five randomly selected com-

munities of moderate size both before and after publicity was given to the suicide of a famous singer. Using the following data on the number of suicides, test the null hypothesis that publicity about a particular suicide had no effect on the incidents of suicide.

Community	Before	After
A	3	6
B	4	7
C	9	10
D	7	9
E	5	8

12. A researcher believes that alcohol intoxication even half the legal limit, that is, .05 blood alcohol instead of .10, might severely impair driving ability. To test this, he subjects 10 volunteers to a driving simulation test first while sober and then after drinking amounts sufficient to raise the blood alcohol level to .05. The researcher measures performance as the number of simulated obstacles with which the driver collides. Thus, the higher the number, the poorer the driving. The obtained results are as follows:

Before drinking	After drinking
1	4
2	2
0	1
0	2
2	5
1	3
4	3
0	2
1	4
2	3

Test the null hypothesis that there is no difference in driving ability before and after alcohol consumption to the .05 blood alcohol level (use the .05 significance level).

13. A national polling organization conducts a telephone survey of American adults concerning whether they believe the president is doing a good job on criminal justice issues. A total of 990 persons surveyed had voted in the previous presidential election. Of the 630 who had voted for the president, 72% said they thought he was doing a good job. Of the 360 who did not vote for the president, 60% reported that they thought he was doing a good job. Test the null hypothesis of no difference in population proportions who believe the president is doing a good job (use a .05 level of significance).

14. A pollster interviews by telephone a statewide random sample of persons aged 18 and over about their attitudes toward stricter gun control. Using the following set of results, test the significance of the difference between the proportions of men and women who support stricter controls.

	Males	Females
Favor	92	120
Oppose	74	85
N	166	205

15. A researcher is interested in gender differences in attitudes toward drug legalization. Polling a sample of 100 men and 80 women, he finds that 36% of the men and 40% of the women approve of legalizing drugs. Test the significance of the difference in sample proportions.

16. A researcher is interested in the differences in attitudes toward drug legalization between prosecutors and public defenders. Polling a random sample of 100 prosecutors and 100 public defenders, he finds that 27% of the prosecutors and 36% of the public defenders approve of legalizing drugs. Test the significance of the difference in sample proportions.

17. The researcher from Question 16 decides to further pursue differences in attitudes and opinions among people in different segments of the criminal justice system. He finds that 52% of his sample of 100 prosecutors and 41% of the 100 public defenders support capital punishment. Test the significance of the difference in sample proportions.

18. The researcher from Questions 16 and 17 asks a sample of 75 police officers and 95 probation officers whether they support capital punishment in their state. He found that 58 of the police officers and 41 of the probation officers supported capital punishment. Test the significance of the difference in sample proportions.

19. A law professor wonders whether male judges dispose of cases more rapidly than do female judges. He obtains a sample of six male and six female judges, and obtains the average daily number of cases disposed of by each. She obtained the following results:

Female judges	Male judges
10	8
9	11
8	8
9	10
12	10
8	9

Test the null hypothesis of no significant gender difference in daily number of disposed cases. What do your results indicate?

20. The anti-black prejudice (racism) of eight white young adults, all convicted of committing a hate crime, was measured both before and after they had seen a film designed to reduce their racist attitudes. Using the following scores on an anti-black prejudice scale obtained by the eight subjects, test the null hypothesis that the film did not result in a reduction of racist attitudes. What do your results indicate?

	Before	After
A	36	24
B	25	20
C	26	26
D	30	27
E	31	18
F	27	19
G	29	27
H	31	30

21. Using Durkheim's theory as a basis, a sociologist calculated the following suicide rates (number of suicides per 100,000 population, rounded to the nearest whole number) for 10 "high-anomie" and 10 "low-anomie" metropolitan areas. Anomie (normlessness) was indicated by the presence of a large number of newcomers or transients in an area.

High anomie	Low anomie
19	15
17	20
22	11
18	13
25	14
29	16
20	14
18	9
19	11
23	14

Test the null hypothesis that high-anomie metropolitan areas do not have higher suicide rates than low-anomie areas. What do your results indicate?

22. The Center for the Study of Violence wants to determine whether a conflict-resolution program in a particular high school alters aggressive behavior among its students. For 10 students, aggression was measured both before and after they participated in the conflict-resolution course. Their scores were the following (higher scores indicate greater aggressiveness):

Before participating	After participating
10	8
3	3
4	1
8	5
8	7
9	8
5	1
7	5
1	1
7	6

Test the null hypothesis that aggression does not differ as a result of participation in the conflict-resolution program. What do your results indicate?

23. A mischievous prosecutor has nicknamed Judge A "Mr. Warm and Fuzzy" in response to his opinion that the judge hands down relatively short sentences for armed robbery. In the same court, Judge B has earned a reputation as "The Hanging Judge" for the relatively harsh sentences she imposes. Are these nicknames deserved? A curious court clerk obtains the last 10 prison sentences imposed on armed robbers by each of the judges. Using the clerk's data, test the null hypothesis that the two judges do not differ in the prison sentence lengths they impose on convicted armed robbers. What do your results indicate?

Judge A	Judge B
3	7
4	4
1	6
1	3
5	10
8	7
2	6
7	9
5	8
4	10

24. A computer company has designed a new "virtual reality" training tool in which a fleeing suspect is being pursued on foot by a law enforcement officer. Similar in concept to flight simulators for pilots, this training device presents officers with a variety of situations where they must decide whether to continue pursuit, whether the suspect is armed, and whether to shoot. Twenty police cadets were randomly split into two groups: 10 received traditional training and 10 received the same training with the addition of the virtual reality exercises. At the end of six weeks, all 20 trainees took the same field test, where they receive scores for decision making and marksmanship. For the following results, test the hypothesis that virtual reality training fails to enhance the field-test performance of police cadets (higher scores indicate better performance).

Traditional training	With Virtual reality
3	8
5	5
7	9
9	3
8	2
9	6
7	4
4	5
9	2
9	5

25. The short-term effect of a lecture on attitudes toward illicit drug use was studied by measuring 10 students' attitudes about drug abuse both before and after they attended a persuasive antidrug lecture given by a former addict. Using the following attitude scores (higher scores indicate more favorable attitudes toward drug use), test the null hypothesis that the antidrug lecture makes no difference in students' attitudes. What do your results indicate?

Student	Before	After
A	5	1
B	9	7
C	6	5
D	7	7
E	3	1
F	9	6
G	9	5
H	8	7
I	4	4
J	5	5

ANALYSIS OF VARIANCE

- **THE LOGIC OF ANALYSIS OF VARIANCE**

- **THE SUM OF SQUARES**

- **MEAN SQUARE**

- **THE *F* RATIO**

- **A MULTIPLE COMPARISON OF MEANS**

- **REQUIREMENTS FOR USING THE *F* RATIO**

- **SUMMARY**

- **TERMS TO REMEMBER**

- **STEP-BY-STEP STUDY GUIDE: TEST OF DIFFERENCES BETWEEN MEANS FOR SEVERAL INDEPENDENT GROUPS USING ANALYSIS OF VARIANCE**

- **PROBLEMS**

Blacks versus whites, males versus females, and liberals versus conservatives represent the kind of two-sample comparisons that occupied our attention in the previous chapter. Yet, reality cannot always be conveniently sliced into two groups; respondents do not always divide themselves in so simple a fashion.

As a result, the criminal justice researcher often seeks to make comparisons among three, four, five, or more samples or groups. To illustrate, he or she may study the influence of racial identity (black, white, or Asian) on job discrimination, degree of economic deprivation (severe, moderate, or mild) on juvenile delinquency, or subjective social class (upper, middle, working, or lower) on support for drug legalization.

The student may wonder whether we use a *series* of t ratios to make comparisons among three or more sample means. Suppose, for example, we want to test the influence of social class on support for drug legalization.Why can we not pair-compare all possible combinations of social class and obtain a t ratio for each comparison? Using this method, four samples generate six paired combinations for which six t ratios must be calculated:

1. Upper class versus middle class
2. Upper class versus working class
3. Upper class versus lower class
4. Middle class versus working class
5. Middle class versus lower class
6. Working class versus lower class

Not only does the procedure of calculating a series of t ratios involve a good deal of work, but it has a statistical limitation as well. This is because it increases the probability of making a Type I error—the error of rejecting the null hypothesis when it should be accepted. Recall that the criminal justice researcher is generally willing to accept a 5% risk of making a Type I error (the .05 level of significance). He or she therefore expects that *by chance alone* 5 out of every 100 sample mean differences will be large enough to be considered as significant. The more statistical tests we conduct, however, the more likely we are to get statistically significant findings by sampling error (rather than by a true population difference) and hence to commit a Type I error. When we run a large number of such tests, the interpretation of our result becomes problematic. To take an extreme example: How would we interpret a significant *t* ratio out of 1,000 such comparisons made in a particular study? We know that at least a few large mean differences can be expected to occur simply on the basis of sampling error.

For a more typical example, suppose a researcher wished to survey and compare voters in eight regions of the country (New England, Middle Atlantic, South Atlantic, Midwest, South, Southwest, Mountain, and Pacific) on their feelings about new federal crime legislation. Comparing the regional samples would require 28 separate *t* ratios (New England vs. Middle Atlantic, New England vs. South Atlantic, Middle Atlantic vs. South Atlantic, and so on). Out of 28 separate tests of difference between sample means, each with a .05 level of significance, 5% or about 1 (1.4 to be exact) would be expected to be significant due to chance or sampling error alone.

Suppose that from his 28 different *t* ratios, the researcher obtains two *t* ratios (New England vs. South, and Middle Atlantic vs. Mountain) that are significant. How should the researcher interpret these two significant differences? Should he go out on a limb and treat both as indicative of real population differences? Should he play it safe by maintaining that both could be the result of sampling error and go back to collect more data? Should he, based on the expectation that one *t* ratio will come out significant by chance, decide that only one of the two significant *t* ratios is valid? If so, in which of the two significant *t* ratios should he have faith? The larger one? The one that seems more plausible? Unfortunately, none of these solutions is particularly sound. The problem is that as the number of separate tests mounts, the likelihood of rejecting a true null hypothesis (Type I error) grows accordingly. Thus, while for each *t* ratio the probability of a Type I error may be .05, overall the probability of rejecting any true null hypothesis is far greater than .05.

To overcome this problem and clarify the interpretation of our result, we need a statistical test that holds Type I error at a constant level by making a *single* overall decision as to whether a significant difference is present among the three, eight, or however many sample means we seek to compare. Such a test is known as the *analysis of variance.*

THE LOGIC OF ANALYSIS OF VARIANCE

To conduct an analysis of variance, we treat the total *variation* in a set of scores as being divisible into two components: the distance or deviation of raw scores from their group mean, known as *variation within groups,* and the distance or deviation of group means from one another, referred to as *variation between groups.*

In order to examine variation within groups, the approval of drug legalization scores of members of four social classes—(1) lower, (2) working, (3) middle, and (4) upper—have been graphically represented in Figure 8.1, where X_1, X_2, X_3, and X_4, are any raw scores in their respective groups, and $\overline{X}_1$, $\overline{X}_2$, $\overline{X}_3$, and $\overline{X}_4$, are the group means. In symbolic terms, we see that variation within groups refers to the distance between X_1 and $\overline{X}_1$, between X_2 and $\overline{X}_2$, between X_3 and $\overline{X}_3$, and between X_4 and $\overline{X}_4$.

We can also visualize variation between groups. With the aid of Figure 8.2, we see that degree of support for drug legalization varies by social class: The upper class group ($\overline{X}_4$) has greater support than the middle-class group ($\overline{X}_3$), which, in turn, has greater support than the working-class group ($\overline{X}_2$), which, in its turn, has greater support than the lower-class group ($\overline{X}_1$).

The distinction between variation *within* groups and variation *between* groups is not peculiar to the analysis of variance. Although not named as such, we encountered a similar distinction in the form of the *t* ratio, wherein a difference *between* $\overline{X}_1$ and $\overline{X}_2$ was compared against the standard error of the difference ($s_{\overline{X}_1 - \overline{X}_2}$), a combined estimate of differences *within* each group. Therefore,

$$t = \frac{\overline{X}_1 - \overline{X}_2}{s_{\overline{X}_1 - \overline{X}_2}} \quad \begin{array}{l} \leftarrow \text{variation between groups} \\ \leftarrow \text{variation within groups} \end{array}$$

In a similar way, the analysis of variance yields an *F ratio,* whose numerator represents variation between the groups being compared, and whose denominator contains an estimate of variation within these groups. As we shall see, the *F* ratio indicates the size of

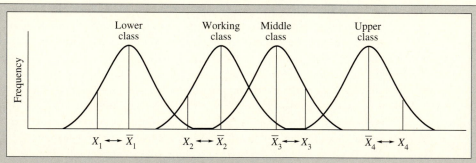

FIGURE 8.1   Graphic representation of variation within four groups of social class

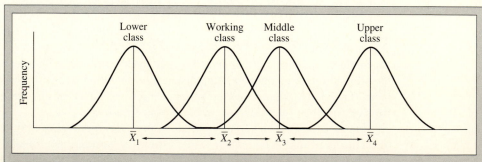

FIGURE 8.2   Graphic representation of variation between four groups of social class

the difference between groups *relative* to the size of the variation within each group. As was true of the *t* ratio, the larger the *F* ratio (the larger the variation between groups relative to the variation within groups), the greater the probability of rejecting the null hypothesis and accepting the research hypothesis.

THE SUM OF SQUARES

At the heart of the analysis of variance is the concept of *sum of squares,* which represents the initial step for measuring total variation as well as variation between and within groups. It may come as a pleasant surprise to learn that only the label "sum of squares" is new to us. The concept itself was introduced in Chapter 4 as an important step in the procedure for obtaining the variance. In that context, we learned to find the sum of squares by squaring the deviations from the mean of a distribution and adding these squared deviations together $\Sigma(X - \overline{X})^2$. This procedure eliminated minus signs, while still providing a sound mathematical basis for the variance and standard deviation.

When applied to a situation in which groups are being compared, there is more than one type of sum of squares, although each type represents *the sum of squared deviations from a mean.* Corresponding to the distinction between total variation and its two components, we have the *total* sum of squares (SS_{total}), *between-groups* sum of squares ($SS_{between}$), and *within-groups* sum of squares (SS_{within}).

Consider the hypothetical results shown in Figure 8.3. Note that only part of the data is shown to help us focus on the concepts of total, within-groups, and between-groups sums of squares.

The respondent with a 7 scored substantially higher than the total mean ($\overline{X}_{total} = 3$). His deviation from the total mean is $(X - \overline{X}_{total}) = 4$. Part of this elevated score represents, however, the fact that his group scored higher on average ($\overline{X}_{group} = 6$) than the overall or total mean ($\overline{X}_{total} = 3$). That is, the deviation of this respondent's group mean from the total mean is $(\overline{X}_{group} - \overline{X}_{total}) = 3$. After accounting for the group difference, this

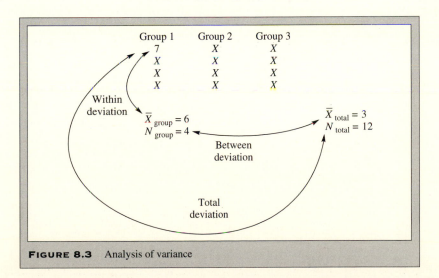

FIGURE 8.3   Analysis of variance

respondent's score remains higher than his own group mean. Within the group, his deviation from the group mean is $(X - \overline{X}_{group}) = 1$.

As we shall see very shortly, we can take these deviations (of scores from the total mean, deviations between group means and the total mean, and deviations of scores from their group means), square them, and then sum them to obtain SS_{total}, SS_{within}, and $SS_{between}$.

A RESEARCH ILLUSTRATION

Let's consider a research situation in which each type of sum of squares might be calculated. Suppose a researcher is interested in comparing self-esteem among different types of criminal offenders. She wants to know if offenders convicted for different kinds of offenses have different levels of self-esteem. She suspects that sex offenders and drug offenders might have lower self-esteem than those convicted of property or violent crimes. She randomly selects five of each type of offender from a state prison: violent, property, sex, and drug offenders. The researcher then administers to each of the offenders a six-item checklist designed to measure self-esteem. The scale scores range from 0 for very low self-esteem to 6 for very high self-esteem.

The researcher sets up her hypotheses as follows:

Null hypothesis: *Self-esteem does not differ by offense type.*
$(\mu_1 = \mu_2 = \mu_3 = \mu_4)$

Research hypothesis: *Self-esteem differs by offense type.*
(some $\mu_i \neq \mu_j$)

The total sum of squares is defined as the sum of the squared deviation of every raw score from the total mean. By formula,

$$SS_{total} = \Sigma (X - \overline{X}_{total})^2$$

where X = any raw score
$\overline{X}_{total}$ = the total mean for all groups combined

Using this formula, we subtract the total mean ($\overline{X}_{total}$) from each raw score (X), square the deviations that result, and then sum. Applying this formula to the data in Table 8.1, we obtain the following results.

$$
\begin{aligned}
SS_{total} = \; & (1 - 2.85)^2 + (0 - 2.85)^2 + (0 - 2.85)^2 + (2 - 2.85)^2 \\
& + (0 - 2.85)^2 + (3 - 2.85)^2 + (1 - 2.85)^2 + (2 - 2.85)^2 \\
& + (2 - 2.85)^2 + (1 - 2.85)^2 + (5 - 2.85)^2 + (6 - 2.85)^2 \\
& + (4 - 2.85)^2 + (2 - 2.85)^2 + (5 - 2.85)^2 + (4 - 2.85)^2 \\
& + (6 - 2.85)^2 + (2 - 2.85)^2 + (5 - 2.85)^2 + (6 - 2.85)^2
\end{aligned}
$$

TABLE 8.1   SELF-ESTEEM BY OFFENDER TYPE

	Sex offenses			Robbery	
X_1	$X_1 - \overline{X}_1$	$(X_1 - \overline{X}_1)^2$	X_2	$X_2 - \overline{X}_2$	$(X_2 - \overline{X}_2)^2$
1	.4	.16	3	1.2	1.44
0	−.6	.36	1	−.8	.64
0	−.6	.36	2	.2	.40
2	1.4	1.96	2	.2	.40
0	−.6	.36	1	−.8	.64
$\Sigma X_1 = 3$	$\overline{X}_1 = \dfrac{3}{5} = .6$	$\Sigma(X_1 - \overline{X}_1)^2 = 3.20$	$\Sigma X_2 = 9$	$\overline{X}_2 = \dfrac{9}{5} = 1.8$	$\Sigma(X_2 - \overline{X}_2)^2 = 2.80$

	Burglary			Drug offenses	
X_3	$X_3 - \overline{X}_3$	$(X_3 - \overline{X}_3)^2$	X_4	$X_4 - \overline{X}_4$	$(X_4 - \overline{X}_4)^2$
5	.6	.36	4	−.6	.36
6	1.6	2.56	6	1.4	1.96
4	−.4	.16	2	−2.6	6.76
2	−2.4	5.76	5	.4	.16
5	.6	.36	6	1.4	1.96
$\Sigma X_3 = 22$	$\overline{X}_3 = \dfrac{22}{5} = 4.4$	$\Sigma(X_3 - \overline{X}_3)^2 = 9.20$	$\Sigma X_4 = 23$	$\overline{X}_4 = \dfrac{23}{5} = 4.6$	$\Sigma(X_4 - \overline{X}_4)^2 = 11.20$

$$\overline{X}_{\text{total}} = 2.85$$

$$= (-1.85)^2 + (-2.85)^2 + (-2.85)^2 + (-.85)^2 + (-2.85)^2$$
$$+ (.15)^2 + (-1.85)^2 + (-.85)^2 + (-.85)^2 + (-1.85)^2$$
$$+ (2.15)^2 + (3.15)^2 + (1.15)^2 (-.85)^2 + (2.15)^2$$
$$+ (1.15)^2 + (3.15)^2 + (-.85)^2 + (2.15)^2 + (3.15)^2$$
$$= 3.42 + 8.12 + 8.12 + .72 + 8.12$$
$$+ .02 + 3.42 + .72 + .72 + 3.42$$
$$+ 4.62 + 9.92 + 1.32 + .72 + 4.62$$
$$+ 1.32 + 9.92 + .72 + 4.62 + 9.92$$
$$= 84.5$$

The within-groups sum of squares is the sum of the squared deviations of every raw score from its group mean. By formula,

$$SS_{\text{within}} = \Sigma(X - \overline{X}_{\text{group}})^2$$

where X = any raw score
$\overline{X}_{\text{group}}$ = mean of the group containing the raw score

Using this formula, we subtract the group mean ($\overline{X}_{\text{group}}$) from each raw score ($X$), square the deviations that result, and then sum. Applying this formula to the data in Table 8.1, we obtain

$$
\begin{aligned}
\text{SS}_{\text{within}} &= (1 - .6)^2 + (0 - .6)^2 + (0 - .6)^2 + (2 - .6)^2 + (0 - .6)^2 \\
&\quad + (3 - 1.8)^2 + (1 - 1.8)^2 + (2 - 1.8)^2 + (2 - 1.8)^2 + (1 - 1.8)^2 \\
&\quad + (5 - 4.4)^2 + (6 - 4.4)^2 + (4 - 4.4)^2 + (2 - 4.4)^2 + (5 - 4.4)^2 \\
&\quad + (4 - 4.6)^2 + (6 - 4.6)^2 + (2 - 4.6)^2 + (5 - 4.6)^2 + (6 - 4.6)^2 \\
&= (.4)^2 + (-.6)^2 + (-.6)^2 + (1.4)^2 + (-.6)^2 \\
&\quad + (1.2)^2 + (-.8)^2 + (.2)^2 + (.2)^2 + (-.8)^2 \\
&\quad + (.6)^2 + (1.6)^2 + (-.4)^2 + (-2.4)^2 + (.6)^2 \\
&\quad + (-.6)^2 + (1.4)^2 + (-2.6)^2 + (.4)^2 + (1.4)^2 \\
&= .16 + .36 + .36 + 1.96 + .36 \\
&\quad + 1.44 + .64 + .40 + .40 + .64 \\
&\quad + .36 + 2.56 + .16 + 5.76 + .36 \\
&\quad + .36 + 1.96 + 6.76 + .16 + 1.96 \\
&= 26.4
\end{aligned}
$$

Notice that the within-groups sum of squares could have been obtained simply by combining the sum of squares within each group. That is, with four groups,

$$
\text{SS}_{\text{within}} = \Sigma(X_1 - \overline{X}_1)^2 + \Sigma(X_2 - \overline{X}_2)^2 + \Sigma(X_3 - \overline{X}_3)^2 + \Sigma(X_4 - \overline{X}_4)^2
$$

From Table 8.1, we have

$$
\text{SS}_{\text{within}} = 3.2 + 2.8 + 9.2 + 11.2 = 26.4
$$

The between-groups sum of squares represents the *sum of the squared deviations of every group mean from the total mean.* Accordingly, we must determine the difference between each group mean and the total mean ($\overline{X}_{\text{group}} - \overline{X}_{\text{total}}$), square this deviation, multiply by the number of scores in that group, and add these quantities. Summing across groups, we obtain the following definitional formula for the between-groups sum of squares:

$$
\boxed{\,\text{SS}_{\text{between}} = \Sigma\,N_{\text{group}}(\overline{X}_{\text{group}} - \overline{X}_{\text{total}})^2\,}
$$

where N_{group} = number of scores in any group
   $\overline{X}_{\text{group}}$ = mean of any group
   $\overline{X}_{\text{total}}$ = mean of all groups combined

Applying the formula to the data in Table 8.1, we obtain

$$SS_{between} = 5(.6 - 2.85)^2 + 5(1.8 - 2.85)^2 + 5(4.4 - 2.85)^2 + 5(4.6 - 2.85)^2$$

$$= 5(-2.25)^2 + 5(-1.05)^2 + 5(1.55)^2 + 5(1.75)^2$$

$$= 5(5.06) + 5(1.10) + 5(2.40) + 5(3.06)$$

$$= 25.3 + 5.5 + 12.0 + 15.3$$

$$= 58.1$$

Thus, the sums of squares are

$$SS_{total} = 84.5$$

$$SS_{within} = 26.4$$

$$SS_{between} = 58.1$$

Notice that the total sum of squares is equal to the within-groups and between-groups sums of squares added together. This relationship among the three sums of squares can be used as a check on your work.

COMPUTING SUMS OF SQUARES

The definitional formulas for total, within-groups, and between-groups sums of squares are based on the manipulation of deviation scores, a time-consuming and difficult process. Fortunately, we may instead employ the following much simpler computational formulas to obtain results that are identical (except for rounding errors) to the lengthier definitional formulas:

$$SS_{total} = \Sigma X^2_{total} - N_{total}\bar{X}^2_{total}$$

$$SS_{within} = \Sigma X^2_{total} - \Sigma N_{group}\bar{X}^2_{group}$$

$$SS_{between} = \Sigma N_{group}\bar{X}^2_{group} - N_{total}\bar{X}^2_{total}$$

where ΣX^2_{total} = all the scores squared and then summed
$\bar{X}_{total}$ = total mean of all groups combined
N_{total} = total number of scores in all groups combined
$\bar{X}_{group}$ = mean of any group
N_{group} = number of scores in any group

The raw scores in Table 8.1 have been set up in Table 8.2 for the purpose of illustrating the use of the computational sum of squares formulas. Note that before applying the formulas, we must first obtain the sum of scores (ΣX_{total}), sum of squared scores (ΣX^2_{total}), number of scores (N_{total}), and mean ($\bar{X}_{total}$) for all groups combined:

$$\Sigma X_{\text{total}} = \Sigma X_1 + \Sigma X_2 + \Sigma X_3 + \Sigma X_4$$

$$= 3 + 9 + 22 + 23$$

$$= 57$$

$$\Sigma X^2_{\text{total}} = \Sigma X_1^2 + \Sigma X_2^2 + \Sigma X_3^2 + X_4^2$$

$$= 5 + 19 + 106 + 117$$

$$= 247$$

$$N_{\text{total}} = N_1 + N_2 + N_3 + N_4$$

$$= 5 + 5 + 5 + 5$$

$$= 20$$

$$\overline{X}_{\text{total}} = \frac{\Sigma X_{\text{total}}}{N_{\text{total}}}$$

$$= \frac{57}{20}$$

$$= 2.85$$

TABLE 8.2   COMPUTATIONS FOR SELF-ESTEEM DATA

Sex offenses		Robbery	
X_1	X_1^2	X_2	X_2^2
1	1	3	9
0	0	1	1
0	0	2	4
2	4	2	4
0	0	1	1
$\Sigma X_1 = 3$	$\Sigma X_1^2 = 5$	$\Sigma X_2 = 9$	$\Sigma X_2^2 = 19$
$\overline{X}_1 = \dfrac{3}{5} = .6$		$\overline{X}_2 = \dfrac{9}{5} = 1.8$	

Burglary		Drug offenses	
X_3	X_3^2	X_4	X_4^2
5	25	4	16
6	36	6	36
4	16	2	4
2	4	5	25
5	25	6	36
$\Sigma X_3 = 22$	$\Sigma X_3^2 = 106$	$\Sigma X_4 = 23$	$\Sigma X_4^2 = 117$
$\overline{X}_3 = \dfrac{22}{5} = 4.4$		$\overline{X}_4 = \dfrac{23}{5} = 4.6$	

$N_{\text{total}} = 20$ $\overline{X}_{\text{total}} = 2.85$ $\Sigma X_{\text{total}} = 57$ $\Sigma X^2_{\text{total}} = 247$

Next, we move on to calculating the following sums of squares:

$$SS_{total} = \Sigma X^2_{total} - N_{total}\overline{X}^2_{total}$$
$$= 247 + (20)(2.85)^2$$
$$= 247 + (20)(8.12)$$
$$= 247 + 162.4$$
$$= 84.5$$

$$SS_{within} = \Sigma X^2_{total} - \Sigma N_{group}\overline{X}^2_{group}$$
$$= 247 - [(5)(.6)^2 + (5)(1.8)^2 + (5)(4.4)^2 + (5)(4.6)^2]$$
$$= 247 - [(5)(.36) + (5)(3.24) + (5)(19.36) + (5)(21.16)]$$
$$= 247 - (1.8 + 16.2 + 96.8 + 105.8)$$
$$= 247 - 220.6$$
$$= 26.4$$

$$SS_{between} = \Sigma N_{group}\overline{X}^2_{group} - N_{total}\overline{X}^2_{total}$$
$$= 220.6 - 162.4$$
$$= 58.1$$

These results agree with the computations obtained using the definitional formulas.

MEAN SQUARE

As we might expect from a measure of variation, the value of the sums of squares tends to become larger as variation increases. For example, $SS = 10.9$ probably designates greater variation than $SS = 1.3$. However, the sum of squares also gets larger with increasing sample size, so that $N = 200$ will yield a larger SS than $N = 20$. As a result, the sum of squares cannot be regarded as an entirely satisfactory "pure" measure of variation, unless, of course, we can find a way to control for the number of scores involved.

Fortunately, such a method exists in a measure of variation known as the *mean square* (or *variance*), which we obtain by dividing $SS_{between}$ or SS_{within} by the appropriate degrees of freedom. Recall that in Chapter 4, we similarly divided $\Sigma(X - \overline{X})^2$ by N to obtain the variance. Therefore,

$$MS_{between} = \frac{SS_{between}}{df_{between}}$$

where $MS_{between}$ = between-groups mean square
$SS_{between}$ = between-groups sum of squares
$df_{between}$ = between-groups degrees of freedom

and

$$MS_{within} = \frac{SS_{within}}{df_{within}}$$

where MS_{within} = within-groups mean square
SS_{within} = within-groups sum of squares
df_{within} = within-groups degrees of freedom

But we must still obtain the appropriate degrees of freedom. For between-groups mean square,

$$df_{between} = k - 1$$

where k = number of groups

To find degrees of freedom for within-groups mean square,

$$df_{within} = N_{total} - k$$

where N_{total} = total number of scores in all groups combined
k = number of groups

Illustrating with the data from Table 8.2, for which $SS_{between} = 58.1$ and $SS_{within} = 26.4$, we calculate our degrees of freedom as follows:

$$df_{between} = 4 - 1$$
$$= 3$$

and

$$df_{within} = 20 - 4$$
$$= 16$$

We are now prepared to obtain the following mean squares:

$$MS_{between} = \frac{58.1}{3}$$
$$= 19.37$$

and

$$MS_{within} = \frac{26.4}{16}$$
$$= 1.65$$

THE *F* RATIO

As previously noted, the analysis of variance yields an *F* ratio in which variation between groups and variation within groups are compared. We are now ready to specify the degree of each type of variation as measured by mean squares. Therefore, the *F* ratio can be regarded as indicating the size of the between-groups mean square relative to the size of the within-groups mean square, or

$$F = \frac{MS_{between}}{MS_{within}}$$

For Table 8.2,

$$F = \frac{19.37}{1.65}$$

$$= 11.74$$

Having obtained an *F* ratio, we must now determine whether it is large enough to reject the null hypothesis and accept the research hypothesis. Does self-esteem differ by offense type? The larger our calculated *F* ratio (the larger the $MS_{between}$ and the smaller the MS_{within}), the more likely we will obtain a statistically significant result.

But exactly how do we recognize a significant *F* ratio? Recall that in Chapter 7 our obtained *t* ratio was compared against a table *t* ratio for the .05 level of significance with the appropriate degrees of freedom. Similarly, we must now interpret our calculated *F* ratio with the aid of Table D in Appendix C. Table D contains a list of critical *F* ratios— *F* ratios that we must obtain to reject the null hypothesis at the .05 and .01 levels of significance. As was the case with the *t* ratio, exactly which *F* value we must obtain depends on its associated degrees of freedom. Therefore, we enter Table D looking for the two df values, between-groups degrees of freedom and within-groups degrees of freedom. Degrees of freedom associated with the numerator ($df_{between}$) have been listed across the top of the page, and degrees of freedom associated with the denominator (df_{within}) have been placed down the left side of the table. The body of Table D presents critical *F* ratios at the .05 and .01 significance levels.

For the data in Table 8.2, we have found $df_{between} = 3$ and $df_{within} = 16$. Thus, we move in Table D to the column marked df = 3 and continue down the page from that point until we arrive at the row marked df = 16. By this procedure, we find that a significant *F* ratio at the $\alpha = .05$ level must exceed 3.24, and at the $\alpha = .01$ level it must exceed 5.29. Our calculated *F* ratio is 11.74. As a result, we reject the null hypothesis and accept the research hypothesis: Self-esteem does appear to differ among offenders convicted of different types of crimes.

The results of our analysis of variance can be presented in a summary table such as the one shown in Table 8.3. It has become standard procedure to summarize an analysis of variance in this manner. The total sum of squares ($SS_{total} = 84.5$) is decomposed into two parts: the between-groups sum of squares ($SS_{between} = 58.1$) and the within-groups sum of squares ($SS_{within} = 26.4$). Each source of sum of squares is converted to mean square by dividing by the respective degrees of freedom. Finally, the F ratio (mean square *between* divided by mean square *within*) is calculated, which can be compared to the table critical value to determine significance.

To review some of the concepts presented thus far, consider Figure 8.4, which shows two contrasting situations. Both Case 1 and Case 2 consist of three samples (A, B, and C) with sample means $\overline{X}_A = 3$, $\overline{X}_B = 7$, and $\overline{X}_C = 11$ and with $N = 3$ in each sample. Because the means are the same in both data sets, the between-groups sums of squares are identical ($SS_{between} = 96$).

TABLE 8.3   ANALYSIS OF VARIANCE SUMMARY TABLE FOR THE DATA IN TABLE 8.2

Source of variation	SS	df	MS	F
Between groups	58.1	3	19.37	11.74
Within groups	26.4	16	1.65	
Total	84.5	19		

Case 1 data

Sample A	Sample B	Sample C
2	6	10
3	7	11
4	8	12
Mean 3	7	11

Analysis-of-variance summary table

Source of variation	SS	df	MS	F
Between groups	96	2	48	48
Within groups	6	6	1	
Total	102	8		

Distributions

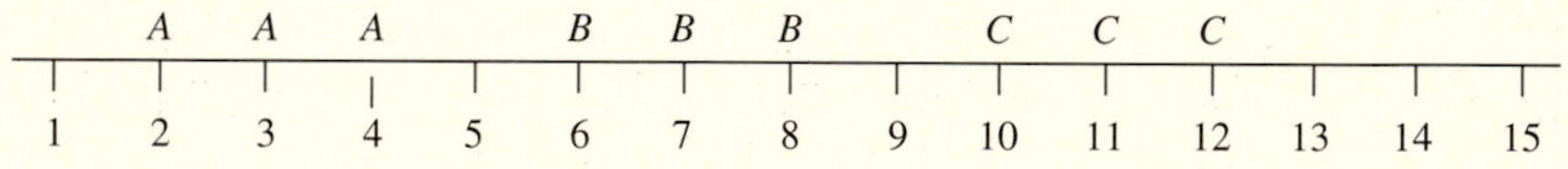

	A	A	A		B	B	B		C	C	C		
1	2	3	4	5	6	7	8	9	10	11	12	13	14	15

Case 2 data

Sample A	Sample B	Sample C
1	3	7
3	5	12
5	13	14
Mean 3	7	11

Analysis-of-variance summary table

Source of variation	SS	df	MS	F
Between groups	96	2	48	3.2
Within groups	90	6	15	
Total	186	8		

Distributions

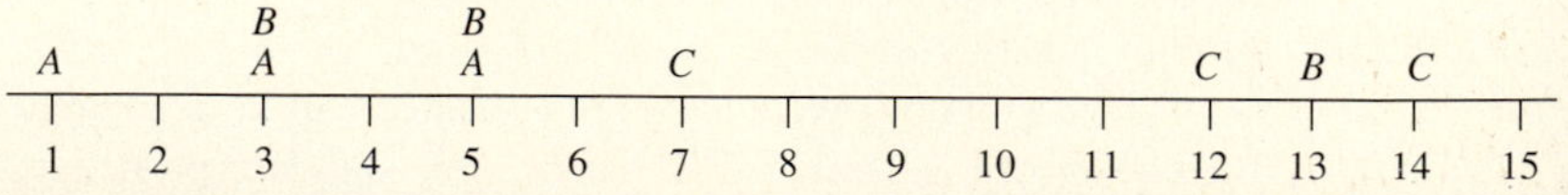

		B		B										
	A	A		A		C					C	B	C	
1	2	3	4	5	6	7	8	9	10	11	12	13	14	15

FIGURE 8.4   Two examples of analysis of variance.

In Case 1, the three samples are clearly different. It would seem then that we should be able to infer that the population means are different. Relative to between-groups variation (the differences between the sample means), the within-groups variation is rather small. Indeed, there is as much as a 48-to-1 ratio of between-groups mean square to within-groups mean square. Thus, $F = 48$ and is significant. Although the sample means and between-groups sum of squares are the same for Case 2, there is far more dispersion within groups, causing the samples to overlap quite a bit. The samples hardly appear as distinct as in Case 1, and so it would seem unlikely that we could generalize the differences between the sample means to differences between population means. The within-groups mean square is 15. The ratio of between to within mean square is then only 48-to-15, yielding a nonsignificant F ratio of 3.2.

STEP-BY-STEP ILLUSTRATION

ANALYSIS OF VARIANCE

To provide a step-by-step illustration of an analysis of variance, suppose that we wish to test the hypothesis that people of different religious affiliations tend to vary with respect to support for concealed weapons laws. Therefore,

Null hypothesis: $(\mu_1 = \mu_2 = \mu_3)$	*support for concealed weapons laws does not differ by religious affiliation.*
Research hypothesis: (some $\mu_i \neq \mu_j$)	*support for concealed weapons laws differ by religious affiliation.*

To investigate this hypothesis, five individuals were selected at random from each of three religious affiliations: Protestant, Catholic, and Jewish. Support for concealed weapons laws was measured on an eight-point scale, with higher scores indicating greater support.

Catholic $(N_1 = 5)$		Jewish $(N_2 = 5)$		Protestant $(N_3 = 5)$	
X_1	X_1^2	X_2	X_2^2	X_3	X_3^2
2	4	6	36	3	9
5	25	7	49	2	4
4	16	8	64	4	16
3	9	6	36	4	16
5	25	4	16	3	9
$\Sigma X_1 = 19$	$\Sigma X_1^2 = 79$	$\Sigma X_2 = 31$	$\Sigma X_2^2 = 201$	$\Sigma X_3 = 16$	$\Sigma X_3^2 = 54$

STEP 1   Find the mean for each sample.

$$\overline{X}_1 = \frac{\Sigma X_1}{N_1}$$

$$= \frac{19}{5}$$

$$= 3.8$$

$$\bar{X}_2 = \frac{\Sigma X_2}{N_2}$$

$$= \frac{31}{5}$$

$$= 6.2$$

$$\bar{X}_3 = \frac{\Sigma X_3}{N_3}$$

$$= \frac{16}{5}$$

$$= 3.2$$

Notice that differences do exist, the tendency being for Jews to have greater support for concealed weapons laws than Protestants or Catholics.

STEP 2   Find the sum of scores, sum of squared scores, number of subjects, and mean for all groups combined.

$$\Sigma X_{total} = \Sigma X_1 + \Sigma X_2 + \Sigma X_3$$

$$= 19 + 31 + 16$$

$$= 66$$

$$\Sigma X_{total}^2 = \Sigma X_1^2 + \Sigma X_2^2 + \Sigma X_3^2$$

$$= 79 + 201 + 54$$

$$= 334$$

$$N_{total} = N_1 + N_2 + N_3$$

$$= 5 + 5 + 5$$

$$= 15$$

$$\bar{X}_{total} = \frac{\Sigma X_{total}}{N_{total}}$$

$$= \frac{66}{15}$$

$$= 4.4$$

STEP 3   Find the total sum of squares.

$$SS_{total} = \Sigma X_{total}^2 - N_{total}\bar{X}_{total}^2$$

$$= 334 - (15)(4.4)^2$$

$$= 334 - (15)(19.36)$$

$$= 334 - 290.4$$

$$= 43.6$$

STEP 4   Find the within-groups sum of squares.

$$SS_{within} = \Sigma X_{total}^2 - \Sigma N_{group} \overline{X}_{group}^2$$

$$= 334 - [(5)(3.8)^2 + (5)(6.2)^2 + (5)(3.2)^2]$$

$$= 334 - [(5)(14.44) + (5)(38.44) + (5)(10.24)]$$

$$= 334 - (72.2 + 192.2 + 51.2)$$

$$= 334 - 315.6$$

$$= 18.4$$

STEP 5   Find the between-groups sum of squares.

$$SS_{between} = \Sigma N_{group} \overline{X}_{group}^2 - N_{total} \overline{X}_{total}^2$$

$$= [(5)(3.8)^2 + (5)(6.2)^2 + (5)(3.2)^2] - (15)(4.4)^2$$

$$= [(5)(14.44) + (5)(38.44) + (5)(10.24)] - (15)(19.36)$$

$$= (72.2 + 192.2 + 51.2) - 290.4$$

$$= 315.6 - 290.4$$

$$= 25.2$$

STEP 6   Find the between-groups degrees of freedom.

$$df_{between} = k - 1$$

$$= 3 - 1$$

$$= 2$$

STEP 7   Find the within-groups degrees of freedom.

$$df_{within} = N_{total} - k$$

$$= 15 - 3$$

$$= 12$$

STEP 8   Find the within-groups mean square.

$$MS_{within} = \frac{SS_{within}}{df_{within}}$$

$$= \frac{18.4}{12}$$

$$= 1.53$$

STEP 9 Find the between-groups means square.

$$MS_{between} = \frac{SS_{between}}{df_{between}}$$

$$= \frac{25.2}{2}$$

$$= 12.6$$

STEP 10 Obtain the F ratio.

$$F = \frac{MS_{between}}{MS_{within}}$$

$$= \frac{12.6}{1.53}$$

$$= 8.24$$

STEP 11 Compare the obtained F ratio with the appropriate F ratio found in Table D.

$$\text{obtained } F \text{ ratio} = 8.24$$

$$\text{table } F \text{ ratio} = 3.88$$

$$df = 2 \text{ and } 12$$

$$\alpha = .05$$

As shown in Step 11, to reject the null hypothesis at the .05 significance level with 2 and 12 degrees of freedom, our calculated F ratio must exceed 3.88. Because we have obtained an F ratio of 8.24, we can reject the null hypothesis and accept the research hypothesis. Specifically, we conclude that people of different religious affiliations differ with respect to support for concealed weapons laws.

A MULTIPLE COMPARISON OF MEANS

A significant F ratio informs us of an *overall difference* among the groups being studied. If we were investigating a difference between only two sample means, no additional analysis would be needed to interpret our result: In such a case, either the obtained difference is statistically significant or it is not, depending on the size of our F ratio. However, when we find a significant F for the differences among three or more means, it may be important to determine exactly where the significant differences lie. For example, in the foregoing illustration, we uncovered statistically significant gun control support differences among three religious affiliations. Consider the possibilities raised by this significant F ratio: $\overline{X}_1$ (Catholics) might differ significantly from $\overline{X}_2$ (Jews); $\overline{X}_1$ (Catholics) might differ significantly from $\overline{X}_3$ (Protestants); or $\overline{X}_2$ (Jews) from $\overline{X}_3$ (Protestants).

As explained earlier in this chapter, obtaining a t ratio for each comparison—$\overline{X}_1$ versus $\overline{X}_2$; $\overline{X}_1$ versus $\overline{X}_3$; $\overline{X}_2$ versus $\overline{X}_3$—would entail a good deal of work and, more importantly, would increase the probability of Type I error. Fortunately, statisticians have developed a number of other tests for making multiple comparisons after a significant F ratio to pinpoint where the significant mean differences lie. We will introduce Tukey's HSD (honestly significant difference), one of the most useful tests for investigating the *multiple comparison of means.*

Tukey's HSD is used *only* after a significant F ratio has been obtained. By Tukey's method, we compare the difference between any two mean scores against HSD. A mean difference is statistically significant only if it exceeds HSD. By formula,

$$\text{HSD} = q\sqrt{\frac{\text{MS}_{\text{within}}}{N_{\text{group}}}}$$

where q = table value at a given level of significance for the total number of group means being compared

$\text{MS}_{\text{within}}$ = within-groups mean square (obtained from the analysis of variance)

N_{group} = number of subjects in each group (assumes the same number in each group)[1]

Unlike the t ratio, HSD takes into account that the likelihood of Type I error increases as the number of means being compared increases. Depending on the value of q, the larger the number of group means, the more conservative HSD becomes with regard to rejecting the null hypothesis. As a result, fewer significant differences will be obtained with HSD than with the t ratio. Moreover, a mean difference is more likely to be significant in a multiple comparison of three means than in a multiple comparison of four or five means.

STEP-BY-STEP ILLUSTRATION

HSD FOR ANALYSIS OF VARIANCE

To illustrate the use of HSD, let us return to a previous example in which support for gun control was found to differ by religious affiliation. More specifically, we obtained a significant F ratio ($F = 8.24$) for the following differences among Protestant, Catholic, and Jewish families:

$$\overline{X}_1 \text{ (Catholic)} = 3.8$$

$$\overline{X}_2 \text{ (Jewish)} = 6.2$$

$$\overline{X}_3 \text{ (Protestant)} = 3.2$$

STEP 1   Construct a table of differences between ordered means.

For the present data, the rank order of means (from smallest to largest) is 3.2, 3.8, and 6.2. These mean scores are arranged in table form so that the difference between each pair of means is shown in a matrix. Thus, the difference between $\overline{X}_3$ (Protestant) and $\overline{X}_1$ (Jewish)

---

[1]Tukey's method can be used for comparisons between groups of unequal size. In such cases, N_{group} is replaced by what is called the harmonic mean of the group sizes. The harmonic mean group size is the reciprocal of the mean of the reciprocal sample sizes.

is .6; the difference between $\overline{X}_3$ (Protestant) and $\overline{X}_2$ (Jewish) is 3.0; and the difference between $\overline{X}_1$ (Catholic) and $\overline{X}_2$ (Jewish) is 2.4. The subscripts for the group means should not change when arranged in order. Thus, for example, $\overline{X}_2$ represents the mean of the group originally designated as number 2, not the second highest group mean.

	$\overline{X}_3 = 3.2$	$\overline{X}_1 = 3.8$	$\overline{X}_2 = 6.2$
$\overline{X}_3 = 3.2$	——	.6	3.0
$\overline{X}_1 = 3.8$	——	——	2.4
$\overline{X}_2 = 6.2$	——	——	——

STEP 2 Find q in Table I in Appendix C.

To find q from Table I, we must have (1) the degrees of freedom (df) for MS_{within}, (2) the number of group means k, and (3) a significance level of either .01 or .05. We already know from the analysis of variance that $df_{within} = 12$. Therefore, we enter the left-hand column of Table I until we arrive at 12 degrees of freedom. Second, because we are pair-comparing three mean scores, we move across Table I to a number of group means (k) equal to three. Assuming a .05 level of significance, we find that $q = 3.77$.

STEP 3 Find HSD.

$$HSD = q\sqrt{\frac{MS_{within}}{N_{group}}}$$

$$= 3.77\sqrt{\frac{1.53}{5}}$$

$$= 3.77\sqrt{.306}$$

$$= (3.77)(.553)$$

$$= 2.08$$

STEP 4 Compare HSD against the table of differences between means.

To be regarded as statistically significant, any obtained difference between means must exceed the HSD (2.08). Referring to the table of differences between means, we find that the support for gun control difference of 3.0 between X_3 (Protestant) and X_2 (Jewish) and the support for gun control scale score difference of 2.4 between $\overline{X}_1$ (Catholic) and $\overline{X}_2$ (Jewish) are greater than HSD = 2.08. As a result, we conclude that these differences between means are statistically significant at the .05 level. Finally, the difference in mean levels of support for concealed weapons laws of .6 between $\overline{X}_3$ (Protestant) and $\overline{X}_1$ (Catholic) is not significant because it is less than the HSD.

REQUIREMENTS FOR USING THE *F* RATIO

The analysis of variance should be made only after the researcher has considered the following requirements:

1. *A comparison between three or more independent means*. The F ratio is usually employed to make comparisons between three or more means from independent samples. It is possible, moreover, to obtain an F ratio rather than a t ratio when a two-sample comparison is made. For the two-sample case, $F = t^2$, and identical results are obtained. However, a single sample arranged in a panel design (the same group studied at several points in time) cannot be tested in this way. Thus, for example, one may not study improvement in class performance across three examinations during the term using this approach.

2. *Interval data*. To conduct an analysis of variance, we assume that we have achieved the interval level of measurement. Categorized or ranked data should not be used.

3. *Random sampling*. We should have taken our samples at random from a given population of scores.

4. *A normal distribution*. We assume the sample characteristic we measure to be normally distributed in the underlying population.

5. *Equal variances*. The analysis of variance assumes that the population variances for the different groups are all equal. The sample variances, of course, may differ as a result of sampling. Moderate differences among the sample variances do not invalidate the results of the F test. When such differences are extreme (for example, when one of the sample variances is many times larger than another), the F test presented here may not be appropriate.

SUMMARY

The analysis of variance can be used to make comparisons among three or more sample means. This test yields an F ratio whose numerator represents variation between groups and whose denominator contains an estimate of variation within groups. The sum of squares represents the initial step for measuring variation. However, it is greatly affected by sample size. To overcome this problem, we divide $SS_{between}$ or SS_{within} by the appropriate degrees of freedom to obtain the mean square. The F ratio indicates the size of the between-groups mean square relative to the size of the within-groups mean square. We interpret our calculated F ratio by comparing it against an appropriate F ratio in Table D. On that basis, we decide whether to reject or accept our null hypothesis. After obtaining a significant F, we can determine exactly where the significant differences lie by applying Tukey's method for the multiple comparison of means.

TERMS TO REMEMBER

Analysis of variance	Mean square
F ratio	Tukey's HSD
Sum of squares	
Within-groups	
Between-groups	
Total	

STEP-BY-STEP STUDY GUIDE

TEST OF DIFFERENCES BETWEEN MEANS FOR SEVERAL INDEPENDENT GROUPS USING ANALYSIS OF VARIANCE

STEP 1   Calculate the mean for each sample ($\overline{X}_1$, $\overline{X}_2$, $\overline{X}_3$, etc.)

STEP 2   Find the sum of scores (ΣX_{total}), the sum of squared scores (ΣX^2_{total}), the total number of cases (N_{total}), and the mean for all groups combined ($\overline{X}_{total}$).

STEP 3   Find the total sum of squares.

$$SS_{total} = \Sigma X^2_{total} - N_{total}\overline{X}^2_{total}$$

STEP 4   Find the within-groups sum of squares.

$$SS_{within} = \Sigma X^2_{total} - \Sigma N_{group}\overline{X}^2_{group}$$

STEP 5   Find the between-groups sum of squares.

$$SS_{between} = \Sigma N_{group}\overline{X}^2_{group} - N_{total}\overline{X}^2_{total}$$

STEP 6   Find the within-groups degrees of freedom.

$$df_{within} = N_{total} - k$$

STEP 7   Find the between-groups degrees of freedom.

$$df_{between} = k - 1$$

STEP 8   Find the within-groups mean square.

$$MS_{within} = \frac{SS_{within}}{df_{within}}$$

STEP 9   Find the between-groups mean square.

$$MS_{between} = \frac{SS_{between}}{df_{between}}$$

STEP 10   Obtain the F ratio.

$$F = \frac{MS_{between}}{MS_{within}}$$

STEP 11   Compare the obtained F ratio with the appropriate critical value for F taken from Table D. If the obtained F ratio exceeds the tabled critical value, then reject the null hypothesis of no differences among the population means and continue with the Tukey's HSD test. Otherwise, accept the null hypothesis of no differences and stop.

STEP 12   If the F ratio is significant, construct a table of differences between the group means, after placing them in order from low to high.

STEP 13   Find q from Table I.

STEP 14   Calculate the honestly significant difference(HSD).

$$\text{HSD} = q\sqrt{\frac{\text{MS}_{\text{within}}}{N_{\text{group}}}}$$

STEP 15   Compare HSD against the table of differences between means. Any difference between two group means that exceeds HSD is significant.

PROBLEMS

1. On the following random samples of social class, test the null hypothesis that support for drug legalization does not vary by social class. (*Note:* Higher scores indicate greater support.)

Lower	Working	Middle	Upper
8	7	6	5
4	3	5	2
7	2	5	1
8	8	4	3

2. A researcher is interested in the effect type of residence has on the beer consumption of college students. She selects samples of students who live in campus dorms, in off-campus apartments, and at home and asks the 12 respondents to record the number of beers they consume per week. Test the null hypothesis that beer consumption does not differ by type of residence.

Dorms	Apartments	At home
8	2	5
9	1	4
7	3	3
8	3	4

3. Construct a multiple comparison of means by Tukey's method to determine precisely where the significant differences occur in Problem 2.

4. A researcher was interested in studying the effects of lighting on feelings of safety. The neighborhoods studied are roughly equivalent in terms of size and crime rate. In the first neighborhood (A), lighting was increased (new poles were installed with high intensity flood lights, and existing lights were replaced with brighter ones). In the second neighborhood (B), existing lights were replaced with moderately brighter lights. In the third neighborhood (C), lighting was not changed. Six months later, five different residents from each neighborhood were randomly selected and given the Fear Survey Schedule, designed to measure feel-

ings of safety (the higher the score the greater the fear). The results are presented below. Test the hypothesis that feelings of safety do not differ in response to changes in street lighting.

A	B	C
10	12	18
13	9	16
11	10	20
12	10	17
9	13	19

5. To learn exactly where the significant differences occur in Problem 4, conduct a multiple comparison of means using Tukey's method.

6. A prison administrator is interested in examining the factors determining whether inmates are classified into maximum, medium, or lower security prisons in his state. One of the factors he examines is the number of separate offenses each inmate has been charged with, according to previous criminal records. He randomly selects eight new inmates from each of the three security levels and compares the number of offenses for which they have ever been charged. Test the null hypothesis that offense history is unrelated to prison security level.

Security Level		
Max.	Med.	Min.
8	4	2
6	4	2
4	3	3
5	6	2
3	5	4
7	6	1
6	3	2
9	3	2

Test the null hypothesis that the number of prior offenses has no effect on the prison security levels in which an offender is placed.

7. Conduct a multiple comparison of means by Tukey's method to determine exactly where the significant differences occur in Problem 6.

8. Based on his own experiences in court, a prosecutor believes that some judges provide more severe penalties than others for people convicted of domestic assault and battery. Five of the most recent domestic assault and battery sentences (in months) handed down by each of three judges are shown here.

Judge #1	Judge #2	Judge #3
1	3	1
1	2	5
3	4	2
2	3	1
2	4	1

Test the null hypothesis that judges do not vary in the sentence lengths imposed on individuals convicted of domestic assault and battery.

9. Conduct a multiple comparison of means by Tukey's method to determine exactly where the significant differences occur in Problem 8.

10. Consider an experiment to determine the effects of alcohol and of marijuana on driving. Five randomly selected subjects are given alcohol to produce legal drunkenness and then are given a simulated driving test (scored from a top score of 10 to a bottom score of 0). Five different randomly selected subjects are given marijuana and then the same driving test. Finally, a control group of five subjects is tested for driving while sober. Given the following driving test scores, test for the significance of differences among means of the following groups:

Alcohol	Drugs	Control
3	1	8
4	6	7
1	4	8
1	4	5
3	3	6

11. Conduct a multiple comparison of means by Tukey's method to determine exactly where the significant differences occur in Problem 9.

12. Using Durkheim's theory as a basis, a sociologist obtained the following suicide rates (the number of suicides per 100,000 population), rounded to the nearest whole number, for five "high-anomie," five "moderate-anomie," and five "low-anomie" metropolitan areas ("anomie" was indicated by the extent to which newcomers and transients were present in the population):

High	Moderate	Low
19	15	8
17	20	10
22	11	11
18	13	7
25	14	8

Test the null hypothesis that high-, moderate-, and low-anomie areas do not differ with respect to suicide rates.

13. Psychologists studied the relative efficacy of three different treatment programs—A, B, and C—on illicit drug abuse. The following data represent the number of days of drug abstinence accumulated by 15 patients (5 in each treatment program) for the 3 months after their treatment program ended. Thus, a larger number of days indicates a longer period free of drug use.

Treatment A	Treatment B	Treatment C
90	81	14
74	90	20
90	90	33
86	90	5
75	85	12

Test the null hypothesis that these drug-treatment programs do not differ in regard to their efficacy.

14. Conduct a multiple comparison of means by Tukey's method to determine exactly where the significant differences occur in Problem 12.

NONPARAMETRIC TESTS OF SIGNIFICANCE

- ONE-WAY CHI-SQUARE TEST

- TWO-WAY CHI-SQUARE TEST

- THE MEDIAN TEST

- THE MANN-WHITNEY *U* TEST

- KRUSKAL-WALLIS ONE-WAY ANALYSIS OF VARIANCE BY RANKS

- SUMMARY

- TERMS TO REMEMBER

- STEP-BY-STEP STUDY GUIDE: TEST OF DIFFERENCES BETWEEN GROUPS FOR NOMINAL-LEVEL DATA USING CHI-SQUARE

- STEP-BY-STEP STUDY GUIDE: TEST OF DIFFERENCES BETWEEN GROUPS FOR ORDINAL-LEVEL DATA USING THE MANN-WHITNEY *U* TEST

- STEP-BY-STEP STUDY GUIDE: TEST OF DIFFERENCES BETWEEN SEVERAL GROUPS FOR ORDINAL-LEVEL DATA USING THE KRUSKAL-WALLIS TEST

- PROBLEMS

As indicated in Chapters 7 and 8, we must ask a good deal of the criminal justice researcher who employs a *t* ratio or an analysis of variance to make comparisons between his or her groups of respondents or subjects. Each of these tests of significance has a list of requirements that includes the assumption that the characteristic studied is normally distributed in a specified population. In addition, each test asks for the interval level of measurement, so that a score can be assigned to every case. When a test of significance, such as the *t* ratio or the analysis of variance, requires (1) normality in the population (or at least large samples so that the sampling distribution is normal) and (2) an interval-level measure, it is referred to as a *parametric test.*[1]

What about the criminal justice researcher who cannot employ a parametric test, that is, who either cannot honestly assume normality, does not work with large numbers of cases, or whose data are not measured at the interval level? Suppose, for example, that he or she is working with a skewed distribution or with data that have been categorized and counted (the nominal level) or ranked (the ordinal level). How does this researcher go about making comparisons between samples without violating the requirements of a particular test?

Fortunately, statisticians have developed a number of *nonparametric* tests of significance—tests whose list of requirements does not include normality or the interval level of measurement. To understand the important position of nonparametric tests in

---

[1]This designation is based on the term *parameter,* which refers to any characteristic of a population.

criminal justice research, we must also understand the concept of the *power of a test,* the probability of rejecting the null hypothesis when it is actually false and should be rejected.

Power varies from one test to another. The most powerful tests—those that are most likely to reject the null hypothesis when it is false—are tests that have the strongest or most difficult requirements to satisfy. Generally, these are parametric tests such as *t* or *F*, which assume that interval data are employed and that the characteristics being studied are normally distributed in their populations. By contrast, the nonparametric alternatives make less stringent demands, but are less powerful tests of significance than their parametric counterparts. As a result, assuming that the null hypothesis is false (and holding constant such other factors as sample size), an investigator is more likely to reject the null hypothesis by the appropriate use of *t* or *F* than by a nonparametric alternative. In a statistical sense, you get what you pay for!

Understandably, criminal justice researchers are eager to reject the null hypothesis when it is false. As a result, many of them would ideally prefer to employ parametric tests of significance, and might even be willing to "stretch the truth" a little bit to meet the assumptions. For example, if ordinal data are fairly evenly spaced and therefore approximate an interval scale, and if the data are not normal but also not terribly skewed, one can "get away with" using a parametric test.

As previously noted, however, it is often not possible—without deceiving yourself to the limit—to come even close to satisfying the requirements of parametric tests. In the first place, much of the data of criminal justice research are nowhere near the interval level. Second, we may know that certain variables or characteristics under study are severely skewed in the population and may not have large enough samples to compensate.

When its requirements have been severely violated, it is not possible to know the power of a statistical test. Therefore, the results of a parametric test whose requirements have gone unsatisfied may lack any meaningful interpretation. Under such conditions, social researchers wisely turn to nonparametric tests of significance.

This chapter introduces some of the best-known nonparametric tests of significance for characteristics measured at the nominal or ordinal level: the chi-square test, the median test, the Mann-Whitney *U* test, and the Kruskal-Wallis one-way analysis of variance.

ONE-WAY CHI-SQUARE TEST

Have you ever tried to psych out your instructor while taking a multiple-choice test? You may have reasoned, "the last two answers were both B; he wouldn't possibly have three in a row." Or you may have thought, "there haven't been very many D answers; maybe I should change a few of the ones I wasn't sure of to D." You are assuming, of course, that your instructor attempts to distribute his correct answers evenly across all categories, A through E.

Suppose your instructor returns the exam and hands out the answer key. You construct a frequency distribution of the correct responses to the 50-item test as follows:

A	12
B	14
C	9
D	5
E	10

Turning to Table E in Appendix C, we find a list of chi-square values that are significant at the .05 and .01 levels. For the .05 significance level, we see that the critical value for chi-square with 4 degrees of freedom is 9.488. This is the value that we must exceed before we can reject the null hypothesis. Because our calculated chi-square is only 4.5 and, therefore, smaller than the table value, we must accept the null hypothesis and reject the research hypothesis. The observed frequencies do not differ enough from the frequencies expected under the null hypothesis of an equal distribution of correct responses. Thus, although we did not observe a perfectly even distribution (10 for each category), the degree of unevenness was not sufficiently large to conclude that the instructor had any underlying preference in designing his answer key.

STEP-BY-STEP ILLUSTRATION
ONE-WAY CHI-SQUARE

To summarize the step-by-step procedure for calculating one-way chi-square, imagine that a researcher is interested in surveying perceptions of juvenile offenders concerning the aggressiveness of police officers. She questions a sample of 60 young offenders about whether they believe that police officers are becoming more aggressive, less aggressive, or staying the same in their law enforcement practices.

We might specify our hypotheses as follows:

Null hypothesis: *Juvenile offenders are equally divided in their perceptions of the aggressiveness of police officers.*

Research hypothesis: *Juvenile offenders are not equally divided in their perceptions of the aggressiveness of police officers.*

Let us say that of the 60 juveniles surveyed, 35 feel that the police have become more aggressive, 10 feel they have become less aggressive, and 15 feel they are about the same.

STEP 1   Arrange the data in the form of a frequency distribution.

Category	Observed frequency
More aggressive	35
Less aggresive	10
About the same	15
Total	60

STEP 2   Obtain the expected frequency for each category.

The expected frequencies (f_e) are those frequencies expected to occur under the terms of the null hypothesis. Under the null hypothesis, we would expect the opinions to divide themselves equally across the three categories. Therefore, with three categories ($k = 3$) and $N = 60$,

$$f_e = \frac{60}{3} = 20$$

Category	Observed frequency (f_o)	Expected frequency (f_e)
More aggressive	35	20
Less aggressive	10	20
About the same	15	20
Total	60	60

STEP 3   Set up a summary table to calculate the chi-square value.

Category	f_o	f_e	$f_o - f_e$	$(f_o - f_e)^2$	$\dfrac{(f_o - f_e)^2}{f_e}$
More aggressive	35	20	15	225	11.25
Less aggressive	10	20	−10	100	5.00
About the same	15	20	−5	25	1.25
					$\chi^2 = 17.50$

STEP 4   Find the degrees of freedom.

$$df = k - 1 = 3 - 1 = 2$$

STEP 5   Compare the calculated chi-square value with the appropriate chi-square value from Table E.

Turning to Table E in Appendix C, we look up the chi-square value required for significance at the .05 level for 2 degrees of freedom, and find that this critical value is 5.99. Because the calculated chi-square ($\chi^2 = 17.50$) is larger than the table value, we reject the null hypothesis. These findings suggest, therefore, that juvenile offenders are not equally divided about their views concerning the changing aggressiveness of police officers. In fact, the majority (35 out of 60) felt they are becoming more aggressive. More to the point, these findings can not be passed off as merely the result of sampling error or chance.

TWO-WAY CHI-SQUARE TEST

Up to this point, we have considered testing whether the categories in an observed frequency distribution differ significantly from one another. To accomplish this, we used a one-way chi-square test to determine whether the observed set of frequencies is significantly different from a set of expected frequencies under the terms of the null hypothesis.

The chi-square test has a much broader use in criminal justice research, namely, in testing whether one observed frequency distribution significantly differs from another observed distribution. For example, the survey of juvenile offenders concerning the aggressiveness of police officers discussed previously could be enhanced by testing to see whether males respond differently than females. Thus, rather than comparing a set of observed frequencies (more aggressive, less aggressive, about the same) against a hypothetically equal distribution, we might compare the observed frequencies (more aggresive, less aggresive, about the same) for both males and females.

As we saw in Chapter 2, nominal and ordinal variables are often presented in the form of a cross-tabulation. Specifically, cross-tabulations are used to compare the distribution of one variable, often called the dependent variable, across categories of some other variable, the independent variable. In a cross-tabulation, the focus is on the differences between groups—such as between males and females—in terms of the dependent variable—for example, perceptions of how aggressively the police pursue their law enforcement obligations.

We are now prepared to consider whether differences in a cross-tabulation—such as gender differences in beliefs regarding the aggressiveness of police officers—are statistically significant. Recall that a one-way chi-square was used to test a single frequency distribution by comparing observed frequencies with expected frequencies under the null hypothesis. Similarly, a *two-way chi-square* can be used for testing a cross-tabulation, also by comparing observed frequencies with expected frequencies under the null hypothesis.

You will be happy to hear that the two forms of chi-square (one-way and two-way) are very similar in both logic and procedure. In fact, the only major difference is the basis for calculating the expected frequencies.

COMPUTING THE TWO-WAY CHI-SQUARE

As in the case of the t ratio and analysis of variance, there is a sampling distribution for chi-square that can be used to estimate the probability of obtaining a significant chi-square value by chance alone rather than by actual population differences. Unlike these earlier tests of significance, however, chi-square is employed to make comparisons between frequencies rather than between mean scores. As a result, the null hypothesis for the chi-square test states that the populations do not differ with respect to the frequency of occurrence of a given characteristic, whereas the research hypothesis says that sample differences reflect actual population differences regarding the relative frequency of a given characteristic.

To illustrate the use of the two-way chi-square for frequency data (or for proportions that can be reduced to frequencies), imagine that we have been asked to investigate the relationship between political orientation and leniency regarding criminal justice punishment. We might categorize our sample members on a strictly either-or basis; that is, we might decide that they are either lenient or punitive. Therefore,

Null hypothesis:	*The relative frequency or percentage of liberals who are lenient is the same as the relative frequency of conservatives who are lenient.*
Research hypothesis:	*The relative frequency or percentage of liberals who are lenient is not the same as the relative frequency of conservatives who are lenient.*

Like its one-way counterpart, the chi-square test of significance for a two-way cross-tab is essentially concerned with the distinction between expected frequencies and observed frequencies. Once again, expected frequencies (f_e) refer to the terms of the null hypothesis, according to which the relative frequency (or proportion) is expected to be the same from one group to another. For example, if a certain percentage of the liberals is expected to be lenient, then we expect the same percentage of the conservatives to be lenient. By contrast, observed frequencies (f_o) refer to the results that we actually obtain when conducting a study and, therefore, may or may not vary from one group to another. Only if the difference between expected and observed frequencies is large enough do we reject the null hypothesis and decide that a true population difference exists.

Let's consider the simplest possible case in which we have equal numbers of liberals and conservatives as well as equal numbers of lenient and punitive respondents. Assuming 40 respondents took part in the survey, the cross-tabulation showing the observed frequencies for each cell (f_o) might be as follows:

Criminal justice punishment attitudes	Political orientation		Total
	Liberals	Conservatives	
Lenient	13	7	20
Punitive	7	13	20
Total	20	20	$N = 40$

In this cross-tabulation, there are four cells and 40 respondents. Therefore, to calculate the expected frequencies (f_e), we might expect 10 cases per cell, as shown in the following:

Criminal justice punishment attitudes	Political orientation		Total
	Liberals	Conservatives	
Lenient	10	10	20
Punitive	10	10	20
Total	20	20	$N = 40$

This straightforward method of calculating expected frequencies works in this cross-tabulation, but *only* because the marginals—both row and column—are identical (they are all 20). Unfortunately, most research situations will not yield cross-tabulations in which both the row and column marginals are evenly split. By sampling technique, it may be possible to control the distribution of the independent variable—for example, to get exactly the same number of liberals and conservatives. But you cannot control the distribution of the dependent variable—for example, the number of lenient and punitive respondents. Thus, we must consider a more general approach to calculating expected frequencies—one that can be used when either or both the row and column marginals are not evenly distributed.

Continuing with the present example in which we drew samples of 20 liberals and 20 conservatives, suppose that we observed more lenient respondents than punitive respondents. Therefore, as shown in Table 9.1, the row marginals would not be equal.

The data in Table 9.1 indicate that lenient criminal justice punishment attitudes were held by 5 out of 20 liberals and 10 out of 20 conservatives. To determine if these frequencies depart from what one would expect by chance alone, we need to determine the expected frequencies under the null hypothesis of no difference.

The observed and expected frequencies for each cell are displayed together in Table 9.2. The expected frequencies are derived purposely to be in line with the null hypothesis, that is, they represent the frequencies one would expect to see if the null hypothesis of no difference were true. Thus, 15 out of 40 of the respondents overall, or 37.5%, are lenient in their punishment attitudes. For there to be no difference between the liberals and the conservatives in this regard, as dictated by the null hypothesis, 37.5% of the liberals and 37.5% of the conservatives should be lenient. Translating the fact that both groups should have the same percentage (or relative frequency) of lenient respondents into expected frequencies, we expect 7.5 liberals (37.5% of 20, or .375 × 20 = 7.5) to be lenient and 7.5 conservatives (37.5% of 20, or .375 × 20 = 7.5) to be lenient, if the null hypothesis were true. Of course, the expected frequencies of respondents who are not lenient are 12.5 for both liberals and conservatives, because the expected frequencies must sum to the marginal totals (in this case, 7.5 + 12.5 = 20). Finally, it is important to note that the expected frequencies, as in the present example, do not have to be whole numbers.

As discussed earlier, chi-square focuses on how close the observed frequencies are to those expected under the null hypothesis. Based on the observed and expected frequencies, the two-way chi-square formula remains the same as in the one-way case. Specifically,

$$\chi^2 = \sum \frac{(f_o - f_e)^2}{f_e}$$

where f_o = observed frequency in any cell
       f_e = expected frequency in any cell

TABLE 9.1 FREQUENCIES OBSERVED IN A CROSS-TABULATION OF CRIMINAL JUSTICE PUNISHMENT ATTITUDES BY POLITICAL ORIENTATIONS

Criminal justice punishment attitudes	Political orientation		Total
	Liberals	Conservatives	
Lenient	5	10	15
Punitive	15	10	25
Total	20	20	$N = 40$

As with one-way chi-square, we subtract each expected frequency from its corresponding observed frequency, square the difference, divide by the expected frequency, and then add up these quotients for all the cells to obtain the chi-square value.

By applying the chi-square formula to the case at hand,

$$\chi^2 = \frac{(5 - 7.5)^2}{7.5} + \frac{(10 - 7.5)^2}{7.5} + \frac{(15 - 12.5)^2}{12.5} + \frac{(10 - 12.5)^2}{12.5}$$

$$= \frac{(-2.5)^2}{7.5} + \frac{(2.5)^2}{7.5} + \frac{(2.5)^2}{12.5} + \frac{(-2.5)^2}{12.5}$$

$$= \frac{6.25}{7.5} + \frac{6.25}{7.5} + \frac{6.25}{12.5} + \frac{6.25}{12.5}$$

$$= .83 + .83 + .50 + .50$$

$$= 2.66$$

Thus, we learn that $\chi^2 = 2.66$. To interpret this chi-square value, we must still determine the appropriate number of degrees of freedom. This can be done for tables that have any number of rows and columns by employing the formula

$$df = (r - 1)(c - 1)$$

where r = number of rows in the table of observed frequencies
         c = number of columns in the table of observed frequencies
        df = degrees of freedom

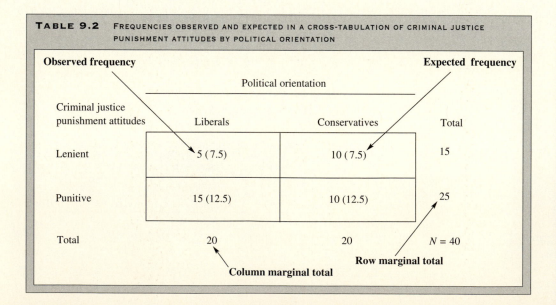

TABLE 9.2   FREQUENCIES OBSERVED AND EXPECTED IN A CROSS-TABULATION OF CRIMINAL JUSTICE PUNISHMENT ATTITUDES BY POLITICAL ORIENTATION

Observed frequency   Expected frequency

Political orientation

Criminal justice punishment attitudes	Liberals	Conservatives	Total
Lenient	5 (7.5)	10 (7.5)	15
Punitive	15 (12.5)	10 (12.5)	25
Total	20	20	N = 40

Row marginal total

Column marginal total

Because the observed frequencies in Table 9.2 form two rows and two columns (2 × 2),

$$df = (2 - 1)(2 - 1)$$

$$= (1)(1)$$

$$= 1$$

Turning to Table E in Appendix C, we find a list of chi-square values that are significant at the .05 and .01 levels. For the .05 significance level, we see that the critical value for chi-square with 1 degree of freedom is 3.84. This is the value that must be exceeded before we can reject the null hypothesis. Because our calculated χ^2 is only 2.66 and, therefore, *smaller* than the table value, we must accept the null hypothesis and reject the research hypothesis. The observed frequencies do not differ enough from the frequencies expected by chance to indicate that actual population differences exist.

FINDING THE EXPECTED FREQUENCIES

The expected frequencies for each cell must reflect the operation of chance under the terms of the null hypothesis. If the expected frequencies are to indicate sameness across all samples, they must be proportional to their marginal totals, both for rows and columns.

To obtain the expected frequency for any cell, we multiply together the column and row marginal totals for a particular cell and divide the product by N. Therefore,

$$f_e = \frac{\text{(row marginal total)(column marginal total)}}{N}$$

For the upper-left cell in Table 9.2 (lenient liberals),

$$f_e = \frac{(15)(20)}{40}$$

$$= \frac{300}{40}$$

$$= 7.5$$

Likewise, for the upper-right cell in Table 9.2 (lenient conservatives),

$$f_e = \frac{(15)(20)}{40}$$

$$= \frac{300}{40}$$

$$= 7.5$$

For the lower-left cell in Table 9.2 (punitive liberals),

$$f_e = \frac{(25)(20)}{40}$$

$$= \frac{500}{40}$$

$$= 12.5$$

For the lower-right cell in Table 9.2 (punitive conservatives),

$$f_e = \frac{(25)(20)}{40}$$

$$= \frac{500}{40}$$

$$= 12.5$$

As we will see, the foregoing method for determining f_e can be applied to any chi-square problem for which the expected frequencies must be obtained.

STEP-BY-STEP ILLUSTRATION
TWO-WAY CHI-SQUARE TEST OF SIGNIFICANCE

To summarize the step-by-step procedure for obtaining chi-square for a cross-tabulation, let us consider a study in which the effectiveness of hypnosis as a means of improving the memory of eyewitnesses to a crime is examined. The hypotheses might be specified as follows:

Null hypothesis: *Hypnosis does not affect the recognition memory of eyewitnesses to a crime.*

Research hypothesis: *Hypnosis does affect the recognition memory of eyewitnesses to a crime.*

To test the null hypothesis at the $\alpha = .05$ level of significance, all subjects first view a videotape of a pickpocket plying his trade. One week later, subjects are randomly assigned to one of two conditions. The subjects in the experimental group are hypnotized and then asked to pick the thief out of a lineup. Subjects in the control group are not hypnotized and attempt the same lineup identification. Suppose the results are as shown in Table 9.3. We can see from the results that the hypnotized group actually did worse in attempting to identify the culprit. Only 7 of the 40 subjects in the experimental group were correct, whereas 17 of the 40 control subjects made the right choice. This difference may suggest that hypnosis does have an effect (although not the kind of effect that one might desire); but is the difference significant?

> **TABLE 9.3**   HYPNOSIS AND ACCURACY OF EYEWITNESS
>   IDENTIFICATION
>
> | | Hypnotized | Control |
> |--------------------------|:----------:|:-------:|
> | Correct identification | 7 | 17 |
> | Incorrect identification | 33 | 23 |
> | Total | 40 | 40 |

STEP 1   Rearrange the data in the form of a 2 × 2 table containing the observed frequencies for each cell.

	Hypnotized	Control	
Correct identification	7 ( )	17 ( )	24
Incorrect identification	33 ( )	23 ( )	56
	40	40	$N = 80$

STEP 2   Obtain the expected frequency for each cell.

	Hypnotized	Control	
Correct identification	7 (12)	17 (12)	24
Incorrect identification	33 (28)	23 (28)	56
	40	40	$N = 80$

(upper-left)
$$f_e = \frac{(24)(40)}{80}$$
$$= \frac{960}{80}$$
$$= 12$$

(upper-right)
$$f_e = \frac{(24)(40)}{80}$$
$$= \frac{960}{80}$$
$$= 12$$

(lower-left) $f_e = \dfrac{(56)(40)}{80}$

$= \dfrac{2{,}240}{80}$

$= 28$

(lower-right) $f_e = \dfrac{(56)(40)}{80}$

$= \dfrac{2{,}240}{80}$

$= 28$

STEP 3   Subtract the expected frequencies from the observed frequencies.

$$f_o - f_e$$

(upper-left) $7 - 12 = -5$
(upper-right) $17 - 12 =\ \ \ 5$
(lower-left) $33 - 28 =\ \ \ 5$
(lower-right) $23 - 28 = -5$

STEP 4   Square this difference.

$$(f_o - f_e)^2$$

(upper-left) $(-5)^2 = 25$
(upper-right) $(5)^2 = 25$
(lower-left) $(5)^2 = 25$
(lower-right) $(-5)^2 = 25$

STEP 5   Divide by the expected frequency.

$$\dfrac{(f_o - f_e)^2}{f_e}$$

(upper-left) $\dfrac{25}{12} = 2.08$

(upper-right) $\dfrac{25}{12} = 2.08$

(lower-left) $\dfrac{25}{28} = .89$

(lower-right) $\dfrac{25}{28} = .89$

STEP 6   Sum these quotients to obtain the chi-square value.

$$\sum \frac{(f_o - f_e)^2}{f_e}$$

$$
\begin{array}{r}
2.08 \\
2.08 \\
.89 \\
.89 \\
\hline
\chi^2 = 5.94
\end{array}
$$

STEP 7   Find the degrees of freedom.

$$df = (r - 1)(c - 1)$$
$$= (2 - 1)(2 - 1)$$
$$= (1)(1)$$
$$= 1$$

STEP 8   Compare the obtained chi-square value with the appropriate chi-square value in Table E.

$$\text{obtained } \chi^2 = 5.94$$
$$\text{table } \chi^2 = 3.84$$
$$df = 1$$
$$\alpha = .05$$

As indicated in Step 8, to reject the null hypothesis at the .05 significance level with 1 degree of freedom, our calculated chi-square value would have to be 3.84 or larger. Because we have obtained a chi-square value of 5.94, we can reject the null hypothesis and accept the research hypothesis. Our results suggest a significant difference in the ability of hypnotized and control subjects to identify a thief. Before you recommend that all crime witnesses be hypnotized, however, take a second look at how the data themselves line up. The hypnotized subjects were *less,* not more, accurate in identifying the thief.

The step-by-step procedure for chi-square just illustrated can be summarized in tabular form as follows:

Cell	f_o	f_e	$f_o - f_e$	$(f_o - f_e)^2$	$\dfrac{(f_o - f_e)^2}{f_e}$
(upper-left)	7	12	−5	25	2.08
(upper-right)	17	12	5	25	2.08
(lower-left)	33	28	5	25	.89
(lower-right)	23	28	−5	25	.89

$$\chi^2 = 5.94$$

STEP-BY-STEP ILLUSTRATION
COMPARING SEVERAL GROUPS

Until now, we have limited our illustrations to the widely employed 2 × 2 problem. It should be emphasized, however, that chi-square is frequently calculated for tables that are larger than 2 × 2 tables in which several groups or categories are to be compared. The step-by-step procedure for comparing several groups is essentially the same as its 2 × 2 counterpart. Let us illustrate with a 3 × 3 problem (3 rows by 3 columns), although any number of rows and columns could be used.

For our purposes, imagine that we are investigating the relationship between religion and attitudes regarding criminal justice punishment. In this example, however, we will be drawing information from three random samples: 32 Protestants, 30 Catholics, and 27 Jews. Suppose, in addition, we are asked to categorize individuals on the basis of their attitudes regarding criminal justice punishments, as either lenient, moderate, or punitive. Therefore

Null hypothesis: *The relative frequency of lenient, moderate, and punitive criminal justice punishment attitudes is the same for Protestants, Catholics, and Jews.*

Research hypothesis: *The relative frequency of lenient, moderate, and punitive criminal justice punishment attitudes is not the same for Protestants, Catholics, and Jews.*

Let us say that we generate the sample differences in criminal justice attitudes shown in Table 9.4. Therein we see that 7 out of 32 Protestants, 9 out of 30 Catholics, and 14 out of 27 Jews could be regarded as lenient in their criminal justice punishment attitudes.

TABLE 9.4   CRIMINAL JUSTICE PUNISHMENT ATTITUDES BY RELIGION: A 3 × 3 PROBLEM

Criminal justice punishment attitudes	Religion		
	Protestant	Catholic	Jewish
Lenient	7	9	14
Moderate	10	10	8
Punitive	15	11	5
Total	32	30	27

In order to determine whether or not there is a significant difference in Table 9.4, we must apply the original chi-square formula as introduced earlier in the chapter:

$$\chi^2 = \sum \frac{(f_o - f_e)^2}{f_e}$$

The chi-square formula can be applied to the 3×3 problem in the following step-by-step procedure:

STEP 1   Rearrange the data in the form of a 3×3 table.

Criminal justice punishment attitudes	Religion				
	Protestant	Catholic	Jewish		
Lenient	7	9	14	30	Row marginal total
Moderate	10	10	8	28	
Punitive	15	11	5	31	Observed frequency
	32	30	27	$N = 89$	

Column marginal total

STEP 2   Obtain the expected frequency for each cell.

(upper-left)

$$f_e = \frac{(30)(32)}{89}$$

$$= \frac{960}{89}$$

$$= 10.79$$

(upper-middle)

$$f_e = \frac{(30)(30)}{89}$$

$$= \frac{900}{89}$$

$$= 10.11$$

(upper-right)

$$f_e = \frac{(30)(27)}{89}$$

$$= \frac{810}{89}$$

$$= 9.10$$

(middle-left) $f_e = \frac{(28)(32)}{89}$

$$= \frac{896}{89}$$

$$= 10.07$$

(middle-middle) $f_e = \frac{(28)(30)}{89}$

$$= \frac{840}{89}$$

$$= 9.44$$

(middle-right) $f_e = \frac{(28)(27)}{89}$

$$= \frac{756}{89}$$

$$= 8.49$$

(lower-left) $f_e = \frac{(31)(32)}{89}$

$$= \frac{992}{89}$$

$$= 11.15$$

(lower-middle) $f_e = \frac{(31)(30)}{89}$

$$= \frac{930}{89}$$

$$= 10.45$$

(lower-right) $f_e = \frac{(31)(27)}{89}$

$$= \frac{837}{89}$$

$$= 9.40$$

STEP 3   Subtract the expected frequencies from the observed frequencies.

$$f_o - f_e$$

(upper-left)	$7 - 10.79 = -3.79$
(upper-middle)	$9 - 10.11 = -1.11$
(upper-right)	$14 - 9.10 = 4.90$
(middle-left)	$10 - 10.07 = -.07$
(middle-middle)	$10 - 9.44 = .56$
(middle-right)	$8 - 8.49 = -.49$
(lower-left)	$15 - 11.15 = 3.85$
(lower-middle)	$11 - 10.45 = .55$
(lower-right)	$5 - 9.40 = -4.40$

STEP 4   Square this difference.

$$(f_o - f_e)^2$$

(upper-left)	$(-3.79)^2 = 14.36$
(upper-middle)	$(-1.11)^2 = 1.23$
(upper-right)	$(4.90)^2 = 24.01$
(middle-left)	$(-.07)^2 = .00$
(middle-middle)	$(.56)^2 = .31$
(middle-right)	$(-.49)^2 = .24$
(lower-left)	$(3.85)^2 = 14.82$
(lower-middle)	$(.55)^2 = .30$
(lower-right)	$(-4.40)^2 = 19.36$

STEP 5   Divide by the expected frequency.

$$\frac{(f_o - f_e)^2}{f_e}$$

(upper-left)	$\dfrac{14.36}{10.79} = 1.33$
(upper-middle)	$\dfrac{1.23}{10.11} = .12$

(upper-right) $\dfrac{24.01}{9.10} = 2.64$

(middle-left) $\dfrac{.00}{10.07} = .00$

(middle-middle) $\dfrac{.31}{9.44} = .03$

(middle-right) $\dfrac{.24}{8.49} = .03$

(lower-left) $\dfrac{14.82}{11.15} = 1.33$

(lower-middle) $\dfrac{.30}{10.45} = .03$

(lower-right) $\dfrac{19.36}{9.40} = 2.06$

STEP 6   Sum these quotients to obtain the chi-square value.

$$\sum \frac{(f_o - f_e)^2}{f_e}$$

1.33
.12
2.64
.00
.03
.03
1.33
.03
2.06

$$\chi^2 = \overline{7.57}$$

STEP 7   Find the number of degrees of freedom.

$$df = (r - 1)(c - 1)$$
$$= (3 - 1)(3 - 1)$$
$$= (2)(2)$$
$$= 4$$

STEP 8   Compare the obtained chi-square value with the appropriate chi-square value in Table E.

$$\text{obtained } \chi^2 = 7.57$$

$$\text{table } \chi^2 = 9.49$$

$$\text{df} = 4$$

$$\alpha = .05$$

Therefore, we need a chi-square value above 9.49 in order to reject the null hypothesis. Because our obtained chi-square is only 7.57, we must accept the null hypothesis. and attribute our sample differences to the operation of chance alone. We have not found statistically significant evidence to indicate that the relative frequency of criminal justice punishment attitudes differs for Protestants, Catholics, and Jews.

The step-by-step procedure for applying the chi-square formula just illustrated can be summarized in tabular form as follows:

Cell	f_o	f_e	$f_o - f_e$	$(f_o - f_e)^2$	$\dfrac{(f_o - f_e)^2}{f_e}$
(upper-left)	7	10.79	−3.79	14.36	1.33
(upper-middle)	9	10.11	−1.11	1.23	.12
(upper-right)	14	9.10	4.90	24.01	2.64
(middle-left)	10	10.07	− .07	.00	.00
(middle-middle)	10	9.44	.56	.31	.03
(middle-right)	8	8.49	− .49	.24	.03
(lower-left)	15	11.15	3.85	14.82	1.33
(lower-middle)	11	10.45	.55	.30	.03
(lower-right)	5	9.40	−4.40	19.36	2.06
					$\chi^2 = 7.57$

CORRECTING FOR SMALL EXPECTED FREQUENCIES

One of the primary reasons why the chi-square test is so popular among criminal justice researchers is that it makes very few demands on the data. That is, the host of assumptions associated with the t ratio and the analysis of variance is absent with the chi-square alternative. Despite this relative freedom from assumptions, however, chi-square cannot be used indiscriminately. In particular, chi-square does impose some rather modest requirements on sample size. Although chi-square does not require the same large samples as some of the parametric tests, an extremely small sample can sometimes yield misleading results, as we will see in what follows.

Generally, chi-square should be used with great care whenever some of the expected frequencies are below 5. There is no hard-and-fast rule concerning just how many expected frequencies below 5 will render an erroneous result. Some researchers contend that all expected frequencies should be at least 5, and others relax this restriction somewhat and only insist that most of the expected frequencies be at least 5. The decision concerning whether to proceed with the test depends on what impact the cells with the small expected frequencies have on the value of chi-square.

Consider, for example, the cross-tabulation in Table 9.5 of murder weapon and gender of offender for 200 homicide cases. The "female/other-weapon" cell has an expected frequency of only 2. For this cell, the observed frequency is 6 (females tend to use poison far more than men), and so its contribution to the chi-square statistic is

$$\frac{(f_o - f_e)^2}{f_e} = \frac{(6 - 2)^2}{2} = 8$$

No matter what happens with the seven other cells, this value of 8 for the female-other cell will cause the null hypothesis to be rejected. That is, for a 4×2 table (df = 3) the critical chi-square value from Table E is 7.815, which is already surpassed because of this one cell alone. One should feel uncomfortable indeed about rejecting the null hypothesis just because there were four more women than expected who used an "other" weapon, such as poison. The problem here is that the expected frequency of 2 in the denominator causes the fraction to be unstable. With even a modest difference between observed and expected frequencies in the numerator, the quotient explodes because of the small divisor. For this reason, small expected frequencies are a concern.

In instances like this in which expected frequencies less than 5 create such problems, you should collapse or merge together some categories, but only if it is logical to do so. One would not want to merge together categories that are substantively very different. But in this instance, we can reasonably combine the "blunt object" and "other" categories into a new category that we can still label "other." The revised cross-tabulation is shown in Table 9.6. Note that now none of the cells has problematically low expected frequencies.

In 2×2 tables, the requirement for having all expected frequencies at least equal to 5 is particularly important. In addition, for 2×2 tables, distortions can also occur if expected frequencies are under 10. Fortunately, however, there is a simple solution for 2×2 tables with any expected frequency less than 10 but greater than 5, known as *Yates's correction*.[2] By using Yates's correction, the difference between observed

TABLE 9.5   CROSS-TABULATION OF MURDER WEAPON AND GENDER OF OFFENDER (EXPECTED FREQUENCIES IN PARENTHESES)

	Male	Female	Total
Gun	100 (90)	20 (30)	120
Knife	39 (45)	21 (15)	60
Blunt object	9 (9)	3 (3)	20
Other	2 (6)	6 (2)	8
Total	150	50	$N = 200$

---

[2]Some researchers recommend that Yates's correction be used for all 2×2 tables, not just those with deficient expected frequencies. Although technically correct, it makes little practical difference when all the expected frequencies are fairly large. That is, the corrected and uncorrected chi-square are very similar with large expected frequencies.

and expected frequencies is reduced by .5. Since chi-square depends on the size of that difference, we also reduce the size of our calculated chi-square value. The following is the corrected chi-square formula for small expected frequencies:

$$\chi^2 = \sum \frac{(|f_o - f_e| - .5)^2}{f_e}$$

In the corrected chi-square formula, the vertical lines surrounding $f_o - f_e$ indicate that we must reduce the absolute value (ignoring minus signs) of each $f_o - f_e$ by .5.

To illustrate, let us suppose that an instructor at an American university close to the Canadian border suspects that his female students are more likely to have experienced sexual aggression than their counterparts at a nearby Canadian university. To test his hypothesis, he distributes questionnaires to random samples of female undergraduate students at each university. The questionnaires ask women whether they have ever had any of several experiences meeting the legal definition of rape or attempted rape. The results are shown in Table 9.7.

If we were to use the original chi-square formula for a 2 × 2 problem ($\chi^2 = 5.13$), we would conclude that the difference between American and Canadian students is significant.

TABLE 9.6   REVISED CROSS-TABULATION OF MURDER WEAPON AND GENDER OF OFFENDER (EXPECTED FREQUENCIES IN PARENTHESES)

	Male	Female	Total
Gun	100 (90)	20 (30)	120
Knife	39 (45)	21 (15)	60
Other	11 (15)	9 (5)	20
Total	150	50	$N = 200$

TABLE 9.7   CROSS-TABULATION OF SEXUAL ASSAULT BY NATIONALITY

Experienced sexual assault	Nationality	
	Americans	Canadians
Yes	15	5
No	6	10
Total	21	15

Before we make much of this result, however, we must be concerned about the potential effects of small expected frequencies and compute Yates's corrected formula.

$$\chi^2 = \frac{(|15 - 11.67| - .5)^2}{11.67} + \frac{(|5 - 8.33| - .5)^2}{8.33}$$

$$+ \frac{(|6 - 9.33| - .5)^2}{9.33} + \frac{(|10 - 6.67| - .5)^2}{6.67}$$

$$= \frac{(3.33 - .5)^2}{11.67} + \frac{(3.33 - .5)^2}{8.33} + \frac{(3.33 - .5)^2}{9.33} + \frac{(3.33 - .5)^2}{6.67}$$

$$= \frac{(2.83)^2}{11.67} + \frac{(2.83)^2}{8.33} + \frac{(2.83)^2}{9.33} + \frac{(2.83)^2}{6.67}$$

$$= \frac{8.01}{11.67} + \frac{8.01}{8.33} + \frac{8.01}{9.33} + \frac{8.01}{6.67}$$

$$= .69 + .96 + .86 + 1.20$$

$$= 3.71$$

The procedure for applying the corrected 2×2 chi-square formula can be summarized in tabular form:

f_o	f_o	$|f_o - f_e|$	$|f_o - f_e| - .5$	$(|f_o - f_e| - .5)^2$	$\dfrac{(|f_o - f_e| - .5)^2}{f_e}$
15	11.67	3.33	2.83	8.01	.69
5	8.33	3.33	2.83	8.01	.96
6	9.33	3.33	2.83	8.01	.86
10	6.67	3.33	2.83	8.01	1.20
					$\chi^2 = \overline{3.71}$

As shown, Yates's correction yields a smaller chi-square value ($\chi^2 = 3.71$) than was obtained by means of the uncorrected formula ($\chi^2 = 5.13$). In the present example, our decision regarding the null hypothesis would depend on whether or not we had used Yates's correction. With the corrected formula, we accept the null hypothesis; without it, we reject the null hypothesis. Given these very different results, one should go with the more conservative formula that uses Yates's correction.

REQUIREMENTS FOR THE USE OF TWO-WAY CHI-SQUARE

The chi-square test of significance has few requirements for its use, which might explain in part why it is applied so frequently. Unlike the t ratio, for example, it does not assume a normal distribution in the population nor interval-level data. The following requirements still need to be considered before using the two-way chi-square:

1. *A comparison between two or more samples.* As illustrated and described in the present chapter, the two-way chi-square test is employed to make comparisons between two or more *independent* samples. This requires that we have at least a 2 × 2 table (at least 2 rows and at least 2 columns). The assumption of independence indicates that chi-square cannot be applied to a single sample that has been studied in a before-after panel design. At least two samples of respondents must be obtained.

2. *Nominal data.* Chi-square does not require data that are ranked or scored. Only frequencies are required.

3. *Random sampling.* We should have drawn our samples at random from a particular population.

4. *The expected cell frequencies should not be too small.* Exactly how large f_e must be depends on the nature of the problem. For a 2 × 2 problem, no expected frequency should be smaller than 5. In addition, Yates's corrected formula should be used for a 2 × 2 problem in which an expected cell frequency is smaller than 10. For a situation wherein several groups are being compared (say, a 3 × 3 or 4 × 5 problem), there is no hard-and-fast rule regarding minimum cell frequencies, although we should be careful to see that few cells contain less than five cases. In such instances, categories with small numbers of cases should be merged together if at all possible.

THE MEDIAN TEST

For ordinal data, the *median test* is a simple nonparametric procedure for determining the likelihood that two or more random samples have been taken from populations with the same median. Essentially, the median test involves performing a chi-square test of significance on a cross-tabulation in which one of the dimensions is whether the scores fall above or below the median of the two groups combined. Just as before, Yates's correction is used for a 2 × 2 problem (comparing two samples) having small expected frequencies.

STEP-BY-STEP ILLUSTRATION

MEDIAN TEST

To illustrate the procedure for carrying out the median test, suppose a police chief wanted to study urban versus rural police officers' reactions to confrontational situations. Specifically, he wondered whether there is a difference in the readiness of officers to call for backup in potentially dangerous confrontations. To examine this, the research division of the police department showed a sample of 15 urban and 12 rural state police officers a videotape of an interaction between a police officer and a citizen who has been pulled over for suspicion of driving while intoxicated. In the videotape, as the officer approaches the car an apparently inebriated man gets out and walks toward the officer, yelling in an angry and aggressive manner. At this point, the tape stops and the officers are asked to predict what they would do if they were the officer in the videotaped scenario. The officers are asked to rate on a 20-point scale the likelihood that they would call for backup in this situation. The following table presents the likelihood scores of each subject, with higher scores indicating greater likelihood:

Urban	Rural	Urban	Rural
15	12	11	9
18	7	10	11
15	15	8	14
17	16	14	9
17	6	9	
16	8	18	
10	10	16	
13	6		

STEP 1   Find the median of the two samples combined.

$$\text{Position of median} = \frac{N + 1}{2}$$

$$= \frac{27 + 1}{2}$$

$$= 14\text{th}$$

The median is the fourteenth score counting from either end of the distribution arranged in order of size. To find the median, we arrange all the scores for police officer in consecutive order (without regard for what sample they have come from) and locate the combined median:

18 18 17 17 16 16 16 15 15 15 14 14 13 12 11 11 10 10 10 9 9 9 8 8 7 6 6

                                                           ▲   Median (the fourteenth score
                                                              from either end)

STEP 2   Count the number in each sample falling above the median and not above the median (Mdn = 12).

	Urban	Rural
Above median	10	3
Not above median	5	9
	$N = 27$	

As shown here, the numbers above and not above the median scores on the Likelihood of Calling for Backup Scale are presented in a 2 × 2 frequency table. In this table, we can see that 10 of the 15 urban officers but only 3 of the 12 rural officers gave ratings that were above the median rating for the group as a whole.

STEP 3   Perform a chi-square test of significance.

If no urban versus rural differences exist with respect to likelihood of calling for backup, we would expect the same median split within each sample, so that half of the urban and half of the rural officers fall above the median. To find out whether the sample differences obtained are statistically significant or merely a product of sampling error, we conduct a chi-square test (using Yates's correction). The following table shows the observed and expected frequencies.

	Urban	Rural
Above median	10 (7.22)	3 (5.78)
Not above median	5 (7.78)	9 (6.22)
	$N = 27$	

$$\chi^2 = \sum \frac{(|f_o - f_e| - .5)^2}{f_e}$$

Setting up the calculations in tabular form:

f_o	f_e	$|f_o - f_e|$	$|f_o - f_e| - .5$	$(|f_o - f_e| - .5)^2$	$\dfrac{(|f_o - f_e| - .5)^2}{f_e}$
10	7.22	2.78	2.28	5.19	.72
3	5.78	2.78	2.28	5.19	.90
5	7.78	2.78	2.28	5.19	.67
9	6.22	2.78	2.28	5.19	.83
					$\chi^2 = 3.12$

Referring to Table E in Appendix C, we learn that chi-square must exceed 3.84 (df = 1) to be regarded as significant at the .05 level. Because our obtained $\chi^2 = 3.12$, we cannot reject the null hypothesis. There is insufficient evidence to conclude on the basis of our results that urban and rural police officers differ in their perceived likelihood of calling for backup in a specific potentially dangerous situation.

In this example, we were interested in comparing two groups on an ordinal level variable. This was accomplished by constructing a chi-square test on the 2 × 2 cross-tab of placement above versus not above the median by group membership (in this case, urban versus rural settings.)

If we were instead interested in comparing three groups on an ordinal level variable, we would need to apply a chi-square for comparing several groups. That is, we would first compute the median for all three groups combined, then construct a 2 × 3 cross-tab of placement above versus not above the median by group membership, and finally calculate the chi-square test of significance.

REQUIREMENTS FOR THE USE OF THE MEDIAN TEST

The following conditions must be satisfied to appropriately apply the median test to a research problem:

1. *A comparison between two or more medians.* The median test is employed to make comparisons between two or more medians from independent samples.
2. *Ordinal data.* To perform a median test, we assume at least the ordinal level of measurement. Nominal data cannot be used.
3. *Random sampling.* We should have drawn our samples on a random basis from a given population.

THE MANN-WHITNEY U TEST

Because its sole criterion is whether a score falls above or below the median, the median test is simple to understand and easy to calculate. For the same reason, the median test also makes inefficient use of data. It ignores the specific rank-order of cases and concentrates only on the middlemost score.

Suppose that you were to rank-order a set of 20 cases from two samples, X_1 and X_2, according to size from high to low as follows:

$$\text{High } X_1$$
$$X_1$$
$$X_1$$
$$X_1$$
$$X_1$$
$$X_2$$
$$X_2$$
$$X_2$$
$$X_2$$
$$X_2$$

—————— Median

$$X_1$$
$$X_1$$
$$X_1$$
$$X_1$$
$$X_1$$
$$X_2$$
$$X_2$$
$$X_2$$
$$X_2$$
$$\text{Low } X_2$$

In this extreme example, half of the cases from each group fall above and below the median. Therefore, though the samples differ sharply in their rankings, the median test would yield a chi-square of zero.

A much more efficient and, therefore, powerful nonparametric test of significance for comparing two samples is the *Mann-Whitney U test*. Like the median test, the Mann-Whitney U test is an appropriate substitute for the t ratio whenever ordinal data are involved. Unlike the median test, however, the Mann-Whitney examines the rank-ordering of *all* cases. Specifically, it determines whether or not the ranked values for a variable are equally distributed throughout two samples.

The formula for the Mann-Whitney U test is

$$U = N_1 N_2 + \frac{N_1(N_1 + 1)}{2} - \Sigma R_1$$

or

$$U' = N_1 N_2 + \frac{N_2(N_2 + 1)}{2} - \Sigma R_2$$

where ΣR_1 = sum of the ranks for the smaller group
       ΣR_2 = sum of the ranks for the larger group
       N_1 = size of the smaller sample
       N_2 = size of the larger sample

STEP-BY-STEP ILLUSTRATION

MANN-WHITNEY U TEST

In order to illustrate the use of the Mann-Whitney U test, consider the situation of the researcher who has been assigned to study the effect of stress on the test scores of candidates for a position as an FBI agent. On a random basis (based on having an odd or even last digit in social security number), the researcher creates two independent groups: 12 candidates take a test after experiencing a stressful situation; 10 candidates take the same test but have not undergone stress. The test scores of the two groups are as follows (note that X_1 should *always* be the smaller-sized group):

X_1 (No stress)	X_2 (Stress)
74	94
90	75
92	92
87	70
79	68
92	83
93	44
82	76
78	88
91	81
	72
	50

STEP 1   Rank-order the scores.

Rank-order all the scores in both groups combined, beginning with the smallest score. All scores must be ranked from lowest to highest (a rank of 1 *must* be assigned to the *smallest* score, 2 to the next smallest score, and so on).

In the case of tied ranks, you take an average of the tied positions; that is, you add the tied positions and then divide by the number of the ties. In the present example, for tied positions 18, 19, and 20 (all of which give scores of 92), we have

$$\frac{18 + 19 + 20}{3} = 19$$

That is, the three scores of 92 are assigned the rank of 19.

Note that more than one set of tied positions can occur in a problem though not in the present illustration. To assign ranks to tied positions at any point, follow the same procedure introduced. If, for example, the two lowest scores are identical, you would split the difference, giving the rank of 1.5 to each. If the same score is in the sixth and seventh places, each would be assigned a rank of 6.5.

Step 2   Sum the ranks for each group.

X_1	R_1	X_2	R_2
74	6	94	22
90	16	75	7
92	19 (18)	92	19 (20)
87	14	70	4
79	10	68	3
92	19 (19)	83	13
93	21	44	1
82	12	76	8
78	9	88	15
91	17	81	11
($N_1 = 10$)	$\Sigma R_1 = 143$	72	5
		50	2
		($N_2 = 12$)	$\Sigma R_2 = 110$

$$\sum R_1 = 143$$

$$\sum R_2 = 110$$

Step 3   Substitute in the formula to obtain U and U'.

$$U = (10)(12) + \frac{(10)(10 + 1)}{2} - 143$$

$$= 120 + 55 - 143$$

$$= 32$$

$$U' = (10)(12) + \frac{(12)(12 + 1)}{2} - 110$$

$$= 120 + 78 - 110$$

$$= 88$$

Step 4   Compare calculated and table values of U.

Take the *smaller* value of U obtained in Step 3 ($U = 32$) and compare it with the appropriate critical value of U in Table J in Appendix C (or Table K for a one-tailed test). Notice that N_1 (the size of the smaller sample) is indicated at the top of the table and that N_2 (the size of the larger sample) is located in the left-hand margin. To reject the null hypothesis, the obtained U (in this case, 32) must be smaller than the table value (in this case, 29). We therefore accept the null hypothesis. We did not find conclusive evidence that stress makes a difference in test scores of potential FBI agents.

Notice that Table J applies only to situations in which the larger group is no larger than 40 and the smaller group is no larger than 20. When the size of samples exceeds the limits of Table J, it is safe to assume that the U statistic is normally distributed, and thus can use a z ratio.

We first obtain U and U' with the formula presented previously and then insert the smaller of U and U' into the following z-score formula:

$$z = \frac{U - \dfrac{N_1 N_2}{2}}{\sqrt{\dfrac{N_1 N_2 (N_1 + N_2 + 1)}{12}}}$$

Suppose that in a particular case, we obtain $U = 202$ and $N_1 = 20$, $N_2 = 45$. The z score is calculated as:

$$z = \frac{202 - \dfrac{(20)(45)}{2}}{\sqrt{\dfrac{(20)(45)(20 + 45 + 1)}{12}}}$$

$$= \frac{202 - 450}{\sqrt{4950}}$$

$$= \frac{-248}{70.36}$$

$$= -3.52$$

To be significant at the .05 level, the obtained z score must exceed the table critical value of ± 1.96. Thus, we reject the null hypothesis and conclude that our difference is significant.

KRUSKAL-WALLIS ONE-WAY ANALYSIS OF VARIANCE BY RANKS

Kruskal-Wallis one-way analysis of variance by ranks is a nonparametric alternative to the analysis of variance (F ratio) that can be used to compare several independent samples, but that requires only ordinal-level data. To apply the Kruskal-Wallis procedure, we find statistic H as follows:

$$H = \frac{12}{N(N + 1)} \Sigma \left(\frac{\Sigma R_i)^2}{n} \right) - 3(N + 1)$$

where N = total number of cases
             n = number of cases in a given sample
         ΣR_i = sum of the ranks for a given sample

STEP-BY-STEP ILLUSTRATION

KRUSKAL-WALLIS TEST

To illustrate the procedure for applying one-way analysis of variance by ranks, consider the effects of observational learning on aggressiveness. Nursery school children were randomly assigned to see one of three film sequences: (1) In the first film, one child attacks another and then is shown enjoying himself (aggressive model rewarded). (2) In a second film, the child engages in the same aggression, but the second child retaliates and overcomes the aggressor (aggressive model punished). Or (3) in the third film, the two children are shown engaged in vigorous but nonaggressive play (nonaggressive model control). The children were then observed in a free-play setting, and the number of aggressive acts that they initiated was recorded.

The researcher felt sure that a greater number of aggressive acts represented greater aggressiveness, and so, the children could be ranked in terms of aggressiveness, but he did not think that the relative differences between aggressiveness scores were meaningful, suggesting that the data were not interval but were ordinal in nature. The following results were obtained:

Aggressive model rewarded ($n = 6$)	Aggressive model punished ($n = 6$)	Nonaggressive model ($n = 6$)
20	14	12
15	8	11
17	11	9
13	10	5
18	6	6
16	9	7

STEP 1   Rank-order the total group of scores.

All scores must be ranked from lowest to highest. In the present illustration, the scores have been ranked from 1 (representing 5 acts of aggression) to 18 (representing 20 acts). (In the case of tied ranks, follow the procedure presented in connection with the Mann-Whitney U test.)

STEP 2   Sum the ranks for each sample.

X_1	Rank	X_2	Rank	X_3	Rank
20	18	14	13	12	11
15	12	8	5	11	9.5
17	14	11	9.5	9	6.5
13	11	10	8	5	1
18	15	6	2.5	6	2.5
16	13	9	6.5	7	4
	$\Sigma R_1 = 92$		$\Sigma R_2 = 44.5$		$\Sigma R_3 = 34.5$

$$\Sigma R_1 = 92$$

$$\Sigma R_2 = 44.5$$

$$\Sigma R_3 = 34.5$$

STEP 3   Substitute in the formula to obtain H.

$$H = \frac{12}{N(N+1)} \Sigma \left(\frac{(\Sigma R_i)^2}{n} \right) - 3(N+1)$$

$$= \left(\frac{12}{(18)(18+1)} \right) \left(\frac{(92)^2}{6} + \frac{(44.5)^2}{6} + \frac{(34.5)^2}{6} \right) - (3)(18+1)$$

$$= \left(\frac{12}{342} \right) \left(\frac{8,464}{6} + \frac{1,980.25}{6} + \frac{1,190.25}{6} \right) - 57$$

$$= (.035)(1,939.08) - 57$$

$$= 68.04 - 57$$

$$= 11.04$$

STEP 4   Find the number of degrees of freedom.

$$df = k - 1$$
$$= 3 - 1$$
$$= 2$$

STEP 5   Compare H with the appropriate chi-square value in Table E.

$$\text{obtained } H = 11.04$$
$$\text{table } \chi^2 = 5.991$$
$$df = 2$$
$$\alpha = .05$$

To reject the null hypothesis at the .05 level of significance with 2 degrees of freedom, our calculated H would have to be larger than 5.991. Because we have obtained an H equal to 11.04, we can reject the null hypothesis and accept the research hypothesis. Our results indicate that there are significant differences, depending on condition of observational learning, in the aggressiveness of nursery school children.

REQUIREMENTS FOR THE USE OF KRUSKAL-WALLIS ONE-WAY ANALYSIS OF VARIANCE BY RANKS

To apply the one-way analysis of variance by ranks, we must consider the following requirements:

1. *A comparison of three or more independent samples.* One-way analysis of variance by ranks cannot be applied to test differences within a single sample of subjects measured more than once.
2. *Ordinal data.* Only data capable of being ranked are required.
3. *Each sample must contain at least six cases.* When there are more than five subjects in each group, the significance of H can be determined by means of the appropriate chi-square value in Table E.

SUMMARY

Statisticians have developed a number of nonparametric tests of significance—tests whose requirements do not include a normal distribution or the interval level of measurement. Although less powerful than their parametric counterparts t and F, nonparametric techniques can be applied to a wide range of research situations. The chi-square test of significance is used to make comparisons between frequencies rather than between mean scores. In a one-way chi-square, the frequencies observed among the categories of a variable are tested to determine whether they differ from a set of hypothetical frequencies.

Next, we discuss the application of chi-square to cross-tabulations of two variables. In a two-way chi-square, when the differences between expected frequencies and observed frequencies are large enough, we reject the null hypothesis and accept the validity of a true population difference. This is the requirement for a significant chi-square value. The chi-square test of significance assumes that the expected frequencies are at least equal to 5. Where several groups are being compared, it may be possible to collapse or merge together some categories. In 2×2 tables, Yates's correction for small expected frequencies is often used.

The median test is used to determine whether there is a significant difference between the medians of two independent samples. The Mann-Whitney U test is a more powerful (sensitive) alternative for testing rank-order differences between two independent samples. Finally, the Kruskal-Wallis one-way analysis of variance by ranks is used for comparing several independent samples.

TERMS TO REMEMBER

Parametric test	Expected frequencies
Nonparametric test	Yates's correction
Power of a test	Median test
One-way chi-square	Mann-Whitney U test
Two-way chi-square	Kruskal-Wallis one-way analysis of variance by ranks
Observed frequencies	

STEP-BY-STEP STUDY GUIDE

TEST OF DIFFERENCES BETWEEN GROUPS FOR NOMINAL-LEVEL DATA USING CHI-SQUARE

STEP 1   Arrange the data in the form of a cross-tabulation. The cell frequencies represent the observed frequencies (f_o).

STEP 2   Obtain the expected frequency for each cell (f_e).

$$f_e = \frac{(\text{row marginal total})(\text{column marginal total})}{N}$$

STEP 3   Subtract each expected frequency from the corresponding observed frequency, square each difference, divide each squared difference by the expected frequency, and then sum the quotients across all cells to derive the chi-square value. If the cross-tabulation is 2×2 and any expected frequency is between 5 and 10, be sure to apply Yates's correction.

$$\chi^2 = \sum \frac{(f_o - f_e)^2}{f_e}$$

$$\chi^2_{\text{Yates}} = \sum \frac{(|f_o - f_e| - .5)^2}{f_e}$$

STEP 4   Determine the degrees of freedom.

$$df = (r - 1)(c - 1)$$

STEP 5   Compare the obtained chi-square to the critical value from Table E. If the obtained value exceeds the tabled critical value, then reject the null hypothesis of no difference; otherwise, accept the null hypothesis.

STEP-BY-STEP STUDY GUIDE

TEST OF DIFFERENCES BETWEEN GROUPS FOR ORDINAL-LEVEL DATA USING THE MANN-WHITNEY U TEST

STEP 1   Rank-order the scores in both groups combined, beginning with the smallest score.

STEP 2   Sum the ranks in each of the groups (ΣR_1 and ΣR_2).

STEP 3   Calculate U and U'.

$$U = N_1 N_2 + \frac{N_1(N_1 + 1)}{2} + \Sigma R_1$$

$$U' = N_1 N_2 + \frac{N_2(N_2 + 1)}{2} + \Sigma R_2$$

STEP 4   Compare the smaller of U and U' to the critical value of U from Table J or K. If the obtained value is smaller than the tabled critical value, then reject the null hypothesis of no difference; otherwise, accept the null hypothesis.

STEP 5   If the values of N_1 and N_2 are such that Tables J and K are unusable, calculate the z score from the following formula. If the obtained z value exceeds the critical value of z found in Table A (or in the bottom row of Table B or C), then reject the null hypothesis of no difference; otherwise, accept the null hypothesis.

$$z = \frac{U - \dfrac{N_1 N_2}{2}}{\sqrt{\dfrac{N_1 N_2 (N_1 + N_2 + 1)}{12}}}$$

STEP-BY-STEP STUDY GUIDE

TEST OF DIFFERENCES BETWEEN SEVERAL GROUPS FOR ORDINAL-LEVEL DATA USING THE KRUSKAL-WALLIS TEST

STEP 1   Rank-order the scores in all groups combined, beginning with the smallest score.

STEP 2   Sum the ranks in each of the groups (ΣR_1, ΣR_2, ΣR_3, etc.).

STEP 3   Calculate H.

$$H = \frac{12}{N(N+1)} + \sum \left[\frac{(\Sigma R_j)^2}{n} \right] - 3(N+1)$$

STEP 4   Determine the degrees of freedom.

PROBLEMS

1. A researcher was interested in studying the phenomenon known as "social distance," the reluctance of people to associate with members of different ethnic and racial groups. She designed an experiment in which students enrolled in a lecture course were asked to choose a discussion group (all meeting at the same time in the same building) based only on the ethnic/racial stereotype associated with the names of the teaching assistant:

Group	Teaching assistant	Room
A	Cheng	106
B	Schultz	108
C	Goldberg	110
D	Rodriguez	112

Based on the following registration counts, use the one-way chi-square to test the null hypothesis that the ethnic/racial name made no difference in students' selection of a discussion group:

Group	Teaching assistant	Enrollment
A	Cheng	10
B	Schultz	24
C	Goldberg	10
D	Rodriguez	16

2. A local judge had recently been complaining about the "liberal press." In order to determine if in fact the press is dominated by left-wing writers, a researcher assesses the political leanings of a random sample of 60 journalists. He found that 15 were conservative, 18 were moderate, and 27 were liberal. Test the null hypothesis that all three political positions are equally represented in the print media.

3. Two groups of students took final exams in statistics. Only one group was given formal course preparation for the exam; the other group read the required text but never attended lectures. Whereas 22 out of the 30 members of the first group (attendance at lectures) passed the final exam, only 10 out of the 28 members of the second group (no attendance at lectures) passed the exam. Test the null hypothesis that the relative frequency of attenders who passed the final exam is the same as the relative frequency of nonattenders who passed the exam. What do your results indicate?

4. The following 2 × 2 cross-tabulation represents whether high school students passed the road test for their driver's license on the first attempt by whether they took a driver's education course. Applying Yates's correction, conduct a chi-square test of significance.

Test results	Driver's education course	
	Yes	No
Pass	16	8
Fail	7	11

5. The following is a 2 × 2 cross-tabulation of approval of capital punishment by gender of respondent. Applying Yates's correction, conduct a chi-square test of significance.

Approval of capital punishment	Gender of respondent	
	Female	Male
Approve	8	12
Disapprove	10	15

6. The Criminal Information Bureau of a particular state conducted a "new and improved" training course for criminal justice agencies designed to improve the quality of offender-related data. Sixty trainees were randomly assigned to two groups: 30 took the customary course and 30 took the new course. At the end of the course, all 60 trainees were given the same exam.

Using chi-square, test the null hypothesis that the new course is no better than the customary course in teaching criminal justice professionals how to collect and process criminal offender data. What do your results indicate?

Skills	Customary	"New and improved"
Excellent	24	23
Good	6	4
Unsatisfactory	0	3

7. For a sample of 100 corrections officers at a particular state prison, a researcher determined years on the job and willingness to help raise money for local charities. Using the following data, test the null hypothesis that willingness to help raise donations does not differ by length of service as a corrections officer. What do your results indicate?

Willingness to help	Years as a corrections officer			
	one	two	three	four or more
Willing	15	16	15	15
Unwilling	15	14	5	5

8. Does self-reported illegal drug use vary by social class? To find out, a criminologist questioned a random sample of 80 state residents about whether they had ever used illegal drugs. The criminologist also asked individuals in her sample questions about their occupation, education, and income, which she then used to categorize them as members of the upper-, middle-, working-, or lower-class. Her results are as follows:

Drug Use	Social class			
	Upper	Middle	Working	Lower
No	14	9	8	6
Yes	10	9	11	13

Using chi-square, test the null hypothesis that self-reported drug use does not differ by social class. What do your results indicate?

9. Do single-parent families tend to be more impoverished than families with two parents? A family researcher studied a sample of 35 one-parent and 65 two-parent families to determine whether their total family income fell below the poverty level. Applying chi-square to the following data, test the null hypothesis that one- and two-parent families do not differ with respect to poverty.

Total family income	Family structure	
	One-parent	Two-parents
Below poverty level	11	20
Not below poverty level	24	45

10. A sample of 118 college students are asked whether they are involved in a new campus crime watch program initiated at several colleges across the country. Using the following cross-tabulation depicting student responses by the region in which their colleges are located, conduct a chi-square test of significance for regional differences.

Region	Campus crime watch participation	
	Involved	Uninvolved
East	19	10
South	25	6
Midwest	15	15
West	8	20

11. A governor running for re-election and considering new legislation to combat youth violence asks his commissioner of probation for a breakdown of offense type by age group, focusing on violent, sex, and property offenders. Using the following cross-tabulation, test the null hypothesis that offense type does not vary by age group.

Offense type	Age		
	Young adult	Middle aged	Older adult
Violent	14	10	3
Sex	4	15	11
Property	7	9	5

12. Conduct chi-square tests of significance for the choice of murder weapon by gender of offender cross-tabulations shown in Tables 9.5 and 9.6. What is the effect of collapsing categories?

13. Two samples of police officers were asked to read and then evaluate a police report written by a rookie officer. Half of the officers were told that the new officer who wrote the report was a woman, and half were told that the officer was a man. The following evaluations were obtained (higher scores indicate more favorable evaluations):

X_1 (told author was a woman)	X_2 (told author was a man)
6	6
5	8
1	8
1	2
3	5
4	6
3	3
6	8
5	6
5	8
1	2
3	2
5	6
6	8
6	4
3	3

Applying the median test, determine whether there is a significant difference between the medians of these groups. Were officer evaluations of the report influenced by the attributed gender of its author?

14. A researcher concerned with racial justice suspects that jurors might perceive the severity of a crime as greater when the victim is white rather than black. She provides mock jurors with videotapes of trials (in which the victim is not shown) and arbitrarily describes the victim as either white or black. Using the following severity scores (1 for less serious to 9 for most serious), apply the median test to determine if there is a significant difference between crimes against white and black victims.

White victim		Black victim	
7	9	4	3
8	5	7	2
7	9	3	2
6	8	2	6
7	9	3	4
7	7	4	5
8	9	7	4
9	9	4	4
7		5	4
6		6	3
9		2	

15. Samples of Republicans and Democrats evaluated the performance of the president on a scale from 1 (poor performance) to 10 (outstanding performance) in terms of his support for measures to combat organized crime. The following performance evaluations were obtained:

X_1 (Republicans)	X_2 (Democrats)
9	8
10	7
5	1
8	2
6	4
8	4
9	3
9	

Applying the Mann-Whitney U test, determine whether there is a significant difference between Republicans and Democrats.

16. In preparation for parole hearings, the staff at the Department of Parole reviews the records of offenders and rates their risk of re-offending on a 12-point scale (based on offense type, number of prior convictions, previous parole and probation performance, drug abuse issues, participation in rehabilitation programs, and the offender's community and family support network). Use the Recidivism Risk Assessment Scale Scores given to determine whether sex offenders and armed robbers differ in their risk of re-offending once released from prison custody:

Recidivism Risk Assessment Scores

Sex offenders	Armed robbers
6	9
2	12
1	4
4	11
8	9
3	8
3	6
2	6
10	11
1	12
5	11
	10
	7
	9

Applying the Mann-Whitney U test, test the null hypothesis of no difference between sex offenders and armed robbers.

17. A state official interested in job satisfaction among criminal justice professionals selected random samples from the police, courts, and corrections and measured how satisfied each person was with his or her job. In the following results, satisfaction is scaled from 1 = very dissatisfied to 7 = very satisfied.

Levels of satisfaction

Courts	Police	Corrections
3	7	4
1	6	2
3	5	5
1	7	1
5	3	6
4	1	7
4	6	
2	4	
	4	
	5	

Applying the Kruskal-Wallis one-way analysis of variance by ranks, determine whether there is a significant difference in job satisfaction as a function of the criminal justice agency for which one works.

18. A manager in a federal law enforcement agency was interested in whether a person's score on an employee screening exam was related to the type of college degree most recently completed. The last 19 applicants were divided into groups based on their most recent degree, and the test score for each group is listed here:

Type of degree		
Law	Bachelor's	Master's
105	101	97
110	90	98
95	91	99
93	107	100
106	94	104
102	96	103
	92	

Applying the Kruskal-Wallis one-way analysis of variance by ranks, determine whether there is a significant difference in test scores by type of degree.

10

CORRELATION

- **STRENGTH OF CORRELATION**

- **DIRECTION OF CORRELATION**

- **CURVILINEAR CORRELATION**

- **THE CORRELATION COEFFICIENT**

- **PEARSON'S CORRELATION COEFFICIENT**

- **THE IMPORTANCE OF SCATTER PLOTS**

- **PARTIAL CORRELATION**

- **SUMMARY**

- **TERMS TO REMEMBER**

- **STEP-BY-STEP STUDY GUIDE: TESTING THE STRENGTH OF ASSOCIATION BETWEEN INTERVAL-LEVEL VARIABLES USING PEARSON'S CORRELATION**

- **PROBLEMS**

Characteristics such as gender, intelligence, and criminal history *vary* from one person to another and, therefore, are referred to as *variables*. In earlier chapters, we have been concerned with establishing the presence or absence of a relationship between any two variables, which we will now label X and Y; for example, between gender (X) and type of offense for which one is convicted (Y), between social class (X) and support for drug legalization (Y), or between nationality (X) and sexual assult victimization (Y). Aided by the t ratio, analysis of variance, or nonparametric tests such as chi-square, we previously sought to discover whether a difference between two or more samples could be regarded as statistically significant— reflective of a true population difference—and not merely the product of sampling error.

STRENGTH OF CORRELATION

Finding that a relationship exists does not indicate much about the degree of association, or *correlation,* between two variables. Many relationships are statistically significant; few express *perfect* correlation. To illustrate, we know that height and weight are associated, since the taller a person is, the more he or she tends to weigh. There are numerous exceptions to the rule, however. Some tall people weigh very little; some short people weigh a lot. In the same way, a relationship between nationality (American vs. Canadian) and sexual assault victimization does not preclude the possibility of finding many victims among Canadian students or many non-victims among American students.

Correlations actually vary with respect to their *strength.* We can visualize differences in the strength of correlation by means of a *scatter plot* or *scatter diagram,* a graph that shows the way scores on any two variables, X and Y, are scattered throughout the range of possible score values. In the conventional arrangement, a scatter plot is set up so that the X variable is located along the horizontal base line, and the Y variable is measured on the vertical line.

Turning to Figure 10.1, we find two scatter plots, each representing the relationship between years of education (X) and income (Y) for a sample of security guards and supervisors in a private security firm. Figure 10.1(a) depicts this relationship for males, and Figure 10.1(b) represents the relationship for females. Note that each and every point in these scatter plots depicts *two* scores, education and income, obtained by *one* respondent. In Figure 10.1(a), for example, we see that a male having 9 years of education earned $14,000, whereas a male with 14 years of education made over $24,000.

We can say that the strength of the correlation between X and Y increases as the points in a scatter plot more closely form an imaginary diagonal line across the center of the graph. Therefore, Figure 10.1(a) represents a stronger correlation than does Figure 10.1(b), although both scatter plots indicate that income tends to increase with greater education. Such data would indeed support the view that the income of women at this security firm (relative to that of men) is less related to the level of education that they attain.

DIRECTION OF CORRELATION

Correlation can often be described with respect to direction as either positive or negative. A *positive correlation* indicates that respondents getting *high* scores on the X variable also tend to get *high* scores on the Y variable. Conversely, respondents who get *low* scores on X also tend to get *low* scores on Y. Positive correlation can be illustrated by the relationship between education and income. As we have previously seen, respondents completing many years of school tend to make large annual incomes, whereas those who complete only a few years of school tend to earn very little annually.

A *negative correlation* exists if respondents who obtain *high* scores on the X variable tend to obtain *low* scores on the Y variable. Conversely, respondents achieving *low* scores on X tend to achieve *high* scores on Y. The relationship between education and income would *not* represent a negative correlation, because respondents completing many years of school *do not* tend to make small annual incomes. A more likely example of negative correlation is

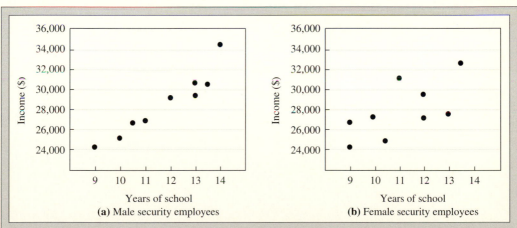

FIGURE 10.1   Scatter plots representing differences in the strength of the relationship between education and income for male and female employees of a private security firm

the relationship between education and prejudice against minority groups. Prejudice tends to diminish as the level of education increases. Therefore, individuals having little formal education tend to hold strong prejudices, whereas individuals completing many years of education tend to be low with respect to prejudice.

A positive or negative correlation represents a type of *straight-line* relationship. Depicted graphically, the points in a scatter plot tend to form a straight line through the center of the graph. If a positive correlation exists, then the points in the scatter plot will cluster around the imaginary straight line indicated in Figure 10.2(a). In contrast, if a negative correlation is present, the points in the scatter plot will surround the imaginary straight line as shown in Figure 10.2(b).

CURVILINEAR CORRELATION

For the most part, criminal justice researchers seek to establish straight-line correlation, whether positive or negative. It is important to note, however, that not all relationships between *X* and *Y* can be regarded as forming a straight line. There are many *curvilinear* relationships, indicating, for example, that one variable increases as the other variable increases until the relationship reverses itself, so that one variable finally decreases while the other continues to increase. That is, a relationship between *X* and *Y* that begins as positive becomes negative; a relationship that starts as negative becomes positive. To illustrate a curvilinear correlation, consider the relationship between age and fear of crime. As shown in Figure 10.3, the points in the scatter plot tend to form a U-shaped curve rather than a straight line. Thus fear of crime tends to decrease with age until people reach their thirties after which fear tends to increase with age.

THE CORRELATION COEFFICIENT

The procedure for finding curvilinear correlation lies beyond the scope of this text. Instead, we turn our attention to *correlation coefficients,* which numerically express both the

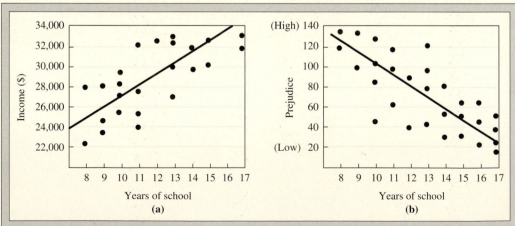

FIGURE 10.2   Scatter plots representing (a) a positive correlation between education and income and (b) a negative correlation between education and prejudice

strength and direction of straight-line correlation. Such correlation coefficients generally range between -1.00 and $+1.00$ as follows:

$-1.00 \leftarrow$ perfect negative correlation

$\vdots$

$-.60 \leftarrow$ strong negative correlation

$\vdots$

$-.30 \leftarrow$ moderate negative correlation

$\vdots$

$-.10 \leftarrow$ weak negative correlation

$\vdots$

$.00 \leftarrow$ no correlation

$\vdots$

$+.10 \leftarrow$ weak positive correlation

$\vdots$

$+.30 \leftarrow$ moderate positive correlation

$\vdots$

$+.60 \leftarrow$ strong positive correlation

$\vdots$

$+1.00 \leftarrow$ perfect positive correlation

We see, then, that negative numerical values such as -1.00, $-.60$, $-.30$, and $-.10$ signify negative correlation, whereas positive numerical values such as $+1.00$, $+.60$, $+.30$, and $+.10$ indicate positive correlation. Regarding degree of association, the closer to 1.00 in either direction, the greater the strength of the correlation. Because the strength of a correlation is independent of its direction, we can say that $-.10$ and $+.10$ are equal in strength (both are weak); $-.80$ and $+.80$ have equal strength (both are very strong).

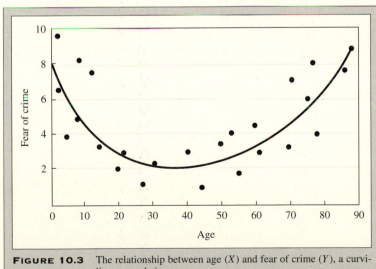

FIGURE 10.3 The relationship between age (X) and fear of crime (Y), a curvilinear correlation

PEARSON'S CORRELATION COEFFICIENT

With the aid of *Pearson's correlation coefficient* (r), we can determine the strength and the direction of the relationship between X and Y variables, both of which have been measured at the interval level. For example, we might be interested in examining the association between height and weight for the following sample of eight children:

Child	Height (in.) (X)	Weight (lb.) (Y)
A	49	81
B	50	88
C	53	87
D	55	99
E	60	91
F	55	89
G	60	95
H	50	90

In the scatter plot in Figure 10.4, the positive association that one would anticipate between height (X) and weight (Y) in fact appears. But note that there are some exceptions. Child C is taller but weighs less than child H; child D is shorter but weighs more than child E. These exceptions should not surprise us because the relationship between height and weight is not perfect. Overall, nonetheless, the general rule that "the taller one is" the heavier one is" holds true: F is taller and heavier than A, as is G compared to H.

Pearson's r does more than just consider if subjects are simply taller or heavier than other subjects; it considers precisely how much heavier and how much taller. The

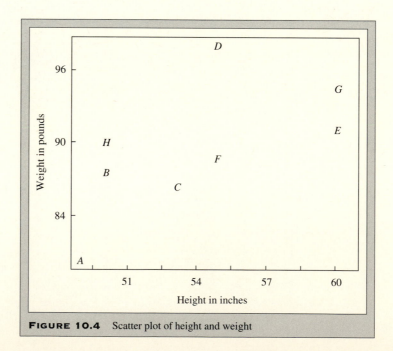

FIGURE 10.4   Scatter plot of height and weight

quantity that Pearson's r focuses on is the product of the X and Y deviations from their respective means. The deviation $(X - \overline{X})$ tells how much taller or shorter than average a particular child is; the deviation $(Y - \overline{Y})$ tells how much heavier or lighter than average a particular child is.

With Pearson's r, we add the products of the deviations to see if the positive products or negative products are more abundant and sizable. Remember, positive products indicate cases in which the variables go in the same direction (that is, both taller and heavier than average or both shorter and lighter than average); negative products indicate cases in which the variables go in opposite directions (that is, taller but lighter than average or shorter but heavier than average).

In Figure 10.5, dashed lines are added to the scatter plot of X and Y to indicate the location of the mean height ($\overline{X} = 54$ inches) and the mean weight ($\overline{Y} = 90$ pounds). Child G is apparently much taller and much heavier than average. His deviations on the two variables are $(X - \overline{X}) = 60 - 54 = 6$ (inches) and $(Y - \overline{Y}) = 95 - 90 = 5$ (pounds), which when multiplied yield $+30$. Child A is much shorter and much lighter than average. Her deviations (-5 and -9) multiply to $+45$. On the other hand, child C is only slightly shorter and lighter than average; her product of deviations ($-1 \times -3 = 3$) is far less dramatic. This is as it would seem intuitively: The more dramatically a child demonstrates the rule "the taller, the heavier," the larger the product of the X and Y deviations. Finally, child F is a slight exception: He is a little taller than average yet lighter than average. As a result his $+1$ deviation on X and -1 deviation on Y produce a negative product (-1).

We can compute the sum of the products for the data as follows. In the following table, columns two and three reproduce the heights and weights for the eight children in the

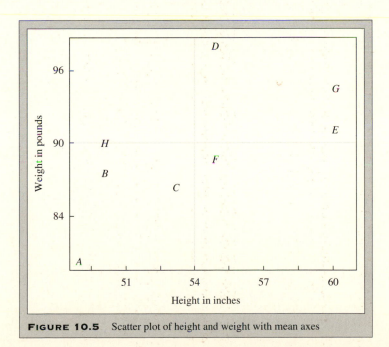

FIGURE 10.5   Scatter plot of height and weight with mean axes

sample. Columns four and five give the deviations from the means for the X and Y values. In column six, these deviations are multiplied and then summed.

Child	X	Y	$(X - \bar{X})$	$(Y - \bar{Y})$	$(X - \bar{X})(Y - \bar{Y})$	
A	49	81	-5	-9	45	$N = 8$
B	50	88	-4	-2	8	$\bar{X} = 54$
C	53	87	-1	-3	3	$\bar{Y} = 90$
D	55	99	1	9	9	
E	60	91	6	1	6	
F	55	89	1	-1	-1	
G	60	95	6	5	30	
H	50	90	-4	0	0	
	$\Sigma X = 432$	$\Sigma Y = 720$			SP = 100	

The sum of the final column (denoted SP, for sum of products) is positive — indicating a positive association between X and Y. But, as we have learned, correlation coefficients are constrained to range from -1 to $+1$ to aid in their interpretation. The formula for r accomplishes this by dividing the SP value by the square root of the product of the sum of squares of both variables (SS_X and SS_Y). Thus, we need to add two more columns to our table in which we square and sum the deviations for X and for Y.

X	Y	$(X - \bar{X})$	$(Y - \bar{Y})$	$(X - \bar{X})(Y - \bar{Y})$	$(X - \bar{X})^2$	$(Y - \bar{Y})^2$
49	81	-5	-9	45	25	81
50	88	-4	-2	8	16	4
53	87	-1	-3	3	1	9
55	99	1	9	9	1	81
60	91	6	1	6	36	1
55	89	1	-1	-1	1	1
60	95	6	5	30	36	25
50	90	-4	0	0	16	0
$\Sigma X = 432$	$\Sigma Y = 720$			SP = 100	$SS_X = 132$	$SS_Y = 202$

The formula for Pearson's correlation is as follows:

$$r = \frac{\Sigma (X - \bar{X})(Y - \bar{Y})}{\sqrt{\Sigma (X - \bar{X})^2 \Sigma (Y - \bar{Y})^2}} = \frac{SP}{\sqrt{SS_X SS_Y}}$$

$$= \frac{100}{\sqrt{(132)(202)}}$$

$$= \frac{100}{\sqrt{26,664}}$$

$$= \frac{100}{163.2}$$

$$= +.61$$

Therefore, Pearson's correlation indicates, as suggested by the scatter plot, that height and weight are fairly strongly correlated in the positive direction.

A COMPUTATIONAL FORMULA FOR PEARSON'S r

Computing Pearson's r from deviations helps relate the topic of correlation to our earlier discussions. However, the previous formula for Pearson's r requires lengthy and time-consuming calculations. Fortunately, there is an alternative formula for Pearson's r that works directly with raw scores, thereby eliminating the need to obtain deviations for the X and Y variables. Similar to the computational formulas for variance and standard deviation in Chapter 4, there are raw-score formulas for SP, SS_X, and SS_Y:

$$SP = \Sigma XY - N\overline{X}\,\overline{Y}$$

$$SS_X = \Sigma X^2 - N\overline{X}^2$$

$$SS_Y = \Sigma Y^2 - N\overline{Y}^2$$

Using these expressions in our formula for Pearson's correlation, we obtain the following computational formula for r :

$$r = \frac{\Sigma XY - N\overline{X}\,\overline{Y}}{\sqrt{(\Sigma X^2 - N\overline{X}^2)(\Sigma Y^2 - N\overline{Y}^2)}}$$

To illustrate the use of Pearson's r computational formula, consider the following data on the number of years of education (X) and the belief that drug treatment for offenders is an effective strategy for preventing crime (Y). Belief (Y) was measured on a 20-point scale, with higher scores indicating greater faith in the crime prevention effectiveness of drug treatment. To apply our formula, we must obtain the sums of X and Y (to calculate the means) and of X^2, Y^2, and XY:

X	Y	X^2	Y^2	XY
12	12	144	144	144
10	8	100	64	80
6	12	36	144	72
16	11	256	121	176
8	10	64	100	80
9	8	81	64	72
12	16	144	256	192
11	15	121	225	165
84	92	946	1,118	981

$N = 8$

$\Sigma X = 84$

$\Sigma Y = 92$

$\overline{X} = \dfrac{\Sigma X}{N} = \dfrac{84}{8} = 10.5$

$\overline{Y} = \dfrac{\Sigma Y}{N} = \dfrac{92}{8} = 11.5$

$\Sigma X^2 = 946$

$\Sigma Y^2 = 1118$

$\Sigma XY = 981$

The Pearson's correlation is then equal to

$$r = \frac{\Sigma\, XY - N\overline{X}\,\overline{Y}}{\sqrt{[\Sigma\, X^2 - N\overline{X}^2][\Sigma\, Y^2 - N\overline{Y}^2]}}$$

$$= \frac{981 - 8(10.5)(11.5)}{\sqrt{[946 - 8(10.5)^2][1118 - 8(11.5)^2]}}$$

$$= \frac{981 - 966}{\sqrt{(946 - 882)(1118 - 1058)}}$$

$$= \frac{15}{\sqrt{(64)(60)}}$$

$$= \frac{15}{\sqrt{3840}}$$

$$= \frac{15}{61.97}$$

$$= +.24$$

Thus, there is a modest positive correlation between education and belief in the efficacy of drug treatment.

Testing the Significance of Pearson's r

Pearson's r gives us a precise measure of the strength and direction of the correlation in the sample being studied. If we have taken a random sample from a specified population, we may still seek to determine whether the obtained association between X and Y exists in the *population* and is not due merely to sampling error.

To test the significance of a measure of correlation, we usually set up the null hypothesis that no correlation exists in the population. With respect to the Pearson correlation coefficient, the null hypothesis states that the population correlation ρ (rho) is zero. That is,

$$\rho = 0$$

whereas the research hypothesis says that

$$\rho \neq 0$$

As was the case in earlier chapters, we test the null hypothesis by selecting the alpha level of .05 or .01 and computing an appropriate test of significance. To test the significance of Pearson's r, we can compute a t ratio with the degrees of freedom equal to $N - 2$ (N equals the number of pairs of scores). For this purpose, the t ratio can be computed by the formula,

$$t = \frac{r\sqrt{N - 2}}{\sqrt{1 - r^2}}$$

where $t = t$ ratio for testing the statistical significance of Pearson's r
$N =$ number of pairs of scores X and Y
$r =$ the obtained Pearson's correlation coefficient

Returning to the previous example, we can test the significance of a correlation coefficient equal to $+.24$ between educational level (X) and the belief that offender drug treatment is an effective strategy for reducing crime (Y).

$$t = \frac{.24\sqrt{8-2}}{\sqrt{1-(.24)^2}}$$

$$= \frac{(.24)(2.45)}{\sqrt{1-.0576}}$$

$$= \frac{.59}{\sqrt{.9424}}$$

$$= \frac{.59}{.97}$$

$$= .61$$

When we turn to Table B in Appendix C, we find that the critical value of t with 6 degrees of freedom and $\alpha = .05$ is 2.447. Because our calculated t value does not even come close to exceeding this critical value, we cannot reject the null hypothesis $\rho = 0$. Although a correlation of $+.24$ is not weak, with a sample size of only 8, it is not nearly statistically significant. That is, given a small sample size of 8, it is very possible that the obtained r of $+.24$ is a result of sampling error. Thus, we are forced to accept the null hypothesis that the population correlation (ρ) is zero, at least until we have more data bearing on the relationship between education and belief in the crime prevention benefits of offender drug treatment.

A SIMPLIFIED METHOD FOR TESTING THE SIGNIFICANCE OF *r*

Fortunately, the process of testing the significance of Pearson's r as previously illustrated has been simplified, so that it becomes unnecessary actually to compute a t ratio. Instead, we turn to Table F in Appendix C, where we find a list of significant values of Pearson's r for the .05 and .01 levels of significance with the number of degrees of freedom ranging from 1 to 90. Directly comparing our calculated value of r with the appropriate table value yields the same result as though we had actually computed a t ratio. If the calculated Pearson's correlation coefficient does not exceed the appropriate table value, we must accept the null hypothesis that $\rho = 0$; if, on the other hand, the calculated r is greater than the table critical value, we reject the null hypothesis and accept the research hypothesis that a correlation exists in the population.

For illustrative purposes, let us return to our previous example in which a correlation coefficient equal to $+.24$ was tested by means of a t ratio and found not to be statistically significant.

Turning to Table F in Appendix C, we now find that the value of r must be at least .7067 to reject the null hypothesis at the .05 level of significance with 6 degrees of freedom. Hence, this simplified method leads us to the same conclusion as the longer procedure of computing a t ratio.

STEP-BY-STEP ILLUSTRATION
PEARSON'S CORRELATION COEFFICIENT

To illustrate the step-by-step procedure for obtaining a Pearson's correlation coefficient (r), suppose that a criminal justice researcher was interested in examining hypotheses about the relationship between education and antisocial beliefs. One such hypothesis asserts that the more people read (and are thus exposed to more information and a wider variety of perspectives about life), the less likely they are to be prejudiced toward people of other racial or ethnic identities. Reading (X) was measured by asking people the number of books they have read in the past year, and prejudice (Y) was measured on a scale from 1 to 10, with higher scores indicating greater prejudice. The data collected from a sample of 10 individuals is presented below:

Respondent	Number of books read (X)	Prejudice (Y)
A	10	1
B	3	7
C	12	2
D	11	3
E	6	5
F	8	4
G	14	1
H	9	2
I	10	3
J	2	10

In order to obtain Pearson's r, we must proceed through the following steps:

STEP 1   Find the values of ΣX, ΣY, ΣX^2, ΣY^2, and ΣXY, as well as $\overline{X}$ and $\overline{Y}$.

X	Y	X^2	Y^2	XY
10	1	100	1	10
3	7	9	49	21
12	2	144	4	24
11	3	121	9	33
6	5	36	25	30
8	4	64	16	32
14	1	196	1	14
9	2	81	4	18
10	3	100	9	30
2	10	4	100	20
85	38	855	218	232

$N = 10$

$\Sigma X = 85$

$\Sigma Y = 38$

$\overline{X} = \dfrac{\Sigma X}{N} = \dfrac{85}{10} = 8.5$

$\overline{Y} = \dfrac{\Sigma Y}{N} = \dfrac{38}{10} = 3.8$

$\Sigma X^2 = 855$

$\Sigma Y^2 = 218$

$\Sigma XY = 232$

STEP 2   Plug the values from Step 1 into Pearson's correlation formula.

$$r = \frac{\Sigma XY - N\bar{X}\bar{Y}}{\sqrt{[\Sigma X^2 - N\bar{X}^2][\Sigma Y^2 - N\bar{Y}^2]}}$$

$$= \frac{232 - (10)(8.5)(3.8)}{\sqrt{[855 - (10)(8.5)^2][218 - (10)(3.8)^2]}}$$

$$= \frac{232 - 323}{\sqrt{(855 - 722.5)(218 - 144.4)}}$$

$$= \frac{-91}{\sqrt{(132.5)(73.6)}}$$

$$= \frac{-91}{\sqrt{9,752}}$$

$$= \frac{-91}{98.75}$$

$$= -.92$$

Our result indicates a rather strong negative correlation between reading and prejudice.

STEP 3   Find the degrees of freedom.

$$df = N - 2$$
$$= 10 - 2$$
$$= 8$$

STEP 4   Compare the obtained Pearson's r with the appropriate value of Pearson's r in Table F.

$$\text{obtained } r = -.92$$
$$\text{table } r = .6319$$
$$df = 8$$
$$\alpha = .05$$

As indicated, to reject the null hypothesis that $\rho = 0$ at the .05 level of significance with 8 degrees of freedom, our calculated value of Pearson's r must exceed .6319. Because our obtained r equals $-.92$, we reject the null hypothesis and accept the research hypothesis. That is, our result suggests that a negative correlation between reading and prejudice is present in the population from which our sample was taken.

REQUIREMENTS FOR THE USE OF PEARSON'S CORRELATION COEFFICIENT

To employ Pearson's correlation coefficient correctly as a measure of association between X and Y variables, the following requirements must be taken into account:

1. *A straight-line relationship.* Pearson's r is only useful for detecting a straight-line correlation between X and Y.
2. *Interval data.* Both X and Y variables must be measured at the interval level, so that scores may be assigned to the respondents.
3. *Random sampling.* Sample members must have been drawn at random from a specified population to apply a test of significance.
4. *Normally distributed characteristics.* Testing the significance of Pearson's r requires both X and Y variables to be normally distributed in the population. In small samples, failure to meet the requirement of normally distributed characteristics may seriously impair the validity of the test. However, this requirement is of minor importance when the sample size equals or exceeds 30 cases.

THE IMPORTANCE OF SCATTER PLOTS

It seems instinctive to look for shortcuts and time-saving devices in our lives. For criminal justice researchers, the development of high-speed computers and simple statistical software has become what the advent of the automatic washer and liquid detergent was for the housekeeper. Unfortunately, these statistical programs have been used too often without sufficient concern for their appropriateness. This is particularly true in correlational analysis.

The correlation coefficient is a very powerful statistical measure. Moreover, for a data set containing several variables, with a very short computer run, one can obtain in just seconds a correlation matrix, such as that in Table 10.1.

A correlation matrix displays in compact form the interrelationships of several variables simultaneously. Along the diagonal from the upper-left corner to the bottom-right corner is a series of 1.00s. These represent the correlation of each variable with itself, and so they are necessarily perfect and therefore equal to one. The off-diagonal entries are the intercorrelations. The entry in the second row, fourth column (.78) gives the correlation of $X2$ and $X4$ (offender's and spouse's education). The matrix is symmetrical—that is, the tri-

---

TABLE 10.1   A CORRELATION MATRIX

	Offender's age X1	Offender's education X2	Family income X3	Spouse's education X4
X1	1.00	−.48	.35	−.30
X2	−.48	1.00	.67	.78
X3	.35	.67	1.00	.61
X4	−.30	.78	.61	1.00

angular portion above the diagonal is identical to that below the diagonal. Thus, the entry for the fourth row, second column is .78 as well.

The value of computer programs that produce results like this is that the researcher can quickly glance at the intercorrelations of a large number of variables—say, 10—and quickly pick out the strong and interesting correlations. One immediate problem, as we discussed earlier in reference to analysis of variance, is that such a fishing expedition of a large number of correlations will tend to pick up correlations that are significant by chance. An even greater pitfall, however, is that correlations may gloss over some major violations of the assumptions of Pearson's r. That is, a correlation matrix only provides (linear) correlation coefficients; it does not tell if the relationships are linear in the first place or whether there are peculiarities in the data that are worth noting. To prevent falling victim to data peculiarities, one really should inspect scatter plots before jumping to conclusions about what is related to what.

It is a far more tedious task to look at scatter plots in conjunction with the correlation matrix, because they must be examined one pair at a time. For example, to inspect scatter plots for all pairs of 10 variables would require 45 plots and a great deal of time and effort. As a result, far too many students and researchers skip over this step, often with misleading or disastrous results. Sometimes, as we shall see, what seems like a strong association on the basis of the correlation coefficient may be proven illusory after seeing the scatter plot. Conversely, truly important associations may be misrepresented by the single summary value of Pearson's r.

Consider, for example, the following data on homicide and suicide rates (per 100,000 population) for the six New England states:

State	Homicide rate	Suicide rate
Maine	3.2	14.3
New Hampshire	2.9	11.3
Vermont	4.3	17.8
Massachusetts	3.6	8.9
Rhode Island	4.2	12.3
Connecticut	5.4	8.6

Source: U.S. Bureau of the Census. *Statistical Abstract of the United States,* Washington, D.C.

The correlation coefficient is $-.17$, suggesting a weak to moderate negative relationship. This would seem to support the contention of some researchers that these two forms of violence (other-directed and self-directed) are tradeoffs; when one rate is high, the other rate is low.

Before we get too excited about this result, however, let's inspect the scatter plot in Figure 10.6. Although the scatter plot appears to show a slight negative association, the lower-right-hand point deserves further consideration. This corresponds to Connecticut. There is some justification for suspecting that Connecticut is in fact systematically different from the rest of the New England states. Suppose, for the sake of argument, we exclude Connecticut and recalculate the correlation. By using only the five other states, $r = .44$. Indeed, Connecticut has both the lowest suicide rate and the highest homicide rate in New England, which seems to have distorted the initial correlation coefficient.

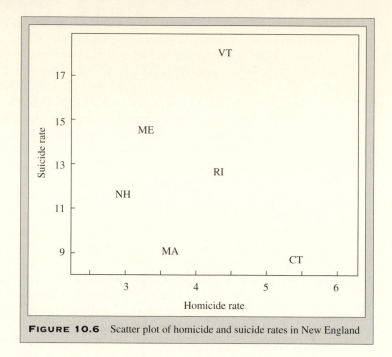

FIGURE 10.6   Scatter plot of homicide and suicide rates in New England

There are statistical procedures for determining if this or any other data point should be excluded; they are, however, beyond the scope of this book. Nevertheless, the importance of inspecting for these so-called *outliers* is a lesson well worth learning. It can be distressing to promote a particular correlation as substantively meaningful, only to find later that the exclusion of one or two observations radically alters the results and interpretation.

PARTIAL CORRELATION

In this chapter, we have considered a powerful method for studying the association or relationship between two interval-level variables. It is important to consider if a correlation between two measures holds up when controlling for additional variables. That is, does our interpretation of the relationship between two variables change in any way when looking at the broader context of other related factors?

To see this most easily, we will focus again on scatter plots. A scatter plot visually displays all the information contained in a correlation coefficient—both its direction (by the trend underlying the points) and its strength (by the closeness of the points to a straight line). We can construct separate scatter plots for different subgroups of a sample to see if the correlation observed for the full sample holds when controlling for the subgroup or control variable. For example, there has been some research in recent years on the relationship between physical characteristics (such as attractiveness) and professional attainment (for example, salary or goal fulfillment). Suppose that within the context of studying the relationship between personal attributes and salary, a criminal justice researcher stumbles upon a strong positive association between height and

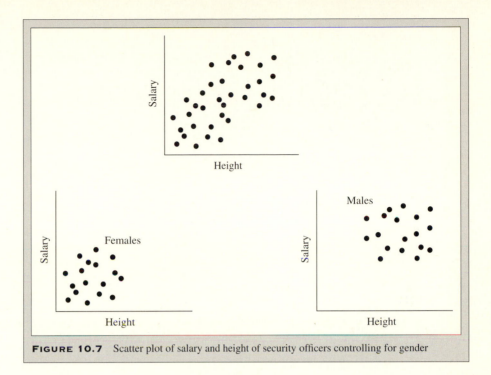

FIGURE 10.7   Scatter plot of salary and height of security officers controlling for gender

salary among security officers, as shown in Figure 10.7. This would make sense to the researcher; he or she reasons that taller people tend to be more assertive and are afforded greater respect from others, which pays off in being successful in requests for raises.

But this researcher could be misled—in total or in part—if he or she fails to bring into the analysis other relevant factors that might alternatively account for the height–salary correlation. Gender is one such possible variable. Male officers tend to be taller than women, and, for a variety of reasons, tend to be paid more. Perhaps this could explain all or part of the strong correlation between height and salary. Figure 10.7 also provides scatter plots of height and salary separately for males and males and females in the sample. It is important to note, first, that if we superimposed these two scatter plots, they would produce the original plot.

Apparently, when we control for sex, the height—salary correlation weakens substantially—in fact, disappears. If any correlation remains in either of the two gender-specific subplots, it is nowhere near as strong as that which we saw at first in the uncontrolled scatter plot. Thus, had the researcher failed to consider the influence of sex, he or she would have been greatly misled.

Figure 10.8 illustrates additional possible outcomes when a control variable is introduced. Each scatter plot represents a positive correlation between X and Y. Observations in subgroup 1 are symbolized by squares and those in subgroup 2 by circles. This allows us to see the X–Y relationship within the two subgroups separately. Note that these are prototypes—in practice, one may not observe such clear-cut situations.

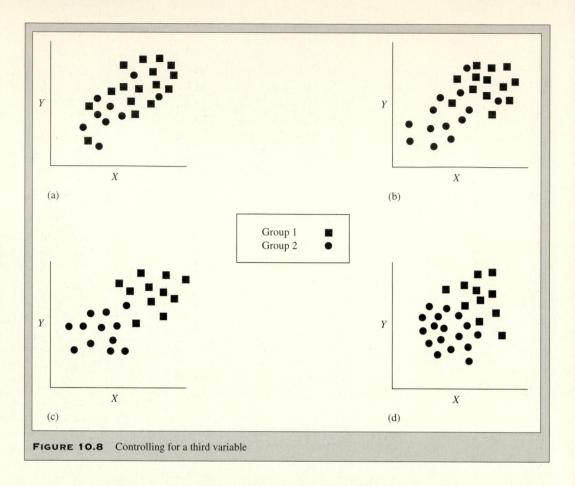

FIGURE 10.8 Controlling for a third variable

In scatter plot (a), we see that the *X*–*Y* association observed overall holds for each subgroup as well. Group 1 tends to exceed Group 2 on both *X* and *Y*, and within these two groups, *X* and *Y* are still related positively and strongly. That is, controlling for the grouping variable does not alter the *X*–*Y* relationship. For example, the positive relationship between education and income holds both for whites and nonwhite. If one observes this kind of outcome when testing for a range of control variables (for example, race, sex, age, etc.), one develops confidence in interpreting the association (for example, between education and income) as causal.

Scatter plot (b) shows a conditional relationship. Again, there is a strong relationship between *X* and *Y* for one group but no relationship for the other. If the grouping variable is ignored, the correlation between *X* and *Y* misrepresents the more accurate picture within the subgroups.

Scatter plot (c) illustrates a spurious or misleading correlation. Within both subgroups, *X* and *Y* are unrelated. Overall, Group 1 tends to be higher on both variables. As a result, when ignoring the subgroup distinction, it appears as if *X* and *Y* are related. Our association noted previously between height and salary among security officers is an example of a spurious correlation. Spurious correlations frequently occur in practice, and one should always be wary that two variables are related only because of their having a common cause.

Finally, scatter plot (d) shows a relationship that changes direction when a third variable is controlled. That is, the original positive association between X and Y becomes negative within the two subgroups. That Group 1 was so much greater than Group 2 on both X and Y overshadowed the negative relationship within each subgroup. This type of situation occurs rarely in practice, but one still should be aware that an apparent finding could be just the opposite of what it should be.

All the comparisons we have considered thus far involve dichotomous (two-category) control variables. The same approach applies to control variables having three or more levels or categories. For example, one could investigate the influence of religion on the relationship between two variables by computing Pearson's r separately for Protestants, Catholics, and Jews.

How would one handle an interval-level control variable like age? There is a temptation to categorize age into a number of subgroups (for example, under 18, 18–34, 35–49, 50 and over) and then to plot the X–Y association separately for each age category. However, this would be both inefficient and a waste of information (for example, the distinction between 18-year-olds and 34-year-olds is lost because these two ages are within the same category). Perhaps, then, we could use narrower age groups, but we still are being less precise than we could be. Fortunately, a simple method exists for adjusting a correlation between two variables for the influence of a third variable, when all three are interval level. That is, we do not have to categorize any variables artificially.

The *partial correlation coefficient* is the correlation between two variables, after removing (or partialing out) the common effects of a third variable. Like simple correlations, a partial correlation can range from -1 to $+1$, and is interpreted exactly the same way as a simple correlation. The formula for the partial correlation of X and Y controlling for Z is

$$r_{XY.Z} = \frac{r_{XY} - r_{XZ}r_{YZ}}{\sqrt{1 - r_{XZ}^2} \sqrt{1 - r_{YZ}^2}}$$

In the notation $r_{XY.Z}$ the variables before the period are those being correlated, and the variable after the period is the control variable. The partial correlation is computed exclusively on the basis of three quantities: the correlations between X and Y, X and Z, and Y and Z.

For example, consider the following correlation matrix for height (X), weight (Y), and age (Z). Not only are height and weight positively correlated, but both increase with age. One might wonder, then, how much of the correlation between height and weight ($r_{xy} = .90$) is due to the common influence of age and how much remains after the influence of age is controlled:

	Height	Weight	Age
Height (X)	1.00	.90	.80
Weight (Y)		1.00	.85
Age (Z)			1.00

$$r_{XYZ} = \frac{r_{XY} - r_{XZ}r_{YZ}}{\sqrt{1 - r_{XZ}^2}\,\sqrt{1 - r_{YZ}^2}}$$

$$= \frac{.90 - (.80)(.85)}{\sqrt{1 - (.80)^2}\,\sqrt{1 - (.85)^2}}$$

$$= \frac{.90 - .68}{\sqrt{1 - .64}\,\sqrt{1 - .7225}}$$

$$= \frac{.22}{\sqrt{.36}\,\sqrt{.2775}}$$

$$= \frac{.22}{(.60)(.5268)}$$

$$= \frac{.22}{.3161}$$

$$= +.70$$

Thus, the strong initial correlation between height and weight ($r_{XY} = .90$) weakens somewhat when the effects of age are removed ($r_{XYZ} = .70$).

We saw in Figure 10.8 that there are many possible patterns when controlling for a third variable. Similarly, partial correlations can be smaller, equal to, or greater than the two-variable simple correlation. Consider, for example, the following correlation matrix for education (X), salary (Y), and age (Z).

	Education	Salary	Age
Education (X)	1.00	.40	−.30
Salary (Y)		1.00	.50
Age (Z)			1.00

The simple correlation between education and salary is .40, but the partial correlation between education and salary controlling for age is even higher:

$$r_{XY.Z} = \frac{r_{XY} - r_{XZ}r_{YZ}}{\sqrt{1 - r_{XZ}^2}\,\sqrt{1 - r_{YZ}^2}}$$

$$= \frac{.40 - (-.30)(.50)}{1 - (.30)^2\ 1 - (.50)^2}$$

$$= \frac{.40 + (-.30)(.50)}{\sqrt{1 - (.30)^2}\,\sqrt{1 - (.50)^2}}$$

$$= \frac{.55}{\sqrt{.91}\,\sqrt{.75}}$$

$$= \frac{.55}{(.9539)(.8660)}$$

$$= \frac{.55}{.8261}$$

$$= +.67$$

Thus, ignoring age suppresses the observed association between education and salary. Younger security officers, because of their low seniority, have lower salaries, despite their higher level of educational attainment. As a result, the influence of education is dwarfed in the simple correlation because highly educated officers, who you would think should be paid more than they are, do not have the salary expected because they tend to be younger and newer employees. By controlling for age, we isolate the effect of education on salary, absent of the influence of age.

The partial correlation coefficient is a very useful statistic for finding spurious relationships, as is demonstrated in this classic case of a "vanishing" correlation.[1] The correlation between the rate of forcible rape (per 100,000) in 1982 and the circulation of *Playboy* (per 100,000) in 1979 for 49 U.S. states (Alaska is an outlier on rape and is excluded) is $r = +40$. Because of this substantial correlation, many observers have asked: If *Playboy* has this kind of effect on sex crimes, imagine what harm may be caused by truly hard-core pornography?

This concern requires the unjustified assumption that the correlation implies cause. Before making such a leap, however, we need to consider whether the two variables have a third variable as a common cause, thereby producing a spurious result.

As it turns out, both the rape and the *Playboy* subscription rate are related to the rate of homes without an adult female (per 1,000 households): For the rape rate (Y) and the rate of homes without an adult female (Z), $r_{YZ} = +.48$; for the rate of subscription to Playboy (X) and the rate of homes without an adult female (Z), $r_{XZ} = +.85$. Apparently both types of sexual outlet (one illegal and one legal) sometimes stem from the absence of adult females in the home.

To determine the correlation of *Playboy* (X) with rape (Y), controlling for homes without adult females (Z), we calculate the partial correlation:

$$r_{XY.Z} = \frac{r_{XY} - r_{XZ}r_{YZ}}{\sqrt{1 - r_{XZ}^2}\sqrt{1 - r_{YZ}^2}}$$

$$= \frac{.40 - (.85)(.48)}{\sqrt{1 - (.85)^2}\sqrt{1 - (.48)^2}}$$

$$= \frac{.40 - 41}{\sqrt{1 - .7225}\sqrt{1 - .2304}}$$

$$= \frac{-.01}{\sqrt{.2775}\sqrt{.7696}}$$

$$= \frac{-.01}{(.53)(.88)}$$

---

[1] We thank Rodney Stark and Cognitive Development, Inc., for this fine illustration and for these data.

$$= \frac{-.01}{.47}$$

$$= -.02$$

As a result, after controlling for one common variable, the original correlation disappears.

SUMMARY

In this chapter, we have presented correlation coefficients that numerically express the degree of association between X and Y variables. With the aid of Pearson's correlation coefficient (r), we can determine both the strength and direction of relationship between variables that have been measured at the interval level. The partial correlation coefficient was also discussed, which allows the researcher to control a two-variable relationship for the effects of a third variable.

TERMS TO REMEMBER

Variable   Correlation coefficient
Correlation   Scatter plot
  Strength   Pearson's correlation coefficient
  Direction (positive versus negative)   Partial correlation coefficient
  Curvilinear versus straight-line

STEP-BY-STEP STUDY GUIDE

TESTING THE STRENGTH OF ASSOCIATION BETWEEN INTERVAL-LEVEL VARIABLES USING PEARSON'S CORRELATION

STEP 1   Arranging the scores (X and Y) in tabular form, with squares (X^2 and Y^2) and products (XY), calculate the sums (ΣX and ΣY), sums of squares (ΣX^2 and ΣY^2), sum of products (ΣXY) and means ($\overline{X}$ and $\overline{Y}$).

STEP 2   Using these sums, calculate Pearson's correlation.

$$r = \frac{\Sigma XY - N\overline{X}\,\overline{Y}}{\sqrt{(\Sigma X^2 - N\overline{X}^2)(\Sigma Y^2 - N\overline{Y}^2)}}$$

STEP 3   Find the degrees of freedom.

$$df = N - 2$$

STEP 4   Compare the obtained Pearson's r with the critical value from Table F. If the obtained value exceeds the tabled critical value, then reject the null hypothesis of no relationship; otherwise, accept the null hypothesis.

PROBLEMS

1. The following six students were questioned regarding (X) their attitudes toward the legalization of prostitution and (Y) their attitudes toward the legalization of marijuana. Compute a Pearson's correlation coefficient for these data and determine whether the correlation is significant.

Student	X	Y
A	1	2
B	6	5
C	4	3
D	3	3
E	2	1
F	7	4

2. A researcher asked a sample of four public defenders about (X) the number of years they have served the court as a public defender, and (Y) their level of anxiety during trials in which they defend accused murderers. Compute a Pearson's correlation coefficient for the following data and indicate whether the correlation is significant.

X	Y
2	5
1	4
5	3
4	1

3. A probation officer is interested in the relationship between the distance an offender lives from where AA meetings are held and attendance at AA meetings. She collects data on distance from home to AA meetings and the number of meetings attended per week for a sample of 10 men under probation supervision. Using the following data, compute a Pearson's correlation coefficient and indicate whether the correlation is significant.

	Distance to AA meeting (miles)	Number of meetings attended per week
Tim	4	3
Stephen	2	1
Mario	7	5
Keivon	1	2
Seamus	4	1
Steve	6	1
Ali	9	9
Alex	7	6
Peter	7	5
Andreas	10	8

4. A prison researcher is interested in the relationship between the number of years incarcerated and inmate anxiety about how well they will function "on the outside" after their release. The researcher obtains the number of years the prisoner has been incarcerated (X), and with a questionnaire measures offenders' anxiety about what will happen to them after their release (Y; high scores indicate greater anxiety). Compute a Pearson's correlation coefficient for these data and determine whether the correlation is significant.

X	Y
1	1
5	4
6	2
1	3
8	5
2	1
5	2
9	6
4	7
2	0

5. The same prison researcher is interested in studying the relationship between length of unemployment and job-seeking activity among offenders recently released from prison. He interviews a sample of 12 unemployed offenders recently released from prison, obtaining from them the number of weeks they have been unemployed (X) and the number of job applications they have submitted during the past week (Y). Compute a Pearson's correlation coefficient for these data and determine whether the correlation is significant.

Offender	X	Y
A	2	8
B	7	3
C	5	4
D	12	2
E	1	5
F	10	2
G	8	1
H	6	5
I	5	4
J	2	6
K	3	7
L	4	1

6. In preparing for an examination, some law students in a class studied more than others. Each student's grade on the 10-point exam and the number of hours studied are listed as follows:

	Hours studied	Exam grade
Robert	4	5
Elias	1	2
Daniel	3	1
Shirley	5	5
Dimitris	8	9
John	2	7
Marika	7	6
Joanna	6	8

Calculate a Pearson's correlation coefficient and determine whether the correlation is significant.

7. A researcher set out to determine whether suicide and homicide rates in metropolitan areas around the country are correlated; and, if so, whether they vary inversely (negative correlation) or together (positive correlation). Using available data for a recent year, he compared the following sample of 10 metropolitan areas with respect to their rates (number per 100,000), rounded to the nearest whole number, of suicide and homicide:

Metropolitan area	Suicide rate	Homicide rate
A	20	22
B	22	28
C	23	15
D	10	12
E	14	12
F	21	19
G	9	13
H	13	16
I	15	17
J	18	20

What is the strength and direction of correlation between suicide and homicide rates among the 10 metropolitan areas sampled? Test the null hypothesis that rates of suicide and homicide are not correlated in the population.

8. A researcher interested in the consistency of school absenteeism over time studied a sample of 8 high school students for whom complete school records were available. The researcher counted the number of days each student had missed while in the sixth grade and then in the tenth grade. He obtained the following results:

Student	Days missed (6th)	Days missed (10th)
A	4	10
B	2	4
C	21	11
D	1	3
E	3	1
F	5	5
G	4	9
H	8	5

What is the strength and direction of the relationship between the number of days these students were absent from elementary school (6th grade) and how many days they missed when they reached high school (10th grade)? Can the correlation be generalized to a larger population of students?

9. A professor of criminal justice is studying the accuracy of eyewitness testimony, and wonders whether particularly gruesome and horrible crimes are recalled accurately. He shows a sample of 10 adults videotapes of crimes that had been pre-tested and rated for the level of horror and disgust that witnesses experience (ranging from "0" for relatively benign crimes such as auto theft to a "7" for a brutal murder). The subjects each view one of the scenarios and are asked a series of questions about its details, such as the race and approximate age of the offender, the length of time the crime took to complete, etc. The researcher's hypothesis was that witnesses would make more factual errors in their recollections of more shocking and horrible crimes.

(X) Crime scenario rating	(Y) Number of errors
0	3
7	1
2	2
1	2
5	0
4	1
3	3
3	2
0	7
1	4

What is the strength and direction of the correlation between the horror and disgust that witnesses experience and factual errors in their recollections of these crimes? Is the correlation significant?

10. In addition to job-seeking activity, the age of a released prisoner may be related to his or her length of unemployment. Suppose then that age (Z) is added to the two variables in Question 5.

Released prisoner	Weeks unemployed (X)	Applications submitted (Y)	Age (Z)
A	2	8	30
B	7	3	42
C	5	4	36
D	12	2	47
E	1	5	29
F	10	2	56
G	8	1	52
H	6	5	40
I	5	4	27
J	2	6	31
K	3	7	36
L	4	1	33

Find the partial correlation of weeks unemployed and the number of applications submitted, holding the age of the offender constant.

11. Besides studying time, intelligence itself may be related to the test performance of law students. Suppose then that IQ (Z) is added to the two variables in Question 6.

	Hours studied (X)	Exam grade (Y)	IQ (Z)
Robert	4	5	100
Elias	1	2	95
Daniel	3	1	95
Shirley	5	5	108
Dimitris	8	9	110
John	2	7	117
Marika	7	6	110
Joanna	6	8	115

Find the partial correlation of studying time and exam grade, holding IQ constant.

12. The following is a correlation matrix among unemployment rate (X), violent crime rate (Y), and divorce rate (Z) for a random sample of 50 cities.

	X	Y	Z
X	1.00	.60	.20
Y	.60	1.00	.30
Z	.20	.30	1.00

a. Which of the correlations are significant at the .05 level?
b. What is the partial correlation between unemployment rate and violent crime rate, holding divorce rate constant? Discuss the difference between the simple correlation r_{XY} and the partial correlation $r_{XY.Z}$.

11

REGRESSION ANALYSIS

- **THE REGRESSION MODEL**

- **INTERPRETING THE REGRESSION LINE**

- **PREDICTION ERRORS**

- **REGRESSION AND PEARSON'S CORRELATION**

- **REGRESSION AND ANALYSIS OF VARIANCE**

- **MULTIPLE REGRESSION**

- **SUMMARY**

- **TERMS TO REMEMBER**

- **STEP-BY-STEP STUDY GUIDE: TESTING THE EFFECT OF AN INDEPENDENT VARIABLE ON A DEPENDENT VARIABLE USING REGRESSION ANALYSIS**

- **PROBLEMS**

Certain concepts of statistics, such as percentages and means, are so commonplace that you may have understood them long before taking a statistics course. Other concepts are new, and in the process of learning statistics thoroughly, you'll begin to see the usefulness of measures that initially you may have learned to calculate by just "plugging into" a formula. It is analogous to becoming fluent in a foreign language: Initially one needs a dictionary to translate words, but later the context of the words also becomes meaningful.

In Chapter 4, we learned a new concept, that of variance. We also saw that in some instances it was an even more important concept than the mean. But still you may not yet have a feel for what the variance signifies and its fundamental role in statistics. In the context of *regression analysis,* the important notion of variance should become clearer.

Let's reconsider the problem in Chapter 4 concerning the length of sentences given criminal defendants. Suppose a criminologist collected data on sentences given defendants convicted under the Massachusetts Bartley-Fox gun law, which mandates a 1-year prison term for the illegal possession of a firearm. Obviously, the entire data set would consist of 12-month sentences. While knowing how many people had been sentenced under the law might be mildly interesting, the mean sentence length of 12 would be of no analytic value: All sentences would be 12 months, and so the variance would be zero.

To learn something about sentencing patterns and the tendencies of judges in handing out their sentences, the criminologist would be far better off focusing on a crime for which the sentences vary. If nothing varies, there is nothing to explain. That is, the goal of research is to explain why variables vary. For example, why do certain defendants obtain short sentences and others long sentences? Can we identify characteristics of defendants or of the nature of their crimes that account for this variation in sentence length? Or, are sentence lengths to some degree random and thus unpredictable?

Suppose that a particular judge, known to be moody at times, has given these sentences (in months) to 10 defendants convicted of assault: 12, 13, 15, 19, 26, 27, 29, 31, 40, and 48. The immediate questions are: Why did certain defendants only receive a term of or near 12 months? Why did one defendant receive as much as 48 months? Was it deserved? Is it because this defendant had a long criminal record or because the crime was particularly vicious? Or was it just a result of how the judge felt that day? Worse, could it have something to do with the defendant's race and the race of the victim?

The mean of these data is 26 months. There is nothing apparently unreasonable (not too harsh or too lenient) about the average sentence given by this judge. But our concern is with his consistency in sentencing—that is, with how disparate his sentences seem. We find that the variance of these data is 125 (you should verify this yourself). This then is a measure of the amount of dissimilarity among the sentences. It may seem large, but, more to the point, is it justified? How much of this 125 value is a result of, say, the number of prior convictions the defendants had?

Regression analysis is used to answer these questions. Each of us might have a theory about what factors encourage stiff prison sentences and which encourage leniency. But regression analysis gives us the ability to quantify precisely the relative importance of any proposed factor or variable. There is little question, therefore, why the regression technique is used more than any other in the social sciences, including criminal justice.

THE REGRESSION MODEL

Regression is closely allied with correlation in that we are still interested in the strength of association between two variables—for example, length of sentence and number of prior convictions. In regression, however, we are also concerned with specifying the nature of this relationship. We specify one variable as dependent and one as independent. That is, one variable is believed to influence the other. In our case, sentence length is dependent and number of prior convictions is independent.

In regression analysis, a mathematical equation is used to predict the value of the dependent variable (denoted Y) on the basis of the independent variable (denoted X):

$$Y = a + bX + e$$

Mathematically, this equation states that the sentence length (Y) received by a given defendant is the sum of three components: (1) a base-line amount given to all defendants (denoted a); (2) an additional amount given for each prior conviction (denoted b); and (3) a residual value (denoted e) that is unpredictable and unique to that individual's case.

The term a is called the *Y-intercept*. It refers to the expected level of Y when $X = 0$ (no priors). This is the base-line amount, because it is what Y should be before we take the level of X into account.

The term b is called the *slope* (or the *regression coefficient*) for X. This represents the amount that Y changes (increases or decreases) for each change of one unit in X. Thus, for example, the difference in sentence length between a defendant with $X = 0$ (no priors) and $X = 1$ (one prior) is expected to be b; the difference in expected sentence length between an offender with $X = 0$ (no priors) and a defendant with $X = 2$ (two priors) is $b + b = 2b$.

Finally, e is called the *error term* or *disturbance term.* It represents the amount of the sentence that cannot be accounted for by a and bX. In other words, e represents the departure of a given defendant's sentence from that which would be expected on the basis of his number of priors (X).

Let's consider this model geometrically. Figure 11.1 gives the scatter plot of the sentence length and prior conviction data of Table 11.1 for the 10 defendants.

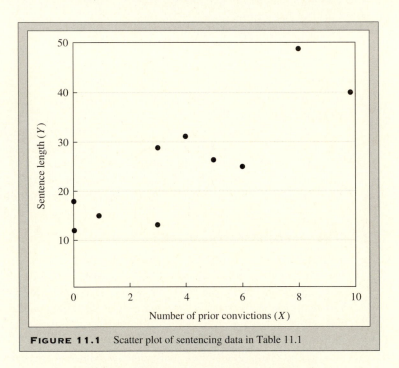

FIGURE 11.1   Scatter plot of sentencing data in Table 11.1

TABLE 11.1	SENTENCE LENGTH AND PRIOR CONVICTIONS FOR 10 DEFENDANTS
Priors (X)	Sentence (in months) (Y)
0	12
3	13
1	15
0	19
6	26
5	27
3	29
4	31
10	40
8	48

Clearly, there is a strong positive association between X and Y. Regression involves placing or fitting a line through the scatter of points: If the line is drawn accurately, the value of a (the Y-intercept) would be the location where the line crosses the Y axis. The value of b (the slope) would correspond to the incline or rise of the line for a unit increase in X. We learned in Chapter 10 that Pearson's correlation coefficient (r) measures the degree to which the points lie close to a straight line; the line to which we were referring is this *regression line*. It falls closest to all the points in a scatter plot.

Because regression is closely allied with correlation, it should not be surprising that the calculations are similar. In fact, almost all the computational steps for regression are the same as those for correlation.

The values of a and b that most closely fit the data are given by

$$b = \frac{SP}{SS_X}$$

or

$$b = \frac{\Sigma (X - \bar{X})(Y - \bar{Y})}{\Sigma (X - \bar{X})^2} \quad \text{for deviations}$$

or

$$b = \frac{\Sigma XY - N\bar{X}\bar{Y}}{\Sigma X^2 - N\bar{X}^2} \quad \text{for raw scores}$$

and the intercept

$$a = \bar{Y} - b\bar{X}$$

The necessary calculations for data given in the previous table are shown in Table 11.2.

First, we compute the means of the two variables ($\bar{X}$ = mean number of priors; $\bar{Y}$ = mean sentence length in months):

$$\bar{X} = \frac{\Sigma X}{N}$$

$$= \frac{40}{10}$$

$$= 4$$

$$\bar{Y} = \frac{\Sigma Y}{N}$$

$$= \frac{260}{10}$$

$$= 26$$

Next, we compute the sum of products and sum of squares:

$$SP = \Sigma\,(X - \overline{X})(Y - \overline{Y})$$

$$= 300$$

$$SS_X = \Sigma\,(X - \overline{X})^2$$

$$= 100$$

$$SS_Y = \Sigma\,(Y - \overline{Y})^2$$

$$= 1{,}250$$

Using these calculations, we now compute b and then a:

$$b = \frac{SP}{SS_X}$$

$$= \frac{300}{100}$$

$$= 3$$

$$a = \overline{Y} - b\overline{X}$$

$$= 26 - (3)(4)$$

$$= 26 - 12$$

$$= 14$$

TABLE 11.2   REGRESSION CALCULATIONS FOR DATA IN TABLE 11.1

X	Y	$X - \overline{X}$	$Y - \overline{Y}$	$(X - \overline{X})(Y - \overline{Y})$	$(X - \overline{X})^2$	$(Y - \overline{Y})^2$	
0	12	−4	−14	56	16	196	$\overline{X} = 4$
3	13	−1	−13	13	1	169	$\overline{Y} = 26$
1	15	−3	−11	33	9	121	SP = 300
0	19	−4	−7	28	16	49	$SS_X = 100$
6	26	2	0	0	4	0	$SS_Y = 1250$
5	27	1	1	1	1	1	$r = +.85$
3	29	−1	3	−3	1	9	$b = 3$
4	31	0	5	0	0	25	$a = 14$
10	40	6	14	84	36	196	
8	48	4	22	88	16	484	
$\Sigma X = 40$	$\Sigma Y = 260$			SP = $\overline{300}$	$SS_X = \overline{100}$	$SS_Y = \overline{1{,}250}$	

The slope (b) and the Y-intercept (a) form the equation for the regression line. Because the regression line represents expected or predicted sentences, rather than the actual sentences, we use $\hat{Y}$ (the caret symbol ^ means *predicted*) on the left side to represent predicted sentence, as opposed to actual sentence (Y):

$$\hat{Y} = a + bX$$

$$\hat{Y} = 14 + 3X$$

The next step is to plot the regression line on the scatter plot. To do this, we only need to find two points on the line and then connect the points (two points uniquely determine a line).

The easiest point to plot is the Y-intercept. That is, the value of a is where the regression line crosses the Y axis. In other words, the regression line always passes through the point ($X = 0$, $Y = a$). The next easiest point to determine is the intersection of the two means. It makes intuitive sense that a case average on X can be predicted to be average on Y. In short, the regression line always passes through the point ($X = \bar{X}$, $Y = \bar{Y}$).

In our example, then, we know immediately that the regression line passes through the points (0,14) and (4,26). And in Figure 11.2, we can connect these points to form this line.

At times, the two easiest points to plot—the Y-intercept and the intersection of the two means—are too close together to allow us to draw the regression line with accuracy. That is, if the points are too near, there is considerable room for error in setting down a ruler between them. In such cases, one needs to select a different point than the intersection of

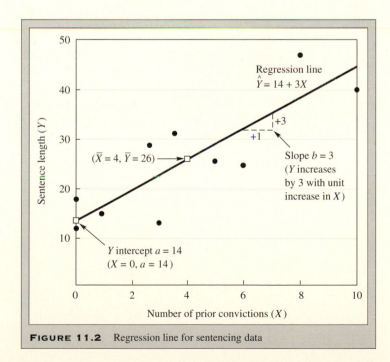

FIGURE 11.2   Regression line for sentencing data

means. One should select a large value of X (so that the point is far from the Y-intercept) and plug it into the equation. In our example, we could select $X = 10$, and so

$$\hat{Y} = a + b(10)$$
$$= 14 + (3)(10)$$
$$= 14 + 30$$
$$= 44$$

Point (10,44) could be used with point (0,14) to plot the line. Besides the advantage of selecting points as far apart as possible to make the drawing simpler, it does not matter which points you choose—all the predicted points will lie on the same line.

REQUIREMENTS FOR REGRESSION

The assumptions underlying regression are the same as those for Pearson's r. In particular:

1. It is assumed that both variables are measured at the interval level.
2. Regression assumes a straight-line relationship. If this is not the case, there are various transformations (which are more advanced than this presentation) that can be used to make the relationship into a straight line. Also, if extremely deviant cases are observed in a scatter plot, these should be removed from the analysis.
3. Sample members must be chosen randomly in order to employ tests of significance.
4. To test the significance of the regression line, one must also assume normality for both variables or else have a large sample.

INTERPRETING THE REGRESSION LINE

Let's consider what the values of a and b mean in substantive terms. The Y-intercept corresponds to the expected or predicted value of Y when X is zero. In our case, then, we can expect that first offenders (that is, those without prior convictions) will be sentenced to $a = 14$ months. Of course, not all first offenders will receive a 14-month sentence—and in our sample, the two such defendants received 12- and 19-month prison terms, respectively. But in the long run, we estimate that the average sentence given first offenders (those with $X = 0$) is 14 months.

The regression coefficient b refers to the increase or decrease in Y expected with each unit change in X. Here, we can say that for each prior conviction a defendant tends to get $b = 3$ additional months. As with the intercept, this rule will not hold in every case; however, 3 months is the long-run cost in terms of prison time for each prior conviction.

With this notion, we can also make predictions of a defendant's sentence on the basis of his number of prior convictions. If a defendant has five priors, for example, we can expect or predict

$$\hat{Y} = a + b(5)$$
$$= 14 + (3)(5)$$
$$= 14 + 15$$
$$= 29$$

In other words, this defendant should or can be expected to receive the base line of 14 months plus 3 additional months for each of his five priors. Note as well that this point (5,29) also lies on the regression line drawn in Figure 11.2. Thus, we could simply use this line to make predictions of the sentence length for any defendant, even defendants outside this sample, as long as they are a part of the population from which this sample was drawn (that is, defendants convicted of aggravated assault in the same jurisdiction). Although we cannot expect to predict sentences exactly, the regression line will make the best prediction possible on the basis of just the number of priors.

Unfortunately, the interpretation of the regression line is not always as direct and meaningful as in this example, particularly in regard to the Y-intercept. In our example, we could interpret the Y-intercept because a value of $X = 0$ was realistic. If, however, we were regressing weight on height (that is, predicting weight from height), the Y-intercept would represent the predicted weight of an individual 0 feet tall. The interpretation would be as foolish as the thought of such a person.

Meaningful or not, the Y-intercept is nevertheless an important part of the regression equation, but never as substantively important as the slope. In the height—weight instance, the slope refers to the expected weight increase for each inch of height. Indeed, the old adage of 5 pounds for every inch of growth is actually a regression slope.

Regression equations are frequently used to project the impact of the independent variable (X) beyond its range in the sample. There were no defendants with more than 10 priors, but we could still predict the sentence given by the judge to a hypothetical defendant with 13 priors (see Figure 11.3):

$$\hat{Y} = a + b(13)$$

$$= 14 + (3)(13)$$

$$= 14 + 39$$

$$= 53$$

One has to be cautious, however, about making predictions that fall far afield from the sample of data points. It would be farfetched to use a height—weight regression to predict the weight of a 10-foot-tall man. Similarly, in our sentencing example, it would be mathematically possible to predict the sentence that would be awarded a defendant with 100 priors:

$$\hat{Y} = a + b(100)$$

$$= 14 + (3)(100)$$

$$= 14 + 300$$

$$= 314$$

A 314-month sentence (over 26 years) for assault is absurd, but then so is the idea of a defendant with 100 prior convictions. Once you exceed the sample range of values too far, the ability to generalize the regression line breaks down. Because the largest value of X in the sample is 10, good sense would dictate against predicting sentences of defendants with more than, say, 15 priors. It would be quite unlikely that the mathematical rule of $b = 3$ months per prior would be applied to someone with as long a criminal record as

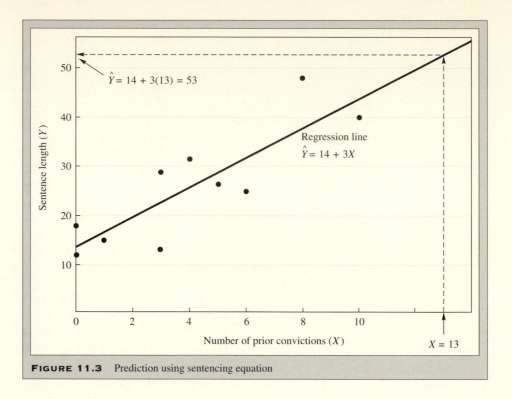

FIGURE 11.3   Prediction using sentencing equation

this. Other considerations would surely intervene that would invalidate such a farfetched prediction.

PREDICTION ERRORS

In the special case in which the correlation is perfect ($r = +1$ or -1), all the points lie precisely on the regression line and all the Y values can be predicted perfectly on the basis of X. In the more usual case, the line only comes close to the actual points (the stronger the correlation, the closer the fit of the points to the line).

The difference between the points (observed data) and the regression line (the predicted values) is the error or disturbance term (e):

$$e = Y - \hat{Y}$$

The concept of a disturbance term is illustrated in Figure 11.4. A positive value of e means that the sentence given a defendant is greater than what you would expect on the basis of his prior record. For example, the defendant with eight priors has a predicted sentence length of

$$\hat{Y} = 14 + (3)(8) = 14 + 24 = 38$$

His actual sentence was as much as 48 months, however, yielding a prediction error of

$$e = Y - \hat{Y} = 48 - 38 = 10$$

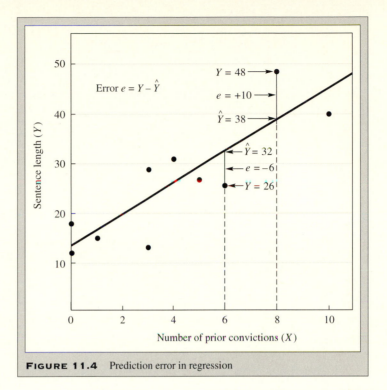

FIGURE 11.4   Prediction error in regression

Thus, on the basis of priors alone, this sentence is underpredicted by 10 months.

Negative prediction errors occur when the data points lie below the regression line. That is, on the basis of the X value, the Y value is overpredicted. For example, for the defendant with six priors, we would predict his sentence to be

$$\hat{Y} = 14 + (3)(6) = 14 + 18 = 32$$

This defendant received only 26 months, producing a prediction error of

$$e = Y - \hat{Y} = 26 - 32 = -6$$

The predictive value of a regression line (say, for predicting sentences on the basis of priors) can be assessed by the magnitude of these error terms. The larger the error, the poorer is the regression line as a prediction device.

It would seem intuitively logical to add the error terms to obtain a measure of predictive ability. However, the negative and positive errors cancel out. That is, $\Sigma e = 0$. To prevent this, we can square the errors before we sum. The so-called *error sum of squares* (or *residual sum of squares*), denoted by SS_{error}, is

$$SS_{error} = \Sigma e^2 = \Sigma (Y - \hat{Y})^2$$

The usefulness of the error sum of squares lies in comparing it to the magnitude of error that would have resulted had one not used X in making predictions. Without knowing anything about a defendant, what would you guess his sentence to be? The best guess would be the average sentence, or $\overline{Y}$. If we guess or predict $\overline{Y}$ for every defendant, the errors would simply be the deviations from the mean:

$$\text{Error without knowing } X = Y - \overline{Y}$$

The sum of squared prediction errors or deviations without using X is called the *total sum of squares:*

$$SS_{\text{total}} = \Sigma\,(Y - \overline{Y})^2$$

The predictive value of the regression equation is in its ability to reduce prediction error—that is, the extent that SS_{error} is smaller than SS_{total}. The difference between the two is the sum of squares that X can explain, and this is termed the *regression sum of squares* (or *explained sum of squares*). The regression sum of squares is then

$$SS_{\text{reg}} = SS_{\text{total}} - SS_{\text{error}}$$

To summarize:

	Not knowing X	Knowing X
Actual value	Y	Y
Predicted value	$\overline{Y}$	$\hat{Y} = a + bX$
Prediction error	$Y - \overline{Y}$	$Y - \hat{Y}$
Sum of squares	$SS_{\text{total}} = \Sigma\,(Y - \overline{Y})^2$	$SS_{\text{error}} = \Sigma\,(Y - \hat{Y})^2$
Difference	$SS_{\text{reg}} = SS_{\text{total}} - SS_{\text{error}}$	

Let's now calculate these sums of squares for the sentencing data. We already have from Table 11.2 the total sum of squares (previously called SS_Y):

$$SS_{\text{total}} = \Sigma\,(Y - \overline{Y})^2 = 1{,}250$$

To calculate the error sum of squares, we need to obtain the predicted sentence length ($\hat{Y}$) for each defendant, subtract it from the actual sentence length (Y), square the difference, and then sum:

X	Y	$\hat{Y} = a + bX$	$e = Y - \hat{Y}$	e^2
0	12	14	-2	4
3	13	23	-10	100
1	15	17	-2	4
0	19	14	5	25
6	26	32	-6	36
5	27	29	-2	4
3	29	23	6	36
4	31	26	5	25
10	40	44	-4	16
8	48	38	10	100
				$\Sigma\,e^2 = 350$

Thus,

$$SS_{\text{error}} = \Sigma\,e^2 = 350$$

and so

$$SS_{reg} = SS_{total} - SS_{error} = 1250 - 350 = 900$$

The ability of a regression line to make predictions can be expressed in what is known as the proportionate reduction in error (PRE), that is, the proportion of the prediction error that can be reduced by knowing the independent variable. The proportionate reduction in error (PRE) due to X is

$$PRE = \frac{SS_{total} - SS_{error}}{SS_{total}}$$

$$= \frac{SS_{reg}}{SS_{total}}$$

$$= \frac{900}{1,250}$$

$$= .72$$

Thus, .72, or 72%, of the error in predicting sentence length is reduced by taking number of priors into account. Put differently, 72% of the variance in sentence length is explained by the number of priors the defendant has on his record. This is precisely the information that we sought from the beginning.

REGRESSION AND PEARSON'S CORRELATION

We approached the problem of sentencing disparity by questioning why some defendants receive longer sentences than others. Using regression, we were able to determine that 72% of the variance in sentence length can be explained by the number of prior convictions. Obtaining the regression equation—the intercept and the slope—was fairly straightforward. It came directly from quantities (SP, SS_X, and SS_Y) derived in calculating the correlation (Pearson's r). However, the steps for computing SS_{error} and SS_{reg} were quite laborious, because they involved making a prediction for each person in the sample. Given the usefulness of determining the proportionate reduction in error (PRE), it would be helpful to employ a far simpler method.

If X and Y are uncorrelated (that is, if Pearson's $r = 0$), SS_{total} and SS_{error} will be the same, because X will not help predict Y. The larger the value of r, the smaller the value of SS_{error} relative to SS_{total}. More precisely, the proportionate reduction in error (PRE) is the square of Pearson's r:

$$r^2 = \frac{SS_{total} - SS_{error}}{SS_{total}}$$

The squared correlation (r^2) is called the *coefficient of determination*. That is, r^2 is the proportion of variance in Y determined or explained by X. The range of possible values for r^2

is from zero to one; r^2 is always positive, because even a negative correlation becomes positive when it is squared.

The complementary quantity $1 - r^2$ is called the *coefficient of nondetermination.* That is, the proportion of variance in Y that is not explained by X is $1 - r^2$:

$$1 - r^2 = \frac{SS_{error}}{SS_{total}}$$

For the sentencing data, using calculations from Table 12.2:

$$r = \frac{SP}{\sqrt{SS_X SS_Y}}$$

$$= \frac{300}{\sqrt{(100)(1,250)}}$$

$$= \frac{300}{\sqrt{125,000}}$$

$$= \frac{300}{353.55}$$

$$= .85$$

The coefficient of determination is then

$$r^2 = (.85)^2 = .72$$

Thus, 72% of the variance in sentence length is explained by the number of priors. This agrees with the results of the long method from the last section.

The coefficient of nondetermination is

$$1 - r^2 = 1 - (.85)^2 = 1 - .72 = .28$$

Thus, 28% of the variance in sentence length is not explained by priors. This 28% residual could be a result of other factors concerning the defendant or his crime. Some portion of the 28% could even be random error—that is, error that cannot be attributed to any factor. We'll discuss this in more detail later in the chapter.

REGRESSION AND ANALYSIS OF VARIANCE

The focus on explained and unexplained variance may remind you of analysis of variance in Chapter 8. In that chapter, we decomposed the total sum of squares (SS_{total}) into sum of squares between groups ($SS_{between}$) and sum of squares within groups (SS_{within}). In regression, we decompose the total sum of squares into regression sum of squares (SS_{reg}) and error sum of squares (SS_{error}). In fact, there are very strong similarities between analysis of variance and regression analysis. In both, we attempt to account for one variable in terms of another. In analysis of variance, the independent variable is categorical or in groups (such as social class or religion), whereas in regression, the independent variable is the interval level (such as number of prior convictions or height).

Fortunately, it is not necessary to calculate a predicted value for every respondent, as we did earlier, in order to decompose the total variation in the dependent variable into portions explained and not explained by the independent variable. Using the coefficients of determination and nondetermination as the proportions of explained and unexplained variation, we can quickly decompose the total sum of squares (SS_{total} or SS_Y) using the formulas:

$$SS_{reg} = r^2 SS_{total}$$

$$SS_{error} = (1 - r^2)SS_{total}$$

Just as in Chapter 8, an analysis of variance summary table is a convenient way of presenting the results of regression analysis. In Table 11.3, for example, we display under the heading "Source of variation" the regression, error, and total sum of squares for our regression of sentence length on the number of priors. Next, the regression and error sums of squares are associated with degrees of freedom. The regression sum of squares has only 1 degree of freedom:

$$df_{reg} = 1$$

For the error sum of squares,

$$df_{error} = N - 2$$

where N is the sample size.

As in Chapter 8, we can next calculate the *mean square regression* (MS_{reg}) and *mean square error* (MS_{error}) by dividing the sums of squares by their respective degrees of freedom:

$$MS_{reg} = \frac{SS_{reg}}{df_{reg}}$$

TABLE 11.3   ANALYSIS OF VARIANCE SUMMARY TABLE FOR SENTENCING DATA

Source of variation	SS	df	MS	F
Regression	900	1	900.00	20.57
Error	350	8	43.75	
Total	1,250			

$$MS_{error} = \frac{SS_{error}}{df_{error}}$$

Finally, by dividing the mean square regression by the mean square error, we obtain an F ratio for testing the significance of the regression—that is, whether the regression explains a significant amount of variation:

$$F = \frac{MS_{reg}}{MS_{error}}$$

To determine if the calculated F ratio is significant, it must exceed the critical value in Table D for 1 and $N - 2$ degrees of freedom.

For our results in Table 11.3 for the sentencing data,

$$F = \frac{900.00}{43.75} = 20.57$$

In Table D, we find that for $\alpha = .05$ with 1 and 8 degrees of freedom, the critical F is 5.32. Thus, the number of prior convictions explains a significant portion of the variance in sentence length.[1]

STEP-BY-STEP ILLUSTRATION

REGRESSION ANALYSIS

To review the steps of regression analysis, let's reconsider the height-weight data of Chapter 10. In this illustration, we will use computational raw-score formulas for sums of squares to simplify the calculations. Height (X), the independent variable, and weight (Y), the dependent variable, for the eight children are given in Table 11.4, along with the squares and products.

STEP 1   Calculate the mean of X and the mean of Y.

$$\overline{X} = \frac{\Sigma X}{N} = \frac{432}{8} = 54$$

$$\overline{Y} = \frac{\Sigma Y}{N} = \frac{720}{8} = 90$$

---

[1]This F-test of the explained variance is equivalent to the test for the significance of the Pearson's correlation presented in Chapter 10. In fact, with one independent variable as we have here, $F = t^2$.

TABLE 11.4   CALCULATIONS FOR HEIGHT-WEIGHT DATA

X	Y	X^2	Y^2	XY	
49	81	2,401	6,561	3,969	$N = 8$
50	88	2,500	7,744	4,400	$\Sigma X = 432$
53	87	2,809	7,569	4,611	$\Sigma Y = 720$
55	99	3,025	9,801	5,445	$\Sigma X^2 = 23,460$
60	91	3,600	8,281	5,460	$\Sigma Y^2 = 65,002$
55	89	3,025	7,921	4,895	$\Sigma XY = 38,980$
60	95	3,600	9,025	5,700	
50	90	2,500	8,100	4,500	
432	720	23,460	65,002	38,980	

STEP 2   Calculate SS_X, SS_Y, and SP.

$$SS_X = \Sigma X^2 - N\overline{X}^2$$
$$= 23,460 - (8)(54)^2$$
$$= 23,460 - 23,328$$
$$= 132$$

$$SS_Y = \Sigma Y^2 - N\overline{Y}^2$$
$$= 65,002 - (8)(90)^2$$
$$= 65,002 - 64,800$$
$$= 202$$

$$SP = \Sigma XY - N\overline{X}\,\overline{Y}$$
$$= 38,980 - (8)(54)(90)$$
$$= 38,980 - 38,880$$
$$= 100$$

STEP 3   Determine the regression line.

$$b = \frac{SP}{SS_X}$$
$$= \frac{100}{132}$$
$$= .76$$

$$a = \overline{Y} - b\overline{X}$$
$$= 90 - (.76)(54)$$
$$= 48.96$$

$$\hat{Y} = 48.96 + .76X$$

STEP 4   Determine correlation and coefficients of determination and nondetermination.

$$r = \frac{SP}{\sqrt{SS_X SS_Y}}$$

$$= \frac{100}{\sqrt{(132)(202)}}$$

$$= \frac{100}{163.29}$$

$$= .6124$$

and thus,

$$r^2 = (.6124)^2$$

$$= .3750$$

$$= 38\%$$

$$1 - r^2 = 1 - (.6124)^2$$

$$= 1 - .3750$$

$$= .6250$$

$$= 62\%$$

STEP 5   Calculate SS_{total}, SS_{reg}, and SS_{error}.

$$SS_{total} = SS_Y = 202$$

$$SS_{reg} = r^2\, SS_{total} = (.3750)(202) = 75.75$$

$$SS_{error} = (1 - r^2)\, SS_{total} = (.6250)(202) = 126.25$$

STEP 6   Calculate regression mean square and error mean square.

$$df_{reg} = 1$$

$$MS_{reg} = \frac{SS_{reg}}{df_{reg}}$$

$$= \frac{75.75}{1} = 75.75$$

$$df_{error} = N - 2 = 8 - 2 = 6$$

$$MS_{error} = \frac{SS_{error}}{df_{error}}$$

$$= \frac{126.25}{6} = 21.04$$

STEP 7 Calculate F and compare with the critical value from Table D.

$$F = \frac{MS_{reg}}{MS_{error}}$$

$$= \frac{75.75}{21.04}$$

$$= 3.60$$

$$df = 1 \text{ and } 6$$

$$\alpha = .05$$

$$F = 5.99 \quad \text{(from Table D)}$$

Because the calculated F is smaller than the critical value, height does not explain a significant amount of variance in weight. Although the correlation was fairly strong ($r = +.61$), the sample was too small to obtain significant results.

STEP 8 Construct an analysis-of-variance summary table.

Source of variation	SS	df	MS	F
Regression	75.75	1	75.75	3.60
Error	126.25	6	21.04	
Total	202.00	7		

MULTIPLE REGRESSION

We have attempted to account for variation in sentence length on the basis of the criminal history of the defendants—that is, to predict sentence length from the number of prior convictions. Overall, 72% of the variance was explained and 28% was not explained by criminal history. This approach is called simple regression—one dependent variable and one independent variable—just as Pearson's correlation is often called simple correlation.

Naturally, prior convictions is not the only factor relevant in analyzing sentencing data. It would be foolish to suggest that sentence length depends on just one factor, even though as much as 72% of the variance was explained. We might want to test multiple-factor theories that include such variables as the age of the defendant and whether there were accomplices to the crime. Perhaps in doing so, we can account for even more of the 28% of variance that sentence length could not.

Let's consider the case of two predictors, prior convictions and age. We add to our set of data another independent variable, the age of the defendant (Z), and calculate a correlation matrix among the three variables.

Priors (X)	Age (Z)	Sentence (Y)
0	18	12
3	22	13
1	27	15
0	29	19
6	30	26
5	35	27
3	36	29
4	29	31
10	34	40
8	31	48

Calculating the Pearson's correlation for each pair of variables yields this correlation matrix:

	Priors (X)	Age (Z)	Sentence (Y)
Priors	1.00	.56	.85
Age	.56	1.00	.68
Sentence	.85	.68	1.00

One might be tempted also to use this regression approach for age of defendant, for example, and then combine the results. Unfortunately, this would produce erroneous results. By squaring the correlations, prior sentences explain $(.85)^2 = .72 = 72\%$ of the variance in sentence length, and age explains $(.68)^2 = .46 = 46\%$ of the variance in sentence length. If we tried to add together these percentages, it would exceed 100%, which is impossible.

The problem is because, to some extent, age and prior convictions overlap: Older defendants have accumulated more priors during their lifetimes. Therefore, because age and priors are themselves correlated $(r = .56)$, part of the percentage of variance in sentences explained by priors is also explained by age, and vice versa. By adding the proportions that they each explain, a certain portion is double counted.

Multiple regression is a generalization of simple regression when one uses two or more predictors. The calculations are quite complex, and so computers are almost always needed. Moreover, it entails a number of issues and complications that are beyond the scope of this book. But just to whet your appetite for your next course in statistics, multiple regression analysis includes a *multiple coefficient of determination* (also known as the squared multiple correlation). Symbolized by R^2 (in contrast to r^2 as in Pearson's coefficient), the multiple coefficient of determination is the proportion of variance in a dependent variable explained by a set of independent variables in combination. For two independent variables (X and Z),

$$R^2 = \frac{r_{YX}^2 + r_{YZ}^2 - 2r_{YX}r_{YZ}r_{XZ}}{1 - r_{XZ}^2}$$

Based on the correlations among sentence length, priors, and age,

$$R^2 = \frac{(.85)^2 + (.68)^2 - (2)(.85)(.68)(.56)}{1 - (.56)^2}$$

$$= \frac{.7225 + .4624 - .6474}{1 - .3136}$$

$$= \frac{.5375}{.6864}$$

$$= .78$$

Thus, age and number of prior convictions together explain 78% of the variance in sentence length. Apparently, the inclusion of age adds only a modest amount to the overall prediction of sentence length. Because the number of prior convictions by itself explains 72%, the inclusion of age as an additional variable increases the percentage of explained variance only by 6%.

As in the case of simple regression, the dependent variable (sentence length) can be expressed as a function of both predictors (priors and age) in a multiple regression equation. Unlike the one predictor case, the calculations are somewhat elaborate, but they are easily and quickly accomplished by using a computer program.

By skipping the calculations, therefore, the regression equation is as follows:

$$\hat{Y} = -.41 + 2.41X + .61Z$$

Notice that each of the two predictors has its own regression coefficient or slope. These slopes indicate the change in the dependent variable associated with a unit increase in a given predictor, holding constant the other predictor.

Based on these results, we can say that each additional prior (X) tends to carry a 2.41-month increase in sentence length (Y), holding constant age (Z). For example, given two defendants of the same age but where one has two more priors than the other, the first defendant can be expected to receive a sentence that is 4.82 months longer than the other defendant.

Also based on these results, we can say that each additional year of age (Z) tends to be associated with a .61-month increase in sentence length (Y), holding constant the number of priors (X). If two defendants have similar criminal records, but one is 5 years older, this defendant can be expected to receive a sentence length that is 3.05 months longer than the other defendant.

Finally, the Y-intercept represents the base line, or expected sentence length when both predictors are equal to zero. It shouldn't bother us in the least that the Y-intercept here is negative ($-.41$ month); after all, how often do we encounter a newborn defendant with no priors?

In this brief discussion of multiple regression, we have only scratched the surface regarding an important but complex topic. Your next course in statistics will likely spend a good deal of time covering this useful technique.

SUMMARY

This chapter extends the concept of Pearson's r to situations in which we are concerned with the effect of one variable (the independent variable) on another variable (the dependent variable). Whereas correlation measures the strength and direction of an association, the regression line, comprising a slope and Y-intercept, specifies the exact nature of the impact of the independent variable on the dependent variable. In addition, regression analysis involves decomposing the sum of squares in the dependent variable into the portion that can be explained by the independent variable (regression sum of squares) and the portion unexplained (error sum of squares). These quantities can be alternatively expressed as the proportion of variance explained (called the coefficient of determination) and the proportion of variance unexplained (called the coefficient of nondetermination). Finally, the logic of multiple regression was introduced, and the multiple coefficient of determination was presented.

TERMS TO REMEMBER

Regression analysis

Y-intercept

Slope (regression coefficient)

Error term

Regression line

Error sum of squares

Regression sum of squares

Coefficient of determination

Coefficient of nondetermination

Mean square regression

Mean square error

Multiple regression

Multiple coefficient of determination

STEP-BY-STEP STUDY GUIDE

TESTING THE EFFECT OF AN INDEPENDENT VARIABLE ON A DEPENDENT VARIABLE USING REGRESSION ANALYSIS

STEP 1   Arranging the scores (X and Y) in tabular form, with squares (X^2 and Y^2) and products (XY), calculate the sums (ΣX and ΣY), sums of squares (ΣX^2 and ΣY^2), sum of products (ΣXY), and means ($\overline{X}$ and $\overline{Y}$).

STEP 2   Compute SS_X, SS_Y, and SP.

$$SS_X = \Sigma X^2 - N\overline{X}^2$$

$$SS_Y = \Sigma Y^2 - N\overline{Y}^2$$

$$SP = \Sigma XY - N\overline{X}\,\overline{Y}$$

STEP 3   Calculate the slope (b) and Y-intercept (a) to derive the regression line.

$$b = \frac{\Sigma XY - N\overline{X}\,\overline{Y}}{\Sigma X^2 - N\overline{X}^2}$$

$$a = \overline{Y} - b\overline{X}$$

STEP 4   Determine Pearson's correlation (r), and the coefficients of determination (r^2) and nondetermination ($1 - r^2$).

$$r = \frac{SP}{\sqrt{SS_x SS_y}}$$

STEP 5   Calculate the sum of squares total, sum of squares due to regression, and the sum of squares error.

$$SS_{total} = SS_Y$$

$$SS_{reg} = r^2 SS_{total}$$

$$SS_{error} = (1 - r^2) SS_{total}$$

STEP 6   Determine the degrees of freedom for regression and the degrees of freedom for error.

$$df_{reg} = 1$$

$$df_{error} = N - 2$$

STEP 7   Calculate the mean square regression and mean square error.

$$MS_{reg} = \frac{SS_{reg}}{df_{reg}}$$

$$MS_{error} = \frac{SS_{error}}{df_{error}}$$

STEP 8   Obtain the F ratio.

$$F = \frac{MS_{reg}}{MS_{error}}$$

STEP 9   Compare the obtained F ratio with the appropriate critical value for F taken from Table D. If the obtained F ratio exceeds the table critical value, then reject the null hypothesis of no effect of X on Y; otherwise, accept the null hypothesis.

PROBLEMS

1. Suppose that a researcher collected the following set of data on years of education (X) and approval of capital punishment (Y), (on a scale of 0 for extremely opposed to 5 for extremely supportive), for a sample of 10 adults:

X	Y
12	2
14	1
17	0
10	3
8	5
9	3
12	4
14	2
18	0
16	2

  a. Draw a scatter plot of the data.
  b. Calculate the regression slope and Y-intercept.
  c. Draw the regression line on the scatter plot.
  d. Predict the approval of capital punishment score for an adult with 11 years of education.
  e. Find the coefficients of determination and nondetermination. What do they mean?
  f. Construct an analysis-of-variance table and perform an F test of the significance of the regression.

2. A researcher was interested in whether offenders' self esteem (Y) was affected by their number of prior convictions (X). She obtained the number of prior convictions and scores on a self-esteem inventory for a sample of eight criminal offenders:

X	Y
1	5
0	3
2	4
4	7
2	5
3	9
1	8
1	4

  a. Draw a scatter plot of the data.
  b. Calculate the regression slope and Y-intercept.
  c. Draw the regression line on the scatter plot.
  d. Predict the self-esteem score of an offender with no prior convictions and an offender with two prior convictions.
  e. Find the coefficients of determination and nondetermination. What do they mean?
  f. Construct an analysis-of-variance table and perform an F test of the significance of the regression.

3. A legal researcher wanted to measure the effect of length of a criminal trial on the length of jury delib-

eration. He observed in a sample of 10 randomly selected courtroom trials the following data on length of trial (in days) and length of jury deliberation (in hours).

X (days)	Y (hours)
2	4
7	12
4	6
1	4
1	1
3	4
2	7
5	2
2	4
3	6

  a. Draw a scatter plot of the data.
  b. Calculate the regression slope and Y-intercept.
  c. Draw the regression line on the scatter plot.
  d. Predict the length of jury deliberation for a recently completed trial that lasted 6 days.
  e. Find the coefficients of determination and nondetermination. What do they mean?
  f. Construct an analysis-of-variance table and preform an F test of the significance of the regression.

4. A personnel specialist for a large bank is interested in determining the effect of seniority (the number of years with the company) on hourly wages for security guards. She randomly selects 10 security guards and compares their years with the bank (X) and hourly wages (Y):

X	Y
0	12
2	13
3	14
6	16
5	15
3	14
4	13
1	12
1	15
2	15

  a. Draw a scatter plot of the data.
  b. Calculate the regression slope and Y-intercept.
  c. Draw the regression line on the scatter plot.
  d. Predict the hourly wage of a randomly selected security guard who has been with the bank for four years.
  e. Find the coefficients of determination and nondetermination. What do they mean?
  f. Construct an analysis-of-variance table and preform an F test of the significance of the regression.

g. Based on these results, what is the typical starting wage per hour, and what is the typical increase in wage for each additional year on the job?

5. A communications researcher wanted to measure the effect of television viewing on aggressive behavior. He questioned a random sample of 14 children as to how many hours of television they watch daily (X) and then, as a measure of aggression, observed the number of schoolmates they physically attacked (shoved, pushed, or hit) on the playground during a 15-minute recess (Y). The following results were obtained:

X	Y
0	0
6	3
2	2
4	3
4	4
1	1
1	0
2	3
5	3
5	2
4	3
0	1
2	3
6	4

a. Draw a scatter plot of the data.
b. Calculate the regression slope and Y-intercept.
c. Draw the regression line on the scatter plot.
d. Predict the number of schoolmates attacked by a child who watches television 3 hours daily.
e. Find the coefficients of determination and non-determination. What do they mean?
f. Construct an analysis-of-variance table and preform an F test of the significance of the regression.

6. The dean of a law school was interested in the effect of academic performance in college on per-formance in law school. She consulted the records of 12 law school graduates, all of whom attended the same college, to determine their college cumulative grade average (X), and their cumulative grade average in law school (Y). The following results were obtained:

X	Y
3.3	2.7
2.9	2.5
2.5	1.9
4.0	3.3
2.8	2.7
2.5	2.2
3.7	3.1
3.8	4.0
3.5	2.9
2.7	2.0
2.6	3.1
4.0	3.2

a. Draw a scatter plot of the data.
b. Calculate the regression slope and Y-intercept.
c. Draw the regression line on the scatter plot.
d. Predict the law school grade average of a student who attains a 3.0 grade average in college.
e. Find the coefficients of determination and nondetermination. What do they mean?
f. Construct an analysis-of-variance table and preform an F test of the significance of the regression.

7. For the variables in Problem 11 in Chapter 10, find the multiple coefficient of determination (with Y the dependent variable).

8. For the correlation matrix in Problem 12 in Chapter 10, find the proportion of variance in the violent crime rate (Y) determined by unempolyment rate (X) alone, by divorce rate (Z) alone, and by unemployment and divorce rates together.

12

CHAPTER

NONPARAMETRIC MEASURES OF CORRELATION

- SPEARMAN'S RANK-ORDER CORRELATION COEFFICIENT
- GOODMAN'S AND KRUSKAL'S GAMMA
- CORRELATION COEFFICIENT FOR NOMINAL DATA ARRANGED IN A 2 × 2 TABLE
- CORRELATION COEFFICIENT FOR NOMINAL DATA IN LARGER THAN 2 × 2 TABLES
- LAMBDA
- ELABORATION
- SUMMARY

- TERMS TO REMEMBER
- STEP-BY-STEP STUDY GUIDE: TESTING THE STRENGTH OF ASSOCIATION BETWEEN ORDINAL-LEVEL VARIABLES USING SPEARMAN'S RANK-ORDER CORRELATION
- STEP-BY-STEP STUDY GUIDE: TESTING THE STRENGTH OF ASSOCIATION BETWEEN CROSS-TABULATED, ORDINAL-LEVEL VARIABLES USING GOODMAN'S AND KRUSKAL'S GAMMA
- PROBLEMS

We saw previously that non parametric alternatives to *t* and *F* were necessary for testing group differences with nominal and ordinal data. Similarly, we need nonparametric measures of correlation to use when the requirements of Pearson's *r* cannot be met. Specifically, these measures are applied if we have nominal or ordinal data or if we cannot assume normality in the population. This chapter introduces some of the best-known nonparametric measures of correlation: Spearman's rank-order correlation coefficient, Goodman's and Kruskal's gamma, phi coefficient, contingency coefficient, Cramér's *V*, and lambda.

SPEARMAN'S RANK-ORDER CORRELATION COEFFICIENT

We turn now to the problem of finding the degree of association for ordinal data—data that have been ranked or ordered with respect to the presence of a given characteristic.

To take an example from criminal justice, consider the relationship between socioeconomic status and the amount of money spent on automobile antitheft devices. Although the amount spent on auto security could be clearly measured at the interval level, socioeconomic status is considered ordinal, and thus a correlation coefficient for ordinal or ranked data is required. Imagine that a sample of eight respondents could be ranked as in Table 12.1.

As shown in the table, Don ranked first with respect to socioeconomic status, but second in the amount of money spent on automobile security; Flora's socioeconomic status rank was second, but first in the amount spent on automobile security devices, and so on.

To determine the degree of association between socioeconomic status and amount spent on automobile security, we apply *Spearman's rank-order correlation coefficient* (r_s). By formula,

$$r_s = 1 - \frac{6 \Sigma D^2}{N(N^2 - 1)}$$

where r_s = rank-order correlation coefficient
        D = difference in rank between X and Y variables
        N = total number of cases

We set up the present example as shown in Table 12.2. By applying the rank-order correlation coefficent to the data in this table,

$$r_s = 1 - \frac{(6)(10)}{(8)(64 - 1)}$$

$$= 1 - \frac{60}{(8)(63)}$$

$$= 1 - \frac{60}{504}$$

$$= 1 - .12$$

$$= +.88$$

TABLE 12.1   SAMPLE RANKED BY SOCIOECONOMIC STATUS AND AMOUNT SPENT ON AUTO SECURITY

Respondent	Socioeconomic status (X) rank		Amount spent on auto security (Y) rank	
Don	1	Highest	2	Most
Flora	2	in socio-	1	spent
Tong	3	economic	3	on auto
Min	4	status	5	security
Juanita	5		4	
Lisa	6		8	
Emma	7		6	
Jason	8		7	

TABLE 12.2   THE RELATIONSHIP BETWEEN SOCIOECONOMIC STATUS AND AMOUNT SPENT ON AUTO SECURITY

Respondent	Socioeconomic status (X)	Amount spent on auto security (Y)	D	D^2
1	1	2	−1	1
2	2	1	1	1
3	3	3	0	0
4	4	5	−1	1
5	5	4	1	1
6	6	8	−2	4
7	7	6	1	1
8	8	7	1	1
				$\Sigma D^2 = \overline{10}$

Therefore, we find a strong positive correlation ($r_s = +.88$) between socioeconomic status and the amount of money spent on automobile security devices: Respondents having high socioeconomic status tend to spend a good deal on auto security; respondents with low socioeconomic status tend to spend little on such devices.

DEALING WITH TIED RANKS

In actual practice, it is not always possible to rank or order our respondents avoiding ties at each and every position. We might find, for instance, that two or more respondents spend exactly the same amount of money on automobile security, that the academic achievement of two or more criminal justice students is indistinguishable, or that several people have the same IQ score.

To illustrate the procedure for obtaining a rank-order correlation coefficient in the case of tied ranks, let us say we are interested in determining the degree of association between position in a graduating class and IQ. Suppose also we are able to rank a sample of 10 graduating criminal justice majors with respect to their class position and to obtain their IQ scores as follows:

Respondent	Criminal justice class standing (X)	IQ (Y)
Katie	10 ←(last)	110
Peter	9	90
Jim	8	104
Marion	7	100
Steven	6	110
Julie	5	110
Liz	4	132
Tom	3	115
Yianna	2	140
Mario	1 ←(first)	140

Before following the standard procedure for obtaining a rank-order correlation coeffi-cient, let us first rank the IQ scores of our 10 graduating seniors:

Respondent	IQ	IQ rank	
Katie	110	7	
Peter	90	10	
Jim	104	8	Positions 5, 6,
Marion	100	9	and 7 are tied
Steven	110	6	
Julie	110	5	
Liz	132	3	
Tom	115	4	
Yianna	140	2	Positions 1 and
Mario	140	1	2 are tied

The table shows that Yianna and Mario received the highest IQ scores and are, therefore, tied for the first and second positions. Likewise, Julie, Steven, and Katie achieved an IQ score of 110, which places them in a three-way tie for the fifth, sixth, and seventh positions.

To determine the exact position in the case of ties, we must *add the tied ranks and divide by the number of ties.* Therefore, the position of a 140 IQ, which has been ranked as 1 and 2, would be the average rank:

$$\frac{1 + 2}{2} = 1.5$$

In the same way, we find that the position of an IQ score of 110 is

$$\frac{5 + 6 + 7}{3} = 6.0$$

Having found the ranked position of each IQ score, we can proceed to set up the problem at hand, as shown in Table 12.3.

We obtain the rank-order correlation coefficient for the problem in Table 12.3 as follows:

$$r_s = 1 - \frac{(6)(24.50)}{(10)(100 - 1)}$$

$$= 1 - \frac{147}{990}$$

$$= 1 - .15$$

$$= +.85$$

TABLE 12.3 THE RELATIONSHIP BETWEEN CLASS STANDING AND IQ

Respondent	Class standing (X)	IQ (Y)	$X - Y = D$	D^2
1	10	6	4.0	16.00
2	9	10	−1.0	1.00
3	8	8	.0	.00
4	7	9	−2.0	4.00
5	6	6	.0	.00
6	5	6	−1.0	1.00
7	4	3	1.0	1.00
8	3	4	−1.0	1.00
9	2	1.5	.5	.25
10	1	1.5	−.5	.25
				$\Sigma D^2 = 24.50$

The resultant rank-order correlation coefficient indicates a rather strong *positive* correlation between class standing and IQ. That is, students having *high* IQ scores tend to rank *high* in their class; students who have *low* IQ scores tend to rank *low* in their class.

TESTING THE SIGNIFICANCE OF THE RANK-ORDER CORRELATION COEFFICIENT

How do we go about testing the significance of a rank-order correlation coefficient? For example: How can we determine whether the obtained correlation of +.85 between class standing in a criminal justice program and IQ can be generalized to a larger population? To test the significance of a computed rank-order correlation coefficient, we turn to Table G in Appendix C, where we find the critical values of the rank-order coefficient of correlation for the .05 and .01 significance levels. Notice that we refer directly to the number of pairs of scores (N) rather than to a particular number of degrees of freedom. In the present case, $N = 10$ and the rank-order correlation coefficient must exceed .648 to be significant. We therefore reject the null hypothesis that $\rho_s = 0$ and accept the research hypothesis that class standing and IQ are actually related in the population of criminal justice majors from which our sample was drawn.

STEP-BY-STEP ILLUSTRATION

SPEARMAN'S RANK-ORDER CORRELATION COEFFICIENT

We can summarize the step-by-step procedure for obtaining the rank-order correlation coefficient with reference to the relationship between the degree of participation in criminal justice professional organizations and number of close friends. This relationship is indicated in the following sample of six respondents working in the field of criminal justice:

Respondent	Criminal justice professional organization participation (X) rank	Number of friends (Y)
A	1 ◄—— Participates most	6
B	2	4
C	3	6
D	4	2
E	5 ——— Participates least	2
F	6 ◄	3

To determine the degree of association between professional organization participation and number of friends, we carry through the following steps:

STEP 1 Rank respondents on the X and Y variables.

As the previous table shows, we rank respondents with respect to X, participation in professional organization, assigning the rank of 1 to the respondent who participates most and the rank of 6 to the respondent who participates least.

Number of friends (Y)	Rank	
6	1	
4	3	Tied for first
6	2	and second
2	5	
2	6	Tied for fifth
3	4	and sixth

We must also rank the respondents in terms of Y, the number of their friends. In the present example, we have instances of tied ranks, as shown in the following:

To convert tied ranks, we take an average of the tied positions:

For first and second positions:

$$\frac{1 + 2}{2} = 1.5$$

For fifth and sixth positions:

$$\frac{5 + 6}{2} = 5.5$$

Therefore, in terms of ranks, where X_R and Y_R denote the ranks on X and Y, respectively,

X_R	Y_R
1	1.5
2	3.0
3	1.5
4	5.5
5	5.5
6	4.0

STEP 2 To find ΣD^2, we must find the difference between X and Y ranks (D), square each difference (D^2), and sum these squares (ΣD^2):

X_R	Y_R	D	D^2
1	1.5	$-.5$	.25
2	3.0	-1.0	1.00
3	1.5	1.5	2.25
4	5.5	-1.5	2.25
5	5.5	$-.5$	.25
6	4.0	2.0	4.00
			$\Sigma D^2 = 10.00$

STEP 3 Plug the result of Step 2 into the formula for the rank-order correlation coefficient.

$$r_s = 1 - \frac{6 \Sigma D^2}{N(N^2 - 1)}$$

$$= 1 - \frac{(6)(10)}{(6)(36 - 1)}$$

$$= 1 - \frac{60}{210}$$

$$= 1 - .29$$

$$= +.71$$

STEP 4 Compare the obtained rank-order correlation coefficient with the critical value of r_s in Table G.

$$\text{Obtained } r_s = .71$$

$$\text{Table } r_s = .886$$

$$N = 6$$

$$\alpha = .05$$

Turning to Table G in Appendix C, we learn that a correlation coefficient of .886 is necessary to reject the null hypothesis at the .05 level of significance with a sample size of 6. Therefore, although we have uncovered a strong positive correlation between profes-sional organization participation and number of friends, we must still accept the null hypothesis that population correlation $\rho_s = 0$. Our result cannot be generalized to the pop-ulation from which our sample was taken.

REQUIREMENTS FOR USING THE RANK-ORDER CORRELATION COEFFICIENT

The rank-order correlation coefficient should be employed when the following conditions can be satisfied:

1. *A straight-line correlation.* The rank-order correlation coefficient detects straight-line relationships between X and Y.
2. *Ordinal data.* Both X and Y variables must be ranked or ordered.
3. *Random sampling.* Sample members must have been taken at random from a larger population to apply a test of significance.

GOODMAN'S AND KRUSKAL'S GAMMA

As we saw in connection with the rank-order correlation coefficient, it is not always possi-ble to avoid tied ranks at the ordinal level of measurement. In fact, criminal justice researchers frequently work with crude ordinal measures that produce large numbers of tied ranks. Typically, this occurs with ordinal variables that are ranked in categories, such as high, medium, and low. When two such ordinal variables are cross-tabulated, Goodman's and Kruskal's *gamma* (G) is a particularly useful measure of association.

The basic formula for gamma is

$$G = \frac{N_a - N_i}{N_i + N_i}$$

where $n_a = $ number of agreements
$n_i = $ number of inversions

Agreements and inversions can be understood as expressing the direction of correla-tion between X and Y variables. Perfect agreement indicates a perfect positive correlation ($+1.00$): All individuals being studied have been ranked in exactly the same order on both variables.

By contrast, perfect inversion indicates a perfect negative correlation (-1.00), so that the individuals being studied are ranked in exactly reverse order on both variables.

The logic of agreements, inversions, and tied pairs can be illustrated by examining the following simple cross-tabulation in which the frequencies are supplemented by the 10 respondents' names:

	X		
	High	Medium	Low
High	$f = 2$ Sam Mary	$f = 1$ Ann	$f = 0$
Y **Low**	$f = 2$ Alex Jack	$f = 3$ Paul John Lisa	$f = 2$ Sue Bob

Mary and John are in agreement because she is higher than he is on both variables. Similarly, the pair Sam and Sue are in agreement because Sam is at a higher level than Sue on both variables. In all, there are 12 agreements ($N_a = 12$). Can you find all 12?

In contrast, the pair Alex and Ann is an inversion because Alex exceeds Ann on X but falls below her on Y. Overall, there are two inversions ($N_i = 2$). Can you find both pairs?

Finally, any pair that is at the same level on one or both variables represents a tie. For example, Alex and Jack are tied on both variables (that is, they are in the same cell). Furthermore, although Alex surpasses Sue on X, they are at the same level on Y (that is, they are in the same row), and thus they are counted as a tied pair. Fortunately you can ignore ties in calculating gamma, because they do not enter into its formula.

STEP-BY-STEP ILLUSTRATION

GOODMAN'S AND KRUSKAL'S GAMMA

Using a larger example, let us now illustrate the procedure for obtaining a gamma coefficient for cross-tabulated ordinal variables. Suppose that a researcher wanting to examine the relationship between social class (X) and faith in the fairness of local police (Y) obtained the following data from a questionnaire study of 80 city residents: Among 29 upper-class respondents, 15 were high, 10 were medium, and 4 were low with respect to faith in the police; among 25 respondents who were middle class, 8 were high, 10 were medium, and 7 were low with respect to faith in the police; and among 26 lower-class respondents, 7 were high, 8 were medium, and 11 were low with respect to faith in the fairness of local police. Notice that tied ranks occur at every position. For instance, there were 29 respondents who tied at the rank of upper social class, the highest rank on the X variable.

STEP 1   Rearrange the data in the form of a cross-tabulation.

Faith in fairness	Social class (X)		
of local police (Y)	Upper	Middle	Lower
High	15	8	7
Medium	10	10	8
Low	4	7	11
	29	25	26
		$N = 80$	

Notice that the preceding table is a 3 × 3 cross-tabulation containing nine cells (3 rows × 3 columns = 9). To ensure that the sign of the gamma coefficient is accurately depicted as either positive or negative, the X variable in the columns must always be arranged in decreasing order from left to right. In the table, for example, social class decreases— upper, middle, lower—from left to right columns. Similarly, the Y variable in the rows must decrease from top to bottom. In the preceding table faith in the fairness of local police decreases—high, medium, low—from top to bottom rows.

STEP 2   Obtain N_a.

To find N_a, begin with the cell ($f = 15$) in the upper left-hand corner. Multiply this number by the sum of all numbers that fall *below and to the right of it*. Reading from left to right, we see that all frequencies below *and* to the right of 15 are 10, 8, 7, and 11. Now repeat this procedure for all cell frequencies that have cells below and to the right of them. By working from left to right in the table,

Upper class/high faith in police	$(15)(10 + 8 + 7 + 11) = (15)(36) = 540$
Middle class/high faith in police	$(8)(8 + 11) = (8)(19) = 152$
Upper class/medium faith in police	$(10)(7 + 11) = (10)(18) = 180$
Middle class/medium faith in police	$(10)(11) = 110$

(Note that none of the other cell frequencies in the table—7 in the top row, 8 in the second row, and 4, 7, and 11 in the bottom row—has cells below *and* to the right.)

N_a is the sum of the products obtained in the previous table.

$$N_a = 540 + 152 + 180 + 110$$

$$= 982$$

STEP 3   Obtain N_i.

To obtain N_i, reverse the procedure for finding agreements and begin in the upper right-hand corner of the table. This time, each number is multiplied by the sum of all numbers that fall *below and to the left of it*. Reading from right to left, we see that frequencies below *and* to the left of 7 are 10, 10, 7, and 4. As before, repeat this procedure for all frequencies having cells below and to the left of them.

Working from right to left,

Lower class/high faith in police	$(7)(10 + 10 + 7 + 4) = (7)(31) = 217$
Middle class/high faith in police	$(8)(10 + 4) = (8)(14) = 112$
Lower class/medium faith in police	$(8)(7 + 4) = (8)(11) = 88$
Middle class/medium faith in police	$(10)(4) = 40$

(Note that none of the other cell frequencies in the table—15 in the top row, 10 in the middle row, 11, 7, and 4 in the bottom row—has cells below and to the left.)

N_i is the sum of the products computed in the previous table. Therefore,

$$N_i = 217 + 112 + 88 + 40$$

$$= 457$$

STEP 4   Plug the results of Steps 2 and 3 into the formula for gamma.

$$G = \frac{N_a - N_i}{N_a + N_i}$$

$$= \frac{982 - 457}{982 + 457}$$

$$= \frac{525}{1439}$$

$$= +.36$$

A gamma coefficient of +.36 indicates a moderate positive correlation between social class and faith in local police. Our result suggests a correlation based on a dominance of agreements. (Note that a gamma coefficient of −.36 would have indicated instead a moderate *negative* correlation based on a dominance of *inversions.*)

Before continuing, let's take another look at how gamma functions in the context of cross-tabulations. Consider, for example, the center ("middle-medium") cell in the cross-tabulation of social class and faith in the fairness of local police. Cases that are below and to the right are agreements because they are lower on both variables. Cases that are below and to the left are inversions because they are lower on Y but greater on X. Why not count the 15 "upper-high" cases as agreements too with respect to our "middle-medium" reference cell? Although these are agreements, they would have already been counted: The

15 "middle-medium" cases are counted as agreements when "upper-high" is the reference cell. Counting agreements and inversions only toward the bottom of the table avoids any mistake of double counting.

TESTING THE SIGNIFICANCE OF GAMMA

To test the null hypothesis that X and Y are not associated in the population—that $Y = O$—we convert our calculated G to a z score by the following formula:

$$z = G \sqrt{\frac{N_a + N_i}{N(1 - G^2)}}$$

where G = calculated gamma coefficient
N_a = number of agreements
N_i = number of inversions
N = sample size

In the foregoing illustration, we found that $G = .36$ for the correlation between social class and faith in the fairness of local police. To test the significance of our finding, we substitute in the formula as follows:

$$z = (.36) \sqrt{\frac{|982 + 457|}{(80)[1 - (.36)^2]}}$$

$$= (.36) \sqrt{\frac{1439}{(80)(.87)}}$$

$$= (.36) \sqrt{\frac{1439}{69.60}}$$

$$= (.36)\sqrt{20.68}$$

$$= (.36)(4.55)$$

$$= 1.64$$

Turning to Table A (or the bottom row of Table B or C) in Appendix C, we see that z must exceed 1.96 to reject the null hypothesis at the .05 level of significance. Because our calculated z (1.64) is smaller than the required table value, we must accept the null hypothesis that faith in police $\gamma = 0$ and reject the research hypothesis that $\gamma \neq 0$. Our obtained correlation cannot be generalized to the population from which our sample was drawn.

REQUIREMENTS FOR USING GAMMA

The following requirements must be taken into account to employ gamma as a measure of association for cross-tabulations.

1. *Ordinal data.* Both X and Y variables must be ranked or ordered.
2. *Random sampling.* To test the null hypothesis ($\gamma = 0$), sample members must have been taken on a random basis from some specified population.

CORRELATION COEFFICIENT FOR NOMINAL DATA ARRANGED IN A 2 × 2 TABLE

In Chapter 9, a test of significance for frequency data known as chi-square was introduced. By a simple extension of the chi-square test, the degree of association between variables at the nominal level of measurement can now be determined. Let us take another look at the null hypothesis that the proportion of sexual assault victims among American female college students is the same as the proportion of sexual assault victims among Canadian female college students.

In Chapter 9, this null hypothesis was tested in a sample of 21 American students and a sample of 15 Canadian students attending universities just across the Canadian/American border from one another. It was determined that 15 out of the 21 American students but only 5 out of the 15 Canadian students were non-sexual assault victims. Thus, we have the 2 × 2 problem shown in Table 12.4.

The relationship between nationality and sexual assault victimization among female college students was tested in Chapter 9 by applying the 2 × 2 chi-square formula (with Yates's correction because of small expected frequencies) as follows:

$$\chi^2 = \Sigma \frac{(|f_o - f_e| - .5)^2}{f_e}$$

$$\chi^2 = \frac{(|15 - 11.67| - .5)^2}{11.67} + \frac{(|5 - 8.33| - .5)^2}{8.33}$$

$$+ \frac{(|6 - 9.33| - .5)^2}{9.33} + \frac{(|10 - 6.67| - .5)^2}{6.67}$$

$$= \frac{(3.33 - .5)^2}{11.67} + \frac{(3.33 - .5)^2}{8.33} + \frac{(3.33 - .5)^2}{9.33} + \frac{(3.33 - .5)^2}{6.67}$$

$$= \frac{(2.83)^2}{11.67} + \frac{(2.83)^2}{8.33} + \frac{(2.83)^2}{9.33} + \frac{(2.83)^2}{6.67}$$

$$= \frac{8.01}{11.67} + \frac{8.01}{8.33} + \frac{8.01}{9.33} + \frac{8.01}{6.67}$$

$$= .69 + .96 + .86 + 1.20$$

$$= 3.71$$

TABLE 12.4 SEXUAL ASSAULT VICTIMIZATION AMONG AMERICAN AND CANADIAN COLLEGE STUDENTS: DATA FROM TABLE 9.7

Sexual assault victim status	Nationality Americans	Canadians	Total
Victim	15	5	20
Non-victim	6	10	16
Total	21	15	$N = 36$

Having calculated a chi-square value of 3.71, we can now obtain the *phi coefficient* (ϕ), which is a measure of the degree of association for 2×2 tables. By formula,

$$\phi = \sqrt{\frac{\chi^2}{N}}$$

where
ϕ = phi coefficient
χ^2 = calculated chi-square value
N = total number of cases

By applying the foregoing formula to the problem at hand,

$$\phi = \sqrt{\frac{3.71}{36}}$$
$$= \sqrt{.1031}$$
$$= .32$$

Our obtained phi coefficient of .32 indicates the presence of a moderate correlation between nationality and sexual assault victimization.

TESTING THE SIGNIFICANCE OF PHI

Fortunately, the phi coefficient can be easily tested by means of chi-square, whose value has already been determined, and Table E in Appendix C:

Obtained $\chi^2 = 3.71$

Table $\chi^2 = 3.84$

df = 1

$\alpha = .05$

Because our calculated chi-square value of 3.71 is less than the required table value, we accept the null hypothesis of no association and reject the research hypothesis that nationality and sexual assault victimization are associated in the population.

REQUIREMENTS FOR USING THE PHI COEFFICIENT

To employ the phi coefficient as a measure of association between X and Y variables, we must consider the following requirements:

1. *Nominal data.* Only frequency data are required.
2. *A 2 × 2 table.* The data must be capable of being cast in the form of a 2 × 2 table (2 rows by 2 columns). It is inappropriate to apply the phi coefficient to tables larger than 2 × 2, in which several groups or categories are being compared.
3. *Random sampling.* To test the significance of the phi coefficient, sample members must have been drawn on a random basis from a larger population.

CORRELATION COEFFICIENTS FOR NOMINAL DATA IN LARGER THAN 2 × 2 TABLES

Until this point, we have considered the correlation coefficient for nominal data arranged in a 2 × 2 table. As we have seen in Chapter 9, there are times when we have nominal data, but are comparing several groups or categories. To illustrate, let us reconsider the null hypothesis that

the relative frequency of lenient, moderate, and punitive criminal justice punishment attitudes is the same for Protestants, Catholics, and Jews.

In Chapter 9, this hypothesis was tested with the data in the 3 × 3 table in Table 12.5.

The relationship between punishment attitudes and religion was tested by applying the chi-square formula as follows:

$$\chi^2 = \frac{(7 - 10.79)^2}{10.79} + \frac{(10 - 10.07)^2}{10.07} + \frac{(15 - 11.14)^2}{11.14}$$

$$+ \frac{(9 - 10.11)^2}{10.11} + \frac{(10 - 9.44)^2}{9.44} + \frac{(11 - 10.45)^2}{10.45}$$

$$+ \frac{(14 - 9.10)^2}{9.10} + \frac{(8 - 8.49)^2}{8.49} + \frac{(5 - 9.40)^2}{9.40}$$

$$= 7.57$$

In the present context, we seek to determine the correlation or degree of association between religion (X) and criminal justice punishment attitudes (Y). In a table larger than 2 × 2, this can be done by a simple extension of the chi-square test, which is referred to as the *contingency coefficient* (C). The value of C can be found by the formula.

$$C = \sqrt{\frac{\chi^2}{N + \chi^2}}$$

TABLE 12.5   CRIMINAL JUSTICE PUNISHMENT ATTITUDES BY RELIGION:
DATA FROM TABLE 9.4

	Protestant	Catholic	Jewish	
Lenient	7	9	14	30
Moderate	10	10	8	28
Punitive	15	11	5	31
	32	30	27	$N = 89$

where χ^2 = calculated chi-square value
N = total number of cases.
C = contingency coefficient

In testing the degree of association between religion and attitudes,

$$C = \sqrt{\frac{7.57}{89 + 7.58}}$$

$$= \sqrt{\frac{7.57}{96.57}}$$

$$= \sqrt{.0784}$$

$$= .28$$

Our obtained contingency coefficient of .28 indicates that the correlation between religion and criminal justice punishment attitudes can be regarded as a rather weak one. Religion and punishment attitudes are related, but many exceptions can be found.

TESTING THE SIGNIFICANCE OF THE CONTINGENCY COEFFICIENT

Just as in the case of the phi coefficient, whether the contingency coefficient is statistically significant can be easily determined from the size of the obtained chi-square value. In the present example, we find that the relationship between religion and criminal justice punishment attitudes is nonsignificant and, therefore, confined to the members of our samples. This is true because the calculated chi-square of 7.57 is smaller than the required table value:

$$\text{Obtained } \chi^2 = 7.57$$

$$\text{Table } \chi^2 = 9.49$$

$$\text{df} = 4$$

$$\alpha = .05$$

REQUIREMENTS FOR USING THE CONTINGENCY COEFFICIENT

To appropriately apply the contingency coefficient, we must be aware of the following requirements:

1. *Nominal data.* Only frequency data are required. These data may be cast in the form of a 2 × 2 table or larger.
2. *Random sampling.* To test the significance of the contingency coefficient, all sample members must have been taken at random from a larger population.

AN ALTERNATIVE TO THE CONTINGENCY COEFFICIENT

Despite its great popularity among researchers, the contingency coefficient has an important disadvantage: The number of rows and columns in a chi-square table will influence the maximum size taken by C. That is, the value of the contingency coefficient will not always vary between 0 and 1.0 (although it will never exceed 1.0). Under certain conditions, the maximum value of C may be .94; at other times, the maximum value of C may be .89; and so on. This situation is particularly troublesome in nonsquare tables; that is, tables that contain different numbers of rows and columns (for example, 2 × 3, 3 × 5, and so on).

To avoid this disadvantage of C, we may decide to employ another correlation coefficient, which expresses the degree of association between nominal-level variables in a table larger than 2 × 2. Known as Cramér's V, this coefficient does not depend on the size of the χ^2 table and has the same requirements as the contingency coefficient. By formula,

$$V = \sqrt{\frac{\chi^2}{N(k - 1)}}$$

where V = Cramér's V
N = total number of cases
k = number of rows *or* columns, whichever is smaller (if the number of rows equals the number of columns as in a 3 × 3, 4 × 4, or 5 × 5 table, either number can be used for k)

Let us return to the relationship between religion and criminal justice punishment attitudes as shown in Table 12.5 (a 3 × 3 table):

$$V = \sqrt{\frac{7.57}{(89)(3 - 1)}}$$

$$= \sqrt{\frac{7.57}{(89)(2)}}$$

$$= \sqrt{\frac{7.57}{178}}$$

$$= \sqrt{.0425}$$

$$= .21$$

As a result, we find a Cramér's *V* correlation coefficient equal to .21, indicating a weak relationship between religion and criminal justice punishment attitudes.

Lambda

As indicated in our previous discussion of Goodman's and Kruskal's gamma, correlation can be regarded as the degree to which the values of one variable are predictable from knowledge of the values of the other variable. Symbolized by the Greek letter λ, the *lambda* coefficient (also known as Guttman's coefficient of predictability) is a *proportionate reduction in error* measure—an index of how much we are able to reduce the error in predicting values of one variable from values of another. This is really another way of measuring to what degree we can improve the accuracy of our prediction. For example, if $\lambda = .60$, we have reduced the error of our prediction about values of the dependent variable by 60%; if $\lambda = .25$, we have reduced the error of our prediction by only 25%.

Like the contingency coefficient and Cramér's *V*, lambda is a measure of association for comparing several groups or categories at the nominal level. Unlike these other coefficients that indicate mutual predictability, however, lambda is asymmetrical—it measures the extent to which values of either variable (serving as the dependent variable) can be guessed or predicted from knowing values of the other variable (serving as the independent variable). If we reverse the designation of independent and dependent variables, the value of λ changes.

To illustrate, consider the relationship between a juvenile offender's placement in remedial education programs and a special needs label (for example, as mentally retarded or learning disabled), either of which could be considered an independent variable for the other: An offender's remedial education placement (for example, in a special class) might help determine whether or not he or she is labeled, or an offender's label might influence his or her placement in remedial programs. In reality, of course, there may be mutual predictability between program placement and label: Either variable probably has some capacity for predicting the other, but which do you think has the *greater* predictive ability, classroom placement or label?

Using lambda, we first treat classroom placement as the independent variable. We ask: To what extent can a juvenile offender's label be predicted by knowing whether he or she is placed in a special class, a regular class, or is tutored?

To find out, we arrange our data in the form of Table 12.6; in this example, a 3×3 table in which the categories of the independent variable (placement) are located in the columns and the categories of the dependent variable (labels) are located in the rows.

The value of λ can be found by the formula

$$\lambda = \frac{F_{iv} - M_{dv}}{N - M_{dv}}$$

where λ = lambda coefficient

F_{iv} = sum of the largest cell frequencies within each category of the independent variable

M_{dv} = largest marginal total among categories of the dependent variable

N = total number of cases

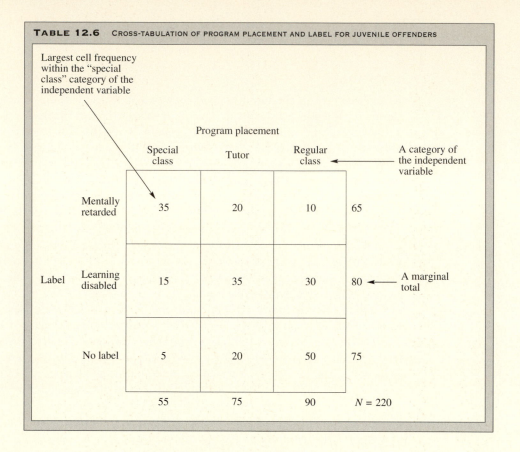

TABLE 12.6 CROSS-TABULATION OF PROGRAM PLACEMENT AND LABEL FOR JUVENILE OFFENDERS

Largest cell frequency within the "special class" category of the independent variable

Program placement

Label		Special class	Tutor	Regular class	
	Mentally retarded	35	20	10	65
	Learning disabled	15	35	30	80
	No label	5	20	50	75
		55	75	90	N = 220

A category of the independent variable

A marginal total

In testing the degree of association between program placement (the independent variable) and label (the dependent variable),

$$\lambda = \frac{(35 + 35 + 50) - 80}{220 - 80}$$

$$= \frac{120 - 80}{140}$$

$$= .29$$

The obtained lambda coefficient indicates that when program placement is treated as the independent variable, we reduce the error of our prediction (increase its accuracy) by 29%.

We next treat label as the independent variable. We now ask: To what degree can an individual's placement be predicted by knowing whether he or she has been labeled as mentally retarded or learning disabled, or has not been labeled? In testing the degree of association between label (the independent variable) and placement (the dependent variable),

$$\lambda = \frac{(35 + 35 + 50) - 90}{220 - 90}$$

$$= \frac{120 - 90}{130}$$

$$= .23$$

Using label as the independent variable, we are able to reduce the error of our prediction (increase its accuracy) by 23%. Thus, program placement more accurately predicts label than label predicts classroom placement.

Let's take another look at lambda as a measure of reduction in error. The following is a cross-tabulation of attitude toward gun control (the dependent variable) by political affiliation (the independent variable) from a survey of 228 people:

	Democrats	Republicans	Total
Favor	78	34	112
Neutral	8	5	13
Oppose	37	66	103
Total	123	105	228

If we attempt to predict opinion on gun control without looking at party affiliation, our best prediction would be Favor, the mode in the margin for this variable. In making these predictions, we would make a total of 13 + 103 = 116 errors. (Any other prediction, again blind to political party, would do no better.) Now let's see what happens if we take into account the political affiliation of the respondent, the independent variable. For Democrats, our best prediction would be the mode Favor, and we would commit 8 + 37 = 45 errors. For Republicans, our best prediction would be the mode Oppose, and we would make 34 + 5 = 39 errors. Together, we would commit 45 + 39 = 84 errors using political party to make the predictions. The formula for the proportionate reduction in error (PRE) is

$$PRE = \frac{\text{errors without independent variable} - \text{errors with independent variable}}{\text{errors without independent variable}}$$

$$= \frac{116 - 84}{116}$$

$$= \frac{32}{116}$$

$$= .28$$

Thus, political affiliation reduces prediction error by 28%. In other words, political party accounts for or explains 28% of the differences in respondents' positions on gun control.

The formula for lambda should, of course, yield the same result. The formula focuses on the correct predictions (the modes), rather than on the errors, but it ends up with the same result.

$$\lambda = \frac{F_{iv} - M_{dv}}{N - M_{dv}}$$

$$= \frac{144 - 112}{228 - 112}$$

$$= \frac{32}{116}$$

$$= .28$$

REQUIREMENTS FOR USING THE LAMBDA COEFFICIENT

To employ the lambda coefficient as a measure of association, the following requirements must be met:

1. *Nominal data.* Only frequency data are required. Lambda can be applied to data cast in the form of a 2 × 2 table or larger.
2. *Random sampling.* To test the significance of the lambda coefficient (for example, with chi-square), sample members must be drawn on a random basis from a specified population.

ELABORATION

In Chapter 10, we saw in the discussion of partial correlation that the relationship between two variables can be dramatically altered when controlling for a third variable. Nonparametric correlation coefficients based on cross-tabulations can similarly be changed by the introduction of a third factor. A wise man must have known this when he said, "Things aren't always what they seem at first glance." This is a lesson recently learned by a social psychologist who conducted a small study of soap opera viewing.

During spring break, this professor got hooked on watching soap operas. While engrossed in their plots, however, he was still able to maintain his scholarly perspective. As he watched, he began noticing a definite antiabortion undertone in the daytime shows. Although the characters did indeed obtain abortions, they usually were punished physically, emotionally, or socially for their choice to terminate a pregnancy. Forever a researcher at heart, this professor designed a study to test if soap opera viewing was associated with opposition to abortion.

The social psychologist conducted telephone interviews with 200 respondents whose numbers were dialed at random. Among other things, the respondents were asked whether or not they watched soap operas fairly regularly and whether they were in favor or opposed to abortion on demand. Because the professor considered soap opera viewing as his independent variable, he used column percentages for his cross-tabulation (see Table 12.7).

The professor was not surprised by the results. Supporting his hypothesis that soap opera viewing would lead to negative views on abortion, he found that proportionately more soap opera viewers were opposed to abortion on demand (54%) than were nonviewers (48%).

As you might expect, our story does not end here. The professor next wondered whether the relationship observed between viewing and abortion position would be the same for both males and females. So he separated the males from the females in his cross-tabulation. Table 12.8 is called a *three-way cross-tabulation,* that is, a frequency table involving three variables at once. Specifically, it shows the relationship between soap opera viewing and abortion position *holding gender constant.* By this we mean that gender does not vary within each of the two subtables. The left subtable only includes women and the right only men. (These are called subtables because they are obtained by subdividing the full table according to gender.)

This process is called *elaboration.* It involves looking deeper into the relationship between the independent and dependent variables by controlling for or holding constant another variable (or variables) that may play a role. By separating the males from the females, we elaborate on the initial finding that ignored gender.

The results in Table 12.8, holding gender constant, are noticeably different from those in the previous table. Among females, there is no difference in the abortion positions of the soap opera viewers and the nonviewers; 40% of each group supports abortion on demand. Among males, there is also no difference between viewers and nonviewers in their position on abortion; 60% of each group supports abortion on demand.

TABLE 12.7   CROSS-TABULATION OF ATTITUDE TOWARD ABORTION ON DEMAND BY SOAP OPERA VIEWING STATUS

Abortion on demand	Soap opera viewer Yes	No	Total
Favor	32	68	100
	46%	52%	50%
Oppose	38	62	100
	54%	48%	50%
Total	70	130	200
	100%	100%	100%

TABLE 12.8   CROSS-TABULATION OF ATTITUDE TOWARD ABORTION ON DEMAND BY SOAP OPERA VIEWING STATUS HOLDING GENDER CONSTANT

	Females Soap opera viewer				Males Soap opera viewer		
Abortion on demand	Yes	No	Total	Abortion on demand	Yes	No	Total
Favor	20	20	40	Favor	12	48	60
	40%	40%	40%		60%	60%	60%
Oppose	30	30	60	Oppose	8	32	40
	60%	60%	60%		40%	40%	40%
Total	50	50	100	Total	20	80	100
	100%	100%	100%		100%	100%	100%

We have then a very curious result. Soap opera viewing and abortion position are unrelated among either the female or the male respondents. However, when you combine the two groups (as in Table 12.7), the soap opera viewers appear to be more opposed than nonviewers toward abortion on demand.

The relationship between soap opera viewing and attitude toward abortion, as seen in Table 12.7, is called a *spurious relationship* (not genuine). That is, soap opera viewing does not influence abortion position, nor does abortion position affect one's television habits. Instead, both variables are influenced by a common factor: gender of respondent.

First, women are more inclined toward soap opera viewing than men: In the column marginals of the subtables in Table 12.8, we see that 50 out of the 100 women (50%) versus 20 out of the 100 men (20%) are soap opera viewers. Second, women are less in favor of abortion on demand than men: According to the row marginals, 40% of the women but 60% of the men support abortions on demand. Thus, it may seem like soap opera viewers tend to oppose abortion more than nonviewers, but it is only because viewers and antiabortion respondents both tend to be female, and nonviewers and abortion proponents both tend to be male. In sum, the relationship between viewing and abortion position is spurious due to the gender of the respondent, and this is exposed when we elaborate on the original two-variable relationship (of Table 12.7) by introducing gender as a control variable in Table 12.8.

Because the relationship between soap opera viewing and abortion position vanishes when gender is controlled, you may have gotten the impression that we played a trick with the numbers—a sort of statistical hocus-pocus. If so, you're only half right. We admit that the numbers in Tables 12.7 and 12.8 were fashioned to illustrate a perfectly spurious relationship. However, one must always be aware of possible contaminating factors that might alter first impressions based on two-variable relationships. With real data, these relationships might not vanish so completely, but they certainly can change in dramatic ways.

One such example comes from survey data regarding the fear of crime in two cities (New York City and San Diego) collected by Skogan and Klecka.[1] Table 12.9 shows a

TABLE 12.9 CROSS-TABULATION OF PERCEPTIONS OF SAFETY WALKING ALONE IN NEIGHBORHOOD AT NIGHT

Perception of safety	Age of respondent				Total
	16–26	27–39	40–64	65+	
Very unsafe	63	56	116	88	323
	11.8%	11.1%	16.8%	34.7%	16.3%
Somewhat unsafe	102	77	146	57	382
	19.0%	15.3%	21.1%	22.4%	19.2%
Reasonably safe	223	239	291	80	833
	41.6%	47.4%	42.1%	31.5%	42.0%
Very safe	148	132	138	29	447
	27.6%	26.2%	20.0%	11.4%	22.5%
Total	536	504	691	254	1,985
	100.0%	100.0%	100.0%	100.0%	100.0%

[1] Wesley G. Skogan and William R. Klecka, *Fear of Crime* (Washington, D.C.: American Political Science Association, 1977).

cross-tabulation by age of the respondent of perceived level of safety when walking alone in the neighborhood at night. Of course, age is the independent variable and so we use column percents, because the age variable is the column variable.

The results of the cross-tabulation are just as one might expect. The older the respondent, the less safe he or she feels when walking alone in the neighborhood at night. The percentage who feel very safe declines with age: 27.6% of the 16–26-year-olds, 26.2% of the 27–39-year-olds, 20.0% of the 40–64-year-olds, and only 11.4% of those aged 65 or over feel safe. Conversely, the percentage who report feelings of unsafeness tends to increase with age. We can use gamma to measure the strength of correlation in this cross-tabulation because both variables are ordinals.[2] This cross-tabulation yields a gamma value of .21, which is significant.

But we're not finished yet. We can fortunately rule out the chance that the relationship is spurious—that is, a mere consequence of age and fear having common causes. Age, obviously, cannot be influenced by other variables. Thus, the effect of age on fear is not an illusion. But there is more to understanding this relationship.

Next we control for race to see if the age–fear relationship holds true for both whites and blacks. This cross-tabulation of perceptions of safety by age, holding race constant, is given in Tables 12.10 and 12.11. Table 12.10, which includes only the white respondents, reveals the same type of relationship we observed for the full sample. Among whites, the older respondents feel less safe than their younger counterparts (gamma is .26 and significant). Among the two younger age categories, for instance, almost 30% reported feeling very safe, as compared to only 11.4% among the oldest age group. A very different picture emerges, however, for the black respondents (see Table 12.11). There does not appear to be any clear increase in fearfulness with increasing age level (gamma is only −.004 and not significant). Apparently all age groups in the black subsample feel rather unsafe. Approximately half of each age group feels on the unsafe side (somewhat unsafe and very unsafe), comparable only to the older whites.

Thus, although one would not necessarily be wrong in concluding from the full sample cross-tabulation in Table 12.9 that fear increases with age, one would not be completely

TABLE 12.10   CROSS-TABULATION OF PERCEPTIONS OF SAFETY WALKING ALONE IN NEIGHBORHOOD AT NIGHT FOR WHITES

Perception of safety	Age of respondent				
	16–26	27–39	40–64	65+	Total
Very unsafe	39	28	101	81	249
	8.4%	6.9%	16.3%	34.2%	14.4%
Somewhat unsafe	90	56	124	54	324
	19.4%	13.8%	20.0%	22.8%	18.8%
Reasonably safe	199	201	269	75	744
	42.9%	49.5%	43.5%	31.6%	43.1%
Very safe	136	121	125	27	409
	29.3%	29.8%	20.2%	11.4%	23.7%
Total	464	406	619	237	1,726
	100.0%	100.0%	100.0%	100.0%	100.0%

[2] The variables are both ordered from low to high rather than from high to low. Either direction is fine as long as both variables are ordered in the same direction.

TABLE 12.11   CROSS-TABULATION OF PERCEPTIONS OF SAFETY WALKING ALONE IN NEIGHBORHOOD AT NIGHT FOR BLACKS

Perception of safety	Age of respondent				Total
	16–26	27–39	40–64	65+	
Very unsafe	24	28	15	7	74
	16.7%	28.6%	20.8%	41.2%	28.6%
Somewhat unsafe	12	21	22	3	58
	33.3%	21.4%	30.6%	17.6%	22.4%
Reasonably safe	24	38	22	5	89
	33.3%	38.8%	30.6%	29.4%	34.3%
Very safe	12	11	13	2	38
	16.7%	11.2%	18.0%	11.8%	14.7%
Total	72	98	72	17	259
	100.0%	100.0%	100.0%	100.0%	100.0%

correct either. A more accurate conclusion would be that this is true only for whites, and that blacks tend to feel relatively unsafe, regardless of age. That is, the nature of the relationship between fear and age is conditional on race; and so we call it a *conditional relationship*. How we view the age-fear relationship depends (or is conditional) upon race.

This result perhaps generates more questions than it answers. Obviously, one would want to determine why fear among blacks is at such a high level (relative to whites). We could suggest that blacks, as a result of their generally lower income level, tend to live in high-crime-rate areas, which explains their higher level of fear. To test these hypotheses about how income and neighborhood conditions interact with race and fear of crime would require an even more elaborate analysis of many variables. However, this goes far beyond the scope of this presentation.

There is a variety of possible scenarios when we elaborate a two-variable relationship by controlling for a third variable. When controlling, the relationship can (a) remain unchanged, (b) strengthen, (c) weaken, (d) disappear (as in our soap opera and view on abortion illustration), (e) disappear or weaken only in part (as in the age and fear example), or even (f) change direction entirely. We have not illustrated each of these, because our intention here is only to introduce the logic of elaboration.

SUMMARY

There are several nonparametric alternatives to Pearson's r. To determine the correlation between variables at the ordinal level of measurement, we can apply Spearman's rank-order correlation coefficient (r_s). To use this measure of correlation, both X and Y variables must be ranked or ordered. When ordinal data are arranged in a cross-tabulation, Goodman's and Kruskal's gamma coefficient (G) is a useful correlation coefficient.

By a simple extension of the chi-square test of significance, we can determine the degree of association between variables at the nominal level of measurement. For a 2 × 2 problem, we employ the phi coefficient (ϕ). For tables larger than 2 × 2, we use the contingency coefficient (for square tables such as 3 × 3 and 4 × 4) or Cramér's V or the asymmetric measure of association called lambda. Finally, we introduce the logic of elaboration in which we consider whether a two-variable cross-tabulation is altered when controlling for a third variable.

TERMS TO REMEMBER

Spearman's rank-order correlation coefficient
Goodman's and Kruskal's gamma
Phi coefficient
Contingency coefficient

Cramér's V
Lambda
Elaboration
Spurious relationship

STEP-BY-STEP STUDY GUIDE

TESTING THE STRENGTH OF ASSOCIATION BETWEEN ORDINAL-LEVEL VARIABLES USING SPEARMAN'S RANK-ORDER CORRELATION

STEP 1   Rank the respondents on both X and Y.

STEP 2   Calculate the differences between ranks (D) for all cases, the squared differences (D^2), and then the sum of squared differences (ΣD^2).

STEP 3   Calculate the rank-order correlation.

$$r_s = 1 - \frac{6 \Sigma D^2}{N(N^2 - 1)}$$

STEP 4   Compare the obtained rank-order correlation with the critical value from Table G. If the obtained value exceeds the table critical value, then reject the null hypothesis of no relationship; otherwise, accept the null hypothesis.

STEP-BY-STEP STUDY GUIDE

TESTING THE STRENGTH OF ASSOCIATION BETWEEN CROSS-TABULATED, ORDINAL-LEVEL VARIABLES USING GOODMAN'S AND KRUSKAL'S GAMMA

STEP 1   Rearrange the data in the form of a cross-tabulation.

STEP 2   Find the total number of agreements among the cases (N_a).

STEP 3   Find the total number of inversions among the cases (N_i).

STEP 4   Calculate G.

$$G = \frac{N_a - N_i}{N_a + N_i}$$

STEP 5   Convert G into a z score.

$$z = G\sqrt{\frac{N_a - N_i}{N(1 - G^2)}}$$

STEP 6   Compare the obtained z to the critical value found in Table A (or in the bottom row of Table B or C). If the obtained value of z exceeds the table critical value, then reject the null hypothesis of no relationship; otherwise, accept the null hypothesis.

PROBLEMS

1. The following five police cadets were ranked in terms of when they completed an exam (1 = first to finish, 2 = second to finish, and so on) and were given an exam grade by the instructor. Test the null hypothesis of no relationship between grade (X) and length of time to complete the exam (Y) (that is, compute a rank-order correlation coefficient and indicate whether it is significant).

X	Y
53	1
91	2
70	3
85	4
91	5

2. In Chapter 10, data were presented on the distance to AA meetings (X) and the number of meetings attended per week (Y) for 10 offenders under probation supervision to which the Pearson's correlation coefficient was applied. One of the probationers (Andreas), who previously lived 10 miles from where meetings are held, has now moved farther away. He is now 17 miles away from his program. Because of the apparent skewness created by this extreme value, Pearson's r may give a distorted result. As an alternative, calculate Spearman's rank-order correlation for the following data, and indicate whether it is significant.

	Distance to AA meeting	Number of meetings attended per week
Tim	4	3
Steven	2	1
Mario	7	5
Keivon	1	2
Seamus	4	1
Steve	6	1
Ali	9	9
Alex	7	6
Peter	7	5
Andreas	17	8

3. A medical sociologist investigated the relationship between severity of illness (X) and length of stay in a hospital (Y). Choosing eight patients at random, she ranked the seriousness of their ailment and determined the number of days they were hospitalized. Her results were as follows:

Patient	X	Y
A	6	12
B	4	19
C	1	18
D	8	3
E	3	21
F	2	21

G	7	5
H	5	10

Compute a rank-order correlation coefficient and indicate whether there is a significant relationship between X and Y.

4. A researcher was interested in the relationship between population density (X) and feelings of personal safety. Ranking 10 major cities on both variables, he obtained the following results:

City	X	Y
A	8	2
B	1	7
C	3	8
D	7	1
E	4	5
F	10	3
G	2	10
H	5	6
I	6	9
J	9	4

Compute a rank-order correlation coefficient and indicate whether there is a significant relationship between X and Y.

5. The director of admissions of a criminal justice program studied 12 recent graduates to determine whether their academic achievement in high school was related to how well they performed in college. As shown, cumulative grade-point average in high school and class rank in college were employed as measures of academic performance:

GPA in high school	College class-rank
3.3	1
2.9	12
2.5	9
4.0	8
2.8	11
2.5	10
3.7	2
3.8	7
3.5	3
2.7	6
2.6	4
4.0	5

Determine the strength and direction of correlation between GPA in high school and college class rank for the 12 criminal justice students. Is it necessary to test the significance of this correlation?

6. A governor commissions a study of the relationship between social class and the level of public faith in the fairness of the state courts in their processing of accused drug dealers. The research team asked a random sample of 105 adults from varying socioeconomic backgrounds how much faith they have in the courts regarding this matter. For the following data, compute a gamma coefficient to determine the degree of association between socioeconomic status (X) and faith in how fairly the courts process cases of alleged drug dealing (Y), and indicate whether the relationship is significant.

Level of faith in fairness of courts	Socioeconomic status			
	Lower	Lower-middle	Upper-middle	Upper
Low	15	12	6	5
Medium	12	8	10	8
High	4	6	9	10

7. A researcher was interested in whether job satisfaction among criminal justice professionals (such as prosecutors, corrections officers, police, defense attorneys, and probation and parole officers) is related to commuting time to work. He interviewed 185 criminal justice professionals concerning their commuting time (X) and their job satisfaction (Y). For the following data, compute a gamma coefficient to determine the degree of association between commuting time and job satisfaction, and indicate whether there is a significant relation between X and Y.

Job satisfaction	Commuting time (minutes)			
	60+	30–59	15–29	Under 15
Very satisfied	8	12	25	22
Somewhat satisfied	9	20	23	11
Dissatisfied	13	18	17	7

$N = 185$

8. The following 96 students were ranked from high to low with respect to their consumption of alcoholic beverages (X) and their daily use of marijuana (Y). For these data, compute a gamma coefficient to determine the degree of association between consumption of alcohol and use of marijuana, and indicate whether there is a significant relation between X and Y.

Use of marijuana	Consumption of alcohol		
	High	Medium	Low
High	5	7	20
Medium	10	8	15
Low	15	6	10

$N = 96$

9. A researcher is interested in determining the degree of association between husbands' and wives' levels of support for legal abortion. For the following cross-tabulation, calculate chi-square and determine the phi coefficient.

Husband supports legal abortion	Wife supports legal abortion	
	Yes	No
Yes	24	6
No	8	22

10. The same researcher is interested in determining the degree of association between the political leanings of husbands and wives. For the following cross-tabulation, calculate chi-square and determine the contingency coefficient.

Husband's political leaning	Wife's political leaning		
	Liberal	Moderate	Conservative
Liberal	10	6	4
Moderate	7	11	5
Conservative	3	5	9

11. The graduating class of 263 criminal justice students were asked to indicate their career preference (X) and their political party affiliation (Y). Using the lambda coefficient, determine by how much we can reduce the error in predicting values of one variable from values of the other. First, indicate to what extent students' career preferences can be predicted by knowing their political party affiliations; then, indicate to what extent students' party affiliations can be predicted by knowing their college majors. Which variable, X or Y, has greater predictive ability?

Career preference (X)	Political party (Y)		
	Democrats	Republicans	Independents
Law/courts	45	31	36
Law enforcement/security	29	42	35
Corrections	22	10	13

$N = 263$

12. A researcher asked 35 males and 35 females to rate their attitude toward legalized drug use (for, neutral, or against). Using the lambda coefficient, determine by how much we are able to reduce the error in predicting

values of one variable from values of the other. First, indicate to what extent people's gender can be predicted by knowing their attitude toward drug legalization. Then, indicate to what extent people's attitude toward drug legalization can be predicted by knowing their gender. Which variable, X or Y, has greater predictive ability?

Gender (X)	Attitude toward drug legalization (Y)		
	For	Neutral	Against
Male	19	12	4
Female	8	11	13
Total	27	23	17

13. A researcher is curious as to whether there is any connection between various behaviors that could be viewed as risk taking. She collects data from her records on 162 patients concerning their usage of seat belts and of cigarettes. For the following cross-tabulation, calculate chi-square and Cramér's V.

Use of seat belts	Use of cigarettes	
	Smoker	Nonsmoker
Always	10	32
Usually	30	26
Seldom	46	18

14. To collect evidence pertaining to gender discrimination, a sample of criminal justice employees was classified by rank and gender. For the following cross-tabulation, calculate chi-square and Cramér's V.

Rank	Gender	
	Male	Female
Executive	8	2
Manager	10	6
Clerical/support	25	20

APPLYING STATISTICAL PROCEDURES TO RESEARCH PROBLEMS

• **RESEARCH SITUATIONS**   • **RESEARCH SOLUTIONS**

Part Three of the text contains a number of statistical procedures that can be applied to various problems in criminal justice research. Chapters 7 to 9 introduced several different procedures for determining whether obtained sample differences are statistically significant or merely a product of sampling error. The procedures in Chapters 10 and 11 are designed to determine the degree of association, the correlation between two variables.

As noted throughout the text, each statistical procedure has a set of assumptions for its appropriate application. In selecting among procedures, any researcher must therefore consider a number of factors such as the following:

1. Whether the researcher seeks to test for statistically significant differences, degree of association, or both
2. Whether the researcher has achieved the nominal, ordinal, or interval level of measurement of the variables being studied
3. Whether or not the variables being studied are normally distributed in the population from which they were drawn

This chapter provides a number of hypothetical research situations in which the foregoing criteria are specified. The reader is asked to choose the most appropriate statistical procedure for each research situation from among the following tests that have been covered in Part Three of the text:

1. t ratio
2. Analysis of variance
3. Chi-square test
4. Median test
5. Mann-Whitney U test
6. Kruskal-Wallis one-way analysis of variance by ranks
7. Pearson's r correlation coefficient
8. Spearman's rank-order correlation coefficient
9. Goodman's and Kruskal's gamma

10. Phi coefficient
11. Contingency coefficient
12. Cramér's *V*
13. Lambda

Table 13.1 locates each statistical procedure with respect to some of the important assumptions that must be considered for its appropriate application. Looking at the columns of the table, we face the first major decision related to the selection of a statistical procedure: Do we wish to determine whether a relationship exists? The tests of significance discussed in Chapter 7 to 9 are designed to determine whether an obtained sample difference reflects a true population difference. Or do we seek instead to establish the strength of the relationship between two variables? This is a question of correlation that can be addressed by means of the statistical procedures introduced in Chapters 10 and 12.

The rows of Table 13.1 direct our attention to the level at which our variables are measured. If we have achieved the interval level of measurement, we may well consider employing a parametric procedure such as *t*, *F*, or *r*. If, however, we have achieved either the nominal or ordinal level of measurement, the choice is limited to several nonparametric alternatives. Finally, for correlation problems involving variables of different levels of measurement, a correlation measure appropriate for the lower level of the two is used. For example, Spearman's rank-order coefficient can be used to measure the correlation between

TABLE 13.1   CHOOSING AN APPROPRIATE STATISTICAL TECHNIQUE

Level of measurement	Test of difference (Chapters 7–9)	Measure of correlation (Chapters 10–12)
Nominal	Chi-square test (nonparametric test for comparing two or more samples)	Phi coefficient (nonparametric measure for 2×2 tables)
Ordinal	Median test and Mann-Whitney *U* test (nonparametric tests for comparing two samples)	Contingency coefficient, Cramér's *V*, and lambda (nonparametric measures for larger than 2×2 tables)
	Kruskal-Wallis one-way analysis of variance by ranks (nonparametric test for comparing three or more samples)	Spearman's rank-order correlation coefficient (nonparametric measure for ranked data)
Interval	*t* ratio (parametric tests for comparing two samples or the same sample measured twice)	Goodman's and Kruskal's gamma (nonparametric measure for cross tabulations)
	Analysis of variance (parametric test for comparing three or more samples)	Pearson's *r* correlation coefficient (parametric measurement for scores)

NOTE: These are the minimal levels of measurement required to apply a particular technique.

an interval and ordinal variable; Cramér's V can be used to measure the association between an ordinal and nominal variable.

The solutions to the following research situations can be found at the end of the chapter.

RESEARCH SITUATIONS

RESEARCH SITUATION 1

A researcher conducted an experiment to determine the effect of a convicted criminal's race on potential juror's judgments of appropriate prison sentence length. In a mock jury experiment, 20 registered voters were presented with information about a hypothetical case of assault with attempt to commit murder. Details about the nature of the offense, the victim, and the offender were presented in a manner like a criminal trial, and a guilty verdict was handed down by a judge. All of the information presented to the "jurors" was identical except that half of the jurors were told the offender was white, and the other half were told the offender was African-American. The 20 experimental subjects in the role of jurors are asked to indicate what they believe would be the appropriate length of prison sentence (in years). The following results were obtained:

Prison sentence length judged appropriate for white offenders	Prison sentence length judged appropriate for African-American offenders
X_1	X_2
8	10
12	7
10	15
20	25
7	20
25	15
10	10
15	12
5	20
10	15

RESEARCH SITUATION 2

A researcher conducted an experiment to determine the effect of a lecturer's age on law student preferences to hear her lecture. In a regular classroom situation, 30 law students were told that the administration wished to know students' preferences regarding a forthcoming visiting lecturer series. In particular, they were asked to evaluate a superior court judge who "might be visiting the campus." The judge was described to all students in the same way with one exception: One-third of the students were told that the judge was 75 years old; one-third were told the judge was 50 years old; and one-third were told the judge was 35 years old. All students were then asked to indicate their willingness to attend the judge's lecture (higher scores indicate greater willingness). The following results were obtained:

X_1 (Scores of students told judge was 35 years old)	X_2 (Scores of students told judge was 50 years old)	X_3 (Scores of students told judge was 75 years old)
65	63	67
38	42	42
52	60	77
71	55	32
69	43	52
72	36	34
55	69	45
78	57	38
56	67	39
80	79	46

Which statistical procedure would you apply to determine whether there is a significant difference between these groups of students with respect to their willingness to attend the lecture?

RESEARCH SITUATION 3

A correctional researcher is evaluating the effectiveness of an offender rehabilitation program, one component of which is remedial education. Part of this evaluation is an attempt to determine whether education skills are being effectively taught. To assess this, the researchers administered a reading examination to a sample of 20 offenders randomly selected from a large population of program participants. She also recorded the number of weeks each of these offenders had been in the program. The following results were obtained (higher reading scores indicated greater skill):

Offender	X (Weeks in program)	Y (Reading score)
A	2	56
B	9	81
C	5	75
D	8	72
E	3	50
F	3	45
G	1	39
H	6	87
I	3	59
J	5	56
K	3	69
L	8	78
M	3	69
N	1	57
O	2	35
P	2	47
Q	5	73
R	12	76
S	6	63
T	8	79

Which statistical procedure would you apply to determine the degree of association between length of time in the program and reading skill?

RESEARCH SITUATION 4

To investigate the validity of the reading test administered to the offenders in Research Situation 3, the researcher gave the reading test to 20 program participants whose reading skills had been previously ranked by their instructor. The test score and instructor's rank for each offender are listed in the following table.

Offender	X (Reading score)	Y (Instructor's rank)
A	28	18
B	50	17
C	92	1
D	85	6
E	76	5
F	69	10
G	42	11
H	53	12
I	80	3
J	91	2
K	73	4
L	74	9
M	14	20
N	29	19
O	86	7
P	73	8
Q	39	16
R	80	13
S	91	15
T	72	14

Which statistical procedure would you apply to determine the degree of association between reading scores and teacher's ranking?

RESEARCH SITUATION 5

To investigate regional differences in willingness of victims of minor property crimes (involving financial losses of less than $500) to report the offense to police, a team of researchers interviewed 400 victims of such crimes from the Northeastern, Southern, Midwestern, and Western regions of the United States. The victims were identified during the course of a large national crime victimization survey, In the interviews, the victims were asked whether they had reported the crime to the police. The results were:

	Region			
	Northeast	South	Midwest	West
Reported	55	69	82	61
Not reported	45	31	18	39
	100	100	100	100

Which statistical procedure would you apply to determine whether these regional differences are statistically significant?

RESEARCH SITUATION 6

To examine the relationship between authoritarianism and prejudice, a researcher administered measures of authoritarianism (the F scale) and prejudice (a checklist of negative adjectives to be assigned to African-Americans) to a national sample of 950 adult Americans. The following results were obtained: Among 500 authoritarian respondents, 350 were prejudiced and 150 were tolerant. Among 450 nonauthoritarian respondents, 125 were prejudiced and 325 were tolerant.

Which statistical procedure would you apply to study the degree of association between authoritarianism and prejudice?

RESEARCH SITUATION 7

To investigate the relationship between year in school and grade average, researchers examined the academic records of 186 criminal justice students who were randomly selected from the undergraduate population of a certain university. The researchers produce the following cross-tabulation:

Grade average	Year in school			
	1st	2nd	3rd	4th
A− or better	6	5	7	10
B− to B+	10	16	19	18
C− to C+	23	20	15	7
D+ or worse	15	7	6	2
	54	48	47	37

Which statistical procedure would you apply to determine the degree of association between grade average and year in school?

RESEARCH SITUATION 8

One of the goals of a particular boot camp prison was to increase inmate self-esteem. To assess whether this goal was being met, a self-esteem inventory was administered to 10 boot camp inmates during their first week in the program, and again during their last week. Scores on the self-esteem scale range from 10 to 40, with higher scores indicating greater self-esteem. The following results were obtained:

Boot camp inmate	X_1 Self-esteem scores at beginning of boot camp	X_2 Self-esteem scores at end of boot camp
A	22	26
B	39	45
C	25	24
D	40	43

E	36	36
F	27	29
G	44	47
H	31	30
I	52	52
J	48	59

Which statistical procedure would you apply to determine whether there is a statistically significant difference in self-esteem scores between the beginning and the end of the boot camp program?

RESEARCH SITUATION 9

A criminologist who was examining the impact of social class on crime and criminal victimization began to wonder about the relationship between "objective" occupational status (as determined by large-scale surveys of occupational prestige and by mean incomes of those in each occupation) and subjective social class (that is, a respondent's own social class identification).

To examine this relationship, 677 individuals were asked to indicate their occupation and the social class in which they belonged. Among 190 respondents with upper-status occupations (professional–technical–managerial), 56 identified themselves as upper class, 122 as middle class, and 12 as lower class; among 221 respondents with middle-status occupations (sales–clerical–skilled labor), 42 identified themselves as upper class, 163 as middle class, and 16 as lower class; among 266 with lower-status occupations (semiskilled and unskilled labor), 15 identified themselves as upper class, 202 as middle class, and 49 as lower class.

Which statistical procedure would you apply to determine the degree of association between occupational status and subjective social class?

RESEARCH SITUATION 10

To investigate the influence of education on the starting salary of people in criminal justice fields, researchers interviewed 21 individuals recently hired at their first jobs in criminal justice. The most recent college degree and starting salary of these criminal justice professionals are:

	Starting salary	
Bachelor's in criminal justice	Master's in criminal justice	Law degree
$19,500	$21,000	$28,336
28,750	18,550	34,000
14,280	36,000	48,650
22,375	28,250	29,000
26,000	32,000	38,400
19,500	24,050	44,950
16,000	19,750	54,000

Which statistical procedure would you apply to determine whether there is a significant difference between these groups of respondents with respect to their starting salaries?

RESEARCH SITUATION 11

A researcher wanted to examine differences in prison sentence lengths received by offenders convicted of "white-collar" versus "street crime." In particular, she was interested in whether criminals who stole money by means of embezzlement or fraud received shorter prison sentences than those who stole money by means of burglary and larceny. The researcher examined court records and selected seven cases of white-collar theft of between $1,000 and $10,000, and 12 cases of burglary or larceny involving dollar amounts in the same range. The data obtained on these offenders is presented here:

Prison sentence length (in months)	
"White-collar" theft of between $1,000 and $10,000	"Street" theft of between $1,000 and $10,000
6	12
12	48
0	6
1	1
30	3
0	0
2	12
	18
	2
	36
	60
	8

Which statistical procedure would you apply to determine whether there is a significant difference in prison sentences for white-collar versus street crimes involving similar financial losses?

RESEARCH SITUATION 12

A researcher conducted an experiment to determine the effect of a judge's age on law student willingness to hear him lecture. In a regular classroom situation, 130 students were told that the administration wished to know their preferences regarding a forthcoming visiting lecturer series. In particular, they were asked to evaluate a judge who "might be visiting the campus." The judge was described to all students in the same way with one exception: One-half of the students were told the judge was 65 years old; one-half were told the judge was 35 years old. All students were then asked to indicate their willingness to attend the judge's lecture with the following results: Among those students told that the judge was 65, 22 expressed their willingness to attend his lecture and 43 expressed their unwillingness; among the students told that the judge was 35, 38 expressed their willingness to attend his lecture and 27 expressed their unwillingness.

Which statistical procedure would you apply to determine whether there is a significant difference between these groups of students with respect to their willingness to attend the judge's lecture?

RESEARCH SITUATION 13

A researcher seized upon an interesting opportunity to study the impact of television on fear of crime. A small, isolated town of 600 residents in a remote part of the Pacific Northwest was beyond the reach of any television broadcast signals, and few households owned satellite dishes. Upon news that a cable television business would soon begin operation in the town, the researcher administered a fear of crime scale to one member of each of 15 randomly selected households. One year after the households received cable television, the 15 individuals were administered the same fear of crime scale. The following results were obtained (higher scores indicate greater fear of crime):

Respondent	X_1 Fear of crime score before cable TV	X_2 Fear of crime score after cable TV
A	4	5
B	2	9
C	2	8
D	0	4
E	4	7
F	1	6
G	1	4
H	2	7
I	1	8
J	1	6
K	3	10
L	7	9
M	1	7
N	2	4
O	1	5

Which statistical procedure would you apply to determine whether there is a statistically significant difference in fear of crime before and after the broad availability of television programs?

RESEARCH SITUATION 14

To investigate the relationship between socioeconomic status and fear of crime, a researcher questioned 500 residents randomly selected from the adult population of a certain city. The respondents were asked questions about their education, occupation, and income, which the researcher used to classify the residents as belonging to the high, medium, or low socioeconomic status. They were also asked a series of questions about their fear of becoming the victim of several kinds of crime, which the researcher used to classify the respondents as having either high, medium or low level. Among the 150 respondents classified as having high socioeconomic status, 45 were high, 65 were medium, and 40 were low in their measured level of fear of crime. Among the 180 respondents of medium socioeconomic status, 55 were high, 110 were medium, and 20 were low in their level of fear of crime. Among those who were classified as having low socioeconomic status, 70 were high, 80 were medium, and 15 were low in their rated level of fear of crime.

Which statistical procedure would you apply to determine the degree of association between socioeconomic status and fear of crime?

RESEARCH SITUATION 15

A great deal of research over the past 20 years indicates that people tend to hold the victims of sexual assault in dating situations at least partially responsible for their assault. A researcher interested in this subject conducted a study examining how the relationship between men and women prior to an episode of date rape affects the level of blame attributed to the victim. A sample of 40 randomly selected college students were given written descriptions of dating scenarios, each describing a date between a young man and woman leading up to a point where the man attempts to have sex with the woman, she resists (both verbally and physically), and he forces her to have intercourse. All of the scenarios meet a legal definition of rape. All of the respondents received date rape scenarios identical in all respects except for the prior relationship between the man and woman. The 40 scenarios presented were evenly divided into those containing each of the following four relationship descriptions: (1) did not know each other, on a blind date set up by friends; (2) acquaintances on a first date; (3) had dated for a month and had not had sex with each other before; (4) had dated for a month and had had sex with each other before. After reading the scenarios, the respondents were asked to rate the level of victim blame on a 10-point scale, with higher scores indicating higher levels of blame attributed to the rape victim.

Victim blame scores

X_1 No prior relationship; blind date	X_2 Acquaintances on first date	X_3 Dating one month, no prior sex	X_4 Dating one month, prior sex
2	1	2	1
1	3	6	8
9	2	4	4
3	6	5	7
1	3	1	3
1	1	3	10
6	4	8	4
2	1	4	5
1	3	2	1
1	2	5	4

Which statistical procedure would you apply to determine whether there is a significant difference in victim blame scores across date rape scenarios with different descriptions of the relationship between the victim and offender?

RESEARCH SITUATION 16

The researcher in Situation 15 was also interested in how the relationship between heterosexual dating partners affects men's perceptions of whether the victim would report to the police that she had been raped. He randomly selected 40 male college students, presenting them with date rape scenarios just as he had in Situation 15, but instead of asking them their level of victim blame, he asked them whether the woman would report to the police that she had been raped. Respondents were instructed to circle "yes" if they believed that she would report her rape to the police, and "no" if they believed she wouldn't.

Report to police	X_1 strangers on blind date	X_2 Acquaintances on first date	X_3 Dating one month, no prior sex	X_4 Dating one month, prior sex
Yes	7	5	3	2
No	3	5	7	8

Which statistical procedure would you use to examine whether there is a significant relationship between the offender-victim relationship and men's judgments of whether the victim would report her rape to the police?

RESEARCH SITUATION 17

The researcher in Situations 15 and 16 wonders whether the number of years of college education affects judgments of appropriate prison sentence lengths for offenders convicted of date rape. He randomly selects 20 college students and presents each with identical scenarios describing a date between a man and a woman where he forces her to have intercourse, she reports it to the police, and he is arrested and convicted. At this point the respondents are asked to indicate their beliefs about the appropriate length of prison sentence (in years) that the convicted rapist should receive. He also asks respondents to report how many years of college they have completed.

Years of College Completed	Appropriate Prison Sentence Length in Years
1	0
3	5
1	3
1	1
4	3
3	7
2	3
3	10
1	2
1	4
4	8
2	3
1	0
2	0
2	4
3	15
3	6
1	2
2	6
2	1

Which statistical procedure would you apply to examine the degree of association between years of college education and perceived appropriate prison sentence length?

RESEARCH SITUATION 18

Suppose that the researcher wanted to determine whether gender affects beliefs about appropriate length of prison sentence for men convicted of date rape. If in Situation 17 the researcher had asked respondents their gender, which statistical procedure would be effective in determining the impact of gender on judgments of appropriate prison sentence length for the offenders described in the date rape scenarios?

Appropriate Sentence Length in Years	
Males	Females
0	5
1	3
3	7
3	10
2	4
0	8
0	3
4	15
2	6
6	1

RESEARCH SITUATION 19

It has been asserted that trying to integrate large numbers of new residents into communities creates conditions favorable for juvenile delinquency (e.g., in many communities new residents take time to find employment, moving is a stressful life event for families, and children have difficulty adjusting to new schools). To assess the relationship between new residency and delinquency, data on seven metropolitan areas were obtained:

Metropolitan area	X (Percentage of the population who moved there within the past year)	Y (Rank with respect to delinquency rates)
A	10	1
B	4	6
C	2	3
D	1	7
E	6	4
F	5	2
G	8	5

Which statistical procedure would you apply to determine the degree of association between the percentage of population who had recently moved and the ranked delinquency rate?

RESEARCH SITUATION 20

A city's police department wanted to determine the most effective method of responding to complaints of domestic violence. They decided to perform an experiment in which police officers responding to domestic violence calls were to randomly select one of three responses: (1) arrest the alleged abuser, (2) attempt to mediate the dispute, or (3) separate the parties for at least 15 minutes to allow them to calm down, then carefully reunite them. The effectiveness of the interventions would be measured as the presence or absence of evidence that additional abuse occurred at any time after the intervention (indicators of abuse would be any of the following: reports to the police, one party seeking a restraining order on the other, and/or future arrests for abuse or violating a restraining order). During the first year of this field experiment, evidence of subsequent abuse was found in 35 of the 138 situations in which the police response was arrest. There was evidence of subsequent abuse in 46 of the 140 situations in which the police mediated, and in 43 of the 139 instances where police separated the alleged abuser and victim.

Which statistical procedure would you apply to determine whether there is a significant difference by the method of police response in terms of subsequent domestic abuse?

RESEARCH SITUATION 21

To investigate the relationship between criminal justice professionals' political party affiliation and occupation, 400 individuals selected from a state's population of court, police, corrections, and private security employees were asked to indicate their political affiliation (Democrat, Republican, or other). Among 100 court employees (attorneys, judges, and support staff), 63 identified themselves as Democrats, 31 as Republicans, and 6 as having other political affiliations. Of the 100 police department employees (officers, administrators, and support staff), 54 were Republicans, 44 were Democrats, and 2 were of other political affiliations. Of the 100 corrections employees (probation, prisons, and parole employees), 61 were Republicans, 36 were Democrats, and 3 were of other affiliations. Of the private security employees, 64 were Republicans, 32 were Democrats, and four were of other affiliations.

Which statistical procedure would you apply to determine degree of association between political party affiliation and occupation?

RESEARCH SITUATION 22

A researcher is interested in whether there is a relationship between racial/ethnic category and the kinds of offenses for which people are arrested. To examine this, she draws a sample of the 475 most recent arrests in her city and examines the offense categories (violent, property, drug, and sex offenses) of the three largest racial/ethnic groups (Caucasian, Latino, African-American). She found that 65 of the 209 Caucasians were arrested for violent offenses, 50 for drug offenses, 32 for sex offenses, and 62 were arrested for property crimes. Of the 156 Latinos, 38 were arrested for violent offenses, 52 for drug offenses, 18 for sex offenses, and 48 for property offenses. Of the 110 African-Americans, 24 were arrested for violent offenses, 39 for drug offenses, 17 for sex offenses, and 30 for property offenses.

Which statistical procedure would you apply to determine the degree of association between the race/ethnicity of a criminal defendant and the type of offense for which he or she has been arrested?

RESEARCH SITUATION 23

A researcher interested in the relationship between marital status and rape collected the following data regarding the frequency of rape and the number of single men in the population for eight cities over a 1-year period:

City	Rapes	Single men (in thousands)
A	55	39
B	72	80
C	12	19
D	34	27
E	98	85
F	23	31
G	3	16
H	16	24

Which statistical procedure would you apply to determine the degree of association between frequency of rape and the number of single men in the population of these eight cities?

RESEARCH SITUATION 24

A criminal justice researcher wanted to examine whether male or female judges are more likely to give harsh prison sentences for females convicted of child abuse. To do so, he obtains from court records the prison sentences of the most recently convicted female child abusers sentenced by male and female judges. He randomly selects 10 sentences for such cases handed down by female judges, and 10 sentences meted out by male judges. The results are as follows:

Prison sentence length (in years)	
Male judges	Female judges
4	10
1	5
20	20
12	7
7	4
10	1
1	15
5	5
2	2
10	8

Which statistical procedure would you apply to determine whether there is a significant difference in the sentence lengths handed down by male and female judges in cases where women are convicted of child abuse?

RESEARCH SITUATION 25

A criminologist was interested in the effects of anomie—normlessness or breakdown of rules in a social setting. She obtained the following suicide rates (the number of suicides per 100,000 population) for five "high-anomie," five "moderate-anomie" and five "low-anomie" cities:

	Anomie	
High	Moderate	Low
19.2	15.6	8.2
17.7	20.1	10.9
22.6	11.5	11.8
18.3	13.4	7.7
25.2	14.9	8.3

Which statistical procedure would you apply to determine whether there is a significant difference by level of anomie in suicide rates?

RESEARCH SITUATION 26

A company accused of gender bias in their employee promotion practices was audited by a team of researchers in preparation for a civil suit. A researcher was commissioned by the court, and then gathered data on the job classification and gender of the company's employees. She found that of the 38 executives and managers in the company, 29 were male and 9 were female. Of the nonmanagement staff (labor, clerical, and part-time), 185 were male and 118 were female.

Which statistical procedure would you apply to determine whether there is a significant difference in employee rank by gender?

RESEARCH SITUATION 27

A state legislature was concerned about rising prison health care, and as part of a large audit of the prison health care system commissioned a study of the relationship between the mental and physical health of prison inmates. A random sample of 250 inmates were questioned regarding their symptoms of depression (for example, insomnia, lack of concentration, suicidal thoughts) and given a physical examination to uncover any symptoms of physical illness (for example, high blood pressure, erratic EKG, high cholesterol). Among the 100 inmates categorized as being in "excellent physical health," only 5 exhibited symptoms of depression; among the 110 inmates categorized in "good health," 14 exhibited symptoms of depression; and among the 40 inmates categorized in "poor health," 20 exhibited symptoms of depression.

Which statistical procedure would you apply to determine the degree of association between depression and physical illness among prison inmates?

RESEARCH SITUATION 28

Another component of the study described in Situation 27 examined the relationship between the gender and physical health of state prison inmates. A random sample of 200 inmates—100 men and 100 women—were given a physical examination to uncover any symptoms of physical illness (for example, high blood pressure, erratic EKG, high cholesterol.) Among the 100 men, 37 were categorized as being in "excellent physical health," 43 were categorized in "good health," and 20 were categorized in "poor health." Among the 100 women, 52 were categorized as being in "excellent physical health," 35 were categorized in "good health," and 13 were categorized in "poor health."

Which statistical procedure would you apply to determine the degree of association between gender and physical illness among state prison inmates?

RESEARCH SITUATION 29

Shortly after the criminal trial of O. J. Simpson ended, black and white Americans were asked by pollsters whether they agreed with the jury's not-guilty verdict. In one of many such studies, a researcher questioned 150 respondents—75 blacks and 75 whites—as to Simpson's guilt or innocence. He determined that 50 blacks but only 24 whites in his sample agreed with the jury that O. J. Simpson was not guilty.

Which statistical procedure would you apply to determine whether black and white Americans differ significantly in their agreement with the jury's verdict?

RESEARCH SITUATION 30

To study the impact of hypnosis on crime witness ability to accurately recall details of crimes, 20 adults were shown a videotape of an armed robbery. Half the subjects were then hypnotized for 15 minutes, and subsequently were asked to recall details of the crime (such as the height, weight, hair color, clothing, and race of the offender, number of bystanders present, physical surroundings, etc.). The other 10 subjects simply waited for 15 minutes after viewing the videotape before they were asked to recall details of the crime. The number of recall errors made by each of the respondents is listed here.

Recall errors	
Hypnotized	Not hypnotized
6	8
2	4
4	9
9	4
2	5
1	0
7	3
0	8
6	2
8	1
3	6
6	9
3	6
7	5
1	3
4	7
5	1
0	6
6	3
8	0

Which statistical procedure would you apply to determine whether the accuracy of crime witness recall is affected by hypnosis?

RESEARCH SOLUTIONS

SOLUTION TO RESEARCH SITUATION 1

(*t* RATIO)

Research Situation 1 represents a comparison between the scores of two independent samples of potential jurors. The *t* ratio (Chapter 7) is employed to make comparisons between two means when interval data have been obtained. The Mann-Whitney *U* test (Chapter 9) is a nonparametric alternative that can be applied when we suspect that the scores are not normally distributed in the population. A quick, but less powerful, nonparametric alternative is the median test.

SOLUTION TO RESEARCH SITUATION 2

(ANALYSIS OF VARIANCE)

Research Situation 2 represents a comparison of the scores of three independent samples of law students. The *F* ratio (analysis of variance—Chapter 8) is employed to make comparisons between three or more independent means when interval data have been obtained. Kruskal-Wallis one-way analysis of variance by ranks (Chapter 9) is a nonparametric alternative that can be applied when we have reason to suspect that the scores are not normally distributed in the population.

SOLUTION TO RESEARCH SITUATION 3

(PEARSON'S *r* CORRELATION COEFFICIENT)

Research Situation 3 is a correlation problem, because it asks for the degree of association between *X* (weeks in program) and *Y* (reading score). Pearson's *r* (Chapter 10) can be employed to detect a straight-line correlation between *X* and *Y* variables when both of these variables have been measured at the interval level. If *X* (weeks in program) and *Y* (reading score) are not normally distributed in the population, we could consider applying a nonparametric alternative such as Spearman's rank-order correlation coefficient (Chapter 12).

SOLUTION TO RESEARCH SITUATION 4

(SPEARMAN'S RANK-ORDER CORRELATION COEFFICIENT)

Research Situation 4 is a correlation problem, asking for the degree of association between *X* (reading score) and *Y* (teacher's rankings of reading ability). Spearman's rank-order correlation coefficient (Chapter 12) can be employed to detect a relationship between *X* and *Y* variables when both of these variables have been ordered or ranked. Pearson's *r* cannot be employed, because it requires interval-level measurement of *X* and *Y*. In the present case, reading scores (*X*) must be ranked from 1 to 20 before rank-order is applied.

SOLUTION TO RESEARCH SITUATION 5

(CHI-SQUARE TEST)

Research Situation 5 represents a comparison between the frequencies (crime reported versus not reported to the police) found in four groups (Northeast, South, Midwest, and West). The chi-square test of significance (Chapter 9) is used to make comparisons between two or more samples. Only nominal data are required. Present results can be cast in the form of a 2 × 4 table, representing 2 rows and 4 columns. Notice that the degree of association between crime reporting rate (X) and region (Y) can be measured by means of Cramér's V (Chapter 12). Note that the contingency coefficient is not a preferred measure here because the contingency table is not square.

SOLUTION TO RESEARCH SITUATION 6

(PHI COEFFICIENT)

Research Situation 6 is a correlation problem that asks for the degree of association between X (authoritarianism) and Y (prejudice). The phi coefficient (Chapter 12) is a measure of association that can be employed when frequency or nominal data can be cast in the form of a 2×2 table (2 rows by 2 columns). In the present problem, such a table would take the following form:

	Level of authoritarianism	
Level of prejudice	Authoritarian	Nonauthoritarian
Prejudiced	350	125
Tolerant	150	325

$$N = 950$$

SOLUTION TO RESEARCH SITUATION 7

(GOODMAN'S AND KRUSKAL'S GAMMA)

Research Situation 7 is a correlation problem that asks for the degree of association in a cross-tabulation of X (grade average) and Y (year in school). Goodman's and Kruskal's gamma coefficient (Chapter 12) is employed to detect a relationship between X and Y, when both variables are ordinal and have been cast in the form of a cross-tabulation. In the present problem, grade average has been ranked from A to D or worse and year in school has been ranked from first to fourth. The contingency coefficient (C) or Cramér's V (Chapter 12) represents an alternative to gamma that assumes only nominal-level data. However, because these variables are ordinal, gamma is preferable.

SOLUTION TO RESEARCH SITUATION 8

(t RATIO)

Research Situation 8 represents a before–after comparison of a single sample measured at two different points in time. The t ratio (Chapter 7) can be employed to compare two means from a single sample arranged in a before–after panel design.

SOLUTION TO RESEARCH SITUATION 9

(GOODMAN'S AND KRUSKAL'S GAMMA)

Research Situation 9 is a correlation problem that asks for the degree of association between X (occupational status) and Y (subjective social class). Gamma (Chapter 12) is especially well-suited to the problem of detecting a relationship between X and Y, when both variables are ordinal and can be arranged in the form of a cross-tabulation. In the present situation, occupational status and subjective social class have been ordered from upper to middle to lower, generating a very large number of tied ranks (for example, 221 respondents had middle-status occupations). To obtain the gamma coefficient, the data must be cast in the form of a cross-tabulation as follows:

Subjective social class (Y)	Occupational status (X)		
	Upper	Middle	Lower
Upper	56	42	15
Middle	122	163	202
Lower	12	16	49
	190	221	266

The contingency coefficient (C) and Cramér's V are alternatives to gamma that assume only nominal data. Because these variables are ordinal, gamma would be far preferable.

SOLUTION TO RESEARCH SITUATION 10

(ANALYSIS OF VARIANCE OR KRUSKAL-WALLIS ONE-WAY ANALYSIS OF VARIANCE BY RANKS)

Research Situation 10 represents a comparison of the scores of three independent samples of respondents. The F ratio (Chapter 8) is used to make comparisons between three or more independent means when interval data have been obtained. Kruskal-Wallis one-way analysis of variance by ranks (Chapter 9) is a nonparametric alternative that can be employed when we suspect that the salaries may not be normally distributed in the population.

SOLUTION TO RESEARCH SITUATION 11

(t RATIO, MANN-WHITNEY U TEST, OR MEDIAN TEST)

Research Situation 11 represents a comparison between the scores of two independent samples of respondents. The t ratio (Chapter 7) is employed to compare two means when interval data have been obtained. The Mann-Whitney U test (Chapter 9) is a nonparametric alternative that can be applied when we cannot assume that the sentence lengths are normally distributed in the population. A quick, but less powerful, nonparametric alternative is the median test.

SOLUTION TO RESEARCH SITUATION 12

(CHI-SQUARE TEST)

Research Situation 12 represents a comparison of the frequencies (willingness versus unwillingness) in two groups of law students (those told the judge was 65 versus those told the judge was 35). The chi-square test of significance (Chapter 9) is used to make comparisons between two or more samples when either nominal or frequency data have been obtained. Present results can be cast in the form of the following 2×2 table, representing two rows and two columns:

Willingness to attend	Experimental condition	
	Students told judge was 65	Students told judge was 35
Willing	22	38
Unwilling	43	27

SOLUTION TO RESEARCH SITUATION 13

(*t* RATIO)

Research Situation 13 represents a before–after comparison of a single sample that is measured at two different points in time. The *t* ratio (Chapter 7) can be used to compare two means drawn from a single sample arranged in a before–after design.

SOLUTION TO RESEARCH SITUATION 14

(GOODMAN'S AND KRUSKAL'S GAMMA)

Research Situation 14 is a correlation problem that asks for the degree of association between X (socioeconomic status) and Y (fear of crime). Goodman's and Kruskal's gamma coefficient (Chapter 12) is applied to detect a relationship between X and Y, when both variables are ordinal and can be arranged in a cross-tabulation. In the present situation, both socioeconomic status and fear of crime have been ranked from high to low.

Socioeconomic status (Y)	Fear of Crime (X)		
	Low	Medium	High
Low	15	80	70
Medium	20	110	55
High	30	80	40
	65	270	165

SOLUTION TO RESEARCH SITUATION 15

(ANALYSIS OF VARIANCE OR KRUSKAL-WALLIS ONE-WAY ANALYSIS OF VARIANCE BY RANKS)

Research Situation 15 represents a comparison of the scores of four independent samples of respondents. The F ratio (Chapter 8) is employed to make comparisons between three or more independent means when interval data have been achieved. Kruskal-Wallis one-way analysis of variance by ranks (Chapter 9) is a nonparametric alternative to be employed if we suspect that the scores may not be normally distributed in the population or if the interval level of measurement has not been achieved.

SOLUTION TO RESEARCH SITUATION 16

(CHI SQUARE TEST)

Research Situation 16 is a comparison of the frequencies (belief that victim would or would not report to the police) of four nominal groups (respondents who read scenarios containing one of four descriptions of the relationship between an offender and victim). The chi-square test of significance (Chapter 9) is employed to compare two or more samples when nominal or frequency data have been obtained. A 2×4 table would be created with the four types of relationships as columns and the judgment of whether the victim would or would not report to the police as rows.

SOLUTION TO RESEARCH SITUATION 17

(PEARSON'S CORRELATION COEFFICIENT)

Research Situation 17 is a correlation problem because it asks for the degree of statistical relationship between X (years of college) and Y (years of prison judged to be an appropriate prison sentence length). Pearson's r (Chapter 10) is employed to examine linear correlation between X and Y variables when both have been measured at the interval level. If the years in college and the perceived appropriate length of prison sentences are not normally distributed in the population, we might consider a nonparametric alternative such as Spearman's rank-order correlation coefficient (Chapter 12).

SOLUTION TO RESEARCH SITUATION 18

(t RATIO)

The t ratio is used to compare two means when interval data have been obtained, and would be an appropriate way to analyze the data in Research Situation 18. Appropriate prison sentence lengths were measured in years (interval data), and two means (for males and females) are compared. The Mann-Whitney U test (Chapter 9) is a nonparametric alternative that can be employed when we believe that the scores are not normally distributed in the population.

SOLUTION TO RESEARCH SITUATION 19

(SPEARMAN'S RANK-ORDER CORRELATION COEFFICIENT)

Research Situation 19 is a correlation problem asking for the degree of association between X (percentage of new population) and Y (delinquency rates). Spearman's rank-order correlation coefficient (Chapter 12) can be applied to detect a relationship between X and Y variables when both have been ranked or ordered. Pearson's r cannot be employed because it requires interval data on X and Y. In the present case, percentage of new population must be ranked from 1 to 7 before rank-order correlation is applied.

SOLUTION TO RESEARCH SITUATION 20

(CHI SQUARE TEST)

Research Situation 20 is a comparison of the frequencies (evidence of subsequent abuse versus no such evidence) of three different samples of domestic violence cases (police response of arrest, mediation, or separation). The chi-square test of significance (Chapter 9) is employed to compare two or more samples when nominal or frequency data have been obtained. A 2×3 table would be created with the type of police response along one axis and evidence of subsequent abuse on the other:

		Evidence of subsequent domestic abuse	
		Yes	No
Police response	Arrest	35	105
to domestic	Mediation	46	94
abuse	Separation	43	97

SOLUTION TO RESEARCH SITUATION 21

(LAMBDA OR CRAMÉR'S V)

Research Situation 21 is a correlation problem that asks for the degree of association between two variables measured at the nominal level: political party affiliation and criminal justice occupation. Like Cramér's V, lambda (Chapter 12) is a measure of association for comparing several groups or categories at the nominal level. Unlike Cramér's *V*, lambda indicates the extent to which values of either variable can be predicted from knowing values of the other variable. To obtain lambda or Cramér's *V*, the data must be arranged in the form of a crosstabulation as follows:

Occupation (*Y*)	Political party affiliation (*X*)		
	Republicans	Democrats	Other
Courts	31	63	6
Police	54	44	2
Corrections	61	36	3
Private Security	64	32	4

SOLUTION TO RESEARCH SITUATION 22

(CRAMÉR'S *V*)

Research Situation 22 is a nonparametric correlation problem (Chapter 12) that asks for the degree of association between two variables measured at the nominal level: racial/ethnic category and offense type. Cramér's *V* is a measure of association for comparing several groups or categories at the nominal level. To obtain Cramér's *V*, the data must be arranged in the form of a crosstabulation as follows:

Offense Type (*Y*)	Racial/ethnic category (*X*)		
	Caucasian	Latino	African-American
Violent	65	38	24
Drug	50	52	39
Sex	32	18	17
Property	62	48	30

SOLUTION TO RESEARCH SITUATION 23

(PEARSON'S *r* CORRELATION COEFFICIENT)

Research Situation 23 is a correlation problem, because it asks for the degree of association between *X* (rape) and *Y* (single men). Pearson's *r* (Chapter 10) is employed to detect a straightline correlation between *X* and *Y* variables when both characteristics have been measured at the interval level. If frequency of occurrence of rape and number of single men are not normally distributed across the populations of cities, we might consider applying a nonparametric alternative such as Spearman's rank-order correlation coefficient (Chapter 12).

SOLUTION TO RESEARCH SITUATION 24

(*t* RATIO)

Research Situation 24 represents a comparison between the prison sentence lengths of two independent samples of judges. The *t* ratio (Chapter 7) is used to compare two means when interval data have been obtained. The Mann-Whitney *U* test (Chapter 9) is a nonparametric alternative that can be employed when we believe that the scores are not normally distributed in the population or that the interval level has not been attained. A simple, but less powerful, nonparametric alternative is found in the median test.

SOLUTION TO RESEARCH SITUATION 25

(ANALYSIS OF VARIANCE)

Research Situation 25 represents a comparison of the suicide rates in cities representing three anomie levels—low, moderate, and high. The F ratio (Chapter 8) is employed to make comparisons between three or more independent means when interval data have been achieved. Kruskal-Wallis one-way analysis of variance by ranks (Chapter 9) is a nonparametric alternative to be employed when we believe that the scores may not be normally distributed in the population.

SOLUTION TO RESEARCH SITUATION 26

(CHI SQUARE TEST)

Research Situation 26 is a comparison of the frequencies (management versus nonmanagement) of two independent samples (males versus females). The chi-square test of significance (Chapter 9) is employed to compare two or more samples when nominal or frequency data have been obtained. A 2×2 table would be created with the job classification along one axis and gender along the other:

Job classification	Gender of employee	
	Male	Female
Management	29	9
Nonmanagement	185	118

SOLUTION TO RESEARCH SITUATION 27

(GOODMAN'S AND KRUSKAL'S GAMMA)

Research Situation 27 is a correlation problem that asks for the degree of association between two variables, X and Y, measured at the ordinal level: physical health and depression (note that an underlying order exists, even though only two levels of depression are indicated). Gamma (Chapter 12) is especially applicable when both variables are ordinal and can be arranged in the form of a cross-tabulation as follows:

Depression	Physical health		
	Excellent	Good	Poor
Depressed	5	14	20
Not depressed	95	96	20

SOLUTION TO RESEARCH SITUATION 28

(CRAMÉR'S V)

Research Situation 28 is a nonparametric correlation problem (Chapter 12) that asks for the degree of association between two variables, one measured at the nominal level (gender) and the other measured at the ordinal level (physical health). Cramér's V is a measure of association for comparing several groups or categories at the nominal level. When variables are measured at two different levels, statistical tests for the lower level are usually appropriate to apply. For example, Spearman's rank-order correlation coefficient is employed when X is an interval measure and Y is an ordinal measure. In the same way, Cramér's V is appropriate when X is nominal and Y is ordinal. To calculate Cramér's V, the data must be arranged in the form of a frequency table as follows:

Gender	Physical health		
	Excellent	Good	Poor
Men	37	43	20
Women	52	35	13

SOLUTION TO RESEARCH SITUATION 29

(CHI-SQUARE TEST)

Research Situation 29 represents a comparison of the frequencies (belief that O. J. Simpson was guilty vs. not guilty) in two groups of people—black and white Americans. The chi-square test of significance (Chapter 9) is used to make comparisons between two or more samples when nominal or frequency data have been obtained. Present results can be cast in the form of the following 2×2 table, representing two rows and two columns:

Belief that	Race of respondent	
O. J. Simpson was	Black	White
Guilty	25	51
Not guilty	50	24

SOLUTION TO RESEARCH SITUATION 30

(t RATIO)

The t ratio is used to compare two means when interval data have been obtained, and would be an appropriate way to analyze the data in Research Situation 30. The number of recall errors was measured at the interval level, and two means (hypnotized versus non-hypnotized subjects) are compared. The Mann-Whitney U test (Chapter 9) is a nonparametric alternative that can be employed when we believe that the scores are not normally distributed in the population. A simple but less powerful nonparametric alternative is the median test.

APPENDIXES

APPENDIX A
SELECTED CRIMINAL JUSTICE SITES ON THE WORLD WIDE WEB

APPENDIX B
A REVIEW OF SOME FUNDAMENTALS OF MATHEMATICS

APPENDIX C
TABLES

APPENDIX D
LIST OF FORMULAS

GLOSSARY

ANSWERS TO SELECTED PROBLEMS

INDEX

A

SELECTED CRIMINAL JUSTICE SITES ON THE WORLD WIDE WEB

What follows is an annotated list of selected World Wide Web (WWW or web) sites containing statistical information of interest to those in criminology and criminal justice[1]. The web is rapidly growing and changing; sites are added, omitted, moved, and changed frequently. The short list provided here is current for the summer of 1998, but there is no guarantee that all of the sites will exist at their current addresses permanently.

Using the web requires software referred to as web browsers, such as Microsoft Internet Explorer, Netscape, or Mosaic. For example, if you would like to visit the Federal Bureau of Investigation (FBI) web site you would open one of the net browsers and then type the address of the FBI site: http://www.fbi.gov/

Once an Internet browser is opened, one can also open an Internet search engine by typing its address: http://www.yahoo.com will access the YAHOO search engine, and http://www.altavista.com will access AltaVista. The search engines are particularly useful when one does not know the address of a particular site, or if one has an interest in a particular subject but does not know which agency or organization would have the information.

NATIONAL CRIMINAL JUSTICE REFERENCE SERVICE

Address: **http://ncjrs.aspensys.com/**

The National Criminal Justice Reference Service (NCJRS) site is one of the most expensive sources of crime and criminal justice data in the world. This site provides links to numerous criminal justice agencies and other organizations providing crime and criminal justice statistics. Click on the "Criminal Justice Statistics" section of the home page, and this will lead to an extensive list of web sites of government agencies and other organizations. Most of the other web sites listed below are accessible through the NCJRS site.

---

1   A useful discussion of criminal justice information available on the Internet is presented by The Criminal Justice Distance Learning Consortium entitled, *The Definitive Guide to Criminal Justice and Criminology on the World Wide Web*, Prentice-Hall, 1999. Another discussion is provided by Phyllis B. Gerstenfeld, entitled *"Net Justice": Using the Internet for Teaching and Research in Criminal Justice.* This article appeared in *ACJS Today* (the newletter of the Academy of Criminal Justice Sciences), volume 16, May/June 1997. Another is provided by Cecil Greek and Deborah B. Henry entitled *Criminal Justice Resources on the Internet,* appearing in the *Journal of Criminal Justice Education,* Volume 8, Spring 1997.

NATIONAL ARCHIVE OF CRIMINAL JUSTICE DATA

Address: **http://www.icpsr.umich.edu/NACJD/index.html**

The National Archive of Criminal Justice Data (NACJD) contains over 550 crime and criminal justice data sets that are available free of charge for purposes of research and instruction. The archive is divided into 11 subject categories: Attitude surveys, community studies, corrections, court case processing, courts, criminal justice system, crime and delinquency, official statistics, police, victimizatin, and drugs, alcohol, and crime. The major crime data sources are available here, such as the National Crime Victimization Survey (NCVS), the Uniform Crime Report (UCR), and the National Incident-Based Reporting System (NIBRS).

Instructions for searching, accessing, and downloading data, abstracts, and codebooks are provided. One of the great advantages of the NACJD is that one can gain access to the actual data, not just to summary statistics. Once one has downloaded the data it is possible to analyze it using most computer statistical packages. The NACJD site provides SPSS and SAS data definitions.

BUREAU OF JUSTICE STATISTICS

Address: **http://www.ojp.usdoj.gov/bjs**

The Burea of Justice Statistics (BJS) is the branch of the U.S. Department of Justice responsible for collecting, analyzing, and disseminating criminal justice information. This site contains data sets available from the NACJD web site, but also contains numerous reports of analyses of criminal justice data in the following general categories: Crimes and victims, drugs and crimes, criminal offenders, law enforcement, prosecution, courts and sentencing, corrections, and justice system expenditures and employment. In addition to downloading data, one can download and/or print BJS publications, press releases, and policies.

FEDERAL BUREAU OF INVESTIGATION

Address: **http://www.fbi.gov**

The site provides a description of and access to the UCR and NIBRS data. Nearly all of the law enforcement agencies in the United States provide to the FBI periodic reports of crimes reported to the police, arrests, offender characteristics and other information. The FBI compiles these reports and from them publishes its annual report, "Crime in the United States" and other reports.

ASSOCIATION OF CERTIFIED FRAUD EXAMINERS

Address: **http://www.acfe.org/**

The Association of Certified Fraud Examiners is a nation-wide professional organization dedicated to fighting fraud and white-collar crime. Its web site provides occupational fraud and abuse statistics such as those about costs, methods, perpetrators, and victims.

BUREAU OF ALCOHOL, TOBACCO, AND FIREARMS

Address: **http://www.atf.treas.gov**

The Bureau of Alcohol, Tobacco, and Firearms (BATF) is a law enforcement organization within the United States Department of Treasury. Its site contains, among other things, the Arson and Explosives National Repository. The Repository contains statistical information contributed by the BATF, the FBI, and the United States Fire Administration.

DRUG ENFORCEMENT ADMINISTRATION

Address: **http://www.usdoj.gov/dea/**

The Drug Enforcement Administration (DEA) is a branch of the U.S. Department of Justice. Its web site contains data on the supply of illegal drugs in the United States, including manufacturing, trafficking, and interdiction efforts.

FEDERAL BUREAU OF PRISONS

Address: **http://www.bop.gov**

This site provides statistics on Federal prison inmate demographics, sentence, and offense. It also contains statistical information about the federal prison system, such as inmate population and staffing of each facility.

FEDERAL JUDICIAL CENTER

Address: **http://www.fjc.gov**

The Federal Judicial Center is the federal courts' agency responsible for research. Its site contains information on judicial administration and reports from the Administrative Office of the U.S. Courts and the U.S. Sentencing Commission, such as mandatory prison sentences and federal appeals.

JUSTICE RESEARCH AND STATISTICS ASSOCIATION

Address: **http://www.jrsainfo.org**

The JRSA is a national nonprofit organization of state Statistical Analysis Center directors and other analysts, researchers, and criminal justice practitioners. Its web site provides information on the collection, analysis, and use of crime and criminal justice data on the state level.

NATIONAL INSTITUTE ON DRUG ABUSE

Address: **http://www.nida.nih.gov**

The National Institute on Drug Abuse (NIDA) is a division of the National Institutes of Health. NIDA's web site provides statistics on drug abuse and addiction, and facts about the use of illegal substances.

B

A REVIEW OF SOME FUNDAMENTALS OF MATHEMATICS

For students of statistics who need to review some of the fundamentals of algebra and arithmetic, this appendix covers the problems of working with decimals and negative numbers. Other problems of mathematics have been discussed at appropriate places throughout the text. For instance, Chapter 1 identifies, defines, and compares the three levels of measurement; Chapter 2 discusses percentages, proportions, ratios, and rates. Finally, this appendix provides a fuller presentation of the summation sign (Σ) than Chapter 3.

WORKING WITH DECIMALS

When adding and subtracting decimals, be sure to place decimal points of the numbers directly below one another. For example, to add 3,210.76, 2.541, and 98.3,

$$
\begin{array}{r}
3{,}210.76 \\
2.541 \\
98.3 \\
\hline
3{,}311.601
\end{array}
$$

To subtract 34.1 from 876.62,

$$
\begin{array}{r}
876.62 \\
-34.1 \\
\hline
842.52
\end{array}
$$

When multiplying decimals, be sure that your answer contains the same number of decimal places as both multiplicand and multiplier combined. For example,

Multiplicand $\longrightarrow$	63.41	2.6	.0003	.5
Multiplier $\longrightarrow$	$\times$ .05	$\times$ 1.4	$\times$ .03	$\times$ .5
Product $\longrightarrow$	3.1705	3.64	.000009	.25

Before dividing, always eliminate decimals from the divisor by moving the decimal point as many places to the right as needed to make the divisor a whole number. Make a corresponding change of the same number of places for decimals in the dividend (that is, if you move the decimal two places in the divisor, then you must move it two places in the dividend). This procedure will indicate the number of decimal places in your answer.

$$\frac{2.44}{.02} = 122$$

$$\frac{.88}{.4} = 2.2$$

$$\frac{10.10}{.10} = 1.01$$

$$\frac{1010}{.10} = 10100$$

quotient

divisor $\longrightarrow$ $.02\overline{)2.44}$ $\longleftarrow$ dividend, quotient 122.

$.4\overline{)\,.88}$ quotient 2.2

$10\overline{)10.10}$ quotient 1.01

$.10\overline{)1010.00}$ quotient 10100.

Arithmetic operations frequently yield answers in decimal form; for instance, 2.034, 24.7, and 86.001. The question arises as to how many decimal places we should have in our answers. A simple rule to follow is to carry every intermediate operation as fully as convenient, and round off the final answer to two more decimal places than found in the original set of numbers.

To illustrate, if data are derived from an original set of whole numbers (for instance, 12, 9, 49, or 15), we might carry out operations to three decimal places (to thousandths) but express our final answer to the nearest hundredth. For example,

$$3.889 = 3.89$$

$$1.224 = 1.22$$

$$7.761 = 7.76$$

Rounding to the nearest decimal place is generally carried out as follows: Drop the last digit if it is less than 5 (in the examples that follow, the last digit is the thousandth digit):

less than 5

$$26.234 = 26.23$$

$$14.891 = 14.89$$

$$1.012 = 1.01$$

Add one to the preceding digit if the last digit is 5 or more (in the examples that follow, the preceding digit is the hundredth digit):

$$26.236 = 26.24$$

5 or more

$$14.899 = 14.90$$

$$1.015 = 1.02$$

The following have been rounded to the nearest whole number:

$$3.1 = 3$$

$$3.5 = 4$$

$$4.5 = 5$$

$$4.8 = 5$$

The following have been rounded to the nearest tenth:

$$3.11 = 3.1$$

$$3.55 = 3.6$$

$$4.45 = 4.5$$

$$4.17 = 4.2$$

The following have been rounded to the nearest hundredth:

$$3.328 = 3.33$$

$$4.823 = 4.82$$

$$3.065 = 3.07$$

$$3.055 = 3.06$$

DEALING WITH NEGATIVE NUMBERS

When adding a series of negative numbers, make sure that you give a negative sign to the sum. For example,

$$
\begin{array}{rr}
-20 & -3 \\
-12 & -9 \\
\underline{-6} & \underline{-4} \\
-38 & -16
\end{array}
$$

To add a series containing both negative and positive numbers, first group all negatives and all positives separately; add each group and then subtract their sums (the remainder gets the sign of the larger number). For example,

$$
\begin{array}{llll}
-6 & +4 & -6 & +6 \\
+4 & +2 & -1 & -10 \\
+2 & \overline{+6} & -3 & \overline{-4} \\
-1 & & \overline{-10} & \\
-3 & & & \\
\overline{-4} & & &
\end{array}
$$

To subtract a negative number, you must first give it a positive sign and then follow the procedure for addition. The remainder gets the sign of the larger number. For example,

$$
\begin{array}{l}
24 \\
-(-6) \\
\overline{30}
\end{array}
$$
-6 gets a positive sign and is therefore added to 24. Because the larger value is a positive number (24), the remainder (30) is a positive value.

$$
\begin{array}{l}
-6 \\
-(-24) \\
\overline{18}
\end{array}
$$
-24 gets a positive sign and is therefore subtracted. Because the larger value is a positive number (remember that you have changed the sign of -24), the remainder (18) is a positive value.

$$
\begin{array}{l}
-24 \\
-(-6) \\
\overline{-18}
\end{array}
$$
-6 gets a positive sign and is therefore subtracted. Because the larger value is a negative number (-24), the remainder (-18) is a negative value.

When multiplying (or dividing) two numbers that have the same sign, always assign a positive sign to their product (or quotient). For example,

$$(+8) \times (+5) = +40 \qquad +5\overline{)+40}^{\;+8} \qquad -5\overline{)-40}^{\;+8}$$

$$(-8) \times (-5) = +40$$

In the case of two numbers having different signs, assign a negative sign to their product (or quotient). For example,

$$(-8) \times (+5) = -40 \qquad -5\overline{)+40}^{\;-8}$$

THE SUMMATION SIGN

The greek letter Σ (capital sigma) is used in statistics to symbolize the sum of a set of numbers. Thus, for example, if the variable X has these values:

$$3 \quad 6 \quad 8 \quad 5 \quad 6$$

then

$$\Sigma X = 3 + 6 + 8 + 5 + 6$$

$$= 28$$

The summation sign Σ is a very convenient way to represent any kind of sum or total. However, there are a couple of basic rules that will enable you to use it properly in computing various statistics. In evaluating a complex formula having a summation sign, any operation involving an exponent (such as a square), multiplication, or division is performed before the summation, *unless* there are parentheses that dictate otherwise. (In math, parentheses always take precedence, meaning that you always perform the operation within them first.)

Applying these rules, the term ΣX^2 means: Square the X scores and then add. In contrast, the notation $(\Sigma X)^2$ dictates: Add the X scores and then square the total. Let's set the preceding X values and their squares in column form and calculate these two expressions.

X	X^2
3	9
6	36
8	64
5	25
6	36
$\Sigma X = 28$	$\Sigma X^2 = 170$

Thus, whereas $\Sigma X^2 = 170$, $(\Sigma X)^2 = (28)^2 = 784$. It is essential that you keep in mind this distinction through many of the calculations in this book.

To illustrate the same concept with multiplication rather than squares, let's add to our X values another variable Y:

$$8 \quad 2 \quad 1 \quad 0 \quad 3$$

We now form three columns: one for X, one for Y, and one for their product (XY).

X	Y	XY
3	8	24
6	2	12
8	1	8
5	0	0
6	3	18
$\Sigma X = 28$	$\Sigma Y = 14$	$\Sigma XY = 62$

Thus, similar to what we found with squares, the sum of products is very different from the product of sums. Whereas, $\Sigma XY = 62$, $(\Sigma X)(\Sigma Y) = (28)(14) = 392$.

TABLES

TABLE A PERCENTAGE OF AREA UNDER THE NORMAL CURVE

Column a gives the distance in standard deviation units from the mean (z). Column b represents the percentage of area between the mean and a given z. Column c represents the percentage at or beyond a given z.

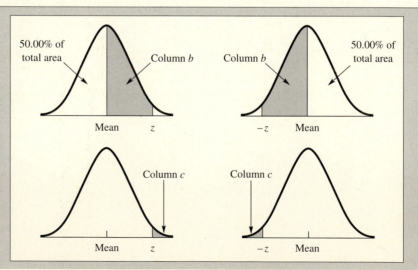

(*continued*)

TABLE A (*continued*)

(a) z	(b) Area between mean and z	(c) Area beyond z	(a) z	(b) Area between mean and z	(c) Area beyond z
.00	.00	50.00	.47	18.08	31.92
.01	.40	49.60	.48	18.44	31.56
.02	.80	49.20	.49	18.79	31.21
.03	1.20	48.80	.50	19.15	30.85
.04	1.60	48.40	.51	19.50	30.50
.05	1.99	48.01	.52	19.85	30.15
.06	2.39	47.61	.53	20.19	29.81
.07	2.79	47.21	.54	20.54	29.46
.08	3.19	46.81	.55	20.88	29.12
.09	3.59	46.41	.56	21.23	28.77
.10	3.98	46.02	.57	21.57	28.43
.11	4.38	45.62	.58	21.90	28.10
.12	4.78	45.22	.59	22.24	27.76
.13	5.17	44.83	.60	22.57	27.43
.14	5.57	44.43	.61	22.91	27.09
.15	5.96	44.04	.62	23.24	26.76
.16	6.36	43.64	.63	23.57	26.43
.17	6.75	43.25	.64	23.89	26.11
.18	7.14	42.86	.65	24.22	25.78
.19	7.53	42.47	.66	24.54	25.46
.20	7.93	42.07	.67	24.86	25.14
.21	8.32	41.68	.68	25.17	24.83
.22	8.71	41.29	.69	25.49	24.51
.23	9.10	40.90	.70	25.80	24.20
.24	9.48	40.52	.71	26.11	23.89
.25	9.87	40.13	.72	26.42	23.58
.26	10.26	39.74	.73	26.73	23.27
.27	10.64	39.36	.74	27.04	22.96
.28	11.03	38.97	.75	27.34	22.66
.29	11.41	38.59	.76	27.64	22.36
.30	11.79	38.21	.77	27.94	22.06
.31	12.17	37.83	.78	28.23	21.77
.32	12.55	37.45	.79	28.52	21.48
.33	12.93	37.07	.80	28.81	21.19
.34	13.31	36.69	.81	29.10	20.90
.35	13.68	36.32	.82	29.39	20.61
.36	14.06	35.94	.83	29.67	20.33
.37	14.43	35.57	.84	29.95	20.05
.38	14.80	35.20	.85	30.23	19.77
.39	15.17	34.83	.86	30.51	19.49
.40	15.54	34.46	.87	30.78	19.22
.41	15.91	34.09	.88	31.06	18.94
.42	16.28	33.72	.89	31.33	18.67
.43	16.64	33.36	.90	31.59	18.41
.44	17.00	33.00	.91	31.86	18.14
.45	17.36	32.64	.92	32.12	17.88
.46	17.72	32.28	.93	32.38	17.62

(*continued*)

TABLE A   (*continued*)

(a) z	(b) Area between mean and z	(c) Area beyond z	(a) z	(b) Area between mean and z	(c) Area beyond z
.94	32.64	17.36	1.43	42.36	7.64
.95	32.89	17.11	1.44	42.51	7.49
.96	33.15	16.85	1.45	42.65	7.35
.97	33.40	16.60	1.46	42.79	7.21
.98	33.65	16.35	1.47	42.92	7.08
.99	33.89	16.11	1.48	43.06	6.94
1.00	34.13	15.87	1.49	43.19	6.81
1.01	34.38	15.62	1.50	43.32	6.68
1.02	34.61	15.39	1.51	43.45	6.55
1.03	34.85	15.15	1.52	43.57	6.43
1.04	35.08	14.92	1.53	43.70	6.30
1.05	35.31	14.69	1.54	43.82	6.18
1.06	35.54	14.46	1.55	43.94	6.06
1.07	35.77	14.23	1.56	44.06	5.94
1.08	35.99	14.01	1.57	44.18	5.82
1.09	36.21	13.79	1.58	44.29	5.71
1.10	36.43	13.57	1.59	44.41	5.59
1.11	36.65	13.35	1.60	44.52	5.48
1.12	36.86	13.14	1.61	44.63	5.37
1.13	37.08	12.92	1.62	44.74	5.26
1.14	37.29	12.71	1.63	44.84	5.16
1.15	37.49	12.51	1.64	44.95	5.05
1.16	37.70	12.30	1.65	45.05	4.95
1.17	37.90	12.10	1.66	45.15	4.85
1.18	38.10	11.90	1.67	45.25	4.75
1.19	38.30	11.70	1.68	45.35	4.65
1.20	38.49	11.51	1.69	45.45	4.55
1.21	38.69	11.31	1.70	45.54	4.46
1.22	38.88	11.12	1.71	45.64	4.36
1.23	39.07	10.93	1.72	45.73	4.27
1.24	39.25	10.75	1.73	45.82	4.18
1.25	39.44	10.56	1.74	45.91	4.09
1.26	39.62	10.38	1.75	45.99	4.01
1.27	39.80	10.20	1.76	46.08	3.92
1.28	39.97	10.03	1.77	46.16	3.84
1.29	40.15	9.85	1.78	46.25	3.75
1.30	40.32	9.68	1.79	46.33	3.67
1.31	40.49	9.51	1.80	46.41	3.59
1.32	40.66	9.34	1.81	46.49	3.51
1.33	40.82	9.18	1.82	46.56	3.44
1.34	40.99	9.01	1.83	46.64	3.36
1.35	41.15	8.85	1.84	46.71	3.29
1.36	41.31	8.69	1.85	46.78	3.22
1.37	41.47	8.53	1.86	46.86	3.14
1.38	41.62	8.38	1.87	46.93	3.07
1.39	41.77	8.23	1.88	46.99	3.01
1.40	41.92	8.08	1.89	47.06	2.94
1.41	42.07	7.93	1.90	47.13	2.87
1.42	42.22	7.78	1.91	47.19	2.81

TABLE A (*continued*)

(a) z	(b) Area between mean and z	(c) Area beyond z	(a) z	(b) Area between mean and z	(c) Area beyond z
1.92	47.26	2.74	2.41	49.20	.80
1.93	47.32	2.68	2.42	49.22	.78
1.94	47.38	2.62	2.43	49.25	.75
1.95	47.44	2.56	2.44	49.27	.73
1.96	47.50	2.50	2.45	49.29	.71
1.97	47.56	2.44	2.46	49.31	.69
1.98	47.61	2.39	2.47	49.32	.68
1.99	47.67	2.33	2.48	49.34	.66
2.00	47.72	2.28	2.49	49.36	.64
2.01	47.78	2.22	2.50	49.38	.62
2.02	47.83	2.17	2.51	49.40	.60
2.03	47.88	2.12	2.52	49.41	.59
2.04	47.93	2.07	2.53	49.43	.57
2.05	47.98	2.02	2.54	49.45	.55
2.06	48.03	1.97	2.55	49.46	.54
2.07	48.08	1.92	2.56	49.48	.52
2.08	48.12	1.88	2.57	49.49	.51
2.09	48.17	1.83	2.58	49.51	.49
2.10	48.21	1.79	2.59	49.52	.48
2.11	48.26	1.74	2.60	49.53	.47
2.12	48.30	1.70	2.61	49.55	.45
2.13	48.34	1.66	2.62	49.56	.44
2.14	48.38	1.62	2.63	49.57	.43
2.15	48.42	1.58	2.64	49.59	.41
2.16	48.46	1.54	2.65	49.60	.40
2.17	48.50	1.50	2.66	49.61	.39
2.18	48.54	1.46	2.67	49.62	.38
2.19	48.57	1.43	2.68	49.63	.37
2.20	48.61	1.39	2.69	49.64	.36
2.21	48.64	1.36	2.70	49.65	.35
2.22	48.68	1.32	2.71	49.66	.34
2.23	48.71	1.29	2.72	49.67	.33
2.24	48.75	1.25	2.73	49.68	.32
2.25	48.78	1.22	2.74	49.69	.31
2.26	48.81	1.19	2.75	49.70	.30
2.27	48.84	1.16	2.76	49.71	.29
2.28	48.87	1.13	2.77	49.72	.28
2.29	48.90	1.10	2.78	49.73	.27
2.30	48.93	1.07	2.79	49.74	.26
2.31	48.96	1.04	2.80	49.74	.26
2.32	48.98	1.02	2.81	49.75	.25
2.33	49.01	.99	2.82	49.76	.24
2.34	49.04	.96	2.83	49.77	.23
2.35	49.06	.94	2.84	49.77	.23
2.36	49.09	.91	2.85	49.78	.22
2.37	49.11	.89	2.86	49.79	.21
2.38	49.13	.87	2.87	49.79	.21
2.39	49.16	.84	2.88	49.80	.20
2.40	49.18	.82	2.89	49.81	.19

(*continued*)

TABLE A   (*continued*)

(a) z	(b) Area between mean and z	(c) Area beyond z	(a) z	(b) Area between mean and z	(c) Area beyond z
2.90	49.81	.19	3.13	49.91	.09
2.91	49.82	.18	3.14	49.92	.08
2.92	49.82	.18	3.15	49.92	.08
2.93	49.83	.17	3.16	49.92	.08
2.94	49.84	.16	3.17	49.92	.08
2.95	49.84	.16	3.18	49.93	.07
2.96	49.85	.15	3.19	49.93	.07
2.97	49.85	.15	3.20	49.93	.07
2.98	49.86	.14	3.21	49.93	.07
2.99	49.86	.14	3.22	49.94	.06
3.00	49.87	.13	3.23	49.94	.06
3.01	49.87	.13	3.24	49.94	.06
3.02	49.87	.13	3.25	49.94	.06
3.03	49.88	.12	3.30	49.95	.05
3.04	49.88	.12	3.35	49.96	.04
3.05	49.89	.11	3.40	49.97	.03
3.06	49.89	.11	3.45	49.97	.03
3.07	49.89	.11	3.50	49.98	.02
3.08	49.90	.10	3.60	49.98	.02
3.09	49.90	.10	3.70	49.99	.01
3.10	49.90	.10	3.80	49.99	.01
3.11	49.91	.09	3.90	49.995	.005
3.12	49.91	.09	4.00	49.997	.003

TABLE B   CRITICAL VALUES OF *t* FOR TWO-TAILED TEST

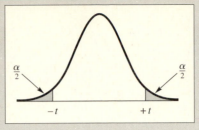

For any given df, the table shows the values of *t* corresponding to various levels of probability. Obtained *t* is significant at a given level if it is *larger than* the value shown in the table.

df	Level of significance for two-tailed test (α)					
	.20	.10	.05	.02	.01	.001
1	3.078	6.314	12.706	31.821	63.657	636.619
2	1.886	2.920	4.303	6.965	9.925	31.598
3	1.638	2.353	3.182	4.541	5.841	12.941
4	1.533	2.132	2.776	3.747	4.604	8.610
5	1.476	2.015	2.571	3.365	4.032	6.859
6	1.440	1.943	2.447	3.143	3.707	5.959
7	1.415	1.895	2.365	2.998	3.499	5.405
8	1.397	1.860	2.306	2.896	3.355	5.041
9	1.383	1.833	2.262	2.821	3.250	4.781
10	1.372	1.812	2.228	2.764	3.169	4.587
11	1.363	1.796	2.201	2.718	3.106	4.437
12	1.356	1.782	2.179	2.681	3.055	4.318
13	1.350	1.771	2.160	2.650	3.012	4.221
14	1.345	1.761	2.145	2.624	2.977	4.140
15	1.341	1.753	2.131	2.602	2.947	4.073
16	1.337	1.746	2.120	2.583	2.921	4.015
17	1.333	1.740	2.110	2.567	2.898	3.965
18	1.330	1.734	2.101	2.552	2.878	3.922
19	1.328	1.729	2.093	2.539	2.861	3.883
20	1.325	1.725	2.086	2.528	2.845	3.850
21	1.323	1.721	2.080	2.518	2.831	3.819
22	1.321	1.717	2.074	2.508	2.819	3.792
23	1.319	1.714	2.069	2.500	2.807	3.767
24	1.318	1.711	2.064	2.492	2.797	3.745
25	1.316	1.708	2.060	2.485	2.787	3.725
26	1.315	1.706	2.056	2.479	2.779	3.707
27	1.314	1.703	2.052	2.473	2.771	3.690
28	1.313	1.701	2.048	2.467	2.763	3.674
29	1.311	1.699	2.045	2.462	2.756	3.659
30	1.310	1.697	2.042	2.457	2.750	3.646
40	1.303	1.684	2.021	2.423	2.704	3.551
60	1.296	1.671	2.000	2.390	2.660	3.460
120	1.289	1.658	1.980	2.358	2.617	3.373
∞	1.282	1.645	1.960	2.326	2.576	3.291

NOTE: The bottom row (df = ∞) also equals critical values for *z*.

TABLE C CRITICAL VALUES OF *t* FOR ONE-TAILED TEST

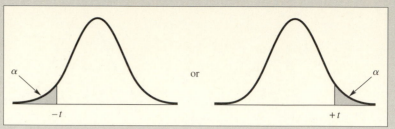

For any given df, the table shows the values of *t* corresponding to various levels of probability. Obtained *t* is significant at a given level if it is *larger than* the value shown in the table.

df	Level of significance for one-tailed test (α)					
	.10	.05	.025	.01	.005	.0005
1	3.078	6.314	12.706	31.821	63.657	636.619
2	1.886	2.920	4.303	6.965	9.925	31.598
3	1.638	2.353	3.182	4.541	5.841	12.941
4	1.533	2.132	2.776	3.747	4.604	8.610
5	1.476	2.015	2.571	3.365	4.032	6.859
6	1.440	1.943	2.447	3.143	3.707	5.959
7	1.415	1.895	2.365	2.998	3.499	5.405
8	1.397	1.860	2.306	2.896	3.355	5.041
9	1.383	1.833	2.262	2.821	3.250	4.781
10	1.372	1.812	2.228	2.764	3.169	4.587
11	1.363	1.796	2.201	2.718	3.106	4.437
12	1.356	1.782	2.179	2.681	3.055	4.318
13	1.350	1.771	2.160	2.650	3.012	4.221
14	1.345	1.761	2.145	2.624	2.977	4.140
15	1.341	1.753	2.131	2.602	2.947	4.073
16	1.337	1.746	2.120	2.583	2.921	4.015
17	1.333	1.740	2.110	2.567	2.898	3.965
18	1.330	1.734	2.101	2.552	2.878	3.922
19	1.328	1.729	2.093	2.539	2.861	3.883
20	1.325	1.725	2.086	2.528	2.845	3.850
21	1.323	1.721	2.080	2.518	2.831	3.819
22	1.321	1.717	2.074	2.508	2.819	3.792
23	1.319	1.714	2.069	2.500	2.807	3.767
24	1.318	1.711	2.064	2.492	2.797	3.745
25	1.316	1.708	2.060	2.485	2.787	3.725
26	1.315	1.706	2.056	2.479	2.779	3.707
27	1.314	1.703	2.052	2.473	2.771	3.690
28	1.313	1.701	2.048	2.467	2.763	3.674
29	1.311	1.699	2.045	2.462	2.756	3.659
30	1.310	1.697	2.042	2.457	2.750	3.646
40	1.303	1.684	2.021	2.423	2.704	3.551
60	1.296	1.671	2.000	2.390	2.660	3.460
120	1.289	1.658	1.980	2.358	2.617	3.373
∞	1.282	1.645	1.960	2.326	2.576	3.291

NOTE: The bottom row (df = ∞) also equals critical values for *z*.

TABLE D   CRITICAL VALUES OF *F* AT THE .05 AND .01 SIGNIFICANCE LEVELS

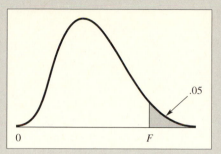

df for the denominator	df for the numerator $\alpha = .05$							
	1	2	3	4	5	6	8	12
1	161.4	199.5	215.7	224.6	230.2	234.0	238.9	243.9
2	18.51	19.00	19.16	19.25	19.30	19.33	19.37	19.41
3	10.13	9.55	9.28	9.12	9.01	8.94	8.84	8.74
4	7.71	6.94	6.59	6.39	6.26	6.16	6.04	5.91
5	6.61	5.79	5.41	5.19	5.05	4.95	4.82	4.68
6	5.99	5.14	4.76	4.53	4.39	4.28	4.15	4.00
7	5.59	4.74	4.35	4.12	3.97	3.87	3.73	3.57
8	5.32	4.46	4.07	3.84	3.69	3.58	3.44	3.28
9	5.12	4.26	3.86	3.63	3.48	3.37	3.23	3.07
10	4.96	4.10	3.71	3.48	3.33	3.22	3.07	2.91
11	4.84	3.98	3.59	3.36	3.20	3.09	2.95	2.79
12	4.75	3.88	3.49	3.26	3.11	3.00	2.85	2.69
13	4.67	3.80	3.41	3.18	3.02	2.92	2.77	2.60
14	4.60	3.74	3.34	3.11	2.96	2.85	2.70	2.53
15	4.54	3.68	3.29	3.06	2.90	2.79	2.64	2.48
16	4.49	3.63	3.24	3.01	2.85	2.74	2.59	2.42
17	4.45	3.59	3.20	2.96	2.81	2.70	2.55	2.38
18	4.41	3.55	3.16	2.93	2.77	2.66	2.51	2.34
19	4.38	3.52	3.13	2.90	2.74	2.63	2.48	2.31
20	4.35	3.49	3.10	2.87	2.71	2.60	2.45	2.28
21	4.32	3.47	3.07	2.84	2.68	2.57	2.42	2.25
22	4.30	3.44	3.05	2.82	2.66	2.55	2.40	2.23
23	4.28	3.42	3.03	2.80	2.64	2.53	2.38	2.20
24	4.26	3.40	3.01	2.78	2.62	2.51	2.36	2.18
25	4.24	3.38	2.99	2.76	2.60	2.49	2.34	2.16
26	4.22	3.37	2.98	2.74	2.59	2.47	2.32	2.15
27	4.21	3.35	2.96	2.73	2.57	2.46	2.30	2.13
28	4.20	3.34	2.95	2.71	2.56	2.44	2.29	2.12
29	4.18	3.33	2.93	2.70	2.54	2.43	2.28	2.10
30	4.17	3.32	2.92	2.69	2.53	2.42	2.27	2.09
40	4.08	3.23	2.84	2.61	2.45	2.34	2.18	2.00
60	4.00	3.15	2.76	2.52	2.37	2.25	2.10	1.92
120	3.92	3.07	2.68	2.45	2.29	2.17	2.02	1.83
∞	3.84	2.99	2.60	2.37	2.21	2.09	1.94	1.75

(*continued*)

TABLE D   (*continued*)

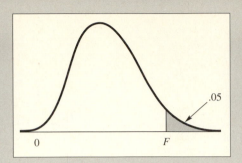

df for the denominator	df for the numerator $\alpha = .01$							
	1	2	3	4	5	6	8	12
1	4052	4999	5403	5625	5764	5859	5981	6106
2	98.49	99.01	99.17	99.25	99.30	99.33	99.36	99.42
3	34.12	30.81	29.46	28.71	28.24	27.91	27.49	27.05
4	21.20	18.00	16.69	15.98	15.52	15.21	14.80	14.37
5	16.26	13.27	12.06	11.39	10.97	10.67	10.27	9.89
6	13.74	10.92	9.78	9.15	8.75	8.47	8.10	7.72
7	12.25	9.55	8.45	7.85	7.46	7.19	6.84	6.47
8	11.26	8.65	7.59	7.01	6.63	6.37	6.03	5.67
9	10.56	8.02	6.99	6.42	6.06	5.80	5.47	5.11
10	10.04	7.56	6.55	5.99	5.64	5.39	5.06	4.71
11	9.65	7.20	6.22	5.67	5.32	5.07	4.74	4.40
12	9.33	6.93	5.95	5.41	5.06	4.82	4.50	4.16
13	9.07	6.70	5.74	5.20	4.86	4.62	4.30	3.96
14	8.86	6.51	5.56	5.03	4.69	4.46	4.14	3.80
15	8.68	6.36	5.42	4.89	4.56	4.32	4.00	3.67
16	8.53	6.23	5.29	4.77	4.44	4.20	3.89	3.55
17	8.40	6.11	5.18	4.67	4.34	4.10	3.79	3.45
18	8.28	6.01	5.09	4.58	4.25	4.01	3.71	3.37
19	8.18	5.93	5.01	4.50	4.17	3.94	3.63	3.30
20	8.10	5.85	4.94	4.43	4.10	3.87	3.56	3.23
21	8.02	5.78	4.87	4.37	4.04	3.81	3.51	3.17
22	7.94	5.72	4.82	4.31	3.99	3.76	3.45	3.12
23	7.88	5.66	4.76	4.26	3.94	3.71	3.41	3.07
24	7.82	5.61	4.72	4.22	3.90	3.67	3.36	3.03
25	7.77	5.57	4.68	4.18	3.86	3.63	3.32	2.99
26	7.72	5.53	4.64	4.14	3.82	3.59	3.29	2.96
27	7.68	5.49	4.60	4.11	3.78	3.56	3.26	2.93
28	7.64	5.45	4.57	4.07	3.75	3.53	3.23	2.90
29	7.60	5.42	4.54	4.04	3.73	3.50	3.20	2.87
30	7.56	5.39	4.51	4.02	3.70	3.47	3.17	2.84
40	7.31	5.18	4.31	3.83	3.51	3.29	2.99	2.66
60	7.08	4.98	4.13	3.65	3.34	3.12	2.82	2.50
120	6.85	4.79	3.95	3.48	3.17	2.96	2.66	2.34
∞	6.64	4.60	3.78	3.32	3.02	2.80	2.51	2.18

SOURCE: R. A. Fisher and F. Yates, *Statistical Tables for Biological, Agricultural, and Medical Research*, 4th ed., Longman Group Ltd., London (previously published by Oliver & Boyd, Edinburgh), Table V, by permission of the authors and the publisher.

TABLE E   CRITICAL VALUES OF CHI-SQUARE AT THE .05 AND .01 LEVELS OF SIGNIFICANCE (α)

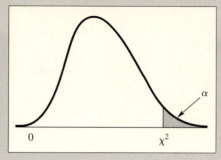

df	α .05	.01	df	α .05	.01
1	3.841	6.635	16	26.296	32.000
2	5.991	9.210	17	27.587	33.409
3	7.815	11.345	18	28.869	34.805
4	9.488	13.277	19	30.144	36.191
5	11.070	15.086	20	31.410	37.566
6	12.592	16.812	21	32.671	38.932
7	14.067	18.475	22	33.924	40.289
8	15.507	20.090	23	35.172	41.638
9	16.919	21.666	24	36.415	42.980
10	18.307	23.209	25	37.652	44.314
11	19.675	24.725	26	38.885	45.642
12	21.026	26.217	27	40.113	46.963
13	22.362	27.688	28	41.337	48.278
14	23.685	29.141	29	42.557	49.588
15	24.996	30.578	30	43.773	50.892

SOURCE: R. A. Fisher and F. Yates, *Statistical Tables for Biological, Agricultural, and Medical Research*, 4th ed., Longman Group Ltd., London (previously published by Oliver & Boyd, Edinburgh), Table IV, by permission of the authors and the publisher.

TABLE F   CRITICAL VALUES OF *r* AT THE .05 AND .01 LEVELS OF SIGNIFICANCE (α)

df	α .05	α .01	df	α .05	α .01
1	.99692	.999877	16	.4683	.5897
2	.95000	.990000	17	.4555	.5751
3	.8783	.95873	18	.4438	.5614
4	.8114	.91720	19	.4329	.5487
5	.7545	.8745	20	.4227	.5368
6	.7067	.8343	25	.3809	.4869
7	.6664	.7977	30	.3494	.4487
8	.6319	.7646	35	.3246	.4182
9	.6021	.7348	40	.3044	.3932
10	.5760	.7079	45	.2875	.3721
11	.5529	.6835	50	.2732	.3541
12	.5324	.6614	60	.2500	.3248
13	.5139	.6411	70	.2319	.3017
14	.4973	.6226	80	.2172	.2830
15	.4821	.6055	90	.2050	.2673

SOURCE: R. A. Fisher and F. Yates, *Statistical Tables for Biological, Agricultural, and Medical Research*, 4th ed., Longman Group Ltd., London (previously published by Oliver & Boyd, Edinburgh), Table VI, by permission of the authors and the publisher.

TABLE G   CRITICAL VALUES OF *rs* AT THE .05 AND .01 LEVELS OF SIGNIFICANCE (α)

N	α .05	α .01	N	α .05	α .01
5	1.000	—	16	.506	.665
6	.886	1.000	18	.475	.625
7	.786	.929	20	.450	.591
8	.738	.881	22	.428	.562
9	.683	.833	24	.409	.537
10	.648	.794	26	.392	.515
12	.591	.777	28	.377	.496
14	.544	.714	30	.364	.478

SOURCE: E. G. Olds, *The Annals of Mathematical Statistics*, "Distribution of the Sum of Squares of Rank Differences for Small Numbers of Individuals," 1938, vol. 9, and "The 5 Percent Significance Levels for Sums of Squares of Rank Differences and a Correction," 1949, vol. 20, by permission of the Institute of Mathematical Statistics.

TABLE H   RANDOM NUMBERS

									Column number									
Row	1	2	3	4	5	6	7	8	9	10	11	12	13	14	15	16	17	18	19
1	9	8	9	6	9	9	0	9	6	3	2	3	3	8	6	8	4	4	2
2	3	5	6	1	7	4	1	3	2	6	8	6	0	4	7	5	2	0	3
3	4	0	6	1	6	9	6	1	5	9	5	4	5	4	8	6	7	4	0
4	6	5	6	3	1	6	8	6	7	2	0	7	2	3	2	1	5	0	9
5	2	4	9	7	9	1	0	3	9	6	7	4	1	5	4	9	6	9	8
6	7	6	1	2	7	5	6	9	4	8	4	2	8	5	2	4	1	8	0
7	8	2	1	3	4	7	4	6	3	0	7	5	0	9	2	9	0	6	1
8	6	9	5	6	5	6	0	9	0	7	7	1	4	1	8	3	1	9	3
9	7	2	1	9	9	8	0	1	6	1	6	2	3	6	9	5	5	8	4
10	2	9	0	7	3	0	8	9	6	3	3	8	5	5	6	5	2	0	9
11	9	3	5	4	5	7	4	0	3	0	1	0	4	3	3	9	5	3	2
12	9	7	5	7	9	4	8	6	8	7	6	1	6	8	2	5	5	5	3
13	4	1	7	8	6	8	1	0	5	8	8	6	1	6	8	2	9	0	4
14	5	0	8	3	3	4	5	4	4	2	5	3	0	4	9	6	1	2	3
15	3	5	0	2	9	4	1	0	0	3	9	0	5	8	6	0	9	9	6
16	0	3	8	2	3	5	1	0	1	0	6	8	5	2	4	8	0	3	8
17	1	7	2	9	1	2	7	8	4	7	0	3	3	1	5	8	2	7	3
18	5	0	5	7	9	5	8	7	8	9	3	5	3	4	4	6	1	1	3
19	7	7	3	3	5	3	6	1	3	2	8	5	4	1	4	8	3	9	0
20	1	0	9	1	3	8	2	5	3	0	3	8	0	9	3	3	0	4	5
21	1	3	8	5	1	8	5	9	4	1	9	3	9	3	6	5	9	8	4
22	8	6	4	7	8	7	5	9	4	1	9	3	9	3	6	5	9	8	4
23	0	6	9	6	5	1	0	3	2	6	7	7	4	9	6	0	3	4	0
24	7	6	7	4	7	0	8	3	8	7	3	2	5	1	2	4	2	9	7
25	3	2	3	8	1	3	1	8	7	4	5	9	0	0	2	4	1	2	1
26	9	2	1	6	4	2	3	8	7	6	2	6	2	6	4	8	1	0	1
27	3	7	4	2	2	8	1	7	8	0	6	0	0	0	3	2	2	9	7
28	0	7	8	0	8	5	1	5	2	6	5	8	7	5	3	0	5	9	6
29	7	4	2	3	3	2	6	0	0	6	5	2	2	3	6	3	9	0	4
30	1	8	2	7	5	9	5	3	6	5	2	9	9	1	1	7	3	4	3
31	4	3	1	8	7	0	6	0	8	6	5	0	1	0	4	0	6	1	5
32	8	5	8	0	6	1	4	1	2	0	4	4	1	4	7	6	3	5	1
33	4	5	8	5	0	4	5	8	3	9	2	8	7	8	9	0	8	4	3
34	5	0	2	5	4	9	2	2	1	1	0	0	5	4	8	7	6	4	0
35	0	8	1	7	0	6	3	3	4	7	6	2	6	8	9	3	4	1	4
36	2	5	9	3	4	6	0	7	5	2	0	0	9	6	0	8	2	2	5
37	2	1	3	1	3	7	8	9	8	4	9	3	8	0	2	2	1	8	1
38	3	8	8	6	8	5	1	3	3	4	6	7	2	6	3	4	8	6	7
39	0	9	9	8	5	9	8	4	4	2	2	1	1	0	1	7	6	1	3
40	2	2	3	5	3	9	7	4	4	2	1	4	0	5	8	2	3	0	8

(*continued*)

Table H (*continued*)

										Column number											
20	21	22	23	24	25	26	27	28	29	30	31	32	33	34	35	36	37	38	39	40	*Row*
0	9	7	1	1	9	1	2	7	3	5	1	8	4	0	4	1	0	6	0	3	1
8	3	7	7	9	1	4	9	9	5	9	2	0	1	6	1	2	6	6	7	0	2
2	5	6	3	7	8	3	3	8	4	3	9	3	9	0	0	9	8	3	5	2	3
4	7	0	8	6	6	5	9	6	2	7	3	5	9	0	1	8	0	9	6	9	4
0	9	8	7	3	5	6	8	8	1	2	0	2	3	2	6	4	3	1	9	7	5
5	1	8	8	4	7	0	1	7	6	8	2	1	6	3	2	1	8	1	8	3	6
1	3	7	8	6	9	5	4	1	7	3	8	7	1	5	6	5	6	4	3	6	7
5	9	0	1	5	2	8	6	5	5	7	8	1	8	7	1	2	4	0	4	1	8
2	2	5	5	2	1	8	6	9	8	9	8	0	5	8	9	9	4	1	3	4	9
1	3	4	2	8	5	0	7	9	8	4	3	5	8	0	9	4	6	6	0	5	10
2	6	8	6	6	4	7	1	5	1	6	4	6	7	6	0	8	7	3	5	2	11
8	6	0	1	4	2	9	8	6	8	0	7	6	5	1	9	1	3	7	0	3	12
9	5	7	0	9	8	7	6	9	0	6	5	4	0	3	6	5	6	3	5	0	13
2	2	3	4	7	8	0	2	0	8	0	3	4	9	2	5	7	7	8	6	4	14
2	4	6	1	0	5	0	6	1	4	9	4	7	3	9	1	7	6	4	5	8	15
6	3	4	8	1	6	9	5	6	2	0	4	6	1	6	8	1	9	9	1	1	16
9	0	5	1	3	6	1	9	5	4	1	2	5	4	2	9	5	6	2	4	0	17
3	6	7	0	3	5	3	7	4	1	7	5	4	8	3	7	4	8	5	7	2	18
4	3	6	6	3	6	3	0	0	9	4	2	2	5	1	8	9	5	1	9	7	19
1	0	6	9	0	2	7	3	9	8	4	0	6	9	8	2	3	2	8	0	4	20
9	1	3	5	7	9	6	2	4	3	4	6	4	9	1	3	1	7	5	2	2	21
6	4	2	2	2	1	4	5	2	2	8	3	2	1	2	6	6	0	1	8	9	22
7	2	6	9	0	7	5	3	2	5	6	2	7	6	3	8	1	4	1	5	1	23
8	2	8	2	4	4	2	9	1	9	8	3	4	4	1	0	4	6	9	9	6	24
7	3	1	4	3	0	4	7	1	3	7	4	8	6	7	3	2	6	6	2	0	25
0	6	4	5	8	3	1	4	8	1	8	3	1	6	4	3	0	2	8	7	3	26
4	2	2	8	3	2	1	9	3	0	1	7	5	9	0	9	1	2	5	8	2	27
2	9	8	7	2	0	6	4	0	2	7	1	3	1	6	8	7	0	9	2	5	28
0	8	0	5	6	8	2	4	3	6	1	3	5	2	3	5	9	8	6	2	1	29
0	1	7	6	1	5	7	9	0	3	5	3	4	2	4	8	5	6	4	0	6	30
5	1	9	8	5	2	4	5	1	7	5	3	2	4	6	7	9	9	6	7	2	31
0	3	6	6	3	7	8	6	9	7	2	8	9	0	7	2	9	4	0	8	6	32
5	0	0	0	2	0	8	9	0	1	0	6	2	0	4	6	9	6	5	4	9	33
1	9	4	4	2	6	4	2	4	1	0	2	7	9	6	8	7	5	6	9	3	34
0	0	5	3	8	3	2	7	5	0	4	7	6	4	6	3	0	4	7	5	3	35
6	2	6	2	0	6	0	1	4	8	9	6	5	9	7	3	6	7	6	5	4	36
6	3	9	0	3	5	0	9	1	2	0	5	9	7	3	2	5	9	3	0	2	37
9	7	3	3	5	4	0	6	4	9	4	7	9	1	4	3	9	7	7	1	8	38
1	9	6	2	9	4	2	9	7	0	3	8	9	5	7	0	6	9	7	2	5	39
5	9	4	5	8	6	2	3	0	6	2	9	8	6	3	0	4	1	0	7	6	40

Source: N. M. Downie and R. W. Heath, *Basic Statistical Methods*, 3rd ed., Harper & Row, New York, 1970. Reprinted by permission of Harper & Row.

TABLE I   PERCENTAGE POINTS OF THE STUDENTIZED RANGE (q) FOR THE .05 AND .01 LEVELS OF SIGNIFICANCE (α)

df for MS$_{within}$	α	2	3	4	5	6	7	8	9	10	11
					$k =$ Number of means						
5	.05	3.64	4.60	5.22	5.67	6.03	6.33	6.58	6.80	6.99	7.17
	.01	5.70	6.98	7.80	8.42	8.91	9.32	9.67	9.97	10.24	10.48
6	.05	3.46	4.34	4.90	5.30	5.63	5.90	6.12	6.32	6.49	6.65
	.01	5.24	6.33	7.03	7.56	7.97	8.32	8.61	8.87	9.10	9.30
7	.05	3.34	4.16	4.68	5.06	5.36	5.61	5.82	6.00	6.16	6.30
	.01	4.95	5.92	6.54	7.01	7.37	7.68	7.94	8.17	8.37	8.55
8	.05	3.26	4.04	4.53	4.89	5.17	5.40	5.60	5.77	5.92	6.05
	.01	4.75	5.64	6.20	6.62	6.96	7.24	7.47	7.68	7.86	8.03
9	.05	3.20	3.95	4.41	4.76	5.02	5.24	5.43	5.59	5.74	5.87
	.01	4.60	5.43	5.96	6.35	6.66	6.91	7.13	7.33	7.49	7.65
10	.05	3.15	3.88	4.33	4.65	4.91	5.12	5.30	5.46	5.60	5.72
	.01	4.48	5.27	5.77	6.14	6.43	6.67	6.87	7.05	7.21	7.36
11	.05	3.11	3.82	4.26	4.57	4.82	5.03	5.20	5.35	5.49	5.61
	.01	4.39	5.15	5.62	5.97	6.25	6.48	6.67	6.84	6.99	7.13
12	.05	3.08	3.77	4.20	4.51	4.75	4.95	5.12	5.27	5.39	5.51
	.01	4.32	5.05	5.50	5.84	6.10	6.32	6.51	6.67	6.81	6.94
13	.05	3.06	3.73	4.15	4.45	4.69	4.88	5.05	5.19	5.32	5.43
	.01	4.26	4.96	5.40	5.73	5.98	6.19	6.37	6.53	6.67	6.79
14	.05	3.03	3.70	4.11	4.41	4.64	4.83	4.99	5.13	5.25	5.36
	.01	4.21	4.89	5.32	5.63	5.88	6.08	6.26	6.41	6.54	6.66
15	.05	3.01	3.67	4.08	4.37	4.59	4.78	4.94	5.08	5.20	5.31
	.01	4.17	4.84	5.25	5.56	5.80	5.99	6.16	6.31	6.44	6.55
16	.05	3.00	3.65	4.05	4.33	4.56	4.74	4.90	5.03	5.15	5.26
	.01	4.13	4.79	5.19	5.49	5.72	5.92	6.08	6.22	6.35	6.46
17	.05	2.98	3.63	4.02	4.30	4.52	4.70	4.86	4.99	5.11	5.21
	.01	4.10	4.74	5.14	5.43	5.66	5.85	6.01	6.15	6.27	6.38
18	.05	2.97	3.61	4.00	4.28	4.49	4.67	4.82	4.96	5.07	5.17
	.01	4.07	4.70	5.09	5.38	5.60	5.79	5.94	6.08	6.20	6.31
19	.05	2.96	3.59	3.98	4.25	4.47	4.65	4.79	4.92	5.04	5.14
	.01	4.05	4.67	5.05	5.33	5.55	5.73	5.89	6.02	6.14	6.25
20	.05	2.95	3.58	3.96	4.23	4.45	4.62	4.77	4.90	5.01	5.11
	.01	4.02	4.64	5.02	5.29	5.51	5.69	5.84	5.97	6.09	6.19
24	.05	2.92	3.53	3.90	4.17	4.37	4.54	4.68	4.81	4.92	5.01
	.01	3.96	4.55	4.91	5.17	5.37	5.54	5.69	5.81	5.92	6.02
30	.05	2.89	3.49	3.85	4.10	4.30	4.46	4.60	4.72	4.82	4.92
	.01	3.89	4.45	4.80	5.05	5.24	5.40	5.54	5.65	5.76	5.85
40	.05	2.86	3.44	3.79	4.04	4.23	4.39	4.52	4.63	4.73	4.82
	.01	3.82	4.37	4.70	4.93	5.11	5.26	5.39	5.50	5.60	5.69
60	.05	2.83	3.40	3.74	3.98	4.16	4.31	4.44	4.55	4.65	4.73
	.01	3.76	4.28	4.59	4.82	4.99	5.13	5.25	5.36	5.45	5.53
120	.05	2.80	3.36	3.68	3.92	4.10	4.24	4.36	4.47	4.56	4.64
	.01	3.70	4.20	4.50	4.71	4.87	5.01	5.12	5.21	5.30	5.37
∞	.05	2.77	3.31	3.63	3.86	4.03	4.17	4.29	4.39	4.47	4.55
	.01	3.64	4.12	4.40	4.60	4.76	4.88	4.99	5.08	5.16	5.23

SOURCE: E. S. Pearson and H. O. Hartley, *Biometrika Tables for Statisticians*, Vol. 1. 3rd ed., Cambridge University Press, New York, 1966, by permission of the Biometrika Trustees.

TABLE J   CRITICAL VALUES OF MANN-WHITNEY U TEST FOR TWO-TAILED TEST AT THE .05 LEVEL OF SIGNIFICANCE (α)

N_2	1	2	3	4	5	6	7	8	9	10	11	12	13	14	15	16	17	18	19	20
1	—																			
2	—	—																		
3	—	—	—																	
4	—	—	—	0																
5	—	—	0	1	2															
6	—	—	1	2	3	5														
7	—	—	1	3	5	6	8													
8	—	0	2	4	6	8	10	13												
9	—	0	2	4	7	10	12	15	17											
10	—	0	3	5	8	11	14	17	20	23										
11	—	0	3	6	9	13	16	19	23	26	30									
12	—	1	4	7	11	14	18	22	26	29	33	37								
13	—	1	4	8	12	16	20	24	28	33	37	41	45							
14	—	1	5	9	13	17	22	26	31	36	40	45	50	55						
15	—	1	5	10	14	19	24	29	34	39	44	49	54	59	64					
16	—	1	6	11	15	21	26	31	37	42	47	53	59	64	70	75				
17	—	2	6	11	17	22	28	34	39	45	51	57	63	69	75	81	87			
18	—	2	7	12	18	24	30	36	42	48	55	61	67	74	80	86	93	99		
19	—	2	7	13	19	25	32	38	45	52	58	65	72	78	85	92	99	106	113	
20	—	2	8	14	20	27	34	41	48	55	62	69	76	83	90	98	105	112	119	127
21	—	3	8	15	22	29	36	43	50	58	65	73	80	88	96	103	111	119	126	134
22	—	3	9	16	23	30	38	45	53	61	69	77	85	93	101	109	117	125	133	141
23	—	3	9	17	24	32	40	48	56	64	73	81	89	98	106	115	123	132	140	149
24	—	3	10	17	25	33	42	50	59	67	76	85	94	102	111	120	129	138	147	156
25	—	3	10	18	27	35	44	53	62	71	80	89	98	107	117	126	135	145	154	163
26	—	4	11	19	28	37	46	55	64	74	83	93	102	112	122	132	141	151	161	171
27	—	4	11	20	29	38	48	57	67	77	87	97	107	117	127	137	147	158	168	178
28	—	4	12	21	30	40	50	60	70	80	90	101	111	122	132	143	154	164	175	186
29	—	4	13	22	32	42	52	62	73	83	94	105	116	127	138	149	160	171	182	193
30	—	5	13	23	33	43	54	65	76	87	98	109	120	131	143	154	166	177	189	200
31	—	5	14	24	34	45	56	67	78	90	101	113	125	136	148	160	172	184	196	208
32	—	5	14	24	35	46	58	69	81	93	105	117	129	141	153	166	178	190	203	215
33	—	5	15	25	37	48	60	72	84	96	108	121	133	146	159	171	184	197	210	222
34	—	5	15	26	38	50	62	74	87	99	112	125	138	151	164	177	190	203	217	230
35	—	6	16	27	39	51	64	77	89	103	116	129	142	156	169	183	196	210	224	237
36	—	6	16	28	40	53	66	79	92	106	119	133	147	161	174	188	202	216	231	245
37	—	6	17	29	41	55	68	81	95	109	123	137	151	165	180	194	209	223	238	252
38	—	6	17	30	43	56	70	84	98	112	127	141	156	170	185	200	215	230	245	259
39	0	7	18	31	44	58	72	86	101	115	130	145	160	175	190	206	321	236	252	267
40	0	7	18	31	45	59	74	89	103	119	134	149	165	180	196	211	227	243	258	274

SOURCE: *Journal of the American Statistical Association* (September 1964), pp. 927–932.

TABLE K Critical values of Mann-Whitney U test for one-tailed test at the .05 level of significance (α)

	N_1																			
N_2	1	2	3	4	5	6	7	8	9	10	11	12	13	14	15	16	17	18	19	20
1	—																			
2	—	—																		
3	—	—	0																	
4	—	—	0	1																
5	—	—	1	2	4															
6	—	0	2	3	5	7														
7	—	0	2	4	6	8	11													
8	—	1	3	5	8	10	13	15												
9	—	1	4	6	9	12	15	18	21											
10	—	1	4	7	11	14	17	20	24	27										
11	—	1	5	8	12	16	19	23	27	31	34									
12	—	2	5	9	13	17	21	26	30	34	38	42								
13	—	2	6	10	15	19	24	28	33	37	42	47	51							
14	—	3	7	11	16	21	26	31	36	41	46	51	56	61						
15	—	3	7	12	18	23	28	33	39	44	50	55	61	66	72					
16	—	3	8	14	19	25	30	36	42	48	54	60	65	71	77	83				
17	—	3	9	15	20	26	33	39	45	51	57	64	70	77	83	89	96			
18	—	4	9	16	22	28	35	41	48	55	61	68	75	82	88	95	102	109		
19	0	4	10	17	23	30	37	44	51	58	65	72	80	87	94	101	109	116	123	
20	0	4	11	18	25	32	39	47	54	62	69	77	84	92	100	107	115	123	130	138
21	0	5	11	19	26	34	41	49	57	65	73	81	89	97	105	113	121	130	138	146
22	0	5	12	20	28	36	44	52	60	68	77	85	94	102	111	119	128	136	145	154
23	0	5	13	21	29	37	46	54	63	72	81	90	98	107	116	125	134	143	152	161
24	0	6	13	22	30	39	48	57	66	75	85	94	103	113	122	131	141	150	160	162
25	0	6	14	23	32	41	50	60	69	79	89	98	108	118	128	137	147	157	167	177
26	0	6	15	24	33	43	53	62	72	82	92	103	113	123	133	143	154	164	174	185
27	0	7	15	25	35	45	55	65	75	86	96	107	117	128	139	149	160	171	182	192
28	0	7	16	26	36	46	57	68	78	89	100	111	122	133	144	156	167	178	189	200
29	0	7	17	27	38	48	59	70	82	93	104	116	127	138	150	162	173	185	196	208
30	0	7	17	28	39	50	61	73	85	96	108	120	132	144	156	168	180	192	204	216
31	0	8	18	29	40	52	64	76	88	100	112	124	136	149	161	174	186	199	211	224
32	0	8	19	30	42	54	66	78	91	103	116	128	141	154	167	180	193	206	218	231
33	0	8	19	31	43	56	68	81	94	107	120	133	146	159	172	186	199	212	226	239
34	0	9	20	32	45	57	70	84	97	110	124	137	151	164	178	192	206	219	233	247
35	0	9	21	33	46	59	73	86	100	114	128	141	156	170	184	198	212	226	241	255
36	0	9	21	34	48	61	75	89	103	117	131	146	160	175	189	204	219	233	248	263
37	0	10	22	35	49	63	77	91	106	121	135	150	165	180	195	210	225	240	255	271
38	0	10	23	36	50	65	79	94	109	124	139	154	170	185	201	216	232	247	263	278
39	1	10	23	38	52	67	82	97	112	128	143	159	175	190	206	222	238	254	270	286
40	1	11	24	39	53	68	84	99	115	131	147	163	179	196	212	228	245	261	278	294

Source: *Journal of the American Statistical Association* (September 1964), pp. 927–932.

D

LIST OF FORMULAS

FORMULAS

$$P = \frac{f}{N}$$

$$\% = (100)\frac{f}{N}$$

$$\text{Ratio} = \frac{f_1}{f_2}$$

$$\text{Rate of change} = (100)\left(\frac{\text{time } 2f - \text{time } 1f}{\text{time } 1f}\right)$$

$$m = \frac{\text{lowest score value} + \text{highest score value}}{2}$$

$$c\% = (100)\frac{cf}{N}$$

$$PR = c\%_b + \left(\frac{X - L}{i}\right)\%$$

$$\text{total } \% = (100)\frac{f}{N_{\text{total}}}$$

$$\text{row } \% = (100)\frac{f}{N_{\text{row}}}$$

$$\text{column } \% = (100)\frac{f}{N_{\text{column}}}$$

$$\text{Position of median} = \frac{N + 1}{2}$$

$$\overline{X} = \frac{\Sigma X}{N}$$

$$\text{Deviation} = X - \overline{X}$$

$$\overline{X} = \frac{\Sigma fX}{N}$$

$$\text{Median} = L + \left(\frac{N/2 - cf_b}{f}\right)i$$

$$\overline{X} = \frac{\Sigma fm}{N}$$

$$\text{MD} = \frac{\Sigma \left|X - \overline{X}\right|}{N}$$

$$s^2 = \frac{\Sigma (X - \overline{X})^2}{N}$$

$$s = \sqrt{\frac{\Sigma (X - \overline{X})^2}{N}}$$

$$s^2 = \frac{\Sigma X^2}{N} - \overline{X}^2$$

$$s = \sqrt{\frac{\Sigma X^2}{N} - \overline{X}^2}$$

$$s^2 = \frac{\Sigma fX^2}{N} - \overline{X}^2$$

$$s = \sqrt{\frac{\Sigma fX^2}{N} - \overline{X}^2}$$

$$s^2 = \frac{\Sigma fm^2}{N} - \overline{X}^2$$

$$s = \sqrt{\frac{\Sigma fm^2}{N} - \overline{X}^2}$$

$$\text{Probability} = \frac{\text{number of times the outcome or event can occur}}{\text{total number of times any outcome or event can occur}}$$

$$z = \frac{X - \mu}{\sigma}$$

$$X = z\sigma + \mu$$

$$z = \frac{\overline{X} - \mu}{\sigma_{\overline{X}}}$$

$$\sigma_{\bar{X}} = \frac{\sigma}{\sqrt{N}}$$

$$95\% \text{ confidence interval} = \bar{X} \pm 1.96\,\sigma_{\bar{X}}$$

$$99\% \text{ confidence interval} = \bar{X} \pm 2.58\sigma_{\bar{X}}$$

$$s_{\bar{X}} = \frac{s}{\sqrt{N-1}}$$

$$t = \frac{\bar{X} - \mu}{s_{\bar{X}}}$$

$$\text{Confidence interval} = \bar{X} \pm ts_{\bar{X}}$$

$$s_P = \sqrt{\frac{P(1-P)}{N}}$$

$$95\% \text{ confidence interval} = P \pm (1.96)\,\sigma_P$$

$$z = \frac{\bar{X}_1 - \bar{X}_2}{\sigma_{\bar{X}_1 - \bar{X}_2}}$$

$$s_{\bar{X}_1 - \bar{X}_2} = \sqrt{\left(\frac{N_1 s_1^2 + N_2 s_2^2}{N_1 + N_2 - 2}\right)\left(\frac{N_1 + N_2}{N_1 N_2}\right)}$$

$$t = \bar{X}_1 - \bar{X}_2 / s_{\bar{X}_1 - \bar{X}_2}$$

$$s_D = \sqrt{\frac{\Sigma D^2}{N} - (\bar{X}_1 - \bar{X}_2)^2}$$

$$s_{\bar{D}} = \frac{s_D}{\sqrt{N-1}}$$

$$t = \frac{\bar{X}_1 - \bar{X}_2}{s_D}$$

$$z = \frac{P_1 - P_2}{s_{P_1 - P_2}}$$

$$s_{P_1 - P_2} = \sqrt{P^*(1 - P^*)\left(\frac{N_1 + N_2}{N_1 N_2}\right)}$$

$$SS_{\text{total}} = SS_{\text{between}} + SS_{\text{within}}$$

$$SS_{\text{total}} = \Sigma\,(X - \bar{X}_{\text{total}})^2$$

$$SS_{\text{within}} = \Sigma\,(X - \bar{X}_{\text{group}})^2$$

$$SS_{between} = \Sigma \, N_{group} \, (\overline{X}_{group} - \overline{X}_{total})^2$$

$$SS_{total} = \Sigma \, X^2_{total} - N_{total} \, \overline{X}^2_{total}$$

$$SS_{within} = \Sigma \, X^2_{total} - \Sigma \, N_{group} \, \overline{X}^2_{group}$$

$$SS_{between} = \Sigma \, N_{group} \, \overline{X}^2_{group} - N_{total} \, \overline{X}^2_{total}$$

$$MS_{between} = \frac{SS_{between}}{df_{between}}$$

$$MS_{within} = \frac{SS_{within}}{df_{within}}$$

$$F = \frac{MS_{between}}{MS_{within}}$$

$$HSD = q \sqrt{\frac{MS_{within}}{N_{group}}}$$

$$\chi^2 = \Sigma \frac{(f_o - f_e)^2}{f_e}$$

$$\chi^2 = \Sigma \, \frac{(|f_o - f_e| - .5)^2}{f_e}$$

$$U = N_1 N_2 + \frac{N_1(N_1 + 1)}{2} - \Sigma \, R_1$$

$$U' = N_1 N_2 + \frac{N_2(N_2 + 1)}{2} - \Sigma \, R_2$$

$$z = \frac{U - \dfrac{N_1 N_2}{2}}{\sqrt{\dfrac{N_1 N_2 (N_1 + N_2 + 1)}{12}}}$$

$$H = \frac{12}{N(N + 1)} \Sigma \left[\frac{(\Sigma R_i)^2}{n} \right] - 3 \, (N + 1)$$

$$r = \frac{SP}{\sqrt{SS_X \, SS_Y}}$$

$$r = \frac{\Sigma \, (X - \overline{X})(Y - \overline{Y})}{\sqrt{\Sigma \, (X - \overline{X})^2 \, (Y - \overline{Y})^2}}$$

$$r = \frac{\Sigma \, XY - N\overline{X}\overline{Y}}{\sqrt{(\Sigma X^2 - N\overline{X}^2)(\Sigma Y^2 - N\overline{Y}^2)}}$$

$$t = \frac{r\sqrt{N-2}}{\sqrt{1-r^2}}$$

$$r_{XY.Z} = \frac{r_{XY} - r_{XZ}\, r_{YZ}}{\sqrt{1-r_{XZ}^2}\ \sqrt{1-r_{YZ}^2}}$$

$$r_s = 1 - \frac{6\,\Sigma\, D^2}{N(N^2-1)}$$

$$G = \frac{N_a - N_i}{N_a - N_i}$$

$$z = G\sqrt{\frac{N_a + N_i}{N(1-G^2)}}$$

$$\phi = \sqrt{\frac{\chi^2}{N}}$$

$$C = \sqrt{\frac{\chi^2}{N + \chi^2}}$$

$$V = \sqrt{\frac{\chi^2}{N(k-1)}}$$

$$\lambda = \frac{F_{iv} - M_{dv}}{N - M_{dv}}$$

$$Y = a + bX + e$$

$$b = \frac{\text{SP}}{\text{SS}_X}$$

$$b = \frac{\Sigma\,(X-\overline{X})\,(Y-\overline{Y})}{\Sigma\,(X-\overline{X})^2}$$

$$b = \frac{\Sigma\,XY - N\overline{X}\,\overline{Y}}{\Sigma\,X^2 - N\overline{X}^2}$$

$$a = \overline{Y} - b\overline{X}$$

$$\hat{Y} = a + bX$$

$$e = Y - \hat{Y}$$

$$\text{SS}_{\text{error}} = \Sigma(Y - \hat{Y})^2$$

$$SS_{total} = \Sigma(Y - \overline{Y})^2$$

$$SS_{reg} = SS_{total} - SS_{error}$$

$$r^2 = \frac{SS_{total} - SS_{error}}{SS_{total}}$$

$$1 - r^2 = \frac{SS_{error}}{SS_{total}}$$

$$MS_{reg} = \frac{SS_{reg}}{df_{reg}}$$

$$MS_{error} = \frac{SS_{error}}{df_{error}}$$

$$F = \frac{MS_{reg}}{MS_{error}}$$

$$R^2 = \frac{r_{YX}^2 + r_{YZ}^2 - 2r_{YX}r_{YZ}r_{XZ}}{1 - r_{XZ}^2}$$

GLOSSARY

accidental sampling   A nonrandom sampling method whereby the researcher includes the most convenient cases in his or her sample.

addition rule   The probability of obtaining any one of several different outcomes equals the sum of their separate probabilities.

alpha   The probability of commiting a Type I Error.

analysis of variance   A statistical test that makes a single overall decision as to whether a significant difference is present among three or more sample means.

area under the normal curve   That area which lies between the curve and the base line containing 100% or all of the cases in any given normal distribution.

bar graph (histogram)   A graphic method in which rectangular bars indicate the frequencies for the range of score values or categories.

between-groups sum of squares   The sum of the squared deviations of every sample mean from the total mean.

bimodal distribution   A frequency distribution containing two or more modes.

central tendency   What is average or typical of a set of data; a value generally located toward the middle or center of a distribution.

chi-square   A nonparametric test of significance whereby expected frequencies are compared against observed frequencies.

class interval   A category in a group distribution containing more than one score value.

class limit   The point midway between adjacent class intervals that serves to close the gap between them.

coefficient of determination   Equal to the Pearson's correlation squared, the proportion of variance in the dependent variable that is explained by the indepedent variable.

coeficient of nondetermination   Equal to one minus the Pearson's correlation squared, the proportion of variance in the dependent variable that is not explained by the independent variable.

column percent   In a cross-tabulation, the result of dividing a cell frequency by the number of cases in the column. Column percents sum to 100 percent for each column of a cross-tabulation.

confidence interval   The range of mean values (proportions) within which the true population mean (proportion) is likely to fall.

contingency coefficient   Based on chi-square, a measure of the degree of association for nominal data arranged in a table larger than 2×2.

converse rule   The probability of an event not occurring equals one minus the probability that it does.

correlation   The strength and direction of the relationship between two variables.

correlation coefficient   Generally ranging between -1.00 and $+1.00$, a number in which both the strength and direction of correlation are expressed.

Cramér's V   An alternative to the contingency coefficient that measures the degree of association for nominal data arranged in a table larger than 2×2.

critical region (rejection region)   The area in the tail(s) of a sampling distribution that dictates that the null hypothesis be rejected.

cross-tabulation   A frequency and percent table of two or more variables taken together.

cumulative frequency   The total number of cases having any given score or a score that is lower.

cumulative frequency polygon   A graphic method in which cumulative frequencies or cumulative percentages are depicted.

cumulative percentage   The percent of cases having any score or a score that is lower.

curvilinear correlation   A relationship between X and Y that begins as either positive or negative and then reverses direction.

deciles   Percentile ranks that divide the 100-unit scale by 10s.

degrees of freedom   In small sample comparisons, a statistical compensation for the failure of the sampling distribution of differences to assume the shape of the normal curve.

deviation   The distance and direction of any raw score from the mean.

elaboration   The process of controlling a two-variable cross-tabulation for additional variables.

error term (disturbance term)   The residual portion of a score that cannot be predicted by the independent variable. Also the distance of a point from the regression line.

expected frequencies   The cell frequencies expected under the terms of the null hypothesis for chi-square.

F ratio   The result of an analysis of variance, a statistical technique that indicates the size of the between-groups mean square relative to the size of the within-groups mean square.

five precent level (0.5) of significance   A level of probability at which the null hypothesis is rejected if an obtained sample difference occurs by chance only 5 times or less out of 100.

frequency distribution   A table containing the categories, score values, or class intervals and their frequency of occurrence.

frequency polygon   A graphic method in which frequencies are indicated by a series of points placed over the score values or midpoints of each class interval and connected with a straight line that is dropped to the base line at either end.

Goodman's and Kruskal's gamma   An alternative to the rank-order correlation coefficient for measuring the degree of association between ordinal-level variables.

grouped frequency distribution   A table that indicates the frequency of occurrence of cases located within a series of class intervals.

hypothesis   An idea about the nature of social reality that is testable through systematic research.

independent outcomes   Two outcomes or events are independent if the probability of one occurring is unchanged by whether the other occurs.

interval level of measurement   The process of assigning a score to cases so that the magnitude of differences between them is know and meaningful.

judgment sampling (purposive sampling)   A nonrandom sampling method whereby logic, common sense, or sound judgment is used to select a sample that is presumed representative of a larger population.

Kruskal-Wallis one-way analysis of variance by ranks   A nonparametric alternative to the analysis of variance that is employed to compare several independent samples but that requires only ordinal-level data.

kurtosis   The peakedness of a distribution.

lambda   A measure association for nominal data that indicates the degree to which we can reduce the error in predicting values of one variable from values of another.

leptokurtic   Characteristic of a distribution that is quite peaked or tall.

level of confidence   How certain we are that a confidence interval covers the true population mean (proportion).

level of significance   A level of probability at which the null hypothesis can be rejected and the research hypothesis can be accepted.

line chart   A graph of the differences between groups or trends across time on some variable(s).

Mann-Whitney U test   A nonparametric alternative to the t ratio, that is employed to compare two independent samples but requires only ordinal-level data.

margin of error   The extent of imprecision expected when estimating the population mean or proportion, obtained by multiplying the standard error times the table value of z or t.

marginal distribution   In a cross-tabulation, the set of frequencies and percents found in the margin that represents the distribution of one of the variables in the table.

mean   The sum of a set of scores divided by the total number of scores in the set. A measure of central tendency.

mean deviation   The sum of the absolute deviations from the mean divided by the number of scores in a distribution. A measure of variability that indicates the average of deviations from the mean.

mean square   A measure of variation used in an F test obtained by dividing the between-group sum of squares or within-group sum of squares (in analysis of variance) or the regression sum of squares or error sum of squares (in regression analysis) by the appropriate degrees of freedom.

measurement   The use of a series of numbers in the data analysis stage of research.

median   The middlemost point in a frequency distribution. A measure of central tendency.

median test   A nonparametric test of significance for determining the probability that two random samples have been drawn from populations with the same median.

mesokurtic   Characteristic of a distribution that is neither very peaked nor very flat.

midpoint   The middlemost score value in a class interval.

mode   The most frequent, typical, or common value in a distribution.

multiple coefficient of determination   The proportional of variance in the dependent variable that is explained by the set of independent variables in combination.

multiplication rule   The probability of obtaining a combination of independent outcomes equals the product of their separate probabilities.

multistage sampling   A random sampling method whereby sample members are selected on a random basis from a number of well-delineated areas known as clusters (or primary sampling units).

mutually exclusive outcomes   Two outcomes or events are mutually exclusive if the occurrence of one rules out the possibility that the other will occur.

negative correlation   The direction of relationship wherein individuals who score high on the X variable score low on the Y variable; individuals who score low on the X variable score high on the Y variable.

negatively skewed distribution   A distribution in which more respondents receive high than low scores, resulting in a longer tail on the left than on the right.

95% confidence interval   The range of mean values (proportions) within which there are 95 chances out of 100 that the true population mean (proportion) will fall.

99% confidence interval   The range of mean values (proportions) within which there are 99 chances out of 100 that the true population mean (proportion) will fall.

nominal level of measurement   The process of placing cases into categories and counting their frequency of occurrence.

nonparametric test   A statistical procedure that makes no assumptions about the way the character being studied is distributed in the population and requires only ordinal or nominal data.

nonrandom sampling   A sampling method whereby each and every population member does not have an equal chance of being drawn into the sample.

normal curve   A smooth, symmetrical distribution that is bell-shaped and unimodal.

null hypothesis   The hypothesis of equal population means. Any observed difference between samples is seen as a chance occurrence resulting from sampling error.

observed frequencies   In a chi-square analysis, the results that are actually observed when conducting a study.

one percent (.01) level of significance   A level of probability at which the null hypothesis is rejeted if an obtained sample difference occurs by chance only 1 time or less out of 100.

one-tailed test   A test in which the null hypothesis is rejected for large differences in only one direction.

ordinal level of measurement   The process of ordering or ranking cases in terms of the degree to which they have any given characteristic.

parametric test   A statistical procedure that requires that the characteristic studied by normally distributed in the population and that the researcher have interval data.

partial correlation coefficient   The correlation between two variables when one or more other variables are controlled.

Pearson's correlation coefficient   A correlation coefficient for interval data.

percentage   A method of standardizing for size that indicates the frequency of occurrence of a category per 100 cases.

percentage distribution   The relative frequency of occurrency of a set of scores or class intervals.

percentile rank   A single number that indicates the percent of cases in a distribution falling below any given score.

phi coefficient   Based on chi-square, a measure of the degree of association for nominal data arranged in a 2×2 table.

pie chart   A circular graph whose pieces add up to 100%.

platykurtic   Characteristic of a distribution that is rather flat.

population (universe)   Any set of individuals who share at least one characteristic.

positive correlation   The direction of a relationship wherein individuals who score high on the X variable also score high on the Y variable; individuals who score low on the X variable also score low on the Y variable.

positively skewed distribution   A distribution in which more respondents receive low than high scores, resulting in a longer tail on the right than on the left.

power of a test   The ability of a statistical test to reject the null hypothesis when it is actually false and should be rejected.

primary sampling unit (cluster)   In multistage sampling, a well-delineated area considered to include characteristics found in the entire population.

probability   The relative frequency of occurrency of an event or outcome. The number of times any given event could occur out of 100.

proportion   A method for standardizing for size that compares the number of cases in any given category with the total number of cases in the distribution.

quartiles   Percentile ranks that divide the 100-unit scale by 25s.

quota sampling   A nonrandom sampling method whereby diverse characteristics of a population are sampled in the proportions they occupy in the population.

random sampling   A sampling method whereby each and every population member has an equal chance of being drawn into the sample.

range   The difference between the highest and lowest scores in a distribution. A measure of variability.

rate   A kind of ratio that indicates a camparison between the number of actual cases and the number of potential cases.

ratio   A method of standardizing for size that compares the number of cases falling into one category with the number of cases falling into another category.

regression analysis   A technique employed in predicting values of one variable (Y) from knowledge of values of another variable (X).

regression line   A straight line drawn through the scatter plot that represents the best possible fit for making predictions of Y from X.

research hypothesis   The hypothesis that regards any observed difference between samples as reflecting a true population difference and not just sampling error.

row percent   In a cross-tabulation, the result of dividing a cell frequency by the number of cases in the row. Row percents sum to 100% for each row of a cross-tabulation.

sample   A smaller number of individuals taken from some population (for the purpose of generalizing to the entire population from which it was taken).

sampling distribution of differences between means   A frequency distribution of a large number of differences between random sample means that have been drawn from a given population.

sampling distribution of means   A frequency distribution of a large number of random sample means that have been drawn from the same population.

sampling error   The inevitable difference between a random sample and its population based on chance alone.

scatter plot   A graph that show the way scores on any two variables X and Y are scattered throughout the range of possible score values.

simple random sampling   A random sampling method whereby a table of random numbers is employed to select a sample that is representative of a larger population.

skewness   Departure from symmetry.

slope   In regression, the change in the regression line for a unit increase in X. The slope is interpreted as the change in the Y variable associated with a unit change in the X variable.

Spearman's rank-order correlation coefficient   A correlation coefficient for data that have been ranked or ordered with respect to the presence of a given characteristic.

spurious relationship   A noncausal relationship between two variables that exists only because of the common influence of a third variable. The spurious relationship disappears if the third variable is held constant.

standard deviation   The square root of the mean of the squared deviations from the mean of a distribution. A measure of variability that reflects the typical deviation from the mean.

standard error of the difference between means   An estimate of the standard deviation of the sampling distribution of differences based on the standard deviations of two random samples.

standard error of the mean   An estimate of the standard deviation of the sampling distribution of means based on the standard deviation of a single random sample.

standard error of the proportion   An estimate of the standard deviation of the sampling distribution of proportions based on the proportion obtained in a single random sample.

statistically significant difference   A sample difference that reflects a real population difference and not just a sampling error.

straight-line correlation   Either a positive or negative correlation, so that the points in a scatter diagram tend to form a straight line through the center of the graph.

stratified sampling   A random sampling method whereby the population is first divided into homogeneous subgroups from which simple random samples are then drawn.

strength of correlation   Degree of association between two variables.

sum of squares   The sum of squared deviations from a mean.

systematic sampling   A random sampling method whereby every nth member of a population is included in the sample.

t **ratio**   A statistical technique that indicates the direction and degree that a sample mean difference falls from zero on a scale of standard error units.

total percent   In a cross-tabulation, the result of dividing a cell frequency by the total number of cases in the sample. Total percents sum to 100% for the entire cross-tabulation.

total sum of squares   The sum of the squared deviations of every raw score from the total mean of the study.

Tukey's HSD (honestly significant difference)   A procedure for the multiple comparison of means after a significant F ratio has been obtained.

two-tailed test   A test that is used when the null hypothesis is rejected for large differences in both directions.

Type I error   The error of rejecting the null hypothesis when it is true.

Type II error   The error of accepting the null hypothesis when it is false.

unimodal distribution   A frequency distribution containing a single mode.

unit of observation   The element that is being studied or observed. Individuals are most often the unit of observation, but sometimes collections or aggregates—such as families, census tracts, or states—are the unit of observation.

variability   The manner in which the scores are scattered around the center of the distribution. Also known as dispersion or spread.

variable   Any characteristic that varies from one individual to another. Hypotheses usually contain an independent variable (cause) and a dependent variable (effect).

variance   The mean of the squared deviations from the mean of a distribution. A measure of variability in a distribution.

within-groups sum of squares   The sum of the squared deviations of every raw score from its sample group mean.

Y-**intercept**   In regression, the point where the regression line crosses the *Y* axis. The *Y*-intercept is the predicted value of *Y* for an *X* value of zero.

Yates's correction   In the chi-square analysis, a factor for small expected frequencies that reduces the overestimate of the chi-square value and yields a more conservative result (only for 2×2 tables).

z **score (standard score)**   A value that indicates the direction and degree that any given raw score deviates from the mean of a distribution on a scale of standard deviation units.

z **score for sample mean differences**   A value that indicates the direction and degree that any given sample mean difference fals from zero (the mean of the sampling distribution of differences) on a scale of standard deviation units.

ANSWERS TO SELECTED PROBLEMS

CHAPTER 1

1. (a) Content analysis; gender; language used in police reports; (b) Experiment; exposure to televised violence; violent behavior; (c) Participant observation; team winning or losing; fan violence; (d) Survey; education level; approval of trying juveniles as adults

2. (a) Nominal; (b) Interval; (c) Interval; (d) Ordinal; (e) Interval; (f) Nominal; (g) Ordinal; (h) Nominal; (i) Ordinal, or interval if one assumes equal intervals between points on scale. (j) Ordinal, or interval if one assumes equal intervals between points on scale.

3. (a) Interval; (b) Interval; (c) Ordinal; (d) Nominal; (e) Nominal; (f) Ordinal; (g) Interval; (h) Ordinal

4. Survey; home environment; gang leadership

5. Experiment; rehabilitation program participation; arrest subsequent to release from prison

CHAPTER 2

1. (a) 49%; (b) 27%; (c) $P = .73$; (d) $P = .51$
2. (a) 53%; (b) 74%; (c) $P = .53$; (d) $P = .74$

3. $\frac{24}{4} = \frac{6}{1}$
4. 156.25
5. $\frac{15}{20} = \frac{3}{4}$
6. There are 85.71 rapes per every 1,000 women.
7. 66.67%
8. (a) 3; (b) 9.5–12.5, 6.5–9.5, 3.5–6.5, .5–3.5; (c) m: 11, 8, 5, 2; (d) %: 27.5, 40.0, 22.5, 10.0; (e) cf: 40, 29, 13, 4; (f) $c\%$: 100, 72.5, 32.5, 10.0
9. (a) 2; (b) 98.5–100.5, 96.5–98.5, 94.5–96.5, 92.5-94.5, 90.5–92.5; (c) m, 99.5, 97.5, 95.5, 93.5, 91.5; (d) %, 15.6, 25.0, 34.4, 17.2, 7.8; (e) cf, 64, 54, 38, 16, 5; (f) $c\%$, 100, 84.4, 59.4, 25.0, 7.8
10. (a) 59.38; (b) 14.59
11. (a) 84.82; (b) 29.64
12. 10.94
13. (a) Social class is the independent variable; crime victim is the dependent variable; (b) 77.5%, 22.5%, 100.0%, 42.7%, 57.3%, 100.0%, 22.0%, 78.0%, 100.0%, 50.0%, 50.0%, 100.0%; (c) 50.0%; (d) 50.0%; (e) 22.5%; (f) 42.7%; (g) Lower class; (h) Upper class; (i) The higher the social class, the lower the chance of victimization.

14. (a) Independent variable is prediction of violence; dependent variable is actual violence;
(b) Left column 11.4%, 88.6%. Right column:
1.4%, 98.6%; (c) 2.5%; (d) 11.0%; (e) 11.4%;
(f) 1.4%; (g) 50.0%; (h) 10.0%; (i) Predictions
are not very accurate.

15.

x	f	%	c%
2	2	40	40
4	1	20	60
5	1	20	80
7	1	20	100

16. (a)

Class Interval	f	%	cf	c%
1.0–1.4	7	23.00	30	100.00
.5–.9	14	47.00	23	77.00
.0–.4	9	30.00	9	30.00
Total	71	100.00		

(b) upper limit = 1.45, lower limit = .95;
(c) upper limit = .95, lower limit = .45;
(d) .2; (e) 77%; yes (25/30, 83%); the highest
class interval has a lower limit of .95, thus
including 2 cases under 1.0 HMR (.96 and .98).

17. (a) Draw pie chart; (b) Draw pie chart; (c) Draw
pie chart.

18. (a) Draw bar graph; (b) Draw bar graph.

19. Draw a cumulative frequency polygon.

20. Draw a bar graph and a line chart.

21. Use blank map to display data on bombing
incidents.

CHAPTER 3

1. (a) medium security; (b) medium security;
(c) level of measurement is ordinal.

2. Room number: mode = 203
Attending physician: mode = Pollock and
Lench
Patient condition: median = fair
Length of stay: mean = 4.78 days

3. (a) 2 times; (b) 2.55 times

4. (a) 3 years; (b) 4 years; (c) 11 years;
(d) Median, because of the skewness of the distribution.

5. (a) 2; (b) 3; (c) 4
6. (a) 6; (b) 7; (c) 7.29
7. (a) 6; (b) 7.50; (c) 7.88
8. (a) 6; (b) 5.5; (c) 5; (d) Students were moderately favorable toward diversity.
9. deviations from mean: $-7; -6; -8; -8; +29$
10. (a) -2.80; (b) -7.80; (c) 6.20; (d) 3.2.
11. (a) Mo = 2; Mdn = 2; Mean = 2.2
(b)

Children	f
6	1
5	1
4	2
3	3
2	6
1	4
0	3

Mo = 2; Mdn = 2; Mean = 2.2
12. (a) Mo = 4; (b) Mdn = 4; (c) Mean = 4.23
13. (a) Mo = 6; (b) Mdn = 6; (c) Mean = 6.26
14. (a) 31; (b) -8; (c) 0; (d) -17;
15. (a) 5; (b) 5; (c) 4.68
16. (a) Mo = 84.5; (b) Mdn = 82.4;
(c) Mean = 80.39
17. (a) 8, 7.5, 6.8; (b) 5, 5.5, 5.6; (c) Knowledge
18. Mean = 15.33; Mdn = 14; Mo = 13
19. Ordinal; Median and mode = completed high
school; can't compute mean using ordinal data.

CHAPTER 4

1. (a) a; (b) b
2. (a) 3 weeks; (b) .67; (c) 1.00; (d) 1.00
3. (a) $A = 5; B = 3$; (b) $A = 1.67; B = 1.00$;
(c) $A = 1.89; B = 1.11$; Class A has greater
variability of attitude scores.
4. (a) 12; (b) 12.86; (c) 3.59
5. (a) 6; (b) 1.52; (c) 3.24, 1.80
6. (a) 7; (b) 1.22; (c) 4.24, 2.06
7. (a) 9; (b) 2.24; (c) 7.35, 2.71
8. (a) 13; (b) 4.16; (c) 22.16, 4.71
9. 1.19

10. 2.37, 1.54

11. 1.90, 1.38

12. 155.01, 12.45

13. 37.76, 6.14

14. 284.49, 16.87

15. 7, 2.44, 3.01, 9.07

16. 2.08, 4.34

17. 115, 85

CHAPTER 5

1. (a) .5; (b) .6; (c) .7; (d) .8

2. .03

3. (a) .5; (b) .2; (c) .1; (d) .4; (e) .4; (f) .1

4. (a) .10; (b) .10; (c) .90; (d) .01; (e) .04; (f) .0004

5. (a) .5; (b) .3; (c) .7; (d) .027

6. (a) .0192; (b) .0385; (c) .0769; (d) .5; (e) .2308; (f) .3077; (g) .3077

7. (a) .25; (b) .25; (c) .50; (d) .0059; (e) .0947

8. (a) .4; (b) .36

9. (a) .98; (b) .96; (c) .94; (d) .92

10. (a) 34.13%; (b) 68.26%; (c) 47.72%; (d) 95.44%

11. (a) 34.13%

    (b) 68.26%

    (c) 47.72%

    (d) 95.44%

    (e) 15.87%

    (f) 2.28%

12. (a) $z = 0$; (b) $z = -1.00$; (c) $z = 1.50$; (d) $z = 0.75$; (e) $z = 2.50$; (f) $z = -1.20$

13. (a) 50.00%; (b) 15.87%; (c) 43.32%; (d) 22.66%; (e) 98.76%; (f) 88.49%

14. (a) 40.82%; (b) $P = .41$; (c) 28.81%; (d) $P = .29$; (e) 25.14%; (f) $P = .25$; (g) $P = .06$; (h) 95th percentile

15. (a) 11.51%; (b) $P = .12$; (c) 28.81%; (d) $P = .29$; (e) 34.46%; (f) $P = .34$; (g) $P = .42$; (h) $P = .25$; (i) $P = .07$

16. (a) 4.01%; (b) $P = .0401$ (c) $P = .0016$

17. (a) 6.68%; (b) 98%, 2.28%; (c) .003%, $P = .00003$

18. (a) $P = .11$; (b) $P = .00002$; (c) Because the probability of randomly selecting five cars with an MPG of 20 or below was less than .05, the company's MPG claim appears to be invalid.

19. (a) .3849; (b) .1151

20. (a) .3944; (9b) .1056; (c) .0012

CHAPTER 6

1. 1.8

2. (a) 9.47–16.53; (b) 8.36–17.64

3. (a) 1.72; (b) 9.33–16.67; (c) 7.93–18.07

4. .27

5. (a) 2.38–3.48; (b) 2.18–3.68

6. (a) 7.35; (b) 2.80; (c) .64; (d) 2.86; (e) 5.51 to 9.19

7. 35

8. (a) 5.08–6.51; (b) 4.83–6.76

9. .39

10. (a) 4.20–5.80; (b) 3.93–6.07

11. (a) .24; (b) 5.51–6.49; (c) 5.34–6.66

12. 16.16–17.44

13. 33.69–42.31

14. (a) 1.22; (b) 39.47–44; (c) 38.59–45.41

15. (a) .0679; (b) .23–.49

16. (a) .0243; (b) .33–.43; (c) .32–.44

17. (a) .014; (b) .42–.48; (c) .41–.49

18. (a) .04; (b) .54–.70; (c) .52–.72

19. Confidence interval of 50% to 58%. Not justified in predicting referendum will pass at .05 level of probability, because confidence intervals for the two candidates overlap at 50%.

20. 2.71–3.29

21. .516–5.084

CHAPTER 7

1. $P = .07$

2. $t = 2.5$, $df = 78$, reject the null hypothesis at .05.

3. $t = 1.48$, $df = 6$, accept the null hypothesis at .05.

4. $t = -0.93$, $df = 16$, accept the null hypothesis at .05.

5. $t = 2.43$, $df = 8$, reject the null hypothesis at .05.

6. $t = -2.98$, $df = 8$, reject the null hypothesis at .05.

7. $t = 1.90$, $df = 13$, accept the null hypothesis at .05.

8. $t = -0.67$, $df = 8$, accept the null hypothesis at .05.

9. $t = 1.97$, $df = 12$, reject the null hypothesis at .05.

10. $t = -2.97$, $df = 4$, reject the null hypothesis at .05.

11. $t = -6.00$, $df = 4$, reject the null hypothesis at .05.

12. $t = -3.75$, $df = 9$, reject the null hypothesis at .05.

13. $z = 3.77$, reject the null hypothesis at .05.

14. $z = -.60$, accept the null hypothesis at .05.

15. $z = -.55$, accept the null hypothesis at .05.

16. $z = -1.37$, accept the null hypothesis at .05.

17. $z = 1.56$, accept the null hypothesis at .05.

18. $z = 4.49$, accept the null hypothesis at .05.

19. $t = 0$, $df = 10$. No significant gender difference. Accept null hypothesis.

20. $t = 3.12$, $df = 7$. indicating that the film was effective in reducing racist attitude scores. Reject null hypothesis.

21. $t = 4.76$, $df = 18$. High anomie areas have significantly higher suicide rates than low anomie areas. Reject null hypothesis.

22. $t = 4.02$, $df = 9$. Aggression declined significantly after participating in the program. Reject null hypothesis.

23. $t = -2.85$, $df = 18$. The two judges differed significantly. Reject null hypothesis.

24. $t = 2.05$, $df = 18$. Those completing the customary course had significantly higher scores than those completing the new course, so the null hypothesis stating that the new course would be no better than the old is accepted.

25. $t = -.59$, $df = 9$. The anti-drug lecture did not significantly affect student attitudes. Accept null hypothesis.

CHAPTER 8

1. $F = 2.72$, $df = 3$, 12, accept the null hypothesis at .05.

2. $F = 46.33$, $df = 2$, 9, reject the null hypothesis at .05.

3. HSD $= 1.71$, all mean differences are significant.

4. (a) $\bar{x}_A = 11$; $\bar{x}_B = 10.8$; $\bar{x}_C = 18$
   (b) $SS_{total} = 197.61$; $SS_{between} = 166.81$; $SS_{within} = 30.8$; (c) $df_{between} = 2$; $df_{within} = 12$;
   (d) $MS_{between} = 83.41$; $MS_{within} = 2.57$;
   (e) 32.46; (f) 3.88; (g) reject H_O

5. (a)

	$\bar{x}_2$	$\bar{x}_1$	$\bar{x}_3$
$\bar{x}_2$		.2	7.2
$\bar{x}_1$			7
$\bar{x}_3$			

(b) 3.77; (c) 2.70; (d) $\bar{x}_1$ vs. $\bar{x}_3$ and $\bar{x}_2$ vs. $\bar{x}_3$; $\bar{x}_1$ vs. $\bar{x}_3$

(e) Adding lighting (A) and changing the type of existing lighting (B) are both equally effective in increasing residents' feelings of safety (these means do not differ significantly from each other), and both adding lighting and changing the type of existing lighting are each significantly different than not changing the lighting (C).

6. $F = 13.14$, $df = 2$, 21, reject the null hypothesis at .05.

7. HSD $= 1.85$, the mean of group 3 differs significantly from the means of groups 1 and 2.

8. (a) $F = 1.97$, critical $F = 3.88$, not significant

9. Since the F is not significant, Tukey's HSD is inappropriate.

10. $F = 11.41$, $df = 2, 12$, reject the null hypothesis at .05.

11. HSD $= 2.54$, the mean of group 3 differs significantly from the means of groups 1 and 2.

12. $F = 19.73$, $df = 2, 12$, reject null hypothesis at .05.

13. $F = 122.85$, $df = 2, 12$, reject null hypothesis at .05.

14. HSD $= 13.43$, the mean of group 3 differs significantly from the means of groups 1 and 2.

CHAPTER 9

1. $x^2 = 8.80$, $df = 3$, reject the null hypothesis at .05.

2. $x^2 = 3.90$, $df = 2$, accept the null hypothesis at .05.

3. $\chi^2 = 8.29$, $df = 1$, reject the null hypothesis at .05.

4. $\chi^2 = 2.17$, $df = 1$, accept the null hypothesis at .05.

5. $\chi^2 = .09$, $df = 1$, accept the null hypothesis at .05.

6. $\chi^2 = 3.42$, $df = 4$, accept the null hypothesis at .05.

7. $\chi^2 = 5.56$, $df = 3$, accept the null hypothesis at .05.

8. $\chi^2 = 3.29$, $df = 3$, accept the null hypothesis at .05.

9. $\chi^2 = .0046$, $df = 1$, accept the null hypothesis at .05.

10. $\chi^2 = 17.74$, $df = 3$, reject the null hypothesis at .05.

11. $\chi^2 = 10.97$, $df = 4$, reject the null hypothesis at .05.

12. Table 9.5—$\chi^2 = 18.31$, $df = 3$, significant at .05. Table 9.6—$\chi^2 = 11.91$, $df = 2$, significant at .05.

13. Mdn $= 5$, $\chi^2 = 2.07$, $df = 1$, accept the null hypothesis at .05.

14. Mdn $= 6$, $\chi^2 = 19.57$, $df = 1$, reject the null hypothesis at .05.

15. $U = 5.0$, reject the null hypothesis at .05.

16. $U = 16.5$, reject the null hypothesis at .05.

17. $H = 4.92$, $df = 2$, accept the null hypothesis at .05.

18. $H = 3.63$, $df = 2$, accept the null hypothesis at .05.

CHAPTER 10

1. $r = .85$, $df = 4$, significant at .05.

2. $r = -.64$, $df = 2$, not significant at .05.

3. $r = .84$, $df = 8$, significant at .05

4. $r = .62$, $df = 8$, not significant at .05

5. $r = -.69$, $df = 10$, significant at .05.

6. $r = .68$, $df = 6$, not significant at .05.

7. $r = .69$, $df = 8$, significant at .05.

8. $r = .61$, $df = 6$, not significant at .05.

9. $r = -.72$, $df = 8$, significant at .05.

10. $r_{XY} = -.69$, $r_{XZ} = .84$, $r_{YZ} = -.61$, $r_{XY.Z} -.42$

11. $r_{XY} = .68$, $r_{XZ} = .42$, $r_{YZ} = .87$, $r_{XY.Z} = .63$

12. (a) r_{XY} and r_{YZ} are significant at .05; (b) $r_{XY.Z} = .58$

CHAPTER 11

1. (a) Draw a scatter plot. (b) $b = -.41$, $a = 7.58$; (c) $\hat{Y} = 7.58 - .41X$; (d) $\hat{Y} = 3.07$; (e) $r^2 = .75$, $1 - r^2 = .25$

(f) Source	SS	df	MS	F
Regression	17.78	1	17.78	24.43($p < .05$)
Error	5.82	8	.73	
Total	23.60	9		

2. (a) Draw a scatter plot. (b) $b = .98$, $a = 3.91$; (c) $\hat{Y} = 3.91 + .98X$; (d) $\hat{Y} = 3.91, 5.87$; (e) $r^2 = .35$, $1 - r^2 = .65$

(f) Source	SS	df	MS	F
Regression	11.01	1	11.01	3.16 not sig.
Error	20.87	6	3.48	
Total	31.88	7		

3. (a) Draw a scatter plot. (b) $b = 1.03$, $a = 1.91$; (c) $\hat{Y} = 1.91 + 1.03X$; (d) $\hat{Y} = 8.09$; (e) $r^2 = .41$, $1 - r^2 = .59$

(f)

Source	SS	df	MS	F
Regression	34.03	1	34.03	5.45$(p < .05)$
Error	49.97	8	6.25	
Total	84.00	9		

4. (a) Draw a scatter plot. (b) $b = .46$, $a = 12.66$; (c) $\hat{Y} = 12.66 + .46X$; (d) $\hat{Y} = \$14.50$; (e) $r^2 = .40$, $1 - r^2 = .60$

(f)

Source	SS	df	MS	F
Regression	6.73	1	6.73	5.30 $(p < .05)$
Error	10.17	8	1.27	
Total	16.90	9		

(g) The average wage per hour when a secretary begins employment is $12.66; each additional year on the job typically earns an employee $.46

5. (a) Draw a scatter plot. (b) $b = .48$, $a = .84$; (c) $\hat{Y} - .84 + .48X$ (d) $\hat{Y} = 2.28$ (e) $r^2 = .59$, $1 - r^2 = .41$.

(f)

Source	SS	df	MS	F
Regression	13.52	1	13.52	17.37
Error	9.34	12	.78	
Total	22.86	13		

6. (a) Draw a scatter plot; (b) $b = .79$, $a = .29$; (c) $\hat{Y} = .29 - .79X$; (d) $\hat{Y} = 2.65$; (e) $r^2 = .60$, $1 - r^2 = .40$.

(f)

Source	SS	df	MS	F
Regression	2.37	1	2.37	14.84
Error	1.59	10	.16	
Total	3.96	11		

7. $R^2 = .86$, $1 - R^2 = .14$

8. $r^2_{XY} = .36$, $r^2_{YZ} = .09$, $R^2 = .39$

CHAPTER 12

1. $r_s = -.53$, $N = 5$, not significant at .05.

2. $r_s = .86$, $N = 10$, significant at .05.

3. $r_s = -.82$, $N = 8$, significant at .05.

4. $r_s = -.71$, $N = 10$, significant at .05.

5. $r_s = .33$. Not necessary, since it is a total enumeration of a population and not a random sample from one.

6. $G = .35$, $z = 1.92$, not significant at .05.

7. $G = -.30$, $z = 1.17$, not significant at .05.

8. $G = -.39$, $z = 1.15$, not significant at .05.

9. phi $= .53$

10. $x^2 = .37$

11. $\lambda = .07$, .08, College major has slightly greater predictive ability.

12. If a person's attitude toward drug legalization is known, gender can be predicted about 28% correctly; using gender as the independent variable in predicting attitudes, we reduce the error of our prediction by .13; Y.

13. $V = .38$, $\chi^2 = 23.53$, significant at .05.

14. $V = .17$, $\chi^2 = 2.08$, not significant at .05.

INDEX

Aggregate, 2
Alpha, 191–196
Analysis of variance
    F ratio, 233–241
    logic, 223–225
    mean square, 231–232
    multiple comparison of means,
       238–240
    requirements, 233–234
    sum of squares, 225–231

Bar graph, 51–57
Becker, Howard S, 5
Bureau of Justice Statistics, 5, 388

Cavender, Gray, 4
Central tendency
    comparison of measures, 74–78
    mean, 71–73
    median, 70–71
    mode, 69–70
Chi-square
    comparing several groups,
       260–265
    degrees of freedom, 254–255
    expected frequencies, 255–256

requirements, 268–269
    small expected frequencies,
       265–268
Class interval, 29–32, 41–44
    flexible, 42–44
    guidelines for constructing, 32
    limits, 30–32
    midpoints, 32
    number, 32
    size, 31–32
Coefficient of determination,
    319–320
Coefficient of nondetermination, 320
Conditional relationship, 300,
    352–356
Confidence intervals, 159–165,
    169–171
Content analysis, 4–5
Contingency coefficient, 346–348
    and Cramer's V, 348–349
    requirements, 348
    testing significance, 347
Correlation
    coefficient, 278–279
    contingency coefficient,
      346–347

Cramer's V, 348–349
    curvilinear, 286
    direction, 285–286
    Goodman's and Kruskal's
      gamma, 339–344
    lambda, 349–352
    partial, 298–304
    Pearson's r, 288–296
    phi coefficient, 344–346
    Spearman's rank-order,
      332–339
    strength, 284–285
Cramer's V, 348–349
Criminal justice research series of
    numbers in, 8 stages of, 8
Cross-tabulation, 44–50
Cumulative distribution, 33–34
Cumulative frequency polygon,
    56–58

Data Sources, 507, 387–390
Deciles, 40
Decimals, 41–42
Dependent variable, 2, 309, 322,
    325–327
Deviation, 72–73

Distribution
    shape of, 75–78

Elaboration, 352–356
Error term, 310, 316
Evans, T. David, 6
Experiment, 3

F ratio, 233–241
Federal Bureau of Investigations,
    6–7, 388
Flanagan, Timothy J., 6
Frequency distribution
    cumulative, 33–34
    grouped, 29–32
    level of measurement, 8–12, 75
    nominal data, 9
    ordinal and interval data, 9–12,
        28–29
    and probability distributions,
        118–120
Frequency polygon, 56–58

Goodman's and Kruskal's gamma,
    339–344
    requirements, 344
    testing significance, 343
Graphs, 50–63

Histogram, 51–57
Hypothesis
    defined, 2
    null, 183–184, 208
    research, 183–184, 208
    testing, 7–8, 188–191

Independent variable, 2
Internet, 5, 387
Interval level of measurement, 10–12

Jankowski, Martin Sanchez, 5

Kruskal-Wallis one-way analysis of
    variance by ranks, 275–277
Kurtosis, 59

Lambda coefficient, 349–352
    requirements, 352
Level of measurement, 8–12, 75

Level of significance, 191–196
Line chart, 60–61

Mann-Whitney *U* test, 272–275
Maps, 62–63
Mean, 71–73
    compared with other central ten-
        dency measures, 74–78
    from grouped frequency distri-
        bution, 80–83
    from simple frequency distribu-
        tion, 78–80
    level of measurement, 75
Mean deviation, 90–92
    compared with other variability
        measures, 100–101
Mean square, 231–232
Median, 70–71
    compared with other central
        tendency measures, 74–78
    from grouped frequency distri-
        bution, 80–83
    from simple frequency distri-
        bution, 78–80
    level of measurement, 75
Median test, 269–271
Mode, 69–70
    in bimodal distributions, 70
    compared with other central ten-
        dency measures, 274–278
    from grouped frequency distri-
        bution, 80–81
    from simple frequency distri-
        bution, 78
Multiple coefficient of determina-
    tion, 326

National Crime Victimization
    Survey, 5–6, 388
Nominal level of measurement, 9
Nonparametric statistics, 245–246
Nonrandom samples, 146–147
Normal curve, 121–140
    area, 124–126, 129, 133–137
    characteristics, 121–122
    model and reality, 122–124
    percentile ranks from, 137–140
    probability under, 133–137
    as probability distribution, 121

and standard scores, 129–133
Null hypothesis, 183–184, 208

One-tailed versus two-tailed tests,
    207–211
One-way chi-square test, 246–250
Ordinal level of measurement, 9–12

Parametric tests, 245–246
Partial correlation, 298–304
Participant observation, 5
Pearson's correlation coefficient
    formula, 290–291
    requirements, 296
    testing significance, 292–294
Percentage, 25–26
Percentile rank, 35–41
    from normal curve, 131–134
Percents
    choice of, 49–50
    column, 48
    row, 47–48
    total, 46–47
Phi coefficient, 344–346
    requirements, 346
    testing significance, 345–346
Pie charts, 50–51
Power, 246
Probability, 113–141
    addition rule, 115
    converse rule, 114
    multiplication rule, 116–117
    under the normal curve, 133–137
Probability distribution, 117–121
    and frequency distribution,
        118–120
    mean, 120
    and normal curve, 121
    standard deviation, 120
    variance, 120
Proportion, 25

Quartiles, 40

Random samples, 147–151
Range, 89–90
    compared with other variability
        measures, 100–101
Rate, 26–28
Rate of change, 28

Ratio, 26–28
Regression analysis
    and analysis of variance, 320–325
    multiple regression, 325–327
    and Pearson's correlation,
        319–320
    prediction, 313–319
    regression line, 314–316
    regression model, 309–314
    requirements, 314
    testing significance, 320–322
Research hypothesis, 183–184
Rounding, 16–17

Samples
    nonrandom, 146–147
    random, 147–150
Sampling distribution of differences
    between means, 184–188
    testing hypotheses, 188–191
Sampling distribution of means,
    151–153
    characteristics, 154–155
    as normal curve, 155–158
Sampling error, 150–151
Sampling methods
    nonrandom samples, 146–147
    random samples, 147–151
Scatter plot, 284, 296–298
Skewness, 59–60
Slope, 309–313
Spearman's rank-order correlation
    coefficient, 332–339
    requirements, 339

testing significance, 336
tied ranks, 334–336
Spurious relationship, 300,
    354–356
Standard deviation
    compared with other variability
        measures, 100–101
    computing, 94–97
    from grouped frequency distri-
        bution, 104–106
    the meaning of, 97–100
    and the normal curve, 126–133
    raw-score formula, 96–97
    from simple frequency distri-
        bution, 101–104
    and variance, 92–94
Standard error of the difference
    between means, 196–200
    requirements, 213–214
    same sample measured twice,
        201–204
    testing, 197–200
Standard error of the difference
    between proportions testing,
    205–207
Standard error of the mean,
    158–159
Standard error of the proportion,
    172–173
Standard scores, 129–133
Statistics
    functions of, 12–16
Sum of squares, 225–239
    computing, 229–231
Survey, 3–6, 388

t distribution, 165–169
Tukey's HSD, 238–240
Two-way chi-square test,
    250–269
Type I error, 192–195
Type II error, 192–195

Unit of observation, 2
Uniform Crime Reports, 6–7, 388

Variability
    comparison of measures,
        100–101
    mean deviation, 90–91
    range, 89–90
    standard deviation, 92–107
    variance, 92–107
Variables, 1–2
Variance
    compared with other variability
        measures, 100–101
    from grouped frequency distri-
        bution, 104–106
    raw-score formula, 96–97
    from simple frequency distri-
        bution, 101–104
    and standard deviation, 92–97

Yates's correction, 265–268
Y-intercept, 309–315

z score, 129–132
    for difference between means,
        189–191